Algorithms of the Intelligent Web

HARALAMBOS MARMANIS
DMITRY BABENKO

MANNING

Greenwich
(74° w. long.)

For online information and ordering of this and other Manning books, please visit
www.manning.com. The publisher offers discounts on this book when ordered in quantity.
For more information, please contact

> Special Sales Department
> Manning Publications Co.
> 180 Broad Street, Suite 1323
> Stamford, CT 06901
> Email: orders@manning.com

Manning Publications Co.
180 Broad Street, Suite 1323
Stamford, CT 06901

Development Editor: Jeff Bleiel
Copyeditor: Benjamin Berg
Typesetter: Gordan Salinovic
Cover designer: Leslie Haimes

ISBN 978-1-933988-66-5

Third, corrected printing January 2011
Printed in the United States of America
4 5 6 7 8 9 10 – MAL – 14 13 12 11

brief contents

v

contents

preface

During my graduate school years I became acquainted with the field of machine learning, and in particular the field of pattern recognition. The focus of my work was on mathematical modeling and numerical simulations, but the ability to recognize patterns in a large volume of data had obvious applications in many fields. The years that followed brought me closer to the subject of machine learning than I ever imagined.

In 1999 I left academia and started working in industry. In one of my consulting projects, we were trying to identify the risk of heart failure for patients based (primarily) on their EKGs. In problems of that nature, an exact mathematical formulation is either unavailable or impractical to implement. Modeling work (our software) had to rely on methods that could adopt their predictive capability based on a given number of patient records, whose risk of heart failure was already diagnosed by a cardiologist. In other words, we were looking for methods that could "learn" from their input.

Meanwhile, during the '90s, a confluence of events had driven the rapid growth of a new industry. The web became ubiquitous! Abiding by Moore's law, CPUs kept getting faster and cheaper. RAM modules, hard disks, and other computer components followed the same trends of capability improvement and cost reduction. In tandem, the bandwidth of a typical network connection kept increasing at the same time that it became more affordable. Moreover, robust technologies for developing web applications were coming to life and the proliferation of open source projects on every aspect of software engineering was accentuating that growth. All these factors contributed to building the vast digital ecosystem that we today call the web.

Naturally, the first task for our profession—the software engineers and web developers of the world—was to establish the technologies that would allow us to build robust, scalable, and aesthetically appealing web applications. Thus, in the last decade a large effort was made to achieve these goals, and significant progress has been made. Of course, perfection is a destination not a state, so we still have room for improvement. Nevertheless, it seems that we're cruising along the plateau of productivity with respect to robustness, scalability, and aesthetic appeal. The era of internet application "plumbing" is more or less over. Mere data aggregation and simple user request/response models based on predetermined logic have reached a state of maturity.

Today, another wave of innovation can be found in certain applications and is passing through the slope of enlightenment fairly quickly. These applications are what we refer to in this book as *intelligent applications*. Unlike traditional applications, intelligent applications adjust their behavior according to their input, much like my modeling software had to predict the risk of heart failure based on the EKG.

Over the last five years, it became clear to me that a lot of the techniques that are used in intelligent applications aren't easily accessible to the vast majority of software professionals. In my opinion, there are primarily two reasons for that. The first is that the commercial potential of innovation in these areas can have huge financial rewards. It makes (financial) sense to protect the proprietary parts of specific applications and hide the critical details of the implementations. The second reason why the underlying techniques remained in obscurity for so long is that nearly all of them originated as scientific research and therefore relied on significant mathematical jargon. There's little that anyone can do about the first reason. But the amount of publicly available knowledge is so large that it raises the question: Is the second reason necessary? My short answer is a loud and emphatic "No!" For the long answer, you'll have to read the book!

I decided to write this book to demonstrate that a number of these techniques can be presented in the form of algorithms, without presuming much about the mathematical background of the reader. The goal of this book is to equip you with a number of techniques that will help you build intelligent behavior in your application, while assuming as little as possible with regard to mathematics. The code contains all the necessary mathematics in algorithmic form.

Initially, I was thinking of using a number of open source libraries for presenting the techniques. But most of these libraries are developed opportunistically and, quite often, without any intention to teach the underlying techniques. Thus, the code tends to become obscure and tedious to read, let alone understand! It was clear that the intended audience of my book would benefit the most from a clean, well-documented code base. At that juncture, Dmitry joined me and he wrote most of the code that you'll find in this book.

Slowly but surely, the number of books that cover this new and exciting area will grow. This book is only an introduction to a field that's already large and keeps growing rapidly. Naturally, the number of algorithms covered had to be limited and the explanations had to be concise. My objective was to select a number of topics and explain them well, rather than attempt to cover as much as possible with the risk of confusing you or simply creating a cookbook.

I hope that we have made a contribution to that end by doing the following four things:

- Staying focused and working on clear examples
- Using high-level scripts that capture the usage of the algorithms, as if you were inserting them in your own application
- Helping you experiment with, and think about, the code through a large number of To Do items
- Writing top-notch and legible code

So, grab your favorite hot beverage, sit back, and test drive some smart apps; they're here to stay!

HARALAMBOS MARMANIS

acknowledgments

We'd like to acknowledge the people at Manning who gave us the opportunity to publish this work. Aside from their contribution in bringing the manuscript to its final form, they patiently waited for its completion, which took much longer than we'd originally planned. In particular, we'd like to thank Marjan Bace, Jeff Bleiel, Karen Tegtmeyer, Megan Yockey, Mary Piergies, Maureen Spencer, Steven Hong, Ron Tomich, Benjamin Berg, Elizabeth Martin, and everyone else on the Manning team who worked on the book but whose names we do not know. Thanks for your hard work.

We'd also like to recognize the time, effort, and valuable feedback that we received from our reviewers and our visitors in the Author Online forum. Your feedback helped make this book better in many ways. We understand how limited and precious "free" time is for every professional so please know that your contributions were greatly appreciated.

We especially thank the following reviewers for reading our manuscript a number of times at various stages during its development and for sharing their comments with us: Robert Hanson, Sumit Pal, Carlton Gibson, David Hanson, Eric Swanson, Frank Wang, Bob Hutchison, Craig Walls, Nicholas C. Heinle, Vlad Gorsky, Alessandro Gallo, Craig Lancaster, Jason Kolter, Martyn Fletcher, and Scott Dawson. Last but not least, thanks to Ajay Bhandari who was the technical proofreader and who read the chapters and checked the code one last time before the book went to press.

H. Marmanis

I'd like to thank my parents, Eva and Alexander. They've instilled in me the appropriate level of curiosity and passion for learning that keeps me writing and researching late into the night. The debt is too large to pay in one lifetime.

I wholeheartedly thank my cherished wife, Aurora, and our three sons: Nikos, Lukas, and Albert—the greatest pride and joy of my life. I'll always be grateful for their love, patience, and understanding. The incessant curiosity of my children has been a continuous inspiration for my studies on learning. A huge acknowledgment is due to my parents-in-law, Cuchi and Jose; my sisters, Maria and Katerina; and my best friends Michael and Antonio for their continuous encouragement and unconditional support.

I'd be remiss if I didn't acknowledge the manifold support of Drs. Amilcar Avendaño and Maria Balerdi, who taught me a lot about cardiology and funded my early work on learning. My thanks also are due to Professor Leon Cooper, and many other amazing people at Brown University, whose zeal for studying the way that our brain works trickled down to folks like me and instigated my work on intelligent applications.

To my past and present colleagues, Ajay Bhandari, Kavita Kanetkar, Alexander Petrov, Kishore Kirdat, and many others, who encouraged and supported all the intelligence related initiatives at work: there are only a few lines that I can write here but my gratitude is much larger than that.

D. Babenko

First and foremost, I want to thank my beloved wife Elena. This book took longer than a year to complete and she had to put up with a husband who was spending all his time at work or working on a book. Her support and encouragement created a perfect environment for me to get this book done.

I'd like to thank all of my past and present colleagues who influenced my professional life and served as an inspiration: Konstantin Bobovich, Paul A. Dennis, Keith Lawless, and Kevin Bedell.

Finally, I'd also like to thank my co-author Dr. Marmanis for including me in this project.

about this book

Modern web application hype revolves around a rich UI experience. A lesser-known aspect of modern applications is the use of techniques that enable the intelligent processing of information and add value that can't be delivered by other means. Examples of success stories based on these techniques abound, and include household names such as Google, Netflix, and Amazon. This book describes how to build the algorithms that form the core of intelligence in these applications.

The book covers five important categories of algorithms: search, recommendations, groupings, classification, and the combination of classifiers. A separate book could be written on each of these topics, and clearly exhaustive coverage isn't a goal of this book. This book is an introduction to the fundamentals of these five topics. It's an attempt to present the basic algorithms of intelligent applications rather than an attempt to cover completely all algorithms of computational intelligence. The book is written for the widest audience possible and relies on a minimum of prerequisite knowledge.

A characteristic of this book is a special section at the end of each chapter. We call it the To Do section and its purpose isn't merely to present additional material. Each of these sections guides you deeper into the subject of the respective chapter. It also aims to implant the seed of curiosity that'll make you think of new possibilities, as well as the associated challenges that surface in real-world applications.

The book makes extensive use of the BeanShell scripting library. This choice serves two purposes. The first purpose is to present the algorithms at a level that's easier to grasp, before diving into the gory details. The second purpose is to delineate the steps that you'd take to incorporate the algorithms in your application. In most cases, you can use the library that comes with this book by writing only a few lines of code! Moreover, in order to ensure the longevity and maintenance of the source code, we've created a new project dedicated to it, on the Google code site: http://code.google.com/p/yooreeka/.

Roadmap

The book consists of seven chapters. The first chapter is introductory. Chapters 2 through 6 cover search, recommendations, groupings, classification, and the combination of classifiers, respectively. Chapter 7 brings together the material from the previous chapters, but it covers new ground in the context of a single application.

While you can find references from one chapter to the next, the material was written in such a way that you can read chapters 1 through 5 on their own. Chapter 6 builds on chapter 5, so it would be hard to read it by itself. Chapter 7 also has dependencies because it touches upon the material of the entire book.

Chapter 1 provides an overview of intelligent applications as well as several examples of their value. It provides a practical definition of intelligent web applications and a number of design principles. It presents six broad categories of web applications that can leverage the intelligent algorithms of this book. It also provides background on the origins of the algorithms that we'll present, and their relation with the fields of artificial intelligence, machine learning, data mining, and soft computing. The chapter concludes with a list of eight design pitfalls that occur frequently in practice.

Chapter 2 begins with a description of searching that relies on traditional information retrieval techniques. It summarizes the traditional approach and paves the way for searching beyond indexing, which includes the most celebrated link analysis algorithm—PageRank. It also includes a section on improving the search results by employing user click analysis. This technique learns the preferences of a user toward a particular site or topic, and can be greatly enhanced and extended to include additional features.

Chapter 2 also covers the searching of documents that aren't web pages by employing a new algorithm, which we call DocRank. This algorithm has shown some promise, but more importantly it demonstrates that the underlying mathematical theory of link analysis can be readily extended and studied in other contexts by careful modifications. This chapter also covers some of the challenges that may arise in dealing with very large networks. Lastly, chapter 2 covers the issue of credibility and validation for search results.

Chapter 3 introduces the vital concepts of distance and similarity. It presents two broad categories of techniques for creating recommendations—collaborative filtering and the content-based approach. The chapter uses a virtual online music store as its context for developing recommendations. It also presents two more general examples. The first is a hypothetical website that uses the Digg API and retrieves the content of our users, in order to recommend unseen articles to them. The second example deals with movie recommendations and introduces the concept of data normalization. In this chapter we also evaluate the accuracy of our recommendations based on the root mean squared error.

Clustering algorithms are presented in chapter 4. There are many application areas for which clustering can be applied. In theory, any dataset that consists of objects that can be defined in terms of attribute values is eligible for clustering. In this chapter, we cover the grouping of forum postings and identifying similar website users. This chapter also offers a general overview of clustering types and full implementations for six algorithms: single link, average link, minimum spanning tree single link, k-means, ROCK, and DBSCAN.

Chapter 5 presents classification algorithms, which are essential components of intelligent applications. The chapter starts with a description of ontologies, which are introduced by employing three fundamental building blocks—concepts, instances, and attributes. Classification is presented as the problem of assigning the "best" concept to a given instance. Classifiers differ from each other in the way that they represent and measure that optimal assignment. The chapter provides an overview of classification that covers *binary* and *multiclass* classification, *statistical* algorithms, and *structural* algorithms. It also presents the three stages in the lifecycle of a classifier: the training, the validation, and the production stage.

Chapter 5 continues with a high-level presentation of regression algorithms, Bayesian algorithms, rule-based algorithms, functional algorithms, nearest-neighbor algorithms, and neural networks. Three techniques of classification are discussed in detail. The first technique is based on the naïve Bayes algorithm as applied to a single string attribute. The second technique deals with the Drools rule engine, an object-oriented implementation of the Rete algorithm, which allows us to declare and apply rules for the purpose of classification. The third technique introduces and employs *computational neural networks*; a basic but robust implementation is provided for building general neural networks. Chapter 5 also alerts you to issues that are related to the credibility and computational requirements of classification, before we introduce it in our applications.

Chapter 6 covers the combination of classifiers—advanced techniques that can improve the classification accuracy of a single classifier. The main example of this chapter is the evaluation of the credit worthiness for a mortgage application. Bagging and boosting are presented in detail. This chapter also presents an implementation of Breiman's arc-x4 boosting algorithm.

Chapter 7 demonstrates the use of the intelligent algorithms in the context of a news portal. We discuss technical issues as well as the new business value that intelligent algorithms can add to an application. For example, a clustering algorithm might be used for grouping similar news stories together, but it can also be used for enhancing the visibility of relevant news stories by *cross-referencing*. In this chapter, we sketch out the adoption of intelligent algorithms and the combination of different intelligent algorithms for a given purpose.

THE SPECIAL TO DO SECTION

The last section of every chapter, beginning with chapter 2, contains a number of to-do items that will guide you in the exploration of various topics. As software engineers, we find the term *to do* quite appealing; it has an imperative flavor to it and is less formal than other terms, such as *exercises*.

Some of these to-do items aim at providing greater depth on a topic that has been covered in the main chapter, while other items present a starting point for exploration on topics that are peripheral to what we've already discussed. The completion of these tasks will provide you with greater depth and breadth on intelligent algorithms.

Whenever appropriate, our code has been annotated with "TODO" tags that you should be able to view in many IDEs; for example, in the Eclipse IDE, click the Tasks panel. By clicking on any of the tasks, the task link will show the portion of the code that's associated with it.

Who should read this book

Algorithms of the Intelligent Web was written for software engineers and web developers who'd like to learn more about this new breed of algorithms that empowers a host of commercially successful applications with intelligence. Since the source code is based on the Java programming language, those who use Java might find it more attractive than those who don't. Nevertheless, people who work with other programming languages should be able to learn from the book, and perhaps transliterate the code into the language of their choice.

The book is full of examples and ideas that can be used broadly, so it may also be of some value to technical managers, product managers, and executive-level people who want a better understanding of the related technologies and the possibilities that they offer from a business perspective.

Finally, despite the term *Web* in the title, the material of the book is equally applicable to many other software applications, ranging from utilities running on mobile telephones to traditional desktop applications such as text editors and spreadsheet applications.

Code Conventions

All source code in the book is in a `monospace` font, which sets it off from the surrounding text. For most listings, the code is annotated to point out key concepts, and numbered bullets are sometimes used in the text to provide additional information about the code. Sometimes very long lines will include line-continuation markers.

The source code of the book can be obtained from the following link: http://code.google.com/p/yooreeka/downloads/list or by following a link provided on the publisher's website at www.manning.com/AlgorithmsoftheIntelligentWeb.

You should unzip the distribution file directly under the C:\ drive. We assume that you're using Microsoft Windows; if not then you should modify our scripts to make them work for your system. The top directory of the compressed file is named `iWeb2`; all directory references in the book are with respect to that root folder. For example, a reference to the `data/ch02` directory, according to our convention, means the absolute directory `C:\iWeb2\data\ch02`.

If you unzipped the file, you're ready to run the Ant build script. Simply go into the build directory and run `ant`. Note that the Ant script will work regardless of the location that you unzipped the file. You're now ready to run the BeanShell script as described in appendix A.

Author Online

Purchase of *Algorithms of the Intelligent Web* includes free access to a private web forum run by Manning Publications where you can make comments about the book, ask technical questions, and receive help from the authors and from other users. To access the forum and subscribe to it, point your web browser to www.manning.com/ AlgorithmsoftheIntelligentWeb. This page provides information on how to get on the forum once you are registered, what kind of help is available, and the rules of conduct on the forum. It also provides links to the source code for the examples in the book, errata, and other downloads.

Manning's commitment to our readers is to provide a venue where a meaningful dialog between individual readers and between readers and the authors can take place. It is not a commitment to any specific amount of participation on the part of the authors, whose contribution to the Author Online remains voluntary (and unpaid). We suggest you try asking the authors some challenging questions lest their interest stray!

The Author Online forum and the archives of previous discussions will be accessible from the publisher's website as long as the book is in print.

About the cover illustration

The illustration on the cover of *Algorithms of the Intelligent Web* is taken from a French book of dress customs, *Encyclopedie des Voyages by J. G. St. Saveur,* published in 1796. Travel for pleasure was a relatively new phenomenon at the time and illustrated guides such as this one were popular, introducing both the tourist as well as the armchair traveler to the inhabitants of other far-off regions of the world, as well as to the more familiar regional costumes of France and Europe.

The diversity of the drawings in the *Encyclopedie des Voyages* speaks vividly of the uniqueness and individuality of the world's countries and peoples just 200 years ago. This was a time when the dress codes of two regions separated by a few dozen miles identified people uniquely as belonging to one or the other, and when members of a social class or a trade or a tribe could be easily distinguished by what they were wearing. This was also a time when people were fascinated by foreign lands and faraway places, even though they could not travel to these exotic destinations themselves.

Dress codes have changed since then and the diversity by region, so rich at the time, has faded away. It is now often hard to tell the inhabitant of one continent from another. Perhaps, trying to view it optimistically, we have traded a world of cultural and visual diversity for a more varied personal life. Or a more varied and interesting intellectual and technical life.

We at Manning celebrate the inventiveness, the initiative, and the fun of the computer business with book covers based on native and tribal costumes from two centuries ago brought back to life by the pictures from this travel guide.

What is the intelligent web?

This chapter covers:
- Leveraging intelligent web applications
- Using web applications in the real world
- Building intelligence in your web

So, what's this book about? First, let's say what it's not. This book isn't about building a sleek UI, or about using JSON or XPath, or even about RESTful architectures. There are several good books for Web 2.0 applications that describe how to deliver AJAX-based designs and an overall rich UI experience. There are also many books about other web-enabling technologies such as XSL Transformations (XSLT) and XML Path Language (XPath), Scalable Vector Graphics (SVG), XForms, XML User Interface Language (XUL), and JSON (JavaScript Object Notation).

The starting point of this book is the observation that most traditional web applications are obtuse, in the sense that the response of the system doesn't take into account the user's prior input and behavior. We refer not to issues related to bad UI but rather to a fixed response of the system to a given input. Our main interest is building web applications that do take into account the input and behavior of

1

every user in the system, over time, as well as any other potentially useful information that may be available.

Let's say that you start using a web application to order food, and every Wednesday you order fish. You'd have a much better experience if, on Wednesdays, the application asked you "Would you like fish today?" instead of "What would you like to order today?" In the first case, the application *somehow realized* that you like fish on Wednesdays. In the second case, the application remains oblivious to this fact. Thus, the data created by your interaction with the site doesn't affect how the application chooses the content of a page or how it's presented. Asking a question that's based on the user's prior selections introduces a new kind of interactivity between the website and its users. So, we could say that websites with that property have a *learning capacity*.

To take this one step further, the interaction of an intelligent web application with a user may adjust due to the input of other users that are somehow related to each other. If your dietary habits match closely those of John, the application may recommend a few menu selections that are common for John but that you never tried; building recommendations is covered in chapter 3.

Another example would be a social networking site, such as Facebook, which could offer a *fact-checking* chat room or electronic forum. By fact checking, we mean that as you type your message, there's a background check on what you write to ensure that your statements are factually accurate and even consistent with your previous messages. This functionality is similar to spell-checking, which may be already familiar to you, but rather than check grammar rules, it checks a set of facts that could be general truths ("the Japanese invasion of Manchuria occurred in 1931"), your own beliefs about a particular subject ("less taxes are good for the economy"), or simple personal facts ("doctor's appointment on 11/11/2008"). Websites with such functional behavior are *inference* capable; we describe the design of such functionality in chapter 5.

We can argue that the era of intelligent web applications began in earnest with the advent of web search engines such as Google. You may legitimately wonder: why Google? People knew how to perform information retrieval (search) tasks long before Google appeared on the world scene. But search engines such as Google take advantage of the fact that the content on the web is interconnected, and this is extremely important. Google's thesis was that the hyperlinks within web pages form an underlying structure that can be mined to determine the importance of the various pages. In chapter 2, we describe in detail the PageRank algorithm that makes this possible.

By extending our discussion, we can say that intelligent web applications are designed from the outset with a collaborative and interconnected world in mind. They're designed to automatically train so that they can understand the user's input, the user's behavior, or both, and adjust their response accordingly. The sharing of the user profiles among colleagues, friends, and family on social networking sites such as MySpace or Facebook, as well as the sharing of content and opinions on newsgroups and online forums, create new levels of connectivity that are central to intelligent web applications and go beyond plain hyperlinks.

1.1   *Examples of intelligent web applications*

Let's review applications that have been leveraging this kind of intelligence over the last decade. As already mentioned, a turning point in the history of the web was the advent of search engines. A lot of what the web had to offer remained untapped until 1998 when *link analysis* (see chapter 2) emerged in the context of search and took the market by storm. Google Inc. has grown, in less than 10 years, from a startup to a dominant player in the technology sector due primarily to the success of its link-based search and secondarily to a number of other services such as Google News and Google Finance.

Nevertheless, the realm of intelligent web applications extends well beyond search engines. The online retailer Amazon was one of the first online stores that offered recommendations to its users based on their shopping patterns. You may be familiar with that feature. Let's say that you purchase a book on JavaServer Faces and a book on Python. As soon as you add your items to the shopping cart, Amazon will recommend additional items that are somehow related to the ones you've just selected; it could recommend books that involve AJAX or Ruby on Rails. In addition, during your next visit to the Amazon website, the same or other related items may be recommended.

Another intelligent web application is Netflix,[1] which is the world's largest online movie rental service, offering more than 7 million subscribers access to 90,000 DVD titles plus a growing library of more than 5,000 full-length movies and television episodes that are available for instant watching on their PCs. Netflix has been the top-rated website for customer satisfaction for five consecutive periods from 2005 to 2007, according to a semiannual survey by ForeSee Results and FGI Research.

Part of its online success is due to its ability to provide users with an easy way to choose movies, from an expansive selection of movie titles. At the core of that ability is a recommendation system called Cinematch. Its job is to predict whether someone will enjoy a movie based on how much he liked or disliked other movies. This is another great example of an intelligent web application. The predictive power of Cinematch is of such great value to Netflix that, in October 2006, it led to the announcement of a million-dollar prize[2] for improving its capabilities. By October 2007, there have been 28,845 contestants from 165 countries. In chapter 3, we offer extensive coverage of the algorithms that are required for building a recommendation system such as Cinematch.

Leveraging the opinions of the collective in order to provide intelligent predictions isn't limited to book or movie recommendations. The company PredictWall-Street collects the predictions of its users for a particular stock or index in order to spot trends in the opinions of the traders and predict the value of the underlying asset. We don't suggest that you should withdraw your savings and start trading based on their predictions, but they're yet another example of creatively applying the techniques of this book in a real-world scenario.

---

[1] Source: Netflix, Inc. website at http://www.netflix.com/MediaCenter?id=5379
[2] Source: http://www.netflixprize.com//rules

1.2   *Basic elements of intelligent applications*

Let's take a closer look at what distinguishes the applications that we referred to in the previous section as intelligent and, in particular, let's emphasize the distinction between collaboration and intelligence. Consider the case of a website where users can collaboratively write a document. Such a website could well qualify as an advanced web application under a number of definitions for the term *advanced*. It would certainly facilitate the collaboration of many users online, and it could offer a rich and easy-to-use UI, a frictionless workflow, and so on. But should that application be considered an intelligent web application?

A document created in that website will be larger in volume, greater in depth, and perhaps more accurate than other documents written by each participant individually. In that respect, the document captures not just the knowledge of each individual contributor but also the effect that the interaction between the users has on the end product. Thus, a document created in this manner captures the collective knowledge of the contributors.

This is not a new notion. The process of defining a standard, in any field of science or engineering, is almost always conducted by a technical committee. The committee creates a first draft of the document that brings together the knowledge of experts and the opinions of many interest groups, and addresses the needs of a collective rather than the needs of a particular individual or vendor. Subsequently, the first draft becomes available to the public and a request for comments is initiated. The purpose of this process is that the final document is going to represent the total body of knowledge in the community and will express guidelines that meet several requirements found in the community.

Let's return to our application. As defined so far, it allows us to capture collective knowledge and is the result of a collective effect, but it's not yet intelligent. Collective intelligence—a term that's quite popular but often misunderstood—requires collective knowledge and is built by collective effects, but these conditions, although necessary, aren't sufficient for characterizing the underlying software system as intelligent.

In order to understand the essential ingredients of what we mean by *intelligence*, let's further assume that our imaginary website is empowered with the following features: As a user types her contribution, the system identifies other documents that may be relevant to the typed content and retrieves excerpts of them in a sidebar. These documents could be from the user's own collection of documents, documents that are shared among the contributors of the work-in-progress, or simply public, freely available, documents.

A user can mark a piece of the work-in-progress and ask the system to be notified when documents pertaining to the content of that excerpt are found on the internet or, perhaps more interestingly, when the consensus of the community about that content has changed according to certain criteria that the user specifies.

Creating an application with these capabilities requires much more than a pretty UI and a collaborative platform. It requires the understanding of freely typed text. It requires the ability to discern the meaning of things within a context. It requires the ability to automatically process and group together documents, or parts of documents, that contain free text in natural (human) language on the basis of whether they're "similar." It requires some structured knowledge about the world or, at least, about the domain of discourse that the document refers to. It requires the ability to focus on certain documents that satisfies certain rules (user's criteria) and do so quickly.

Thus, we arrive at the conclusion that applications such as Wikipedia or other public portals are different from applications such as Google search, Google Ads, Netflix Cinematch, and so on. Applications of the first kind are collaborative platforms that facilitate the aggregation and maintenance of collective knowledge. Applications of the second kind generate abstractions of patterns from a body of collective knowledge and therefore generate a new layer of opportunity and value.

We conclude this section by summarizing the elements that are required in order to build an intelligent web application:

- *Aggregated content*—In other words, a large amount of data pertinent to a specific application. The aggregated content is dynamic rather than static, and its origins as well as its storage locations could be geographically dispersed. Each piece of information is typically associated with, or linked to, many other pieces of information.
- *Reference structures*—These structures provide one or more structural and semantic interpretations of the content. For example, this is related to what people call *folksonomy*—the use of tags for annotating content in a dynamic way and continuously updating the representation of the collective knowledge to the users. Reference structures about the world or a specific domain of knowledge come in three big flavors: dictionaries, knowledge bases, and ontologies (see the related references at the end).
- *Algorithms*—This refers to a layer of modules that allows the application to harness the information, which is hidden in the data, and use it for the purpose of abstraction (generalization), prediction, and (eventually) improved interaction with its users. The algorithms are applied on the aggregated content, and sometimes require the presence of reference structures.

These ingredients, summarized in figure 1.1, are essential for characterizing an application as an intelligent web application, and we'll refer to them throughout the book as the *triangle of intelligence.*

It's prudent to keep these three components separate and build a model of their interaction that best fits your needs. We'll discuss more about architecture design in the rest of the chapters, especially in chapter 7.

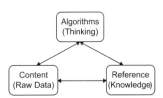

Figure 1.1   The triangle of intelligence: the three essential ingredients of intelligent applications.

1.3   What applications can benefit from intelligence?

The ingredients of intelligence, as described in the previous section, can be found across a wide spectrum of applications, from social networking sites to specialized counterterrorism applications. In this section, we'll describe examples from each category. Our list is certainly not complete, but it'll demonstrate that the techniques of this book can be widely useful, if not irreplaceable in certain cases.

1.3.1   Social networking sites

The websites that have marked the internet most prominently in the last few years are the social networking sites. These are web applications that provide their users with the ability to establish an online presence using nothing more than a browser and an internet connection. The users can share files (presentations, video files, audio files) with each other, comment on current events or other people's pages, build their own social network, or join an existing one based on their interests. The two most-visited[3] social networking sites are MySpace and Facebook, with hundreds of millions and tens of millions of registered users, respectively.

These sites are content aggregators by construction, so the first ingredient for building intelligence is readily available. The second ingredient is also present in those sites. For example, on MySpace, the content is categorized using top labels such as "Books," "Movies," "Schools," "Jobs," and so on that are clearly visible on the site (see figure 1.2).

In addition, these top-level categories are further refined by lower-level structures that differentiate content related to "Classifieds" from content related to "Polls" or

Figure 1.2   This snapshot shows the categories on the MySpace websites.

---

[3]   Based on traffic data captured by Alexa.com on December 2007.

"Weather." Finally, most social networking sites are able to recommend to their users new friends and new postings that may be of interest. In order to do that, they rely on advanced algorithms for making predictions and abstractions of the collected data, and therefore contain all three ingredients of intelligence.

1.3.2 Mashups

The IBM DeveloperWorks site (http://www.ibm.com/developerworks/spaces/mashups) has a whole section dedicated to *mashups*, and the definition is particularly apt: "Mashups are an exciting genre of interactive web applications that draw upon content retrieved from external data sources to create entirely new and innovative services." In other words, you're building a site by using content and UI elements "borrowed" from others. Another interesting site, in the context of mashups, is ProgrammableWeb (http://www.programmableweb.com). It's a convenient place for starting your exploration of the mashups world (see figure 1.3).

In our context, mashups are important because they're based on aggregated content, but unlike social networking sites, they don't own the content that they display—at least, a big part of it. The content is physically stored in geographically dispersed locations and is pulled together from its various sources to create a unique presentation based on your interaction with the application.

But not all mashups are intelligent. In order to build intelligent mashups, we need the ability to reconcile differences or identify similarities of the content that we try to collage. In turn, the reconciliation and classification of the content require one or

Figure 1.3   To learn more about mashups, visit sites like ProgrammableWeb.

more reference structures for interpreting the meaning of the content, as well as a number of algorithms that can identify what elements of the reference structures are contained within the various pieces or how content that has been retrieved from different sites should be categorized for viewing purposes.

1.3.3   Portals

Portals and in particular news portals are another class of web applications where the techniques of this book can have a large impact. By definition, these applications are gateways to content that's distributed throughout the internet or, in the case of a corporate network, throughout an intranet. This is another case in which the aggregated content is dispersed but accessible.

The best example in this category is Google News (http://news.google.com). This site gathers news stories from thousands of sources and automatically groups similar news stories under a common heading. Moreover, each group of news stories is assigned to one of the news categories that are available by default, such as Business, Health, World, Sci/Tech, and so on (see figure 1.4).

You can even define your own categories and determine what kind of stories are of interest to you. Once again, we see that the underlying theme is aggregated content coupled with a reference structure and a number of algorithms that can perform the required tasks automatically or, at least, semiautomatically.

A promising project for building intelligence in your portal—especially for social application kinds of portals—is OpenSocial (http://code.google.com/apis/opensocial/)

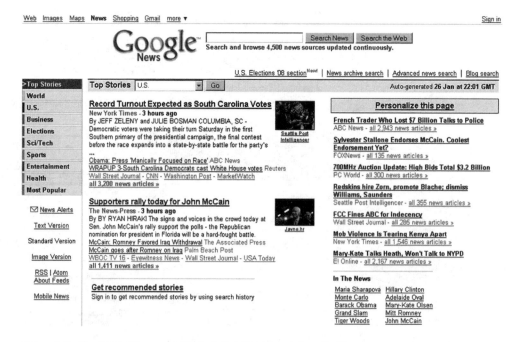

Figure 1.4 The Google News website is an intelligent portal application.

and a number of projects that are developed around it such as the Apache project Shindig. The premise of OpenSocial is to build a common API base that will allow the development of applications that interact with a large, and continuously growing, number of websites such as Engage , Friendster, hi5, Hyves, imeem, LinkedIn, MySpace, Ning, Oracle, orkut, Plaxo, Salesforce , Six Apart, Tianji, Viadeo, and XING.

1.3.4 *Wikis*

Wikipedia shouldn't require much introduction; you've probably visited that website already, or at least heard of it. It's a wiki site that has been consistently in the top 10 most visited websites. A *wiki* is a repository of knowledge that's accessible online. Wikis are used by social communities on the internet and by corporations internally for knowledge-sharing purposes.

These sites are clearly content aggregators. In addition, a lot of these sites, due to the page creation workflow, have a built-in structure that annotates the content. In Wikipedia, you can assign an article to a *category* and link articles that refer to the same subject. Wikis are a promising area for applying the techniques of this book. For example, you could build or modify your wiki site so that it automatically categorizes the pages that you write. The wiki pages could have an inlet, or another panel, of recommended terms that you can link to—pages on a wiki are supposed to be linked to each other whenever the link provides an explanation or additional information on a term or topic. Finally, the natural linkage of the pages provides fertile ground for advanced search (chapter 2), clustering (chapter 4), and other analytical techniques.

1.3.5 *Media-sharing sites*

YouTube is the hallmark of the internet media-sharing sites, but other websites such as RapidShare (http://www.rapidshare.com) and MegaUpload (http://www.megaupload.com/) enjoy a high percentage of visitors. The unique feature of these sites is that most of their content is in binary format—video or audio files. In most cases, the size of the smallest unit of information is larger on these sites than on text-based site aggregators; the sheer volume of data to be processed, at the unit level, poses some of the greatest challenges in the context of gathering intelligence.

In addition, two of the most difficult problems of intelligent applications (and also most interesting from a business perspective) are intimately related to the processing of binary information. These two problems are voice and pattern recognition. Companies such as Clearspring (http://www.clearspring.com/) and ScanScout (http://www.scanscout.com/), working together, enable advertisers to enhance the distribution of their brand and message to a broader audience. ScanScout provides advertisers with intelligence about the distribution of, and engagement with, their widgets across more than 25 sites, including MySpace, Facebook, Google, and Yahoo!

The same pattern we described in the earlier sections can be found in these sites as well. We have aggregated content; we typically want to have the content categorized; and we want to have algorithms that can help us extract value from that content. We'd

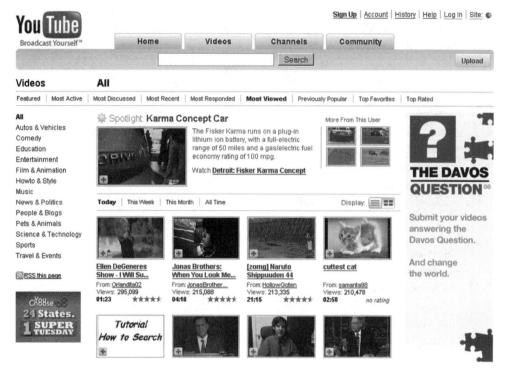

Figure 1.5   The YouTube categories for videos. The reference schema for the categorization of content is shown on the left panel.

like to have our binary files categorized in terms of the themes that we define—"Autos & Vehicles," "Education," "Entertainment," "Politics," and so on (see figure 1.5).

Similarly to other cases of intelligent applications, these categories may be structured as a hierarchy. For example, the category of "Autos & Vehicles" may be further divided into subcategories such as "Sedan," "Trucks," "Luxury," "SUV," and so on.

1.3.6   *Online gaming*

Massive multiplayer online games have all the ingredients required to create intelligence in the game. They have ample aggregated content and reference structures that reflect the rules, and they can certainly use the algorithms that we describe in this book to introduce new levels of sophistication in the game. Characters that are played by the computer can assimilate the input of the human players so that the experience of the game as perceived by the humans becomes more entertaining.

Online gaming is an exciting area for applying intelligent techniques, and it can become a key differentiator among competitors, as the computational power that's available for playing games and the expectations of the human players with respect to game complexity and innovation increase. Techniques that we describe in chapters 4, 5, and 6, as well as a lot of the material in the appendices, are directly applicable in online games.

1.4   *How can I build intelligence in my own application?*

We've provided many reasons for embedding intelligence in your application. We've also described a number of areas where the intelligent behavior of your software can drastically improve the experience and value that your users get from your application. At this point, the natural question is "How can I build intelligence in my own application?"

This entire book is an introduction to the design and implementation of intelligent components, but to make the best use of it, you should also address two prerequisites of building an intelligent application.

The first prerequisite is a review of your functionality. What are your users doing with your application? How does your application add consumer or business value? We provide a few specific questions that are primarily related to the algorithms that we'll develop in the rest of the book. The importance of these questions will vary depending on what your application does. Nevertheless, these specific questions should help you identify the areas where an intelligent component would add most value to your application.

The second prerequisite is about data. For every application, data is either internal to an application (immediately available within the application) or external. First examine your internal data. You may have everything that you need, in which case you're ready to go. Conversely, you may need to insert a workflow or other means of collecting some additional data from your users. You may want, for example, to add a "five star" rating UI element to your pages, so that you can build a recommendation engine based on user ratings.

Alternatively, you might want or need to obtain more data from external sources. A plethora of options is available for that purpose. We can't review them all here, but we present four large categories that are fairly robust from a technology perspective, and are widely used. You should look into the literature for the specifics of your preferred method for collecting the addition data that you want to obtain.

1.4.1   *Examine your functionality and your data*

You should start by identifying a number of use cases that would benefit from intelligent behavior. This will obviously differ from application to application, but you can identify these cases by asking some very simple questions, such as:

- Does my application serve content that's collected from various sources?
- Does it have wizard-based workflows?
- Does it deal with free text?
- Does it involve reporting of any kind?
- Does it deal with geographic locations such as maps?
- Does our application provide search functionality?
- Do our users share content with each other?
- Is fraud detection important for our application?
- Is identity verification important for our application?
- Does our application make automated decisions based on rules?

This list is, of course, incomplete but it's indicative of the possibilities. If the answer to any of these questions is yes, your application can benefit greatly from the techniques that we'll describe in the rest of the book.

Let's consider the common use case of searching through the data of an imaginary application. Nearly all applications allow their users to search their site. Let's say that our imaginary application allows its users to purchase different kinds of items based on a catalog list. Users can search for the items that they want to purchase. Typically, this functionality is implemented by a direct SQL query, which will retrieve all the product items that match the item description. That's nice, but our database server doesn't take into account the fact that the query was executed by a specific user, for whom we probably know a great deal within the context of his search. We can probably improve the user experience by implementing the ranking methods described in chapter 2 or the recommendation methods described in chapter 3.

1.4.2   *Get more data from the web*

In many cases, your own data will be sufficient for building intelligence that's relevant and valuable to your application. But in some cases, providing intelligence in your application may require access to external information. Figure 1.6 shows a snapshot from the mashup site HousingMaps (http:www.housingmaps.com), which allows the

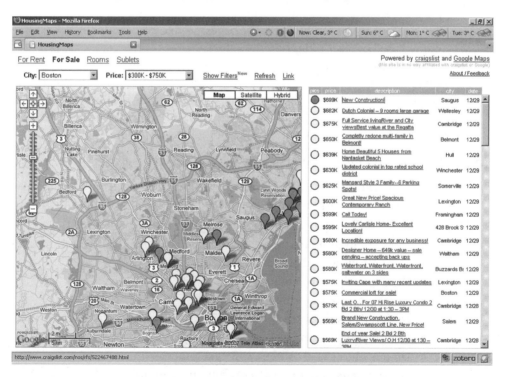

Figure 1.6   A screenshot that shows the list of available houses on craigslist combined with maps from the Google maps service (source: http://www.housingmaps.com).

user to browse the houses available in a geographic location by obtaining the list of houses from craigslist (http://www.craigslist.com) and maps from the Google maps service (http://code.google.com/apis/maps/index.html).

Similarly, a news site could associate a news story with the map of the area that the story refers to. The ability to obtain a map for a location is already an improvement for any application. Of course, that doesn't make your application intelligent unless you do something intelligent with the information that you get from the map.

Maps are a good example of obtaining external information, but more information is available on the web that's unrelated to maps. Let's look at the enabling technologies.

CRAWLING AND SCREEN SCRAPING

Crawlers, also known as *spiders*, are software programs that can roam the internet and download content that's publicly available. Typically, a crawler would visit a list of URLs and attempt to follow the links at each destination. This process can repeat for a number of times, usually referred to as the *depth of crawling*. Once the crawler has visited a page, it stores its content locally for further processing. You can collect a lot of data in this manner, but you can quickly run into storage or copyright-related issues. Be careful and responsible with crawling. In chapter 2, we present our own implementation of a web crawler. We also include an appendix that provides a general overview of web crawling, a summary of our own web crawler, as well as a brief description of a few open source implementations.

Screen scraping refers to extracting the information that's contained in HTML pages. This is a straightforward but tedious exercise. Let's say that you want to build a search engine exclusively for eating out (such as http://www.foodiebytes.com). Extracting the menu information from the web page of each restaurant would be one of your first tasks. Screen scraping itself can benefit from the techniques that we describe in this book. In the case of a restaurant search engine, you want to assess how good a restaurant is based on reviews from people who ate there. In some cases, ratings may be available, but most of the time these reviews are plain, natural language, text. Reading the reviews one-by-one and ranking the restaurants accordingly is clearly not a scalable business solution. Intelligent techniques can be employed during screen scraping and help you automatically categorize the reviews and assess the ranking of the restaurants. An example is Boorah (http://www.boorah.com).

RSS FEEDS

Website syndication is another way to obtain external data and it eliminates the burden of revisiting websites with your crawler. Usually, syndicated content is more machine-friendly than regular web pages because the information is well structured. There are three common feed formats: RSS 1.0, RSS 2.0, and Atom.

RDF Site Summary (RSS) 1.0, as the name suggests, was born out of the Resource Description Framework[4] (RDF) and is based on the idea that information on the web can be harnessed by humans and machines. However, humans can usually infer the

---

[4] http://www.w3.org/RDF

semantics of the content (the meaning of a word or phrase within a context) whereas machines can't do that easily. RDF was introduced to facilitate the semantic interpretation of the web. You can use it to extract useful data and metadata for your own purposes. The RSS 1.0 specification can be found at http://web.resource.org/rss/1.0/.

Really Simple Syndication (RSS 2.0 is based on Netscape's Rich Site Summary 0.91—there's significant overloading of the acronym RSS, to say the least—and its primary purpose was to alleviate the complexity of the RDF-based formats. It employs a syndication-specific language that's expressed in plain XML format, without the need for XML namespaces or direct RDF referencing. Nearly all major sites provide RSS 2.0 feeds today; these are typically free for individuals and nonprofit organizations for noncommercial use. Yahoo!'s RSS feeds site (http://developer.yahoo.com/rss) has plenty of resources for a smooth introduction in the subject. You can access the RSS 2.0 specification and other related information at http://cyber.law.harvard.edu/rss.

Finally, you can use Atom-based syndication. A number of issues with RSS 2.0 led to the development of an Internet Engineering Task Force (IETF) standard expressed in RFC 4287 (http://tools.ietf.org/html/rfc4287). Atom is not RDF-based; it's neither as flexible as RSS 1.0 nor as easy as RSS 2.0. It was in essence a compromise between the features of the existing standards under the constraint of maximum backward compatibility with the other syndication formats. Nevertheless, Atom enjoys widespread adoption like RSS 2.0. Most big web aggregators (such as Yahoo! and Google) offer news feeds in these two formats. Read more about the Atom syndication format at the IBM Developer Works website: http://www.ibm.com/developerworks/xml/standards/x-atomspec.html.

RESTFUL SERVICES

Representational State Transfer (REST) was introduced in the doctoral dissertation of Roy T. Fielding.[5] It's a software architecture style for building applications on distributed, hyperlinked, media. REST is a stateless client/server architecture that maps every service onto a URL. If your nonfunctional requirements aren't complex and a formal contract between you and the service provider isn't necessary, REST may be a convenient way for obtaining access to various services across the web. For more information on this important technology, you can consult *RESTful Web Services* by Leonard Richardson and Sam Ruby.

Many websites offer RESTful services that you can use in your own application. Digg offers an API (http://apidoc.digg.com/) that accepts REST requests and offers several response types such as XML, JSON, JavaScript, and serialized PHP. Functionally, the API allows you to obtain a list of stories that match various criteria, a list of users, friends, or fans of users, and so on.

The Facebook API is also a REST-like interface. This makes it possible to communicate with that incredible platform using virtually any language you like. All you have to do is send an HTTP GET or POST request to the Facebook API REST server. The Facebook API is well documented, and we'll make use of it later in the book. You can read more about it at http://wiki.developers.facebook.com/index.php/API.

---

[5]　http://www.ics.uci.edu/~fielding/pubs/dissertation/rest_arch_style.htm

WEB SERVICES

Web services are APIs that facilitate the communication between applications. A large number of web services frameworks are available and many of them are open source. Apache Axis (http://ws.apache.org/axis/) is an open source implementation of the Simple Access Object Protocol (SOAP), which "can be used for exchanging structured and typed information between peers in a decentralized, distributed environment."[6] Apache Axis is a popular framework and it was completely redesigned in version 2. Apache Axis2 supports SOAP 1.1 and SOAP 1.2 as well as the widely popular REST style of web services, and contains a staggering number of features.

Another Apache project worth mentioning is Apache CXF (http://incubator. apache.org/cxf/), the result of the merger of Celtix by IONA and Codehaus XFire. Apache CXF supports the following standards: JAX-WS 2.0, JAX-WSA, JSR-181, SAAJ, SOAP 1.1, 1.2, WS-I Basic Profile, WS-Security, WS-Addressing, WS-RM, WS-Policy, WSDL 1.1 and 2.0. It also supports multiple transport mechanisms, bindings, and formats. If you're considering using web services, you should have a look at this project.

Aside from the many frameworks available for web services, there are even more web service providers. Nearly every company uses web services for integrating applications that are quite different, in terms of their functionality or their technology stack. That situation could be the result of companies merging or uncoordinated parallel development efforts in a single, typically large, company. In the vertical space, nearly all big financial and investment institutions use web services for seamless integration. Xignite (http://preview.xignite.com/Default.aspx) offers a variety of financial web services. Software giants (such as SAP, Oracle, and Microsoft) also offer support for web services. In summary, web services-based integration is ubiquitous and, as one of the major integration enablers, it's an important infrastructure element in the design of intelligent applications.

At this point, you must have thought of the possible enhancements in your existing applications or you got a new idea for the next smashing startup! You checked that you have all the required data or that, at least, you can access the data. Now, let's look at the kind of intelligence that we plan to inject in our applications and its relationship to some terms that may be already familiar to you.

1.5 *Machine learning, data mining, and all that*

We talk about "intelligence" throughout this book, but what exactly do we mean? Are we talking about the field of artificial intelligence? How about machine learning? Is it about data mining and soft computing? Academics of the respective fields may argue for years about the precise definition of what we're about to present. From a practical perspective, most distinctions are benign and mainly a matter of context rather than substance. This book is a distillation of techniques that belong to all these areas. So, let's discuss them.

---

[6] http://www.w3.org/TR/soap12-part0/ - L1153

Artificial intelligence, widely known by its acronym *AI*, began as a computational field around 1950. Initially, the goals of AI were quite ambitious and aimed at developing machines that can think like humans (Russell and Norvig, 2002; Buchanan, 2005). Over time, the goals became more practical and concrete. Megalomania yielded to pragmatism and that, in turn, gave birth to many of the other fields that we mentioned, such as machine learning, data mining, soft computing, and so on.

Today, the most advanced system of computational intelligence can't comprehend simple stories that a four-year-old can easily understand. So, if we can't make computers "think," can we make them "learn"? Can we teach a computer to distinguish an animal based on its characteristics? How about a bad subprime mortgage application? How about something more complicated, such as recognizing your voice and replying in your native language—can a computer do that? The answer to these questions is a resounding yes. Nevertheless, you may wonder, "What's all the fuss about?" After all, you can always build a huge lookup table and get answers to your questions based on the data that you have in your database.

You can certainly follow the lookup table approach, but there are a few problems with it. First, for any problem of consequence in a real production system, your lookup table would be enormous; so, based on efficiency considerations, this isn't an optimal solution. Second, if the question that you form is based on data that doesn't exist in your database, you'd get no answer at all. If a person behaved in that manner, you'd be quick to adorn him with adjectives that censorship wouldn't allow us to print on these pages. Last, someone would have to build and maintain your lookup table, and the number of these people would grow with the size of your table: a feature that may not sit well with the financial department of your organization. So we need something better than a lookup table.

Machine learning refers to the capability of a software system to generalize based on past experience, and use these generalizations to provide answers to questions that relate to data that it has encountered in the past as well as new data that the system has never encountered before. Some learning algorithms are transparent to humans—a human can follow the reasoning behind the generalization. Examples of transparent learning algorithms are decision trees and, more generally, any rule-based learning method. Other algorithms, though, aren't transparent to humans—neural networks and support vector machines (SVM) fall in this category.

Always remember that machine intelligence, like human intelligence, isn't infallible. In the world of intelligent applications, you'll learn to deal with uncertainty and fuzziness; just like in the real world, any answer given to you is valid with a certain degree of confidence but not with certainty. In our everyday life, we simply assume that certain things will happen for sure. For that reason, we'll address the issues of credibility, validity, and the cost of being wrong when we use intelligent applications.

1.6 *Eight fallacies of intelligent applications*

We've covered all the introductory material. By now, you should have a fairly good, although only high-level, idea of what intelligent applications are and how you're going to use them. You're probably sufficiently motivated and anxious to dive into the code. We won't disappoint you. Every chapter other than the introduction is loaded with new and valuable code.

But before we embark on our journey into the exciting and financially rewarding (for the more cynical among us) world of intelligent applications, we'll present a number of mistakes, or fallacies, that are common in projects that embed intelligence in their functionality. You may be familiar with the eight fallacies of distributed computing (if not, see the industry commentary by Van den Hoogen); it's a set of common but flawed assumptions made by programmers when first developing distributed applications. Similarly, we'll present a number of fallacies, and consistent with the tradition, we'll present eight of them.

1.6.1   *Fallacy #1: Your data is reliable*

There are many reasons your data may be unreliable. That's why you should always examine whether the data that you'll work with can be trusted before you start considering specific intelligent algorithmic solutions to your problem. Even intelligent people that use very bad data will typically arrive at erroneous conclusions.

The following is an indicative, but incomplete, list of the things that can go wrong with your data:

- The data that you have available during development may not be representative of the data that corresponds to a production environment. For example, you may want to categorize the users of a social network as "tall," "average," and "short" based on their height. If the shortest person in your development data is six feet tall (about 184 cm), you're running the risk of calling someone short because they're "just" six feet tall.

- Your data may contain missing values. In fact, unless your data is artificial, it's almost certain that it'll contain missing values. Handling missing values is a tricky business. Typically, you either leave the missing values as missing or you fill them in with some default or calculated value. Both conditions can lead to unstable implementations.

- Your data may change. The database schema may change or the semantics of the data in the database may change.

- Your data may not be normalized. Let's say that we're looking at the weight of a set of individuals. In order to draw any meaningful conclusions based on the value of the weight, the unit of measurement should be the same for all individuals—in pounds or kilograms for every person, not a mix of measurements in pounds and kilograms.

- Your data may be inappropriate for the algorithmic approach that you have in mind. Data comes in various shapes and forms, known as *data types*. Some datasets are numeric and some aren't. Some datasets can be ordered and some can't. Some numeric datasets are discrete (such as the number of people in a room) and some are continuous (the temperature of the atmosphere).

1.6.2   Fallacy #2: Inference happens instantaneously

Computing a solution takes time, and the responsiveness of your application may be crucial for the financial success of your business. You shouldn't assume that all algorithms, on all datasets, will run within the response time limits of your application. You should test the performance of your algorithm within the range of your operating characteristics.

1.6.3   Fallacy #3: The size of data doesn't matter

When we talk about intelligent applications, size does matter! The size of your data comes into the picture in two ways. The first is related to the responsiveness of the application as mentioned in fallacy #2. The second is related to your ability to obtain meaningful results on a large dataset. You may be able to provide excellent movie or music recommendations for a set of users when the number of users is around 100, but the same algorithm may result in poor recommendations when the number of users involved is around 100,000.

Conversely, in some cases, the more data you have, the more intelligent your application can be. Thus, the size of the data matters in more than one way and you should always ask: Do I have enough data? What's the impact to the quality of my intelligent application if I must handle 10 times more data?

1.6.4   Fallacy #4: Scalability of the solution isn't an issue

Another fallacy that's related to, but distinct from, fallacies #2 and #3 is the assumption that an intelligent application solution can scale by simply adding more machines. Don't assume that your solution is scalable. Some algorithms are scalable and others aren't. Let's say that we're trying to find groups of similar headline news among billions of titles. Not all clustering algorithms (see chapter 4) can run in parallel. You should consider scalability during the design phase of your application. In some cases, you may be able to split the data and apply your intelligent algorithm on smaller datasets in parallel. The algorithms that you select in your design may have parallel (concurrent) versions, but you should investigate this from the outset, because typically, you'll build a lot of infrastructure and business logic around your algorithms.

1.6.5   Fallacy #5: Apply the same good library everywhere

It's tempting to use the same successful technique many times over to solve diverse problems related to the intelligent behavior of your application. Resist that temptation at all costs! I've encountered people who were trying to solve every problem under the sun using the Lucene search engine. If you catch yourself doing something like that, remember the expression: When you're holding a hammer, everything looks like a nail.

Intelligent application software is like every other piece of software—it has a certain area of applicability and certain limitations. Make sure that you test thoroughly your favorite solution in new areas of application. In addition, it's recommended that you examine every problem with a fresh perspective; a different problem may be solved more efficiently or more expediently by a different algorithm.

1.6.6 *Fallacy #6: The computation time is known*

Classic examples in this category can be found in problems that involve optimization. In certain applications, it's possible to have a large variance in solution times for a relatively small variation of the parameters involved. Typically, people expect that, when we change the parameters of a problem, the problem can be solved consistently with respect to response time. If you have a method that returns the distance between any two geographic locations on Earth, you expect that the solution time will be independent of any two specific geographic locations. But this isn't true for all problems. A seemingly innocuous change in the data can lead to significantly different solution times; sometimes the difference can be hours instead of seconds!

1.6.7 *Fallacy #7: Complicated models are better*

Nothing could be further from the truth. Always start with the simplest model that you can think of. Then gradually try to improve your results by combining additional elements of intelligence in your solution. KISS is your friend and a software engineering invariant.

1.6.8 *Fallacy #8: There are models without bias*

There are two reasons why you'd ever say that—either ignorance or bias! The choice of the models that you make and the data that you use to train your learning algorithms introduce a bias. We won't enter here into a detailed scientific description of bias in learning systems. But we'll note that bias balances generalization in the sense that our solution will gravitate toward our model description and our data (by construction). In other words, bias constrains our solution inside the set of things that we do know about the world (the facts) and sometimes how we came to know about it, whereas generalization attempts to capture what we don't know (factually) but it's reasonable to presume true given what we do know.

1.7 *Summary*

In this chapter, we gave a broad overview of intelligent web applications with a number of specific examples based on real websites, and we provided a practical definition of intelligent web applications, which can act as a design principle. The definition calls for three different components: (1) data aggregation, (2) reference structures, and (3) algorithms that offer learning capabilities and allow the manipulation of uncertainty.

We provided a reality check by presenting six broad categories of web applications for which our definition can be readily applied. Subsequently, we presented the enabling technologies that allow us to aggregate data or get access to data aggregation platforms. We also provided background on the origins of the techniques that we will present in the next chapters and, in particular, their relation with the fields of artificial intelligence, machine learning, data mining, and soft computing.

Finally, we presented a list of eight design pitfalls that occur frequently in practice. These are given as broad empirical guidelines rather than as rigorously established facts. We believe that knowing these eight guidelines can save you a lot of time and reduce your caffeine consumption. In the rest of the book we will examine, one by one, a number of techniques that can add intelligent behavior in your own application. Additional material for each of these techniques is provided in the end of each chapter in a "To Do" section.

1.8   References

Buchanan, B.G. "A (Very) Brief History of Artificial Intelligence." *AI Magazine.* Volume 26. issue 4, 2005.

Gómez-Pérez, A., M. Fernández-López, O. Corcho. *Ontological Engineering: With Examples from the Areas of Knowledge Management, E-commerce and the Semantic Web.* Springer, 2005.

Hart, P.E., N.J. Nilsson, and B. Raphael. "A Formal Basis for the Heuristic Determination of Minimum Cost Paths." *IEEE Transactions on Systems Science and Cybernetics.* Volume 4, issue 2, 1968.

Hart, P.E., N.J. Nilsson, and B. Raphael. Correction to "A Formal Basis for the Heuristic Determination of Minimum Cost Paths." *SIGART Newsletter* 37, 1972.

Richardson, L. and S. Ruby. *RESTful Web Services.* O'Reilly Media, 2007.

Russell, S. and P. Norvig. *Artificial Intelligence: A Modern Approach (2nd Edition).* Prentice Hall, 2002.

Van Den Hoogen, I. "Deutsch's fallacies, 10 Years After." *Java Developer's Journal,* 2004. http://java.sys-con.com/read/38665.htm.

Searching

2

Let's say that you have a list of documents and you're interested in reading about those that are related to the phrase "Armageddon is near"—or perhaps something less macabre. How would you implement a solution to that problem? A brute force, and naïve, solution would be to read each document and keep only those in which you can find the term "Armageddon is near." You could even count how many times you found each of the words in your search term within each of the documents and sort them according to that count in descending order. That exercise is called *information retrieval (IR)* or simply searching. Searching isn't new functionality; nearly every application has some implementation of search, but intelligent searching goes beyond plain old searching.

Experimentation can convince you that the naïve IR solution is full of problems. For example, as soon as you increase the number of documents, or their size, its performance will become unacceptable for most purposes. Fortunately, there's an enormous amount of knowledge about IR and fairly sophisticated and robust libraries are available that offer scalability and high performance. The most successful IR library in the Java programming language is Lucene, a project created by Doug Cutting almost 10 years ago. Lucene can help you solve the IR problem by indexing all your documents and letting you search through them at lightning speeds! *Lucene in Action* by Otis Gospodnetić and Erik Hatcher, published by Manning, is a must-read, especially if you want to know how to index data and introduces search, sorting, filtering and highlighting search results.

State-of-the-art searching goes well beyond indexing. The fiercest competition among search engine companies doesn't involve the technology around indexing but rather subjects such as link analysis, user click analysis, and natural-language processing. These techniques strengthen the searching functionality, sometimes to the tune of billions of dollars, as was the case with Google.

In this chapter, we'll summarize the features of the Lucene library and demonstrate its use. We'll present the PageRank algorithm, which has been the most successful link analysis algorithm so far, and we'll present a probabilistic technique for conducting user click analysis. We'll combine all these techniques to demonstrate the improvement in the search results due to the synergies among them. The material is presented in a successive manner, so you can learn as much as you want about searching and come back to it later if you don't have enough time now. Without further ado, let's collect a number of documents and search for various terms in them by using Lucene.

2.1   Searching with Lucene

Searching with Lucene will be our baseline for the rest of the chapter. So, before we embark on advanced intelligent algorithms, we need to learn the traditional IR steps. On our journey, we'll show you how to use Lucene to search a set of collected documents, we'll present some of the inner workings of Lucene, and we'll provide an overview of the basic stages for building a search engine.

The data that you want to search could be in your database, on the internet, or on any other network that's accessible to your application. You can collect data from the internet by using a crawler. A number of crawlers are freely available, but we'll use a crawler that we wrote for the purposes of this book. We'll use a number of pages that we collected on November 6, 2006, so we can modify them in a controlled fashion and observe the effect of these changes in the results of the algorithms.

These pages have been cleaned up and changed to form a tiny representation of the internet. You can find these pages under the `data/ch02/` directory. It's important to know the content of these documents, so that you can appreciate what the algorithms do and understand how they work. Our 15 documents are (the choice of content was random):

- Seven documents related to business news; three are related to Google's expansion into newspaper advertisement, another three discuss primarily about the NVidia stock, and one about stock price and index movements.
- Three documents related to Lance Armstrong's attempt to run the marathon in New York.
- Four documents related to U.S. politics and, in particular, the congressional elections (circa 2006).
- Five documents related to world news; four about Ortega winning the elections in Nicaragua and one about global warming.

Lucene can help us analyze, index, and search these and any other document that can be converted into text, so it's not limited to web pages. The class that we'll use to quickly read the stored web pages is called `FetchAndProcessCrawler`; this class can also retrieve data from the internet. Its constructor takes three arguments:

- The base directory for storing the retrieved data.
- The depth of the link structure that should be traversed.
- The maximum number of total documents that should be retrieved.

Listing 2.1 shows how you can use it from the BeanShell.

Listing 2.1   Reading, indexing, and searching the default list of web pages

```
FetchAndProcessCrawler crawler =
➥ new FetchAndProcessCrawler("C:/iWeb2/data/ch02",5,200);

crawler.setDefaultUrls();      ⟵ Load files

crawler.run();                 ⟵┐ Gather and
                                 │ process content
LuceneIndexer luceneIndexer =  ┘
➥ new LuceneIndexer(crawler.getRootDir());

luceneIndexer.run();      ⟵ Index content in directory

MySearcher oracle = new MySearcher(luceneIndexer.getLuceneDir());

oracle.search("armstrong",5);    ⟵ Search based on index just created
```

The crawling and preprocessing stage should take only a few seconds, and when it finishes you should have a new directory under the base directory. In our example, the base directory was `C:/iWeb2/data/ch02`. The new directory's name will start with the string `crawl-` and be followed by the numeric value of the crawl's timestamp in milliseconds—for example, `crawl-1200697910111`.

You can change the content of the documents, or add more documents, and rerun the preprocessing and indexing of the files in order to observe the differences in your search results. Figure 2.1 is a snapshot of executing the code from listing 2.1 in the BeanShell, and it includes the results of the search for the term "armstrong."

```
bsh % FetchAndProcessCrawler c =
new FetchAndProcessCrawler("c:/iWeb2/data/ch02",5,200);
bsh % c.setDefaultUrls();
bsh % c.run();
There are no unprocessed urls.
Timer (s): [Crawler fetched data] -> 5.5
Timer (s): [Crawler processed data] -> 0.485
bsh %
bsh % LuceneIndexer lidx = new LuceneIndexer(c.getRootDir());
bsh % lidx.run();
Starting the indexing ... Indexing completed!

bsh % MySearcher oracle = new MySearcher(lidx.getLuceneDir());
bsh % oracle.search("armstrong",5);

Search results using Lucene index scores:
Query: armstrong

Document Title: Lance Armstrong meets goal in painful marathon
debut
Document URL: file:/c:/iWeb2/data/ch02/sport-01.html ->
Relevance Score: 0.397706508636475
_____

Document Title: New York 'tour' Lance's toughest
Document URL: file:/c:/iWeb2/data/ch02/sport-03.html ->
Relevance Score: 0.312822639942169
_____

Document Title: New York City Marathon
Document URL: file:/c:/iWeb2/data/ch02/sport-02.html ->
Relevance Score: 0.226110160350800
_____
```

Figure 2.1   An example of retrieving, parsing, analyzing, indexing, and searching a set of web pages with a few lines of code

Those are the high-level mechanics: load, index, search. It doesn't get any simpler than that! But how does it really work? What are the essential elements that participate in each stage?

2.1.1   *Understanding the Lucene code*

Let's examine the sequence of events that allowed us to perform our search. The job of the FetchAndProcessCrawler class is to retrieve the data and parse it. The result of that processing is stored in the subdirectory called processed. Take a minute to look in that folder. For every group of documents that are processed, there are four subdirectories—fetched, knownurls, pagelinks, and processed. Note we've dissected the web pages by separating metadata from the core content and by extracting the links from one page to another—the so-called *outlinks*. The FetchAndProcessCrawler class doesn't use any code from the Lucene API.

The next thing that we did was create an instance of the `LuceneIndexer` class and call its `run()` method. This is where we use Lucene to index our processed content. The Lucene index files will be stored in a separate directory called `lucene-index`. The `LuceneIndexer` class is a convenience wrapper that helps us invoke the `LuceneIndex-Builder` class from the Bean shell. The `LuceneIndexBuilder` class is where the Lucene API is used. Figure 2.2 shows the complete UML diagram of the main classes involved in retrieving and indexing the documents.

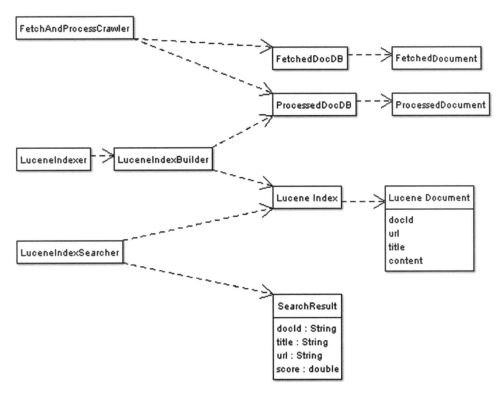

Figure 2.2   A UML diagram of the classes that we used to crawl, index, and search a set of web pages

Listing 2.2 shows the entire code from the `LuceneIndexBuilder` class.

Listing 2.2   The `LuceneIndexBuilder` creates a Lucene index

```
public class LuceneIndexBuilder implements CrawlDataProcessor {
  private File indexDir;
  public LuceneIndexBuilder(File indexDir) {
    this.indexDir = indexDir;
    try {                                          Create Lucene index
        IndexWriter indexWriter =
        new IndexWriter(indexDir, new StandardAnalyzer(), true);
        indexWriter.close();
```

```
    } catch(IOException ioX) {
          throw new RuntimeException("Error: ", ioX);
        }
    }
    public void run(CrawlData crawlData) {

        List<String> allGroups =                                    Get all document
          crawlData.getProcessedDocsDB().getAllGroupIds();    ←──┘  groups

        for(String groupId : allGroups) {
          buildLuceneIndex(groupId, crawlData.getProcessedDocsDB());
        }
    }

    private void buildLuceneIndex(String groupId,
➡ ProcessedDocsDB parsedDocsService) {

        try {                                             Get all documents
                                                      ┌── for group
            List<String> docIdList =          ←──────┘
parsedDocsService.getDocumentIds(groupId);

            IndexWriter indexWriter =

new IndexWriter(indexDir, new StandardAnalyzer(), false);

            for(String docId : docIdList) {    ←──┐   Index all
                indexDocument(indexWriter,           documents
➡ parsedDocsService.loadDocument(docId));
            }

            indexWriter.close();

        } catch(IOException ioX) {
            throw new RuntimeException("Error: ", ioX);
        }
    }

    private void indexDocument(IndexWriter iw,
➡ ProcessedDocument parsedDoc) throws IOException {

        org.apache.lucene.document.Document doc =
➡ new org.apache.lucene.document.Document();

        doc.add(new Field("content", parsedDoc.getText(),
➡ Field.Store.NO, Field.Index.TOKENIZED));

        doc.add(new Field("url",
➡ parsedDoc.getDocumentURL().toExternalForm(),
➡ Field.Store.YES, Field.Index.NO));

        doc.add(new Field("docid", parsedDoc.getDocumentId(),
➡ Field.Store.YES, Field.Index.NO));

        doc.add(new Field("title", parsedDoc.getDocumentTitle(),
➡ Field.Store.YES, Field.Index.NO));

        doc.add(new Field("doctype", parsedDoc.getDocumentType(),
➡ Field.Store.YES,Field.Index.NO));
        iw.addDocument(doc);
    }
}
```

The `IndexWriter` class is what Lucene uses to create an index. It comes with a large number of constructors, which you can peruse in the Javadocs. The specific constructor that we use in our code takes three arguments:

- The directory where we want to store the index.
- The analyzer that we want to use—we'll talk about analyzers later in this section.
- A Boolean variable that determines whether we need to override the existing directory.

As you can see in listing 2.2, we iterate over the groups of documents that our crawler has accumulated. The first group corresponds to the content of the initial URL list. The second group contains the documents that we found while reading the content of the initial URL list. The third group will contain the documents that are reachable from the second group, and so on. Note that the structure of these directories changes if you vary the parameter `maxBatchSize` of the `BasicWebCrawler` class. To keep the described structure intact, make sure that the value of that parameter is set to a sufficiently large number; for the purposes of this book, it's set to 50.

This directory structure will be useful when you use our crawler to retrieve a much larger dataset from the internet. For the simple web page structure that we'll use in the book, you can see the effect of grouping if you add only a few URLs—by using the `addUrl` method of the `FetchAndProcessCrawler` class—and let the crawler discover the rest of the files.

For each document within a group, we index its content. This takes place inside the `indexDocument` method, which is shown at the bottom of listing 2.2. The Lucene `Document` class encapsulates the documents that we've retrieved so that we can add them in the index; that same class can be used to encapsulate not only web pages but also emails, PDF files, and anything else that you can parse and transform into plain text. Every instance of the `Document` class is a virtual document that represents a collection of fields. Note that we're using our dissection of the retrieved documents to create various `Field` instances for each document:

- The `content` field, which corresponds to the text representation of each document, stripped of all the formatting tags and other annotations. You can find these documents under the subdirectory `processed/1/txt`.
- The `url` field represents the URL that was used to retrieve this document.
- The `docid` field, which uniquely identifies each document.
- The `title` field, which stores the title of each document.
- The `doctype` field, which stores the document type of each document, such as HTML or Microsoft Word.

The field content of every document is indexed but isn't stored with the index files; the other fields are stored with the index files but they aren't indexed. The reason being we want to be able to query against the content but we want to retrieve from the index files the URL, the ID, and the title of each retrieved document.

This practice is common. You typically store a few pointers that allow you to identify what you've found in the index, but you don't include the content inside the index files unless you have good reasons for doing so (you may need part of the content immediately and the original source isn't directly accessible). In that case, pay attention to the size of the files that you're creating during the indexing stage.

We use the `MySearcher` class to search through our newly created index. Listing 2.3 shows all the code in that class. It requires a single argument to construct it—the directory where we stored the Lucene index—and then it allows us to search through the search method, which uses two arguments:

- A string that contains the query that we want to execute against the index
- The maximum number of documents that we want to retrieve

Listing 2.3 MySearcher: retrieving search results based on Lucene indexing

```
public class MySearcher {

  private static final Logger log =
➥ Logger.getLogger(MySearcher.class);

  private String indexDir;

  public MySearcher(String indexDir) {
    this.indexDir = indexDir;
  }

  public SearchResult[] search(String query, int numberOfMatches) {

    SearchResult[] docResults = new SearchResult[0];
    IndexSearcher is = null;

    try {

      is = new IndexSearcher(FSDirectory.getDirectory(indexDir));    ◁──┐ Open
                                                                         Lucene
    } catch (IOException ioX) {                                          index
      log.error(ioX.getMessage());
    }
QueryParser qp = new QueryParser("content",                       ◁──┐ Create query
                    new StandardAnalyzer());                            parser
    Query q = null;
    try {
                                                                  ◁──┐ Transform text query
      q = qp.parse(query);                                             into Lucene query
    } catch (ParseException pX) {
      log.error(pX.getMessage());
    }

    Hits hits = null;
    try {
                                                                  ◁──┐ Search index
      hits = is.search(q);

      int n = Math.min(hits.length(), numberOfMatches);
      docResults = new SearchResult[n];
```

```
    for (int i = 0; i < n; i++) {                          ◁──┐ Collect first
                                                              │ N search
        docResults[i] = new SearchResult(hits.doc(i).get("docid"),  │ results
                        hits.doc(i).get("doctype"),
                        hits.doc(i).get("title"),
                        hits.doc(i).get("url"),
                        hits.score(i));         ◁──┐ Score for i-th
    // report the results                          │ document
        System.out.println(docResults[i].print());
        }
        is.close();

    } catch (IOException ioX) {
        log.error(ioX.getMessage());
    }
    return docResults;
    }
}
```

Let's review the steps in listing 2.3:

1 We use an instance of the Lucene `IndexSearcher` class to open our index for searching.

2 We create an instance of the Lucene `QueryParser` class by providing the name of the field that we query against and the analyzer that must be used for tokenizing the query text.

3 We use the `parse` method of the `QueryParser` to transform the human-readable query into a `Query` instance that Lucene can understand.

4 We search the index and obtain the results in the form of a Lucene `Hits` object.

5 We loop over the first *n* results and collect them in the form of our own `SearchResult` objects. Note that Lucene's `Hits` object contains only references to the underlying documents. We use these references to collect the required fields; for example, the call `hits.doc(i).get("url")` will return the URL that we stored in the index.

6 The *relevance score* for each retrieved document is recorded. This score is a number between 0 and 1.

Those elements constitute the mechanics of our specific implementation. Let's take a step back and view the bigger picture of conducting searches based on indexing. This will help us understand the individual contributions of index-based search engines, and will prepare us for a discussion about more advanced search features.

2.1.2 Understanding the basic stages of search

If we could travel back in time (let's say to 1998), what would be the basic stages of work we'd need to perform to build a search engine? These stages are the same today as they were in 1998 but we've improved their effectiveness and computational performance. Figure 2.3 depicts the basic stages in conventional searching:

- Crawling
- Parsing
- Analyzing
- Indexing
- Searching

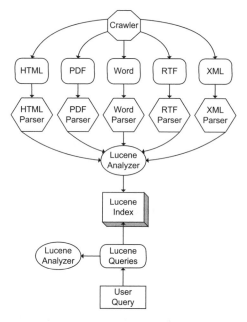

Figure 2.3   An overview of searching for a set of documents with different formats

Crawling refers to the process of gathering the documents on which we want to enable the search functionality. It may not be necessary if the documents exist or have been collected already. Parsing is necessary for transforming the documents (XML, HTML, Word, PDF) into a common structure that will represent the fields of indexing in a purely textual form. For our examples, we're using the code from the NekoHTML project. NekoHTML contains a simple HTML parser that can scan HTML files and "fix" many common mistakes that occur in HTML documents, adding missing parent elements, automatically closing elements with optional end tags, and handling mismatched inline element tags. NekoHTML is fairly robust and sufficiently fast, but if you're crawling special sites, you may want to write your own parser.

If you plan to index PDF documents, you can use the code from the PDFBox project (http://www.pdfbox.org/); it's released under the BSD license and has plenty of documentation. PDFBox includes the class LucenePDFDocument, which can be used to obtain a Lucene Document object immediately with a single line of code such as the following:

```
Document doc = LucenePDFDocument.convertDocument(File file)
```

Look at the Javadocs for additional information. Similar to PDF documents, there are also parsers for Word documents. For example, the Apache POI project (http://poi.apache.org/) provides APIs for manipulating file formats based on Microsoft's OLE 2 Compound Document format using pure Java. In addition, the TextMining code, available at http://www.textmining.org/, provides a Java library for extracting text from Microsoft Word 97, 2000, XP, and 2003 documents.

The stage of analyzing the documents is very important. In listing 2.2 and listing 2.3, the Lucene class StandardAnalyzer was used in two crucial places in the code, but we didn't discuss it before now. As figure 2.3 indicates, our parsers will be used to extract text from their respective documents, but before the textual content is indexed, it's processed by a Lucene analyzer. The work of an analyzer is crucial because analyzers are responsible for tokenizing the text that's to be indexed. This means that they'll keep some words from the text that they consider to be important while they ignore everything else. If you ignore something that's of interest to you during the analysis stage then you'll never find it during your search, no matter how sophisticated your indexing algorithm is.

Of course, analyzers can't select the appropriate fields for you. As an example, in listing 2.2, we've explicitly defined the four fields that we're interested in. The `StandardAnalyzer` will process the `content` field, which is the only field indexed. This default analyzer is the most general purpose built-in analyzer for Lucene. It intelligently tokenizes alphanumerics, acronyms, company names, email addresses, computer host names, and even CJK (Chinese, Japanese, and Korean) characters, among other things.

The latest version of Lucene (2.3 at the time of this writing) uses a lexical analyzer that's written in Java and called JFlex (http://jflex.de/). The Lucene `StandardTokenizer` is a grammar-based tokenizer that's constructed with JFlex, and it's used in the `StandardAnalyzer`. To convince you of the analyzer's importance, replace the `StandardAnalyzer` with the `WhitespaceAnalyzer` and observe the difference in the resulting scores. Lucene analyzers provide a wealth of capabilities, such as the ability to add synonyms, modify stop words (words that are explicitly removed from the text before indexing), and deal with non-English languages. We'll use Lucene analyzers throughout the book, even in chapters that don't deal with search. The general idea of identifying the unique characteristics of a text description is crucial when we deal with documents. Thus, analyzers become very relevant in areas such as the development of spam filters, recommendations that are based on text, enterprise, or tax compliance applications, and so on.

The Lucene indexing stage is completely transparent to the end user but it's also powerful. In a single index, you can have Lucene `Documents` that correspond to different entities (such as emails, memos, legal documents) and therefore are characterized by different fields. You can also remove or update `Documents` from an index. Another interesting feature of Lucene's indexing is *boosting*. Boosting allows you to mark certain documents as more or less important than other documents. In the method `indexDocument` described in the listing 2.2, you could add a statement such as the following:

```
if ( parsedDoc.getDocumentId().equals("g1-d14")) {
    doc.setBoost(2);
}
```

You can find this statement in the code, commented out and marked as "To Do." If you remove the comments, compile the code, and run again the script of listing 2.1, you'll notice that the last document is now first. Boosting has increased—in fact, it has doubled—the score of every `Field` for this document. You can also boost individual `Field`s in order to achieve more granular results from your boosting.

Searching with Lucene can't be easier. As you've seen, using our `MySearcher` wrapper, it's a matter of two lines of code. Although we used a simple word in our example of listing 2.1, Lucene provides sophisticated query expression parsing through the

QueryParser class. Sometimes you may have to use different means for creating the Lucene Query. To search for the term "nasdaq index" and allow for the possibility of results that refer to "nasdaq composite index," you'd use the class PhraseQuery. In this case, the term "index" can be a term apart from the term "nasdaq". The maximum number of terms that can separate "nasdaq" and "index" is set by a parameter called *slope*. By setting the slope equal to 1, we can achieve the desired result. For this and more powerful features of searching with Lucene, we encourage you to explore the Lucene APIs and documentation.

2.2 *Why search beyond indexing?*

Now that we've showed you how to quickly index your documents with Lucene and execute queries against those indices, you're probably convinced that using Lucene is easy and wonderful. You may wonder: "If Lucene is so sophisticated and efficient, why bother with anything else?" In this section we'll demonstrate why searching beyond indexing is necessary. We mentioned the reasons in passing in chapter 1, but in this section we'll discuss the issue in more depth. Let's add a new document to our list of seeding URLs. Listing 2.4 is similar to listing 2.1, but it now includes a URL that contains spam.

> **Listing 2.4   Reading, indexing, and searching web pages that contain spam**

```
FetchAndProcessCrawler crawler =
➥ new FetchAndProcessCrawler("C:/iWeb2/data/ch02",5,200);

crawler.setDefaultUrls();

crawler.addUrl("file:///c:/iWeb2/data/ch02/spam-01.html");    ⟵── Add web page
                                                                    with spam
crawler.run();

LuceneIndexer luceneIndexer =                      Build Lucene
➥ new LuceneIndexer(crawler.getRootDir());    ⟵── index        Build
                                                                plain
luceneIndexer.run();                                            search
                                                                engine
MySearcher oracle = new MySearcher(luceneIndexer.getLuceneDir());   ⟵──

oracle.search("armstrong",5);
```

Figure 2.4 shows the results of the search for "Armstrong." You can see that the carefully crafted spam web page catapulted to first place in our ranking. You can create three or more similar spam pages and add them to your URL list to convince yourself that pretty soon the truly relevant content will be lost in a sea of spam pages!

Unlike a set of documents in a database or on your hard drive, the content of the Web isn't regulated. Hence, the deliberate creation of deceptive web pages can render traditional IR techniques practically useless. If search engines relied solely on traditional IR techniques then web surfing for learning or entertainment—our national online sport—wouldn't be possible. Enter a new brave world: *link analysis*! Link analysis was the first (and a significant) contribution toward fast and accurate searching on a set of documents that are linked to each other explicitly, such as internet web pages.

```
bsh % oracle.search("armstrong",5);

Search results using Lucene index scores:
Query: armstrong

Document Title: Cheap medicine--low interest loans
Document URL: file:/c:/iWeb2/data/ch02/spam-01.html --> Relevance
Score: 0.591894507408142
_____

Document Title: Lance Armstrong meets goal in painful marathon
debut
Document URL: file:/c:/iWeb2/data/ch02/sport-01.html ->
Relevance Score: 0.370989531278610
_____

Document Title: New York 'tour' Lance's toughest
Document URL: file:/c:/iWeb2/data/ch02/sport-03.html ->
Relevance Score: 0.291807949542999
_____

Document Title: New York City Marathon
Document URL: file:/c:/iWeb2/data/ch02/sport-02.html ->
Relevance Score: 0.210920616984367
_____

bsh %
```

Figure 2.4　A single deceptive web page significantly altered the ranking of the results for the query "Armstrong."

It propelled Google from anonymity to world domination in that space and advanced many other areas of research and development.

Link analysis is a structural characteristic of the internet. Another characteristic of the internet is *user click analysis*, which is behavioral. In short, user click analysis refers to the recording of the user's clicks as she navigates the search pages, and the subsequent processing of these recordings for the purpose of improving the ranking of the results for this particular user. It's based on the premise that if you search for a term and find a page that's relevant (based on your criteria) you'll most likely click on that page. Conversely, you wouldn't click pages that are irrelevant to your search term and your *search intention*. We emphasize the term because this is a deviation from traditional applications, where the response of the system was based on the user's direct input alone. If the application can detect your intentions then it has achieved a major milestone toward intelligence, which is the ability to learn about the user without the programmer entering the answer from a "back door."

2.3　*Improving search results based on link analysis*

In our effort to search beyond indexing, we'll present the link analysis algorithm that makes Google special—PageRank. The PageRank algorithm was introduced in 1998, at the seventh international World Wide Web conference (WWW98), by Sergey Brin and

Larry Page in a paper titled "The anatomy of a large-scale hypertextual Web search engine." Around the same time, Jon Kleinberg at IBM Almaden had discovered the *Hypertext Induced Topic Search (HITS)* algorithm. Both algorithms are link analysis models, although HITS didn't have the degree of commercial success that PageRank did.

In this section, we'll introduce the basic concepts behind the PageRank algorithm and the mechanics of calculating ranking values. We'll also examine the so-called *teleportation mechanism* and the inner workings of the *power method*, which is at the heart of the PageRank algorithm. Lastly, we'll demonstrate the combination of index scores and PageRank scores for improving our search results.

2.3.1   *An introduction to PageRank*

The key idea of PageRank is to consider hyperlinks from one page to another as recommendations or endorsements. So, the more endorsements a page has the higher its importance should be. In other words, if a web page is pointed to by other, important pages, then it's also an important page. Hold on a second! If you need to know what pages are important in order to determine the important pages, how does it work? Let's take a specific example and work out the details.

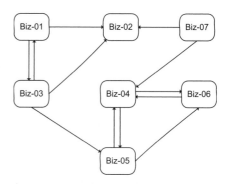

Figure 2.5   A directed graph that represents the linkage between the "biz" web pages.

Figure 2.5 shows the directed graph for all our sample web pages that start with the prefix *biz*. The titles of these articles and their file names are given in table 2.1.

If web page *A* has a link to web page *B*, there's an arrow pointing from *A* to *B*. Based on this figure, we'll introduce the *hyperlink matrix H* and a row vector *p* (the PageRank vector). Think of a matrix as nothing more than a table (a 2D array) and a vector as a

Table 2.1   The business news documents and their connection (see also figure 2.5)

Title	File name	Links to
Google Expands into Newspaper Ads	biz-01.html	biz-02, biz-03
Google's Sales Pitch to Newspapers	biz-02.html	(No outlink; *dangling node*)
Google Sells Newspaper Ads	biz-03.html	biz-01, biz-02, biz-05
NVidia Now a Supplier for MP3 Players	biz-04.html	biz-05, biz-06
Nvidia Shares Up on PortalPlayer Buy	biz-05.html	biz-04, biz-06
Chips Snap: Nvidia, Altera Shares Jump	biz-06.html	biz-04
Economic Stimulus Plan Helps Stock Prices	biz-07.html	biz-02, biz-04

single array in Java. Each row in the matrix *H* is constructed by counting the number of all the outlinks from page P_i, say $N(i)$ and assigning to column *j* the value *1/N(i)* if there's an outlink from page P_i to page P_j, or assigning the value 0 otherwise. Thus, for the graph in Figure 2.5, our *H* matrix would look like table 2.2.

Table 2.2   The H matrix for the business news pages and their connection (see also figure 2.5)

0	1/2	1/2	0	0	0	0
0	0	0	0	0	0	0
1/3	1/3	0	0	1/3	0	0
0	0	0	0	1/2	1/2	0
0	0	0	1/2	0	1/2	0
0	0	0	1	0	0	0
0	1/2	0	1/2	0	0	0

A couple of things stand out:

- There are a lot of zeros in that matrix—we call these matrices *sparse*. That's not a curse; it's actually a good thing. It's the result of the fact that a web page typically links to only a small number of other web pages—small with respect to the total number of web pages on the internet. Sparse matrices are desirable because their careful implementation can save a lot of storage space and computational time.
- All values in the matrix are less than or equal to 1. This turns out to be very important. There's a connection between the "random" surfer that Brin and Page envisioned (see section 2.3.2) and the theory of transition probability matrices, also known as *Markov chain theory*. That connection guarantees certain desirable properties for the algorithm.

2.3.2   *Calculating the PageRank vector*

The PageRank algorithm calculates the vector *p* using the following iterative formula:

$$p(k+1) = p(k) * H$$

The values of *p* are the PageRank values for every page in the graph. You start with a set of initial values such as *p(0) = 1/n*, where *n* is the number of pages in the graph, and use the formula to obtain *p(1)*, then *p(2)*, and so on, until the difference between two successive PageRank vectors is small enough; that arbitrary smallness is also known as the *convergence criterion* or *threshold*. This iterative method is the *power method* as applied to *H*. That, in a nutshell, is the PageRank algorithm.

For technical reasons—the *convergence* of the iterations to a *unique* PageRank vector—the matrix *H* is replaced by another matrix, usually denoted by *G* (the Google matrix), which has better mathematical properties. We won't review the mathematical details of the PageRank algorithm here, but let's describe the rationale behind Page-Rank and the problems that lead us to alter the matrix so that you have a better idea of what's going on.

The PageRank algorithm begins by envisioning a user who "randomly" surfs the Web. Our surfer can start from any given web page with outlinks. From there, by following one of the provided outlinks, he lands on another page. Then, he selects a new outlink to follow, and so on. After several clicks and trips through the graph, the proportion of time that our surfer spends on a given page is a measure of the relative importance that the page has with respect to the other pages on the graph. If the surfing is truly random—without an explicit bias—our surfer will visit pages that are pointed to by other pages, thus rendering those pages more important. That's all good and straightforward, but there are two problems.

The first problem is that on the internet there are some pages that don't point to any other pages; in our example, such a web page is biz-02 in figure 2.5. We call these pages of the graph *dangling nodes*. These nodes are a problem because they trap our surfer; without outlinks, there's nowhere to go! They correspond to rows that have value equal to zero for all their cells in the *H* matrix. To fix this problem, we introduce a random *jump*, which means that once our surfer reaches a dangling node, he may go to the address bar of his browser and type the URL of any one of the graph's pages. In terms of the *H* matrix, this corresponds to setting all the zeros (of a dangling node row) equal to *1/n*, where *n* is the number of pages in the graph. Technically, this correction of the *H* matrix is referred to as the *stochasticity adjustment*.

The second problem is that sometimes our surfer may get bored, or interrupted, and may jump to another page without following the linked structure of the web pages; the equivalent of *Star Trek*'s teleportation beam. To account for these arbitrary jumps, we introduce a new parameter that, in our code, we call alpha. This parameter determines the amount of time that our surfer will surf by following the links versus jumping arbitrarily from one page to another page; this parameter is sometimes referred to as the *damping factor*. Technically, this correction of the *H* matrix is referred to as the *primitivity adjustment*.

In the code, you'll find explicit annotations for these two problems. You don't need to worry about the mathematical details, but if you do, *Google's PageRank and Beyond: The Science of Search Engine Rankings* by Amy Langville and Carl Meyer is an excellent reference. So, let's get into action and get the *H* matrix by running some code. Listing 2.5 shows how to load just the web pages that belong to the business news and calculate the PageRank that corresponds to them.

Listing 2.5 Calculating the PageRank vector

```
FetchAndProcessCrawler crawler =
    new FetchAndProcessCrawler("C:/iWeb2/data/ch02",5,200);

crawler.setUrls("biz");        <--- Load business web pages
crawler.run();
```

```
PageRank pageRank = new PageRank(crawler.getCrawlData());   ⊲──┐ Build PageRank
                                                               │ instance
pageRank.setAlpha(0.8);

pageRank.setEpsilon(0.0001);

pageRank.build();   ⊲── Find PageRank values
```

Figure 2.6 shows a screenshot of the results. The page with the lowest relevance is biz-07.html; the most important page, according to PageRank, is biz-04.html. We've calculated a measure of relevance for each page that doesn't depend on the search term! We've calculated the PageRank values for our network.

```
Iteration: 8,    PageRank convergence error:
1.4462733376210263E-4
Index: 0-->  PageRank: 0.03944811976367004
Index: 1-->  PageRank: 0.09409188129468615
Index: 2-->  PageRank: 0.32404719855854225
Index: 3->  PageRank: 0.24328037107628753
Index: 4->  PageRank: 0.18555028886849476
Index: 5-->  PageRank: 0.05593157626783124
Index: 6->  PageRank: 0.061816733771795335

 Iteration: 9,    PageRank convergence error:
5.2102415715682415E-5
Index: 0-->  PageRank: 0.039443819850858625
Index: 1->  PageRank: 0.09407831778282823
Index: 2->  PageRank: 0.3240636997004271
Index: 3->  PageRank: 0.24328782624042117
Index: 4->  PageRank: 0.18555238603685822
Index: 5->  PageRank: 0.0559269660757835
Index: 6->  PageRank: 0.06181315844717868

_____ Calculation Results _____
Page U RL: file:/c:/iWeb2/data/ch02/biz-04.html  -->  Rank:
0.324063699700427
Page URL: file:/c:/iWeb2/data/ch02/biz-06.html  -->  Rank:
0.243287826240421
Page URL: file:/c:/iWeb2/data/ch02/biz-05.html  -->  Rank:
0.185552386036858
Page URL: file:/c:/iWeb2/data/ch02/biz-02.html  -->  Rank:
0.094078317782828
Page URL: file:/c:/iWeb2/data/ch02/biz-03.html  -->  Rank:
0.061813158447179
Page URL: file:/c:/iWeb2/data/ch02/biz- 01.html  -->  Rank:
0.055926966075784
Page URL: file:/c:/iWeb2/data/ch02/biz-07.html  -->  Rank:
0.039443819850859
```

Figure 2.6   The calculation of the PageRank vector for the small network of the business news web pages

2.3.3   *alpha: The effect of teleportation between web pages*

Let's vary the value of alpha from 0.8 to some other value between 0 and 1, in order to observe the effect of the teleportation between web pages on the PageRank values. As alpha approaches zero, the PageRank values for all pages tends to the value 1/7 (approximately equal to the decimal value 0.142857), which is exactly what you'd expect because our surfer is choosing his next destination at random, not on the basis of the links. On the other hand, as alpha approaches one, the PageRank values will converge to the PageRank vector that corresponds to a surfer who closely follows the links.

Another effect you should observe as the value of alpha approaches one is the number of iterations, which are required for convergence, increases. In fact, for our small web page network, we have table 2.3 (we keep the error tolerance equal to 10^{-10}).

Alpha	Number of iterations
0.50	13
0.60	15
0.75	19
0.85	23
0.95	29
0.99	32

Table 2.3   Effect of increasing alpha values on the number of iterations for the biz set of web pages

As you can see, the number of iterations grows rapidly as the value of alpha increases. For seven web pages, the effect is practically insignificant, but for 8 billion pages (roughly the number of pages that Google uses), a careful selection of alpha is crucial. In essence, the selection of alpha is a trade-off between adherence to the structure of the Web and computational efficiency. The value that Google is allegedly using for alpha is equal to 0.85. A value between 0.7 and 0.9 should provide you with a good trade-off between effectiveness and efficiency in your application, depending on the nature of your graph and user browsing habits.

There are techniques that can accelerate the convergence of the power method as well as methods that don't rely on the power method at all, the so-called *direct methods*. The latter are more appropriate for smaller networks (such as a typical intranet) and high values of alpha (for example, 0.99). We'll provide references at the end of this chapter, if you're interested in learning more about these methods.

2.3.4   *Understanding the power method*

Let's examine the code that calculates the PageRank values in more detail. Listing 2.6 shows an excerpt of the code responsible for evaluating the matrix *H* based on the link information; it's from the class iweb2.ch2.ranking.PageRankMatrixH.

Listing 2.6 Evaluating the matrix *H* based on the links between web pages

```
public void addLink(String pageUrl) {
   indexMapping.getIndex(pageUrl);
}

public void addLink(String fromPageUrl,
   String toPageUrl, double weight) {

   int i = indexMapping.getIndex(fromPageUrl);
   int j = indexMapping.getIndex(toPageUrl);

   try {

      matrix[i][j] = weight;

   } catch(ArrayIndexOutOfBoundsException e) {
     System.out.println("fromPageUrl:" + fromPageUrl
   + ", toPageUrl: " + toPageUrl);
   }
 }

public void addLink(String fromPageUrl, String toPageUrl) {
      addLink(fromPageUrl, toPageUrl, 1);
   }

public void calculate() {

   for(int i = 0, n = matrix.length; i < n; i++) {

      double rowSum = 0;

      for(int j = 0, k = matrix.length; j < k; j++) {

         rowSum += matrix[i][j];
      }

      if( rowSum > 0 ) {

         for(int j = 0, k = matrix.length; j < k; j++) {

            if( matrix[i][j] > 0 ) {

                matrix[i][j] =
   (double)matrix[i][j] / (double) rowSum;
            }
         }
      } else {

         numberOfPagesWithNoLinks++;
      }
   }
}

/**
 * A dangling node corresponds to a web page that has no outlinks.
 * These nodes result in an H row that has all its values equal to 0.
 */
public int[] getDangling() {

  int  n = getSize();
  int[] d = new int[n];
```

1 Assign initial values

2 Calculate substochastic version of matrix

3 Handle dangling node entries

```
    boolean foundOne = false;

    for (int i=0; i < n; i++) {

      for (int j=0; j < n; j++) {

      if (matrix[i][j] > 0) {

        foundOne = true;
        break;
      }
      }

      if (foundOne) {
        d[i] = 0;
      } else {
        d[i] = 1;
      }

      foundOne = false;
    }
    return d;
}
```

❶ The addLink methods allow us to assign initial values to the matrix variable, based on the links that exist between the pages.

❷ The calculate method sums up the total number of weights across a row (outlinks) and replaces the existing values with their weighted counterparts. Once that's done, if we add up all the entries in a row, the result should be equal to 1 for every nondangling node. This is the substochastic version of the original matrix.

❸ The dangling nodes are treated separately, since they have no outlinks. The getDangling() method will evaluate what rows correspond to the dangling nodes and will return the dangling vector.

Recall that we've separated the final matrix composition into three parts: the basic link contribution, the dangling node contribution, and the teleportation contribution. Let's see how we combine them to get the final matrix values that we'll use for the evaluation of the PageRank. Listing 2.7 shows the code that's responsible for assembling the various contributions and executing the power method. This code can be found in the iweb2.ch2.ranking.Rank class.

Listing 2.7 Applying the power method for the calculation of PageRank

```
public void findPageRank(double alpha, double epsilon) {

  // A counter for our iterations
  int k = 0;

  // auxiliary variable
  PageRankMatrixH matrixH = getH();

  // The H matrix has size nxn and the PageRank vector has size n
  int n = matrixH.getSize();

  //auxiliary variable - inverse of n
  double inv_n = (double)1/n;
```

```
// This is the actual nxn matrix of double values
double[][] H = matrixH.getMatrix();

// A dummy variable that holds our error, arbitrarily set to a value of 1
double error = 1;

// This holds the values of the PageRank vector
pR = new double[n];

// PageRank copy from the previous iteration
// The only reason that we need this is for evaluating the error
double[] tmpPR = new double[n];

// Set the initial values (ad hoc)
for (int i=0; i < n; i++) {
  pR[i] = inv_n;
}

// Book Section 2.3 -- Altering the H matrix: Dangling nodes

double[][] dNodes= getDanglingNodeMatrix();

// Book Section 2.3 -- Altering the H matrix: Teleportation

double tNodes=(1 - alpha) * inv_n;

//Replace the H matrix with the G matrix
for (int i=0; i < n; i++) {
  for (int j=0; j < n; j++) {

    H[i][j] = alpha*H[i][j] + dNodes[i][j] + tNodes;
  }
}

// Iterate until convergence!
// If error is smaller than epsilon then we've found the PageRank values
while ( error >= epsilon) {

  // Make a copy of the PageRank vector before we update it
  for (int i=0; i < n; i++) {
    tmpPR[i] = pR[i];
  }

  double dummy =0;

  // Now we get the next point in the iteration
  for (int i=0; i < n; i++) {

    dummy =0;

    for (int j=0; j < n; j++) {

      dummy += pR[j]*H[j][i];
    }

    pR[i] = dummy;
  }

  // Get the error, so that we can check convergence
  error = norm(pR,tmpPR);

  //increase the value of the counter by one
  k++;
```

```
}

// Report the final values
System.out.println(
"\n_____ Calculation Results _____\n");
for (int i=0; i < n; i++) {
  System.out.println("Page URL: "+
matrixH.getIndexMapping().getValue(i)+"  --> Rank: "+pR[i]);
  }
}
```

Given the importance of this method, we've gone to great lengths to make this as easy to read as possible. We've removed some Javadoc associated with a to-do topic, but otherwise this snippet is intact. So, we start by getting the values of the matrix *H* based on the links and then initialize the PageRank vector. Subsequently, we obtain the dangling node contribution and the teleportation contribution. Note that the dangling nodes require a full 2D array, whereas our teleportation contribution requires only a single double variable. Once we have all three components, we add them together. This is the most efficient way to prepare the data for the power method, but instead of full 2D arrays, you should use sparse matrices; we describe this enhancement in one of the to-do topics at the end of the chapter.

Once the new *H* matrix has been computed, we begin the power method—the code inside the while loop. We know that we've attained the PageRank values if our error is smaller than the arbitrarily small value epsilon. Of course, that makes you wonder: What if I change epsilon? Will the PageRank values change? If so, what should the value of epsilon be? Let's take these questions one by one. First, let's say that the error is calculated as the absolute value of the term by term difference between the new and the old PageRank vectors. Listing 2.8 shows the method norm, from the iweb2.ch2.ranking.Rank class, which evaluates the error.

Listing 2.8   Evaluation of the error between two consecutive PageRank vectors

```
private double norm(double[] a, double[] b) {

  double norm = 0;

  int n = a.length;

  for (int i=0; i < n; i++) {
    norm += Math.abs(a[i]-b[i]);
  }

  return norm;
}
```

If you run the code a few times, or observe figure 2.6 closely, you'll realize that the values of the PageRank at the time of convergence change at the digit that corresponds to the smallness of epsilon. So, the value of epsilon ought to be small enough to allow us to separate all web pages according to the PageRank values. If we have 100 pages then a value of epsilon equal to 0.001 should be sufficient. If we have the entire internet, about 10^{10} web pages, then we need a value of epsilon that is about 10^{-10} small.

2.3.5 Combining the index scores and the PageRank scores

Now that we've showed you how to implement the PageRank algorithm, we're ready to show you how to combine the Lucene search scores with the relevance of the pages as given by the PageRank algorithm. We'll use the same seven web pages that refer to business news, but this time we'll introduce three spam pages (called spam-biz-0x.html, where x stands for a numeral). The spam pages will fool the index-based search, but they won't fool PageRank.

Let's run this scenario and see what happens. Listing 2.9 shows you how to

- Load the business web pages, as we did before.
- Add the three spam pages, one for each subject.
- Index all the pages.
- Build the PageRank.
- Compute a hybrid ranking score that incorporates both the index relevance score (from Lucene) and the PageRank score.

Listing 2.9 Combining the Lucene and PageRank scores for ranking web pages

```
FetchAndProcessCrawler crawler =
⇒ new FetchAndProcessCrawler("C:/iWeb2/data/ch02",5,200);

crawler.setUrls("biz");                                          Add spam
crawler.addUrl("file:///c:/iWeb2/data/ch02/spam-biz-01.html"); ⟵ pages
crawler.addUrl("file:///c:/iWeb2/data/ch02/spam-biz-02.html");
crawler.addUrl("file:///c:/iWeb2/data/ch02/spam-biz-03.html");
crawler.run();

LuceneIndexer luceneIndexer =
⇒ new LuceneIndexer(crawler.getRootDir());       Index all
                                                 pages
luceneIndexer.run();                           ⟵

PageRank pageRank = new PageRank(crawler.getCrawlData());
pageRank.setAlpha(0.99);
pageRank.setEpsilon(0.00000001);
pageRank.build();                    ⟵ Build PageRank

MySearcher oracle = new MySearcher(luceneIndexer.getLuceneDir());

oracle.search("nvidia",5, pageRank);   ⟵ Search using combined score
```

The results of our search for "nvidia" are shown in figure 2.7. First, we print the result set that's based on Lucene alone, then we print the resorted results where we took into account the PageRank values. As you can see, we have a talent for spamming! The deceptive page comes first in our result set when we use Lucene alone. But when we apply the hybrid ranking, the most relevant pages come up first. The spam page went down in the abyss of irrelevance where it belongs! You've just written your first Google-like search engine. Congratulations!

The code that combines the two scores can be found in the class `MySearcher` inside the overloaded method `search` that uses the `PageRank` class as an argument.

```
bsh % oracle.search("nvidia",5,pr);

Search results using Lucene index scores:
Query: nvidia

Document Title: NVIDIA shares plummet into cheap medicine for
you!
Document URL: file:/c:/iWeb2/data/ch02/spam-biz-02.html   ->
Relevance Score: 0.519243955612183
_____
Document Title: Nvidia shares up on PortalPlayer buy
Document URL: file:/c:/iWeb2/data/ch02/biz-05.html
Relevance Score: 0.254376530647278
_____
Document Title: NVidia Now a Supplier for MP3 Players
Document URL: file:/c:/iWeb2/data/ch02/biz-04.html   ->
Relevance Score: 0.190782397985458
_____
Document Title: Chips Snap: Nvidia, Altera Shares Jump
Document URL: file:/c:/iWeb2/data/ch02/biz-06.html   ->
Relevance Score: 0.181735381484032

Document Title: Economic stimulus plan helps stock prices
Document URL: file:/c:/iWeb2/data/ch02/biz-07.html   ->
Relevance Score: 0.084792181849480
_____

Search results using combined Lucene scores and page rank scores:
Query: nvidia

Document URL: file:/c:/iWeb2/data/ch02/biz-04.html   ->
Relevance Score: 0.087211910261991
Document URL: file:/c:/iWeb2/data/ch02/biz-06.html   ->

Document URL: file:/c:/iWeb2/data/ch02/biz-05.html   ->
Relevance Score: 0.062737066556678
Document URL: file:/c:/iWeb2/data/ch02/spam-biz-02.html   ->

Document URL: file:/c:/iWeb2/data/ch02/biz-07.html   ->
Relevance Score: 0.000359708275446
_____
```

Figure 2.7   Combining the Lucene scores and the PageRank scores allows you to eliminate spam.

The snippet of code in listing 2.10 is from that method and captures the combination of the two scores.

Listing 2.10 Combining the Lucene scores and the PageRank scores

```
double m = 1 - (double) 1/pR.getH().getSize();        ⊲── Calculate scaling factor

for (int i = 0; i < numberOfMatches; i++) {

  url = docResults[i].getUrl();

  double hScore =                                                      Calculate
⇒ docResults[i].getScore() *Math.pow(pR.getPageRank(url),m);   ⊲─┘ hybrid score

  docResults[i].setScore(hScore);

  urlScores.put(hScore, url);        ⊲── Create map between scores and URLs
}
```

Now, a number of reasonable questions may come to your mind. Why did we introduce the variable m? Why didn't we take the average of the two scores? Why didn't we use a more complicated formula for combining the indexing score and the PageRank score? These are good questions to ask, and the answers may surprise you. Apart from the fact that our formula retains the value of the score between 0 and 1, our selections have been arbitrary. We may as well have taken the product of the two scores in order to combine them.

The rationale for raising the PageRank value to power m is that the small number of pages that we've indexed may cause the relevance score of indexing to be too high for the spam pages, thus artificially diluting the effectiveness of the PageRank. As the number of pages increases, the value of the scaled PageRank (the second term of the hybrid score) tends to the original PageRank value, because m quickly becomes approximately equal to 1. We believe that in small networks, such a power-law scaling can help you increase the importance of the link structure over that of the index. This formula should work well for small as well as large sets of documents. There's a deep mathematical connection between power laws and graphs similar to the internet, but we won't discuss it here (see Adamic et al.). The corollary is that when you deal with a small number of pages, and if the search term appears in the document a large number of times (as it happens with spam pages), the index page score (the number that Lucene returns as the score of a search result) will be close to 1; therefore a rescaling is required to balance that effect.

2.4 *Improving search results based on user clicks*

In the previous section, we showed that link analysis allows us to take advantage of the structural aspects of the internet. In this section, we'll talk about a different way of leveraging the nature of the internet: user clicks. As you know, every time a user executes a query, he'll either click one of the results or click the link that shows the next page of results, if applicable. In the first case, the user has identified something of interest and clicks the link either because that's what he was looking for or because the result is interesting and he wants to explore the related information, in order to decide if it is indeed what he was looking for. In the second case, the best results weren't what the user wanted to see and he wants to look at the next page just in case the search engine is worth a dime!

Kidding aside, one reason why evaluating relevance is a difficult task is because relevance is subjective. If you and I are looking results for the query "elections," you may be interested in the U.S. elections, while I may be interested in the UK elections, or even in my own town's elections. It's impossible for a search engine to know the intention (or the context) of your search without further information. So, the most relevant results for one person can be, and quite often are, different from the most relevant results for another person, even though the query terms may be identical!

We're going to introduce user clicks as a way of improving the search results for each user. This improvement is possible due to an algorithm that we'll study in great detail later in the book—the `NaiveBayes` classifier. We'll demonstrate the combination of index scores, PageRank scores, and the scores from the user clicks for improving our search results.

2.4.1   *A first look at user clicks*

User clicks allow us to take as input the interaction of each user with the search engine. Aristotle said, "We are what we repeatedly do," and that's the premise of user clicks analysis: your interaction with the search engine defines your own areas of interest and your own subjectivity. This is the first time that we describe an intelligent technique responsible for the *personalization* of a web application. Of course, a necessary condition for this is that the search engine can identify which queries come from a particular user. In other words, the user must be logged in to your application or must have otherwise established a session with the application. It should be clear that our approach for user-click analysis is applicable to every application that can record the user's clicks, and it's not specific to search applications.

Now, let's assume that you've collected the clicks of the users as indicated in the file user-clicks.csv, which you can find in the `data/ch02` directory together with the rest of the files that we've been using in this chapter. Our goal is to write code that can help us leverage that information, much like the PageRank algorithm helped us to leverage the information about our network. That is, we want to use this data to *personalize* the results of the search by appropriately modifying the ranking, depending on who submits the query. The comma separated file contains values in three fields:

- A string that identifies the user
- A string that represents the search query
- A string that contains the URL that the user has selected in the past, after reviewing the results for that query

If you don't know the user (no login/no session of any kind), you can use some default value such as "anonymous"—of course, you should ensure that anonymous isn't actually a valid username in your application! If your data has some other format, it's okay. You shouldn't have any problems adopting our code for your specific data. In order to personalize our results, we need to know the user, her question, and her past selections of links for that question. If you have that information available then you should be ready to get in action!

You may notice that, in our data, for the same user and the same query there is more than one entry. That's normal and you should notice it in your data as well. The number of times that a click appears in that file makes its URL a better or worse candidate for our search results. Typically, the same user will click a number of different links for the same query because his interest at the time may be different or because he may be looking for additional information on a topic. An interesting attribute that you should consider is a *timestamp*. Time-related information can help you identify temporal structure in your data. Some user clicks follow periodic patterns; some are event-driven; others are completely random. A timestamp can help you identify the patterns or the correlations with other events.

First let's see how we can obtain personalized results for our queries. Listing 2.11 shows our script, which is similar to listing 2.9, but this time we load the information about the user clicks and we run the same query "google ads" twice, once for user dmitry and once for user babis.

Listing 2.11   Accounting for user clicks in the search results

```
FetchAndProcessCrawler crawler =
➥ new FetchAndProcessCrawler("C:/iWeb2/data/ch02",5,200);

crawler.setUrls("biz");
crawler.addUrl("file:///c:/iWeb2/data/ch02/spam-biz-01.html");
crawler.addUrl("file:///c:/iWeb2/data/ch02/spam-biz-02.html");
crawler.addUrl("file:///c:/iWeb2/data/ch02/spam-biz-03.html");
crawler.run();

LuceneIndexer luceneIndexer =
➥ new LuceneIndexer(crawler.getRootDir());

luceneIndexer.run();
MySearcher oracle = new MySearcher(luceneIndexer.getLuceneDir());

PageRank pageRank = new PageRank(crawler.getCrawlData());
pageRank.setAlpha(0.9);
pageRank.setEpsilon(0.00000001);
pageRank.build();                                          Load user clicks

UserClick aux = new UserClick();
UserClick[] clicks =aux.load("C:/iWeb2/data/ch02/user-clicks.csv");   ⟵

TrainingSet tSet = new TrainingSet(clicks);   ⟵ Create training set

NaiveBayes naiveBayes = new NaiveBayes("Naïve Bayes", tSet);   ⟵  Define
                                                                  classifier
naiveBayes.trainOnAttribute("UserName");   ⟵  Select
naiveBayes.trainOnAttribute("QueryTerm_1");     attributes
naiveBayes.trainOnAttribute("QueryTerm_2");

naiveBayes.train();                     ⟵ Train classifier

oracle.setUserLearner(naiveBayes);

UserQuery dmitryQuery = new UserQuery("dmitry","google ads");
oracle.search(dmitryQuery,5, pageRank);

UserQuery babisQuery = new UserQuery("babis","google ads");
oracle.search(babisQuery,5, pageRank);
```

You've seen the first part of this script in listing 2.9. First, we load the pages that we want to search. After that, we index them with Lucene and build the PageRank that corresponds to their structure. The part that involves new code comes with the class `UserClick`, which represents the click of a specific user on a particular URL. We also defined the class `TrainingSet`, which holds all the user clicks. Of course, you may wonder, what's wrong with the array of `UserClicks`? Why can't we just use these objects? The answer lies in the following: in order to determine the links that are more likely to be desirable for a particular user and query, we're going to load the user clicks onto a *classifier*—in particular, the `NaiveBayes` classifier.

2.4.2   *Using the NaiveBayes classifier*

We'll address classification extensively in chapters 5 and 6, but we'll describe fundamentals here for clarity. Classification relies on reference structures that divide the space of all possible data points into a set of classes (also known as *categories* or *concepts*) that are (usually) non-overlapping. We encounter classification on a daily basis. From our everyday experience, we know that we can list food items according to a restaurant's menu, for example salads, appetizers, specialties, pastas, seafood, and so on. Similarly, the articles in a newspaper, or in a newsgroup on the internet, are classified based on their subject—politics, sports, business, world, entertainment, and so on. In short, we can say that classification algorithms allow us to automatically identify objects as part of this or that class.

In this section, we'll use a probabilistic classifier that implements what's known as the *naïve Bayes algorithm*; our implementation is provided by the `NaiveBayes` class. Classifiers are agnostic to `UserClicks`, they're only concerned with `Concepts`, `Instances`, and `Attributes`. Think of `Concepts`, `Instances`, and `Attributes` as the analogues of directories, files, and file attributes on your filesystem.

A classifier's job is to assign a `Concept` to an `Instance`; that's all a classifier does. In order to know what `Concept` should be assigned to a particular `Instance`, a classifier reads a `TrainingSet`—a set of `Instances` that already have a `Concept` assigned to them. Upon loading those `Instances`, the classifier *trains* itself, or *learns,* how to map a `Concept` to an `Instance` based on the assignments in the `TrainingSet`. The way that each classifier trains depends on the classifier.

Our intention is to use the `NaiveBayes` classifier as a means of obtaining a relevance score for a particular URL based on the user and submitted query. The good thing about the `NaiveBayes` classifier is that it provides something called the *conditional probability* of X given Y—a probability that tells us how likely is it to observe event X provided that we've already observed event Y. In particular, this classifier uses as input the following:

- The probability of observing concept X, in general, also known as the *prior* probability and denoted by $p(X)$.
- The probability of observing instance Y if we randomly select an instance from concept X, also known as the *likelihood* and denoted by $p(Y|X)$.
- The probability of observing instance Y in general, also known as the *evidence* and denoted by $p(Y)$.

The essential part of the classifier is the calculation of the probability that an observed instance *Y* belongs in concept *X*, which is also known as the *posterior probability* and denoted by $p(X|Y)$. The calculation is performed based on the following formula (known as Bayes theorem):

$$p(X|Y) = p(Y|X)\,p(X)\,/\,p(Y)$$

The NaiveBayes classifier can provide a measure of how likely it is that user *A* wants to see URL *X* provided that she submitted query *Q*; in our case, $Y = A + Q$. In other words, we won't use the NaiveBayes classifier to classify anything. We'll only use its capacity to produce a measure of relevance, which exactly fits our purposes. Listing 2.12 shows the relevant code from the class NaiveBayes; for a complete description, see section 5.3.

Listing 2.12 Evaluating the relevance of a URL with the NaiveBayes classifier

```
public class NaiveBayes implements Classifier {
  private String name;                                        ❶
  private TrainingSet tSet;                                   ❷

  private HashMap<Concept,Double> conceptPriors;              ❸

  protected Map<Concept,Map<Attribute, AttributeValue>> p;    ❹

  private ArrayList<String> attributeList;                    ❺

  public double getProbability(Concept c, Instance i) {
    double cP=0;
    if (tSet.getConceptSet().contains(c)) {

     cP = (getProbability(i,c)*getProbability(c))/getProbability(i);   ❻
    } else {

     cP = 1/(tSet.getNumberOfConcepts()+1);                  ❼
    }
    return cP;
  }

  public double getProbability(Instance i) {
    double cP=0;

    for (Concept c : getTset().getConceptSet()) {

     cP += getProbability(i,c)*getProbability(c);
    }
    return (cP == 0) ? (double)1/tSet.getSize() : cP;         ❽
  }

  public double getProbability(Concept c) {
    Double trInstanceCount = conceptPriors.get(c);
    if( trInstanceCount == null ) {
       trInstanceCount = 0.0;
    }
    return trInstanceCount/tSet.getSize();                    ❾
  }

  public double getProbability(Instance i, Concept c) {
    double cP=1;
    for (Attribute a : i.getAtrributes()) {
```

```
     if ( a != null && attributeList.contains(a.getName()) ) {

       Map<Attribute, AttributeValue> aMap = p.get(c);
       AttributeValue aV = aMap.get(a);
       if ( aV == null) {                                    ❿
           cP *= ((double) 1 / (tSet.getSize()+1));
       } else {
         cP *= (double)(aV.getCount()/conceptPriors.get(c));
       }
     }
   }
 }
   return (cP == 1) ? (double)1/tSet.getNumberOfConcepts() : cP;
 }
}
```

First, let's examine the main points of the listing:

❶ This is a name for this instance of the `NaiveBayes` classifier.

❷ Every classifier needs a training set. The name of the classifier and its training set are intentionally set during the Construction phase. Once you've created an instance of the `NaiveBayes` classifier, you can't set its `TrainingSet`, but you can always get the reference to it and add instances.

❸ The `conceptPriors` map stores the counts for each of the concepts that we have in our training set. We could've used it to store the *prior* probabilities, not just the counts. But we want to reuse these counts, so in the name of computational efficiency, we store the counts; the priors can be obtained by a simple division.

❹ The variable p stores the conditional probabilities—the probability of observing concept *X* given that we observed instance *Y*, or in the case of the user clicks, the probability that a user *A* wants to see URL *X* provided that he submitted query *Q*.

❺ This is the list of attributes that should be considered by the classifier for training. The instances of a training set may have many attributes and it's possible that only a few of these attributes are relevant (see chapter 5), so we keep track of what attributes should be used.

❻ If we've encountered the concept in our training set, use the formula that we mentioned earlier and calculate the posterior probability.

❼ It's possible that we haven't encountered a particular instance before, so the `getProbability(i)` method call wouldn't be meaningful. In that case, we assign something reasonable as a *posterior* probability. Setting that value equal to one over the number of all known concepts is reasonable, in the absence of information for assigning higher probability to any one concept. We've also added unity to that number. That's an arbitrary modification, intended to lower the probability assigned to each concept, especially for a small number of observed concepts. Think about why, and under what conditions, this can be useful.

❽ This method of the `NaiveBayes` class isn't essential for the pure classification problem because its value is the same for all concepts. In the context of this example, we decided to keep it. Feel free to modify the code so that you get back only the numerator of the Bayes theorem; what do your results look like?

⑨ The prior probability for a given concept c is evaluated based on the number of times that we encountered this concept in the training set. Note that we arbitrarily assign probability zero to unseen concepts. This can be good and bad. If you're pretty confident that you have all related concepts in your training set then this ad hoc choice helps you eliminate flukes in your data. In a more general case, where you might not have seen a lot of concepts, you should replace the zero value with something more reasonable—one over the total number of known concepts. What other choices do you think are reasonable? Is it important to have a sharp estimate of that quantity? Regardless of your answer, try to rationalize your decision and justify it as best as you can.

⑩ We arrive at the heart of the `NaiveBayes` class. The "naïve" part of the Bayes theorem is the fact that we evaluate the likelihood of observing `Instance i`, as the product of the probabilities of observing each of the attribute values. That assumption implies that the attributes are statistically independent. We used quotes around the word *naïve* because the naïve Bayes algorithm is very robust and widely applicable, even in problems where the attribute independence assumption is clearly violated. It can be shown that the naïve Bayes algorithm is optimal in the exact opposite case—cases in which there's a completely deterministic dependency among the attributes (see Rish).

If you recall the script in listing 2.11, we've created a training set and an instance of the classifier with that training set, and before we assign the classifier to the `MySearcher` instance, we do the following two things:

- We tell the classifier what attributes should be taken into account for training purposes.
- We tell the classifier to train itself on the set of user clicks that we just loaded and for the attributes that we specified.

The attribute with label `UserName` corresponds to the user. The attributes `QueryTerm_1` and `QueryTerm_2` correspond to the first and second term of the query, respectively. These terms are obtained by using Lucene's `StandardAnalyzer` class. During training, we're assigning probabilities based on the frequency of occurrence for each instance. The important method, in our context, is `getProbability(Concept c, Instance i)`, which we'll use to obtain the relevance of a particular URL (`Concept`) when a specific user executes a specific query (`Instance`).

2.4.3 Combining Lucene indexing, PageRank, and user clicks

Armed with the probability of a user preferring a particular URL for a given query, we can proceed and combine all three techniques to obtain our enhanced search results. The relevant code is shown in listing 2.13.

Listing 2.13 Lucene indexing, PageRank values, and user click probabilities

```
public SearchResult[] search(UserQuery uQuery,
    int numberOfMatches, Rank pR) {

  SearchResult[] docResults =
    search(uQuery.getQuery(), numberOfMatches);    ⟵— Results based on index
```

```
String url;

StringBuilder strB = new StringBuilder();

int docN = docResults.length;                                      Collect at most
                                                           numberOfMatches documents
if (docN > 0) {

  int loop = (docN<numberOfMatches) ? docN : numberOfMatches;   ◁

  for (int i = 0; i < loop; i++) {

    url = docResults[i].getUrl();                              Collect all user
                                                               click scores
    UserClick uClick = new UserClick(uQuery,url);    ◁

      double indexScore = docResults[i].getScore();

    double pageRankScore  = pR.getPageRank(url);

    BaseConcept bC = new BaseConcept(url);

    double userClickScore = learner.getProbability(bC, uClick);

    double hScore;                      Evaluate final
                                        (hybrid) score
    if (userClickScore == 0) {   ◁

      hScore = indexScore * pageRankScore * EPSILON;

    } else {

        hScore = indexScore * pageRankScore * userClickScore;
      }

      docResults[i].setScore(hScore);

    strB.append("Document URL   : ")
➡   .append(docResults[i].getUrl()).append(" --> ");
    strB.append("Relevance Score: ")
➡   .append(docResults[i].getScore()).append("\n");
    }
  }
  strB.append(PRETTY_LINE);
  System.out.println(strB.toString());

  return docResults;
}
```

Figure 2.8 shows the results for user dmitry. As you can see, due to the fact that dmitry clicked several times on the page biz-03.html in the past, the relevance score for that page is the highest. The second best hit is page biz-01.html, which is also in the user clicks file. The spam page appears third, but that's a side effect of the small number of pages; we intentionally didn't include our scaling m factor to demonstrate its impact on the results.

In figure 2.9, we execute the same query—"google ads"—but this time we do it as user babis. We've reversed the order of dmitry's clicks to create the clicks for the user babis. The results show that the first hit is page biz-01.html; page biz-03.html is second. Everything else is the same. The only difference in the result set comes from the fact that the query was executed by different users, and that difference reflects exactly what the application *learned* from the file user-clicks.csv.

```
bsh % UserQuery dQ = new UserQuery("dmitry", "google ads");
bsh % oracle.search(dQ,5,pr);

Search results using Lucene index scores:
Query: google ads

Document Title: Google Ads and the best drugs
Document URL: file:/c:/iWeb2/data/ch02/spam-biz-01.html ->
Relevance Score: 0.788674294948578
_____

Document Title: Google Expands into Newspaper Ads
Document URL: file:/c:/iWeb2/data/ch02/biz-01.html ->
Relevance Score: 0.382
_____

Document Title: Google sells newspaper ads
Document URL: file:/c:/iWeb2/data/ch02/biz-03.html ->
Relevance Score: 0.317
_____

Document Title:Google's sales pitch to newspapers
Document URL: file:/c:/iWeb2/data/ch02/biz-02.html ->
Relevance Score: 0.291
_____

Document Title: Economic stimulus plan helps stock prices
Document URL: file:/c:/iWeb2/data/ch02/biz-07.html ->
Relevance Score: 0.031
_____


Search results using combined Lucene scores, page rank scores and
user clicks:
Query: user=dmitry, query text=google ads

Document URL: file:/c:/iWeb2/data/ch02/biz-03.html   ->
Relevance Score: 0.0057

Document URL: file:/c:/iWeb2/data/ch02/biz-01.html   ->
Relevance Score: 0.0044

Document URL: file:/c:/iWeb2/data/ch02/spam-biz-01.html->
Relevance Score: 0.0040

Document URL: file:/c:/iWeb2/data/ch02/biz-02.html   ->
Relevance Score: 0.0012

Document URL: file:/c:/iWeb2/data/ch02/biz-07.html   ->
Relevance Score: 0.0002
```

Figure 2.8   Combining Lucene, PageRank, and user clicks to produce high-relevance search results for dmitry.

```
bsh % UserQuery bQ = new UserQuery("babis", "google ads");
bsh % oracle.search(bQ,5,pr);


Search results using Lucene index scores:
Query: google ads


Document Title: Google Ads and the best drugs
Document URL: file:/c:/iWeb2/data/ch02/spam-biz-01.html ->
Relevance Score: 0.788674294948578

_____

Document Title: Google Expands into Newspaper Ads
Document URL: file:/c:/iWeb2/data/ch02/biz-01.html ->
Relevance Score: 0.382

_____

Documen t Title: Google sells newspaper ads
Document URL: file:/c:/iWeb2/data/ch02/biz-03.html ->
Relevance Score: 0.317

_____

Document Title: Google's sales pitch to newspapers
Document URL: file:/c:/iWeb2/data/ch02/biz-02.html ->
Relevance Score: 0.291

_____

Document Title: Economic stimulus plan helps stock prices
Document URL: file:/c:/iWeb2/data/ch02/biz-07.html ->
Relevance Score: 0.0314

_____

Search results using combined Lucene scores, page rank scores
and user clicks:
Query: user=babis, query text=google ads

Document URL: file:/c:/iWeb2/data/ch02/biz-01.html    ->
Relevance Score: 0.00616

Document URL: file:/c:/iWeb2/data/ch02/biz-03.html    ->
Relevance Score: 0.00407

Document URL: file:/c:/iWeb2/data/ch02/spam-biz-01.html ->
Relevance Score: 0.00393

Document URL: file:/c:/iWeb2/data/ch02/biz-02.html    ->    .
Re levance Score: 0.00117
```

Figure 2.9   Lucene, PageRank, and user clicks together produce high-relevance search results for Babis.

That's great! We now have a powerful improvement over the pure index-based search that accounts for the structure of the hyperlinked documents and the preferences of the users based on their clicks. But a large number of applications must search among documents that aren't explicitly linked to each other. Is there anything that we can do to improve our search results in that case? Let's examine exactly that case in what follows.

2.5 Ranking Word, PDF, and other documents without links

Let's say that you have hundreds of thousands of Word or PDF documents, or any other type of document that you want to search through. At first, it may seem that indexing is your only option and, at best, you may be able to do some user-click analysis too. But we'll show you that it's possible to extend the same ideas of link analysis that we applied to the Web. Hopefully, we'll get you thinking and develop an even better method. By the way, to the best of our knowledge, the technique that we describe here has never been published before.

To demonstrate that it's possible to introduce ranking in documents without links, we'll take the HTML documents and create Word documents with identical content. This willl allow us to compare our results with those in section 2.3 and identify any similarities or differences in the two approaches. Parsing Word documents can be done easily using the open source library *TextMining*; note that the name has changed to *tm-extractor*. The license of this library starting with the 1.0 version is LGPL, which makes it business friendly. You can obtain the source code from http://code.google.com/p/text-mining/source/checkout. We've written a class called `MSWordDocumentParser` that encapsulates the parsing of a Word document in that way.

2.5.1 An introduction to DocRank

In listing 2.14 we use the same classes to read the Word documents as we did to read the HTML documents (the `FetchAndProcessCrawler` class) and we use Lucene to index the content of these documents.

Listing 2.14 Ranking documents based on content

```
FetchAndProcessCrawler crawler =
  new FetchAndProcessCrawler("C:/iWeb2/data/ch02",5,200);      Load business
                                                               Word documents
crawler.setUrls("biz-docs");

crawler.addDocSpam();
crawler.run();

LuceneIndexer luceneIndexer =                  Build Lucene
  new LuceneIndexer(crawler.getRootDir());     index           Create
                                                               plain
luceneIndexer.run();                                           search
                                                               engine
MySearcher oracle = new MySearcher(luceneIndexer.getLuceneDir());
oracle.search("nvidia",5);

DocRank docRank = new DocRank(luceneIndexer.getLuceneDir(),7);
```

```
docRank.setAlpha(0.9);
docRank.setEpsilon(0.00000001);           Create DocRank
docRank.build();                     <──┘  engine

oracle.search("nvidia",5, docRank);
```

Figure 2.10 shows that a search for "nvidia" returns as the highest ranked result the undesirable spam-biz-02.doc file—a result similar to the case of the HTML documents. Of course, in the case of Word, PDF, and other text documents, the chance of having spam documents is fairly low, but you could have documents with unimportant repetitions of terms in them.

So far, everything has been the same as in listing 2.9. The new code is invoked by the class DocRank. That class is responsible for creating a measure of relevance between documents that's equivalent to the relevance which PageRank assigns between web pages. Unlike the PageRank class, it takes an additional argument whose role we'll explain later on. Similar to the previous sections, we want to have a matrix that represents the importance of page Y based on page X. Our problem is that, unlike with web pages, we don't have an explicit linkage between our documents. Those web links were only used to create a matrix whose values told us how important page Y is according to page X. If we could find a way to assign a measure of importance for document Y according to document X we could use the same mathematical theory that underpins the PageRank algorithm. Our code provides such a matrix.

```
bsh % oracle.search("nvidia", 5);

Search results using Lucene index sco
Query: nvidia

Document Title: NVIDIA shares plummet into cheap medicine for
you!
Document URL: file:/c:/iWeb2/data/ch02/spam-biz-02.doc -->
Relevance Score: 0.458221405744553
────────────────────────────────────────────────────────────
Document Title: Nvidia shares up on PortalPlayer buy
Document URL: file:/c:/iWeb2/data/ch02/biz-05.doc   -->
Relevance Score: 0.324011474847794
────────────────────────────────────────────────────────────
Document Title: NVidia Now a Supplier for MP3 Players
Document URL: file:/c:/iWeb2/data/ch02/biz-04.doc   -->
Relevance Score: 0.194406896829605
────────────────────────────────────────────────────────────
Document Title: Nov. 6, 2006, 2:38PM?Chips Snap: Nvidia, Altera
Shares Jump
Document URL: file:/c:/iWeb2/data/ch02/biz-06.doc   -->
Relevance Score: 0.185187965631485
────────────────────────────────────────────────────────────
```

Figure 2.10   Index based searching for "nvidia" in the Word documents that contain business news and spam

2.5.2   *The inner workings of DocRank*

Our measure of importance is to a large degree arbitrary, and its viability depends crucially on two properties that are related to the elements of our new *H* matrix. The elements of that matrix should be such that:

- They are all positive numbers.
- The sum of the values in any row is equal to 1.

Whether our measure will be successful depends on the kind of documents that we're processing. Listing 2.15 shows the code from class `DocRankMatrixBuilder` that builds matrix *H* in the case of our Word documents.

Listing 2.15   DocRankMatrixBuilder: Ranking text documents based on content

```
public class DocRankMatrixBuilder implements CrawlDataProcessor {
   private final int TERMS_TO_KEEP = 3;

   private int termsToKeep=0;
   private String indexDir;
   private PageRankMatrixH matrixH;

   public void run() {
      try {
         IndexReader idxR =
 ➥ IndexReader.open(FSDirectory.getDirectory(indexDir));
         matrixH = buildMatrixH(idxR);
      }
      catch(Exception e) {
         throw new RuntimeException("Error: ", e);
      }
   }

   // Collects doc ids from the index for documents with matching doc type
   private List<Integer> getProcessedDocs(IndexReader idxR)
      throws IOException {
      List<Integer> docs = new ArrayList<Integer>();
      for(int i = 0, n = idxR.maxDoc(); i < n; i++) {
         if( idxR.isDeleted(i) == false ) {
            Document doc = idxR.document(i);
            if( eligibleForDocRank(doc.get("doctype") ) ) {
               docs.add(i);
            }
         }
      }
      return docs;
   }

// Is the index entry eligible?

   private boolean eligibleForDocRank(String doctype) {
      return ProcessedDocument.DOCUMENT_TYPE_MSWORD
 ➥    .equalsIgnoreCase(doctype);
   }

   private PageRankMatrixH buildMatrixH(IndexReader idxR)
```

```
        throws IOException {

     // consider only URLs with fetched and parsed content
        List<Integer> allDocs = getProcessedDocs(idxR);

        PageRankMatrixH docMatrix =
➥   new PageRankMatrixH( allDocs.size() );

        for(int i = 0, n = allDocs.size(); i < n; i++) {

            for(int j = 0, k = allDocs.size(); j < k; j++) {

                double similarity = 0.0d;

              Document docX = idxR.document(i);
                String xURL= docX.get("url");

                if ( i == j ) {

                   // Avoid shameless self-promotion ;-)
                   docMatrix.addLink(xURL, xURL, similarity);

                } else {

                   TermFreqVector x =
➥   idxR.getTermFreqVector(i, "content");
                   TermFreqVector y =
➥   idxR.getTermFreqVector(j, "content");

                   similarity = getImportance(x.getTerms(),
➥   x.getTermFrequencies(), y.getTerms(), y.getTermFrequencies());

                   // add link from docX to docY
                   Document docY = idxR.document(j);
                   String yURL = docY.get("url");

                   docMatrix.addLink(xURL, yURL, similarity);
               }
           }
        }
        docMatrix.calculate();

        return docMatrix;
     }

     // Calculates importance of document Y in the context of document X
     private double getImportance(String[] xTerms, int[] xTermFreq,
                        String[] yTerms, int[] yTermFreq){

     // xTerms is an array of the most frequent terms for first document
        Map<String, Integer> xFreqMap =
➥   buildFreqMap(xTerms, xTermFreq);

       // yTerms is an array of the most frequent terms for second document
        Map<String, Integer> yFreqMap =
➥   buildFreqMap(yTerms, yTermFreq);

        // sharedTerms is the intersection of the two sets
        Set<String> sharedTerms =
➥   new HashSet<String>(xFreqMap.keySet());
        sharedTerms.retainAll(yFreqMap.keySet());
```

```
       double sharedTermsSum = 0.0;

       // Note that this isn't symmetrical.
       // If you swap X with Y then you get a different value;
       // unless the frequencies are equal, of course!

       double xF, yF;
       for(String term : sharedTerms) {

           xF = xFreqMap.get(term).doubleValue();
           yF = yFreqMap.get(term).doubleValue();

           sharedTermsSum += Math.round(Math.tanh(yF/xF));
       }

       return sharedTermsSum;
   }

   private Map<String, Integer> buildFreqMap(String[] terms, int[] freq) {
int topNTermsToKeep = (termsToKeep == 0)? TERMS_TO_KEEP: termsToKeep;

Map<String, Integer> freqMap =
➥  TermFreqMapUtils.getTopNTermFreqMap(terms, freq, topNTermsToKeep);

       return freqMap;
   }
}
```

There are two essential ingredients in our solution. First, note that we use the Lucene *term vectors*, which are pairs of terms and their frequencies. If you recall our discussion about indexing documents with Lucene, we mentioned that the text of a document is first parsed, then analyzed before it's indexed. During the analysis phase, the text is dissected into *tokens* (terms); the way that the text is tokenized depends on the analyzer that's used. The beautiful thing with Lucene is that we can retrieve that information later on and use it. In addition to the terms of the text, Lucene also provides us with the number of times that each term appears in a document. That's all we need from Lucene: a set of terms and their frequency of occurrence in each document.

The second ingredient of our solution is the choice of assigning importance to each document. The method getImportance in listing 2.15 shows that, for each document X, we calculate the importance of document Y by following two steps: (1) we find the intersection between the most frequent terms of document X and the most frequent terms of document Y and (2) for each term in the set of shared terms (intersection), we calculate the ratio of the number of times the term appears in document Y (Y-frequency of occurrence) over the number of times the term appears in document X (X-frequency of occurrence). The importance of document Y in the context of document X is given as the sum of all these ratios and filtered by the hyperbolic tangent function (Math.tanh) as well as the rounding function (Math.round). The end result of these operations will be the entry in the H matrix for row X and column Y.

We use the hyperbolic tangent function because we want to gauge whether a particular term between the two documents should be considered a good indicator for assigning importance. We aren't interested in the exact value; we're interested only in keeping the importance factor within reasonable limits. The hyperbolic tangent takes values between 0 and 1, so the final rounding will ensure that each term can either be neglected or count for one unit of importance. That's the rationale behind building the formula by using these functions.

Figure 2.11 shows that a search for "nvidia" returns the file biz-05.doc as the highest-ranked result; that's a legitimate file (not spam) and related to nvidia! The spam

```
bsh % oracle.search("nvidia",5,dr);

Search results using Lucene index scores:
Query: nvidia

Document Title: NVIDIA shares plummet into cheap medicine for
you!

Document URL: file:/c:/iWeb2/data/eh02/spam-biz-02.doc   ->
Relevance Score: 0.4582
_____

Document Title: Nvidia shares up on PortalPlayer buy

Document URL: file:/c:/iWeb2/data/ch02/biz-05.doc   ->
Relevance Score: 0.3240
_____

Document Title: NVidia Now a Supplier for MP3 Players

Document URL: file:/c:/iWeb2/data/ch02/biz-04.doc   ->
Relevance Score: 0.1944
_____

Document Title: Chips Snap: Nvidia, Altera Shares Jump

Document URL: file:/c:/iWeb2/data/ch02/biz-06.doc   ->
Relevance Score: 0.1852
_____


Search results using combined Lucene scores and page rank scores:
Query: nvidia

Document URL: file:/c:/iWeb2/data/ch02/biz-05.doc   ->
Relevance Score: 0.03858

Document URL: file:/c:/iWeb2/data/eh02/spam-biz-02.doc   ->
Relevance Score: 0.03515

Document URL: file:/c:/iWeb2/data/ch02/biz-04.doc   ->
Relevance Score: 0.02925

Document URL: file:/c:/iWeb2/data/ch02/biz-06.doc   ->
Relevance Score: 0.02233
_____
```

Figure 2.11   Index and ranking based search for "nvidia" on the Word documents

page survived because the number of our documents is small, but we did get additional value. The Lucene index had the exact same information all along, but its metric of relevance has been skewed by the ersatz news document. DocRank helped us to increase the relevance of the biz-05.doc document, and in more realistic situations it can help you identify the most pertinent documents in a collection. The DocRank values, like the PageRank values, need to be calculated only once, but can be reused for all queries.

There are other means of enhancing the search of plain documents, and we provide the related references at the end of this chapter. DocRank is a more powerful algorithm when applied to data from a relational database. To see this, let's say that we have two tables—table *A* and table *B*—that are related to each other through table *C*; this is a common case. For example, you may have a table that stores users, another table that stores groups, and another that stores the relationship between users and groups by relating the IDs of each entry. In effect, you have one graph that connects the users based on their groups and another graph that connects the groups based on their users. Every time you have a linked representation of entities, it's worthwhile to try the DocRank algorithm or a similar variant. Don't be afraid to experiment! There's no single answer to this kind of problem, and sometimes the answer may surprise you.

2.6 Large-scale implementation issues

Everything that we've discussed so far can be used across the functional areas and the various domains of web applications. But if you're planning to process vast amounts of data, and you have the computational resources to do it, you're going to face issues that fall largely into two categories. The first category is related to the mathematical properties of the algorithms; the second is related to the software engineering aspects of manipulating data on the scale of terabytes or even petabytes!

The first symptom of large-scale computing constraints is the lack of addressable memory. In other words, your data is so large that the data structures don't fit in memory anymore; that would be particularly true for an interpreted language, like Java, because even if you manage to fit the data, you'd probably have to worry about garbage collection. In large-scale computing, there are two basic strategies for dealing with that problem. The first is the construction of more efficient data structures, so that the data does fit in memory; the second is the construction of efficient, distributed, I/O infrastructure for accessing and manipulating the data *in situ*. For very large datasets, with sizes similar to what Google handles, you should implement both strategies because you want to squeeze every bit of efficiency out of your system.

In terms of representing data more efficiently, consider the structures that we used for storing the *H* matrix. The part of the original link structure required a double[n][n] and the part of the dangling node matrix required another double[n][n], where n is the number of pages (or documents for DocRank). If you think about it, that's a huge waste of resources when n is very large, because most of these double values are zero. A more efficient way to store that information would be by means of an *adjacency list*. In Java, you can easily implement an adjacency list using a `Hashtable` that will contain `HashSets`. So, the definition of the variable `matrix` in the class `PageRankMatrixH` would look as follows:

```
Hashtable<Integer, Hashtable <Integer,Double>> matrix;
```

One of the exercises that we propose is to rewrite our algorithmic implementation using these efficient structures. You could even compress the data in the adjacency list by *reference encoding* or other techniques (see Boldi and Vigna). Reference encoding relies on the similarity of web pages and sacrifices simplicity of implementation for memory efficiency.

Another implementation aspect for large-scale searching is the accuracy that you're going to have for the PageRank values (or any other implementation of the `Rank` base class). To differentiate between values of the PageRank for any two web pages among *N*, you'll need a minimum of $1/N$ accuracy in your numerical calculation. So, if you deal with *N = 1000* pages then even 10^{-4} accuracy should suffice. If you want to get the rankings of billions of pages, the accuracy should be on the order of 10^{-10} for the PageRank values.

Consider a situation where the dangling nodes make up a large portion of your fetched web pages. This could happen if you want to build a dedicated search engine for a central site such as the Apache set of projects, or something less ambitious such as the Jakarta project alone. Brin and Page realized that handling a large number of nodes that are, in essence, artificial—because their entries in the *H* matrix don't reflect the link structure of the web but rather help the matrix to conform with certain nice mathematical properties—isn't going to be very efficient. They suggested you could remove the dangling nodes during the computation of the PageRank, and add them back after the values of the remaining PageRanks have converged sufficiently.

We don't know, of course, the actual implementation of the Google search engine—such secrets are closely guarded—but we can say with certainty that an equitable treatment of all pages will require inclusion of the dangling nodes from the beginning to the end of the calculation of PageRank. In an effort to be both fair and efficient, we can use methods that rely on the symmetric reordering of the *H* matrix. These techniques appear to converge at the same rate as the original PageRank algorithm while acting on a smaller problem, which means that you can have significant gains in computational time; for more details see *Google's PageRank and Beyond: The Science of Search Engine Rankings*.

Implicit in all discussions with respect to large-scale computations of search are concerns about memory and speed. One speed factor is the number of iterations for the power method, which as we've seen depends on the value of `alpha` as well as the number of the linked pages. Unfortunately, in practitioner's books similar to ours, we found statements asserting that the initial value of the PageRank vector doesn't matter and that you could set all the values equal to 1. Strictly speaking, that's not true and it can have dramatic implications when you work with large datasets whose composition changes periodically. The closer the initial vector is to the unique PageRank values, the fewer the number of iterations required. A number of techniques, known collectively as *approximate aggregation techniques,* to compute the PageRank vector of a smaller matrix in order to generate an estimate of the true updated distribution of the PageRank vector. That estimate, in turn, will be used as the initial vector for the final computation. The mathematical underpinnings of these methods won't be covered in this book. For more information on these techniques, see the references at the end of this chapter.

While we're discussing acceleration techniques for the computation of the PageRank vector, we should mention the Aitken extrapolation, a quadratic extrapolation technique by Kamvar et al., as well as more advanced techniques such as the application of spectral methods (such as Chebyshev polynomial spectral methods). These techniques aim at obtaining a better approximation of the PageRank vector between iterations. They may be applicable in the calculation of your ranking, and it may be desirable to implement them; see the references for more details.

With regard to the software aspects of an implementation for large-scale computations, we should mention Hadoop (http://hadoop.apache.org/). Hadoop is a full-blown, top-level project of the Apache Software Foundation and it offers an open source software platform that's scalable, economical, efficient, and reliable. Hadoop implements MapReduce (see Dean and Ghemawat), by using its own distributed file-system (HDFS). MapReduce divides applications into many small blocks of work. HDFS creates multiple copies of data blocks for reliability, and places them on computational nodes around a computational cluster (see figure 2.12). MapReduce can then process the data where it's located. Hadoop has been demonstrated on clusters with 2,000 nodes. The current design target for the Hadoop platform is 10,000 node clusters.

The ability to handle large datasets is certainly of great importance in real-world production systems. We gave you a glimpse of the issues that can arise and pointed you to some appropriate projects and the relevant literature on that subject. When you design a search engine, you need to consider not just your ability to scale and handle a larger volume of data, but the quality of your search results. At the end of the day, your users want your results to be fast and accurate. So, let's see a few quantitative ways of measuring whether what we have is what we want.

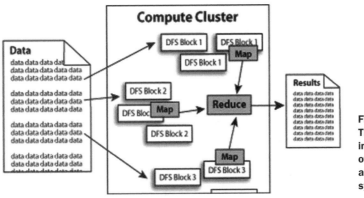

Figure 2.12 The MapReduce implementation of Hadoop using a distributed file system

2.7   *Is what you got what you want? Precision and recall*

Google and Yahoo! spend a considerable amount of time studying the quality of their search engines. Similar to the process of validation and verification (QA) of software systems, search quality is crucial to the success of a search engine. If you submit a query to a search engine, you may or may not find what you want. There are various metrics that quantify the degree of success for a search engine. The two most common metrics—*precision* and *recall*—are easy to implement and understand qualitatively.

Figure 2.13 shows the possibilities of results from a typical query. That is, provided a set of documents, a subset of these documents will be relevant to your query and another subset will be retrieved. Clearly the goal is to retrieve all the relevant documents, but that's rarely the case. So, our attention turns quickly to the intersection between these two sets, as indicated in figure 2.13.

In information retrieval, precision is the ratio of the number of relevant documents that are retrieved (RR) divided by the total number of retrieved documents (Rd)—*precision = RR/Rd*. In figure 2.13, precision would be about 1/5 or 0.2. That's measured with the "eye norm"; it's not exact, we're engineers after all! On the other hand, recall is the ratio of the number of relevant documents that are retrieved divided by the total number of relevant documents (Rt)—*recall = RR/Rt*.

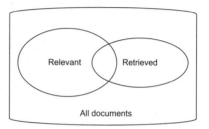

Figure 2.13   This diagram shows the set of relevant documents and the set of retrieved documents; their intersection is used to define the search metrics precision and recall.

Qualitatively, these two measures answer different questions. Precision answers, "To what extent do I get what I want?" Recall answers, "Does what I got include everything that I can get?" Clearly it's easier to find precision than it is to find recall, because finding recall implies that we already know the set of all relevant documents for a given query. In reality, that's hardly ever the case. We plot these two measures together so that we can assess to what extent the good results blend with bad results. If what I get is the truth, the whole truth, and nothing but the truth, then the precision and recall values for my queries will both be close to one.

During the evaluation of the algorithms and tweaks involved in tuning a search engine, you should employ plots of these two quantities for representative queries that span the range of questions that your users are trying to answer. Figure 2.14 shows a typical plot of these quantities. For each query, we enter a point that corresponds to the precision and recall values of that query. If you execute many queries and plot these points, you'll get a line that looks like the one shown in figure 2.14. Be

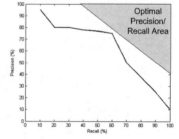

Figure 2.14   A typical precision/ recall plot for a search engine

aware that interpolating the values, if you have a small number of queries, may not be a good idea. It would be better to leave the values as points without connecting them.

Good precision-recall points are located in the upper-right corner of the graph because we want to have high precision and high recall. These plots can help you establish, objectively, the need for a particular tweak in an algorithm or the superiority of one approach versus another. It could help you convince your ever-skeptical upper management team to use the algorithms of this book! You can practice by using the three approaches that we presented in this chapter (search with Lucene; Lucene and PageRank; Lucene, PageRank, and user clicks). You can apply them on the dataset that we provided you or another dataset that you can create yourself, and you can create a precision/recall plot that includes the results of 10–20 queries.

In section 5.5, we'll discuss many aspects of credibility that can be evaluated for a particular algorithm and how to compare two algorithms. We'll also talk about the way that the validation experiments must be carried out in order to enhance the confidence that we have in our results. Precision and recall are the tip of the iceberg when we consider the quality of our search results. We'll postpone a more detailed analysis of credibility until after we cover all the basic intelligent algorithms that we want to present. This approach will allow us to use a general framework for assessing the quality of intelligence.

2.8 *Summary*

Since early 2000, a lot of online news article have proclaimed: "Search is king!" This kind of statement could've been insightful, and perhaps prophetic, in the last millennium, but it's a globally accepted truth today. If you don't believe us, Google it!

This chapter has shown that intelligently answering user queries on content-rich material that's spread across the globe deserves attention and effort beyond indexing. We've demonstrated a searching strategy that starts with building on traditional information retrieval techniques provided by the Lucene library. We talked about collecting content from the Web (web crawling) and provided our own crawler implementation. We used a number of document parsers such as NekoHTML and the TextMining library (tm-extractor), and passed the content to the Lucene analyzers. The standard Lucene analyzers are powerful and flexible, and should be adequate for most purposes. If they're not suitable for you, we've discussed a number of potential extensions and modifications that are possible. We also hinted at the power of the Lucene querying framework and its own extensibility and flexibility.

More importantly, we've described in great detail the most celebrated link analysis algorithm—PageRank. We provided a full implementation that doesn't have any dependencies and adopts the formulation of the G(oogle) matrix that's amenable to the large-scale implementation of sparse matrices. We also provided hints that'll allow you to complete this step and feel the pride of that great accomplishment yourself! We've touched upon a number of intricacies of that algorithm and explained its key characteristics, such as the teleportation component and the power method, in detail.

We also presented user-click analysis, which introduced you to intelligent probabilistic techniques such as our `NaiveBayes` classifier implementation. We've provided wrapper classes that expose all the important steps involved, but we've also analyzed the code under the hood to a great extent. This kind of technique allows us to learn the preferences of a user toward a particular site or topic, and it can be greatly enhanced and extended to include additional features.

Since one size doesn't fit all, we've provided material that'll help you deal with documents that aren't web pages, by employing a new algorithm that we called DocRank. This algorithm has shown some promise, but more importantly it demonstrates that the underlying mathematical theory of PageRank can be readily extended and studied in other contexts by careful modifications. Lastly, we talked about some of the challenges that may arise in dealing with very large networks, and we provided a simple yet robust way of qualifying your search results and add credibility to your search engine.

The statement "search is king" might be true, but recommendation systems also have royal blood! The next chapter covers exclusively the creation of suggestions and recommendations. Adding both to your application can make a big difference in the user experience of your application. But before you move on, make sure that you read the To do items for search, if you haven't done so already. They're full of interesting and valuable information.

2.9   *To do*

The last section of every chapter in the rest of this book will contain a number of to-do items that will guide you in the exploration of various topics. Whenever appropriate, our code has been annotated with "TODO" tags that you should be able to view in the Eclipse IDE in the Tasks panel. By clicking on any of the tasks, the task link will show the portion of the code associated with it. If you don't use Eclipse then simply search the code for the term "TODO".

Some of these to-do items aim at providing greater depth on a topic that's been covered in the main chapter, while others present a starting point for exploration on topics that are peripheral to what we've already discussed. The completion of these tasks will provide you with greater depth and breadth on intelligent algorithms. We highly encourage you to peruse them.

With that in mind, here is our to do list for chapter 2.

1   *Build your own web search engine.*   Use the crawler of your choice and crawl your favorite site, such as http://jakarta.apache.org/, then use our crawler to process the retrieved data, build an index for it, and search through its pages.

How do the results vary if you add PageRank to them?

How about user clicks?

You could write your own small web search engine by applying the material of this chapter. Try it and let us know!

2   *Experiment with boosting.*   Uncomment the code between lines 83 to 85 in the class `LuceneIndexBuilder` and see how the results of the Lucene ranking

change. Depending on your application, you can devise a unique strategy of boosting your documents that depends on factors that are specific to the domain of your application.

3   *Scaling the PageRank values.*   In our example of a combined Lucene (index) and PageRank (ranking) search, we use a scaling factor that boosted the value of the PageRank. Our choice of function for the exponent had only one parameter—m = (1 - 1/n), where *n* is the size of the *H* matrix—and its behavior was such that for large networks our scaling factor is approaching the value 1, while for small networks the value is between 0 and 1. In reality, you get zero only in the degenerate case where you have a single page, but that's not a very interesting network anyway!

Experiment with such scaling factors and observe the impact on the rankings. You may want to change that value to a higher power of *n*—another valid formula would be m = (1 - 1 / Math.pow(n,k)), because as *k* takes on values greater than 1, the PageRank value approaches its calculated value faster.

4   *Altering the* G *matrix: Dangling nodes.*   We've assigned a value of 1/n to all the nodes for each entry in a dangling node row. In the absence of additional information about the browsing habits of our users, or under the assumption that there's a sufficient number of users that covers all browsing habits, that's a reasonable assignment. But what if we make different kind of assumptions that are equally reasonable would the whole mechanism work?

Let's assume that a user encounters a dangling node. Upon arriving at the dangling node, it seems natural to assume that the user is more likely to select a search engine as his next destination, or a website similar to the dangling node, rather than a website that's dissimilar to the content of the dangling node. That kind of assumption would result in an adjustment of the dangling node values: higher values for search engines and similar content pages, and lower values for everybody else. How does that change affect the PageRank values? How about the results of the queries? Did your precision recall graph change in that case?

5   *Altering the* G *matrix: Teleportation.*   In our original implementation, the teleportation contribution has been assigned in an egalitarian manner—all pages are assigned a contribution equal to *(1-alpha)/n*, where *n* is the number of the pages. But the potential of that component is enormous. If chosen appropriately, it can create an online bourgeois, and if it's chosen at a user level, it can target the preferences of each user much like the technique of user clicks allowed us to do. The latter reason is why the teleportation contribution is also known as the *personalization vector*.

Try to modify it so that certain pages get more weight than others. Does it work? Are your PageRank values higher for these pages? What issues do you see with such an implementation? If we assume that we assign a personalization vector to each user, what does this imply in terms of computational effort? Is it worth it? Is it feasible? The papers by Haveliwala, Jeh & Widom, and Richardson

& Domingos are related to this and can provide you with more information and insight on this important topic.

6 *Combining different scores.*   In section 2.4.3, we showed one way to combine the three different scores, in order to provide the final ranking for the results of a particular query. That's not the only way. This is a case where you can devise a balancing of these three terms in a way that best fits your needs. Here's an idea: introduce weighing terms for each of the three scores and experiment with different allocations of weight to each one of them.

Provided that you consider a fixed network of pages or documents, how do the results change based on different values of these weight coefficients? Plot 20 precision/recall values that correspond to 20 different queries, and do that for three different weight combinations, for example (0.6, 0.2, 0.2), (0.2, 0.6, 0.2), (0.2, 0.2, 0.6). What do you see? How do these points compare to the equal weight distribution (1,1,1)? Can you come up with different formulas for balancing the various contributions?

2.10   References

Adamic, L.A., R.M. Lukose, A.R. Puniyani, and B.A. Huberman. "Search in power-law networks." *Physical Review E*, vol. 64, 046135. 2001.

Boldi, P., and S. Vigna. "The WebGraph Framework I: Compression Techniques." *WWW 2004*, New York.

Dean, J. and S. Ghemawat. "MapReduce: Simplified Data Processing on Large Clusters." *Sixth Symposium on Operating System Design and Implementation*, San Francisco, CA, 2004. http://labs.google.com/papers/mapreduce-osdi04.pdf.

Haveliwala, T.H. "Topic-sensitive PageRank: A context-sensitive ranking algorithm for web search." *IEEE transactions on Knowledge and Data Engineering*, 15 (4): 784. 2004. http://www-cs-students.stanford.edu/~taherh/papers/topic-sensitive-pagerank-tkde.pdf.

Jeh, G. and J. Widom. "Scaling personalized web search." Technical report, Stanford University, 2002. http://infolab.stanford.edu/~glenj/spws.pdf.

Kamvar, S.D., T.H. Haveliwala, Christopher D. Manning, and Gene H. Golub. Extrapolation Methods for Accelerating PageRank Computations. WWW 2003. http://www.kamvar.org/code/paper-server.php?filename=extrapolation.pdf.

Langville, A.N. and C.D. Meyer. *Google's PageRank and Beyond: The Science of Search Engine Rankings*. Princeton University Press, 2006.

Richardson, M. and P. Domingos. The intelligent surfer: Probabilistic combination of link and content information in PageRank. *Advances in Neural Information Processing Systems*, 14:1441, 2002. http://research.microsoft.com/users/mattri/papers/nips2002/qd-pagerank.pdf.

Rish, I. An empirical study of the naïve Bayes classifier." *IBM Research Report*, RC22230 (W0111-014), 2001. http://www.cc.gatech.edu/~isbell/classes/reading/papers/Rish.pdf.

Creating suggestions and recommendations

In today's world, we're overwhelmed with choices; a plethora of options are available for nearly every aspect of our lives. We need to make choices on a daily basis, from automobiles to home theatre systems, from finding Mr. or Ms. "Perfect" to selecting attorneys or accountants, from books and newspapers to wikis and blogs, from movies to songs, and so on. In addition, we're constantly being bombarded by information—and occasionally misinformation! Under these conditions, the ability to recommend a choice is valuable, even more so if that choice doesn't deviate significantly from the preferences of the person who receives the recommendation.

In the business of influencing your choice, no one is interested in good results more than advertising companies. The *raison d'être* of these entities is to convince you that you really *need* product *X* or service *Y*. If you have no interest in products like *X* or services like *Y*, they'll be wasting their time and you'll be annoyed! The "broadcasting" approach of traditional advertising methods (such as billboards, TV ads, radio ads) suffers from that problem. The goal of broadcasting is to alter your preferences by incessantly repeating the same message. An alternative, more pleasant, and more effective approach would be targeting to your preferences. It would entice you to select a product based on its relevance to your personal wants and desires. That's where the online world and the intelligent advertisement business on the internet distinguish themselves. It may be the searching functionality that made Google famous, but advertisements are what make Google rich!

In this chapter, we'll tell you everything you need to know about building a recommendation engine. You'll learn about *collaborative filtering* and content-based recommendation engines. You'll also learn how to optimize the classical algorithms and how to extend them in more realistic applications. We'll start by describing the problem of recommending songs in an online music store, and we'll generalize it so that our proposed solutions are applicable to a variety of circumstances. The online music store is a simple example, but it's concrete and detailed, making it easy to understand all the basic concepts involved in the process of writing a recommendation engine.

Once we cover all the basic concepts in our online music store, we'll make things a lot more interesting by presenting more complicated cases. We'll adhere to the important principle of commercial proselytism and we'll cover recommendation engines that are crucial in online movie rentals (see our coverage of Netflix in the introduction), online bookstores, and general online stores.

3.1 An online music store: the basic concepts

Let's say that you have an online store that sells music downloads. Registered users log in to your application and can play samples of the available songs. If a user likes a particular song, she can add it to her shopping cart and purchase it later when she's ready to check out from your store. Naturally, when users complete their purchase, or when they land on the pages of our hypothetical application, we want to suggest more songs to them. There are millions of songs available, myriad artists, and dozens of music styles of broad interest to choose from—classical, ecclesiastical, pop, heavy metal, country, and many others more or less refined! In addition, many people are quite sensitive to the kind of music that they don't like. You'd be better off throwing me in the middle of the Arctic Ocean than showing me anything related to rap! Someone else could be allergic to classical music, and so on.

The moral of the story is that, when you display content for a user, you want to target the areas of music that the user likes and avoid the areas of music that the user doesn't like. If that sounds difficult, fear not! Recommendation engines are here to help you deliver the right content to your users!

A recommendation engine examines the selections that a user has made in the past, and can identify the degree to which he would like a certain item that he hasn't seen yet. It can be used to determine what types of music your user prefers, and the extent to which he does so, by comparing the *similarity* of his preferences with the characteristics of music types. In a more creative twist, we could help people establish a social network on that site based on the *similarity* of their musical taste. So, it quickly becomes apparent that the crucial functional element of recommendation engines is the ability to define how similar to each other two (or more) users or two (or more) items are. That similarity can later be leveraged to provide recommendations.

3.1.1 *The concepts of distance and similarity*

Let's take some data and start exploring these concepts in detail. The basic concepts that we'll work with are Items, Users, and Ratings. In the context of recommendation engines, similarity is a measure that allows us to compare the proximity of two items in much the same way that the proximity between two cities tells us how close they are to each other geographically. For two cities, we'd use their longitude and latitude coordinates to calculate their geographical proximity. Think of the Ratings as the "coordinates" in the space of Items or Users. Let's demonstrate these concepts in action. We'll select three users from a list of MusicUsers and will associate a list of songs (items) and their hypothetical rankings with each user.

As it is typically the case on the internet, ratings will range between 1 and 5 (inclusive). The assignments for the first two users (Frank and Constantine) involve ratings that are either 4 or 5—these people really like all the songs that we selected! But the third user's ratings (Catherine) are between 1 and 3. So clearly, we expect the first two users to be similar to each other and be dissimilar to the third user. When we load our example data in the script (the second line in the script of listing 3.1), we have available the users, songs, and ratings shown in table 3.1.

Table 3.1 The ratings for the users show that Frank and Constantine agree more than Frank and Catherine (see also figure 3.2).

User	Song	Rating
Frank	Tears In Heaven	5
	La Bamba	4
	Mrs. Robinson	5
	Yesterday	4
	Wizard of Oz	5
	Mozart: Symphony #41 (Jupiter)	4
	Beethoven: Symphony No. 9 in D	5

Table 3.1   The ratings for the users show that Frank and Constantine agreemore than Frank and Catherine (see also figure 3.2). *(continued)*

User	Song	Rating
Constantine	Tears in Heaven	5
	Fiddler on the Roof	5
	Mrs. Robinson	5
	What a Wonderful World	4
	Wizard of Oz	4
	Let It Be	5
	Mozart: Symphony #41 (Jupiter)	5
Catherine	Tears in Heaven	1
	Mrs. Robinson	2
	Yesterday	2
	Beethoven: Symphony No. 9 in D	3
	Sunday, Bloody Sunday	1
	Yesterday	1
	Let It Be	2

We can execute all these steps in the shell using the script shown in listing 3.1.

Listing 3.1   A small list of `MusicUsers` and their `Ratings` on `MusicItems`

```
MusicUser[] mu = MusicData.loadExample();

mu[0].getSimilarity(mu[1],0);

mu[0].getSimilarity(mu[1],1);

mu[0].getSimilarity(mu[2],0);

mu[1].getSimilarity(mu[2],0);     ◁— Similarity is symmetrical
mu[2].getSimilarity(mu[1],0);

mu[0].getSimilarity(mu[0],0);     ◁— Similarity of a user with itself
mu[0].getSimilarity(mu[0],1);
```

We've provided two definitions of similarity, which are invoked by providing a different value in the second argument of the `getSimilarity` method of the `MusicUser` class. We'll describe the detailed implementation of that code shortly, but first look at figure 3.1, which shows the results that we get for the comparisons between the three users.

According to our calculations, shown in figure 3.1, Frank's preferences in songs are more similar to Constantine's than they are to Catherine's. The similarity between

```
bsh % MusicUser[] mu = MusicData.loadExample();

bsh % mu[0].getSimilarity(mu[1],0);

 User Similarity between Frank and Constantine is equal to
0.3911406349860862

bsh % mu[0].getSimilarity(mu[1],1);

 User Similarity between Frank and Constantine is equal to
0.22350893427776353

bsh % mu[0].getSimilarity(mu[2],0);

 User Similarity between Frank and Catherine is equal to 0.
004197074413470947

bsh % mu[1].getSimilarity(mu[2],0);

 User Similarity between Constantine and Catherine is equal to
0.0023790682635077554

bsh % mu[2].getSimilarity(mu[1],0);

 User Similarity between Catherine and Constantine is equal to
0.0023790682635077554

bsh % mu[0].getSimilarity(mu[0],0);

 User Similarity between Frank and Frank is equal to 1.0

bsh % mu[0].getSimilarity(mu[0],1);

User Similarity between Frank and Frank is equal to 1.0
```

Figure 3.1   Calculating the similarity of users for the data that are shown in table 3.1. It's clear that Frank and Constantine agree more than Frank and Catherine (see also table 3.1).

two users doesn't depend on the order in which we pass the arguments in the get-Similarity method. The similarity of Frank with himself is equal to 1.0, which we take to be the maximum value of similarity between any two entities. These properties stem from the fact that many similarity measures are based on distances, like the geometric distance between two points on a plane that we learned in high school.

In general, mathematical distances have the following four important properties:

- All distances are greater than or equal to zero. In most cases, as with the Music-User, we constrain the similarities to be nonnegative like distances. In fact, we constrain the similarities within the interval [0,1].

- The distance between any two points, say A and B, is zero if and only if A is the same point as B. In our example, and based on our implementation of similarity, this property is reflected in the fact that when two users have exactly the same ratings, the similarity between them will be equal to 1.0. That's true in figure 3.1, where we used the same user twice to show that the similarity is 1.0. Of course, you can create a fourth user and prove that the similarity will be equal to 1, provided that the users have listened to the same songs.

- The third property of distances is *symmetry*—the distance between A and B is exactly the same as the distance between B and A. This means that if Catherine's musical taste is similar to the musical taste of Constantine, the reverse will also be true by exactly the same amount. So, quite often we want the measure of similarity to preserve the symmetric property of distances, with respect to its arguments.

- The fourth property of mathematical distances is the *triangle inequality* because it relates the distances between three points. In mathematical terms, if $d(A,B)$ denotes the distance between points A and B, then the triangle inequality states that $d(A,B) <= d(A,C) + d(C,B)$, for any third point C. In figure 3.1, Frank is similar to Constantine by 0.391 and Constantine is similar to Catherine by 0.002, while Frank is similar to Catherine by 0.004, which is less than the sum of the first two similarities. Nevertheless, that property doesn't hold, in general, for our similarities.

Relaxing the fourth fundamental property of distances when we pass on to similarities is fine; there's no imperative to carry over the properties of distances to similarities. We should always be cautious to ensure that the mathematics involved is in agreement with what we consider to be reasonable. There's a century-old counterexample to the triangle inequality, when it comes to similarities, that's attributed to William James:[1] "A flame is similar to the moon because they are both luminous, and the moon is similar to a ball because they are both round, but in contradiction to the triangle inequality, a flame is not similar to a ball." For an interesting account of similarities in relation to cognition, we recommend *Classification and Cognition* by W.K. Estes.

At the top of figure 3.2, we show a visual representation of the similarity between Frank and Constantine by plotting their ratings for the songs they both rated. The closer the lines of the ratings, the more similar the users are; the further apart the lines, the less the similarity. On the bottom plot of figure 3.2, where we show the ratings of Frank versus those of Catherine, the lines diverge and are far apart, which is in accordance with the low similarity value that we got during our calculation.

The lines for Frank and Constantine are close, depicting the similarity between them. If you look at the code in the `plot` method of `MusicUser`, you'll see that we sort these ratings in order of increasing difference. If you have a lot of these ratings, you'll see the difference between the two lines increase as you look at the plot from left to right.

---

[1] Source: ScholarPedia (http://www.scholarpedia.org/article/Similarity_measures)

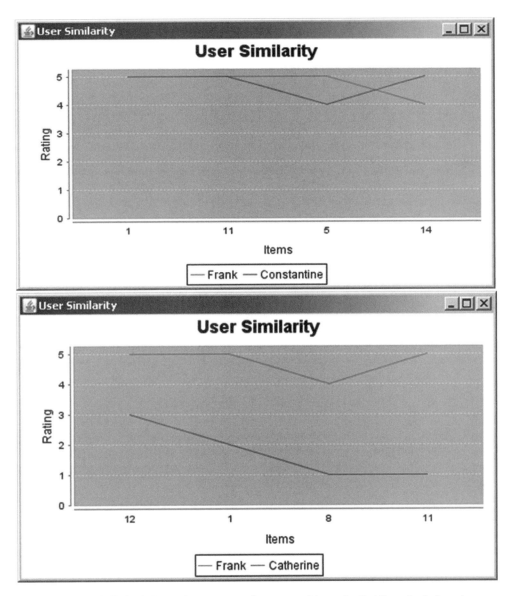

Figure 3.2 The similarity between two users can be measured by evaluating the extent of overlap between the two lines in plots like this. Thus, Frank and Constantine (top) are more similar than Frank and Catherine (bottom).

The plots of the ratings in figure 3.2 clearly display the somewhat reciprocal nature of distance and similarity. The greater the distance between the two curves, the smaller the similarity between the two users; the smaller the distance between the two curves, the greater the similarity between the two users. As we'll see in the next section, the evaluation of similarity often involves the evaluation of some kind of distance; although that's not necessary. The concept of distance is more familiar. The concept of distance and the concept of similarity are special cases of the general concept of a metric.

3.1.2   *A closer look at the calculation of similarity*

Now, let's examine the code that helped us find the similarity between the users and look closely at how we can calculate similarity. The code in listing 3.2 shows the details of the getSimilarity method, which accepts two arguments. The first provides a reference to another user, the second specifies the kind of similarity that we want to use.

Listing 3.2   Two similarity measures in `getSimilarity` of `MusicUser`

```
public double getSimilarity(MusicUser u, int simType) {

  double sim=0.0d;
  int commonItems=0;

  switch(simType) {

  case 0:
    for (Rating r : this.ratingsByItemId.values()) {          ⟵—┐ Identify all
                                                                 │ common items
        for (Rating r2 : u.ratingsByItemId.values()) {

        //Find the same item
        if ( r.getItemId() == r2.getItemId() ) {               ┌─ Square
         commonItems++;                                        │  differences of
         sim += Math.pow((r.getRating()-r2.getRating()),2);  ⟵─┘  ratings and
        }                                                        sum them
      }
    }
  }

// If there are no common items, we cannot tell whether
// the users are similar or not. So, we let it return 0.
if (commonItems > 0) {

    sim = Math.sqrt(sim/(double)commonItems);

    // Similarity should be between 0 and 1
    // For the value 0, the two users are as dissimilar as they come
    // For the value 1, their preferences are identical.
    //
    sim = 1.0d - Math.tanh(sim);
}

break;

case 1:
  for (Rating r : this.ratingsByItemId.values()) {           ⟵—┐ Identify all
    for (Rating r2 : u.ratingsByItemId.values()) {              │ common items

      //Find the same item
      if ( r.getItemId() == r2.getItemId() ) {                 ┌─ Square
       commonItems++;                                          │  differences of
       sim += Math.pow((r.getRating()-r2.getRating()),2);  ⟵───┘  ratings and
      }                                                          sum them
    }
  }
```

```
// If there are no common items, we cannot tell whether
// or not the users are similar. So, we let it return 0.
if (commonItems > 0) {

    sim = Math.sqrt(sim/(double)commonItems);

    // Similarity should be between 0 and 1
    // For the value 0, the two users are as dissimilar as they come
    // For the value 1, their preferences are identical.
    //
    sim = 1.0d - Math.tanh(sim);

    // Find the max number of items that the two users can have in common
    int maxCommonItems =
➥   Math.min(this.ratingsByItemId.size(), u.ratingsByItemId.size());

    // Adjust similarity to account for the importance of common terms
    // through the ratio of common items over all possible common items

    sim = sim * ((double)commonItems/(double)maxCommonItems);
}
break;

} //switch block ends

//Let us know what it is
System.out.print("\n"); //Just for pretty printing in the Shell
System.out.print(" User Similarity between");
System.out.print(" "+this.getName());
System.out.print(" and "+u.getName());
System.out.println(" is equal to "+sim);
System.out.print("\n"); //Just for pretty printing in the Shell

return sim;
}
```

We included two similarity formulas in the code to show that the notion of similarity is fairly flexible and extensible. Let's examine the basic steps in the calculation of these similarity formulas. First we take the differences between all the ratings of songs that the users have in common, square them, and add them together. The square root of that value is called the *Euclidean distance* and, as it stands, it's not sufficient to provide a measure of similarity. As we mentioned earlier, the concept of distance and similarity are somewhat reciprocal, in the sense that the smaller the value of the Euclidean distance, the more similar the two users. We can argue that the ordering incompatibility with the concept of similarity is easy to rectify. For instance, we could say that we'll add the value 1 to the Euclidean score and invert it.

At first sight, it appears that inverting the distance (after adding the constant value 1) might work. But this seemingly innocuous modification suffers from shortcomings. If two users have listened to only one song and one of them rated the song with 1 and the other rated the song with 4, the sum of their differences squared is 9. In that case, the naïve similarity, based on the Euclidean distance, would result in a similarity value of 0.25. The same similarity value can be obtained in other cases. If the two users listened to three songs and among these three songs, their ratings differed by 1 (for each song), their similarity would also be 0.25, according to the naïve similarity metric. Intuitively we expect these two users to be more similar than those who listened to a single song and their opinions differed by 3 units (out of 5!).

The naïve similarity "squeezes" the similarity values for small distances (because we add 1) while leaving large distances (values of the distance much larger than 1) unaffected. What if we add another value? The general form of the naïve similarity is $y = beta / (beta + x)$, where beta is our free parameter and x is the Euclidean distance. Figure 3.3 shows what the naïve similarity would look like for various values, between 1 and 2, of the parameter `beta`.

Keeping in mind the shortcomings of the naïve similarity, let's look at the first similarity definition between two users as shown in listing 3.2, in the `case 0` block. If the users have some songs in common we divide the sum of their squared differences by the number of common songs, take the positive square root, and pass on that value to a special function. We've seen that function before: it's the hyperbolic tangent function. We subtract the value of the hyperbolic tangent from 1, so that our final value of similarity ranges between 0 and 1, with zero implying dissimilarity and 1 implying the highest similarity. Voilà! We've arrived at our first definition of similarity of users based on their ratings.

The second similarity definition that we present in listing 3.2, in the `case 1` block, improves on the first similarity by taking into account the ratio of the common items versus the number of all possible common items. That's a heuristic that intuitively makes sense. If I've listened to 30 songs and you've listened to 20, we could have up to 20 common songs. Let's say that we have only 5 songs in common and we agree fairly well on

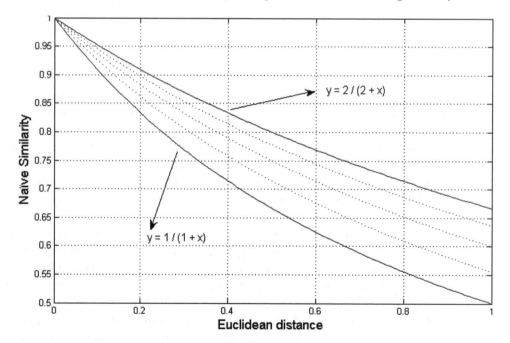

Figure 3.3 Naïve similarity curves as functions of the Euclidean distance

these songs, which is nice, but why don't we have more songs in common? Shouldn't that somehow be reflected in our similarity? This is exactly the aspect of the problem that we're trying to capture in the second similarity formula. In other words, the extent to which we listen to the same songs should somehow affect the degree of our similarity as music listeners.

3.1.3 *Which is the best similarity formula?*

It may be clear by now that there are many formulas you can use to establish the similarity between two users, or between two items for that matter. In addition to the two similarities that we introduced in the MusicUser class, we could've used a metric formula known as the *Jaccard similarity* between users, which is defined by the ratio of the intersection over the union of their item sets—or, in the case of item similarity, the ratio of the intersection over the union of the user sets. In other words, the Jaccard similarity between two sets, A and B, is defined by the following pseudocode: *Jaccard = intersection(A,B) / union(A,B)*. We'll use the Jaccard similarity in the next sections and will also present a few more similarity formulas in our "To do" section at the end of this chapter.

Of course, you may naturally wonder: "which similarity formula is more appropriate?" The answer, as always, is it depends. In this case, it depends on your data. In one of the few large-scale comparisons of similarity metrics (conducted by Spertus, Sahami, and Buyukkokten), the simple Euclidean distance-based similarity showed the best empirical results among seven similarity metrics, despite the fact that other formulas were more elaborate and intuitively expected to perform better. Their measurements were based on 1,279,266 clicks on related community recommendations from September 22, 2004, through October 21, 2004, on the social networking website Orkut (http://www.orkut.com); for more details, see the related reference.

We don't advise that you choose randomly your similarity metric, but if you're in a hurry, use a formula similar to the two that we included in the MusicUser class—the Euclidean or the Jaccard similarity. It should give you decent results. You should try to understand the nature of your data and what it means for two users or two items to be similar. If you don't understand the reasons why a particular similarity metric (formula) is good or bad, you're setting yourself up for trouble. To stress this point, think of the common misconception that "the shortest path between two points is a straight line that joins them." That statement is true only for what we call "flat" geometries, such as the area of a football field. To convince yourself, compare the distance of going over a tall but not wide hill versus going around the hill's base. The "straight" line will not be the shortest path for a wide range of hill sizes.

In summary, one of the cornerstones of recommendations is the ability to measure the similarity between any two users and the similarity between any two items. We've provided a number of similarity measures that you can use off-the-shelf, and the music store exemplified the typical structure of the data that you'd deal with in order to create recommendations. We'll now pass on to examine the types of recommendation engines and how they work.

3.2 *How do recommendation engines work?*

Armed with a good understanding of what similarity between two users or two items means, we can proceed with our description of recommendation engines. Generally speaking, there are two categories of recommendation engines. The first goes under the label *collaborative filtering (CF)*. The first incarnation of CF appeared in an experimental mail system (circa 1992) developed at the Xerox Palo Alto Research Center (PARC) by Goldberg et al. CF relies on the breadcrumbs that a user leaves behind through the interaction with a software system. Typically, these breadcrumbs are the user's ratings, such as the song ratings that we described in the previous section. Collaborative filtering isn't limited to one-dimensional or only discrete variables; its main characteristic is that it depends on the user's past behavior rather than the content of each item in the collection of interest. CF requires neither domain knowledge nor preliminary gathering and analysis work to produce recommendations.

The second broad category of recommendation engines is based on the analysis of the content—associated with the items or the users, or both. The main characteristic of this content-based approach is the accumulation and analysis of information related to both users and items. That information may be provided either by the software system or through external sources. The system can collect information about the users *explicitly* through their response to solicited questionnaires or *implicitly* through the mining of the user's profile or news reading habits, emails, blogs, and so on.

In the category of CF, we'll describe recommendations based on the similarity of users and of items. We'll also describe the category of content-based recommendations, thus covering all known recommendation engine systems.

3.2.1 *Recommendations based on similar users*

There's an ancient Greek proverb (with similar variants in nearly every culture of the world) that states: "Show me your friends and I'll tell you who you are." Collaborative filtering based on neighborhoods of similar users is more or less an algorithmic incarnation of that proverb. In order to evaluate the rating of a particular user for a given item, we look for the ratings of similar users (neighbors or friends, if you prefer) on the same item. Then, we multiply the rating of each friend by a weight and add them up. Yes, it's that simple, in principle!

Listing 3.3 shows a series of steps that demonstrate the creation and usage of a recommendation engine, which we called Delphi. First, we need to build data to work with. We create a sample of data by assigning ratings to songs for all users. For each user, we randomly pick a set of songs that corresponds to 80% of all the songs in our online music store. For each song assigned to a user, we assign a random rating that's either 4 or 5 if the username starts with the letters A through D (inclusive), and 1, 2, or 3 otherwise.

Thus, we establish two large groups of users with similar preferences; this allows us to quickly assess the results of our engine.

Listing 3.3   Creating recommendations based on similar users

```
BaseDataset ds = MusicData.createDataset();        ⊲── Create music dataset

ds.save("C:/iWeb2/deploy/data/ch3_2_dataset.ser");   ⊲── Save it for later

Delphi delphi = new Delphi(ds,RecommendationType.USER_BASED);    ⊲─┐
delphi.setVerbose(true);                                Create
                                                        recommendation
MusicUser mu1 = ds.pickUser("Babis");                      engine
delphi.findSimilarUsers(mu1);          Find similar
                                       users
MusicUser mu2 = ds.pickUser("Lukas");
delphi.findSimilarUsers(mu2);

delphi.recommend(mu1);     ⊲── Recommend a few songs
```

The first line creates the dataset of our users and the ratings for the songs, in the way we described earlier. The code is straightforward and you can modify the data in the MusicData class as you see fit. In the second line, we store the dataset that we use in our example so we can refer to it later on. The third line creates an instance of our Delphi recommendation engine, and the fourth line sets it to verbose mode so that we can see the details of the results. Note that the constructors of Delphi use the interface Dataset rather than our example classes. You can use it with your own implementation straight out of the box—or more precisely out of the Java Archive (JAR).

Figure 3.4 shows the results of our script for the findSimilarUsers method. In the first case, the username starts with the letter B, and all the friends that are selected have names that start with the letters A through D. In the second case, the username starts with the letter J, and all the friends that are selected have names that start with the letters E through Z. In both cases, we obtain results that are in agreement with what we expected.

So, it seems that our recommendation engine is working well! Note also that the similarities between the friends of the first case are higher than the similarities of the group that corresponds to the second case because the ratings were distributed between only two values (4 and 5) in the first case, but in the second case were distributed among three values (1, 2, and 3). These kinds of sanity checks are useful, and you should always be alert of what an intelligent algorithm returns; it wouldn't be very intelligent if it didn't meet common sense criteria, would it?

In addition, figure 3.4 shows the results of the song recommendations for one of the users, as well as the predicted ratings for each recommendation. Note that although the ratings of the users are integers, the recommendation engine uses a double for its prediction. That's because the prediction expresses only a degree of belief about the rating rather than an actual rating. You may wonder why websites don't allow you to give a rating that's not an integer, or equally liberating, offer a rating between larger ranges of values, such as between 1 and 10 or even 1 and 100. We'll revisit this point in one of our to-do items at the end of the chapter.

Observe that the recommendation engine is correctly assigning values between 4 and 5, since the users whose letters start with the letters A through D have all given ratings that are either 4 or 5.

```
bsh % MusicUser mu1 = ds.pickUser("Bob");
bsh % delphi.findSimilarUsers(mu1);

Top Friends for user Bob:

name: Babis                          , similarity: 0.692308
name: Alexandra                      , similarity: 0.666667
name: Bill                           , similarity: 0.636364
name: Aurora                         , similarity: 0.583333
name: Charlie                        , similarity: 0.583333

bsh % MusicUser mu2 = ds.pickUser("John");
bsh % delphi.findSimilarUsers(mu2);

Top Friends for user John:

name: George                         , similarity: 0.545455
name: Jack                           , similarity: 0.500000
name: Elena                          , similarity: 0.461538
name: Lukas                          , similarity: 0.454545
name: Frank                          , similarity: 0.416667

bsh % delphi.recommend(mu1);

Recommendations for user Bob:

Item: I Love Rock And Roll        , predicted rating: 4.922400
Item: La Bamba                    , predicted rating: 4.758600
Item: Wind Beneath My Wings       , predicted rating: 4.540900
Item: Sunday, Bloody Sunday       , predicted rating: 4.526800
```

Figure 3.4 **Discovering friends and providing recommendations with Delphi based on user similarity**

How did the Delphi class arrive at these conclusions? How can it find the similar users (friends) for any given user? How can it recommend songs from the list of songs that a user never listened to? Let's go through the basic steps to understand what happens. Recommendation engines that are based on collaborative filtering proceed in two steps. First, they calculate the similarity between either users or items. Then, they use a weighted average to calculate the rating that a user would give to a yet-unseen item.

CALCULATING THE USER SIMILARITIES

Since we're dealing with recommendations that are based on user similarity, the first thing that Delphi does for us is to calculate the similarity between the users. This is shown in listing 3.4, where we show the code from the method calculate of the class UserBasedSimilarity, an auxiliary class that's used in Delphi. Note that the double loop has been optimized to account for the symmetry of the similarity matrix; we discuss this and one more optimization after the code listing.

Listing 3.4 UserBasedSimilarity: calculating the user similarity

```
protected void calculate(Dataset dataSet) {

   int nUsers = dataSet.getUserCount();        ⟵── Defines size of similarity matrix

   int nRatingValues = 5;                                    ⟵┐ Defines size of
   similarityValues = new double[nUsers][nUsers];              │ rating count matrix

   if( keepRatingCountMatrix ) {
      ratingCountMatrix = new RatingCountMatrix[nUsers][nUsers];
   }

   // if mapping from userId to index then generate index for every userId
   if( useObjIdToIndexMapping ) {

      for(User u : dataSet.getUsers() ) {
         idMapping.getIndex(String.valueOf(u.getId()));
      }
   }

   for (int u = 0; u < nUsers; u++ ) {

      int userAId = getObjIdFromIndex(u);
      User userA = dataSet.getUser(userAId);

      for (int v = u + 1; v < nUsers; v++) {      ⟵─❶ Similarity matrix

         int userBId = getObjIdFromIndex(v);
         User userB = dataSet.getUser(userBId);

         RatingCountMatrix rcm =                              ⟵┐ Agreement of
      new RatingCountMatrix(userA, userB, nRatingValues);       │ ratings between
                                                                │ two users
         int totalCount = rcm.getTotalCount();         ⟵┐ Calculate
         int agreementCount = rcm.getAgreementCount();    │ similarity or
                                                          │ set it to zero
         if (agreementCount > 0) {                     ⟵┘

            similarityValues[u][v] =
      (double) agreementCount / (double) totalCount;

         } else {
            similarityValues[u][v] = 0.0;
         }

         // For large datasets
         if( keepRatingCountMatrix ) {
            ratingCountMatrix[u][v] = rcm;
         }
      }

      // for u == v assign 1.
      // RatingCountMatrix wasn't created for this case
      similarityValues[u][u] = 1.0;                 ⟵─❶ Similarity matrix
   }
}
```

❶ Here is the optimization that we mentioned earlier. You'd expect the first loop to select the first user and the second loop to select all other users. But in the listing, the second loop uses the fact that the similarity matrix is symmetrical. This simply means that if user *A* is similar to user *B* with a similarity value *X* then user *B* will be similar to user *A* with a similarity value equal to *X*. The code avoids evaluating the similarity of a user object with itself, because that should always be equal to 1. These two code optimizations are simply a reflection of the fundamental properties that every similarity measure should obey, as stated in section 3.1.1.

As you can see, the definition of similarity is given by the Jaccard metric, where the agreement on the ratings represents the intersection between the two sets of ratings, and the total count of ratings represents the union of the two sets of ratings. Similarity values are held in a two-dimensional array of type double. But similarity is a symmetrical property, which simply means that if I'm similar to you then you're similar to me, regardless of how similarity was defined. So clearly, we can use the similarity values much more efficiently by either using sparse matrices or by using some other structure that's designed to store only half the number of values; the latter structure is technically known as the *upper triangular form* of the matrix. From a computational perspective, we're already leveraging that fact in the code of listing 3.4. Once again, note that the second loop doesn't run over all users, but starts with the user that follows the outer loop user in our list.

The calculation of similarity for each pair of users relies on an auxiliary class that we called RatingCountMatrix. The purpose of the class is to store the rating of one user with respect to another in a nice tabular format and allow us to calculate the final similarity value easily and transparently. Listing 3.5 contains the code for Rating-CountMatrix.

Listing 3.5   Storing the agreement distribution of two users in a tabular form

```
public class RatingCountMatrix implements Serializable {

    private int matrix[][] = null;

    public RatingCountMatrix(Item itemA, Item itemB,
        int nRatingValues) {

        init(nRatingValues);

        calculate(itemA, itemB);           ⟵  Calculate item-
    }                                          based similarity

    public RatingCountMatrix(User userA, User userB,
        int nRatingValues) {

        init(nRatingValues);

        calculate(userA, userB);           ⟵  Calculate user-
    }                                          based similarity

    private void init(int nSize) {
        // starting point - all elements are zero
        matrix = new int[nSize][nSize];
    }
```

Initialize rating count matrix

```
    private void calculate(Item itemA, Item itemB) {         ◁──┐  Calculate item-
                                                               │  based similarity
        for (Rating ratingForA : itemA.getAllRatings()) {

            // check if the same user rated itemB
            Rating ratingForB =
➡    itemB.getUserRating(ratingForA.getUserId());

            if (ratingForB != null) {

                int i = ratingForA.getRating() - 1;
                int j = ratingForB.getRating() - 1;

                matrix[i][j]++;
            }
        }
    }

    private void calculate(User userA, User userB) {         ◁──┐  Calculate user-
                                                               │  based similarity
        for (Rating ratingByA : userA.getAllRatings()) {

            Rating ratingByB =
➡    userB.getItemRating(ratingByA.getItemId());

            if (ratingByB != null) {

                int i = ratingByA.getRating() - 1;
                int j = ratingByB.getRating() - 1;

                matrix[i][j]++;
            }
        }
    }

    public int getTotalCount() {                             ◁──┐

        int ratingCount = 0;
        int n = matrix.length;

        for (int i = 0; i < n; i++) {
            for (int j = 0; j < n; j++) {
                ratingCount += matrix[i][j];
            }
        }

        return ratingCount;
    }

    public int getAgreementCount() {                         ◁──┤  Auxiliary
                                                                  methods
        int ratingCount = 0;                                      for various
        for (int i = 0, n = matrix.length; i < n; i++) {          counters
            ratingCount += matrix[i][i];
        }

        return ratingCount;
    }

    public int getBandCount(int bandId) {                    ◁──┘
        int bandCount = 0;
        for (int i = 0, n = matrix.length; (i + bandId) < n; i++) {
            bandCount += matrix[i][i + bandId];
```

```
      bandCount += matrix[i + bandId][i];
    }
    return bandCount;
  }
}
```

The heart of that class is the two-dimensional int array (5-by-5, in this case) that stores the agreement rate of two users based on their ratings. Let's say that user *A* and user *B* both listened to 10 songs, and agreed on 6 and disagreed on the rest. The matrix is initialized to zero for all its elements; for every agreement, we add the value 1 in the row and column that corresponds to the rating. So, if three of the agreements were for a rating with value 4, and another three were for the rating 5, then the matrix[3][3] and the matrix[4][4] elements will both be equal to 3. In general, if you add the diagonal elements of the matrix array, you'll find the number of times that the two users agreed on their ratings.

This way of storing the ratings of your users has several advantages. First, you can treat ratings that are from 1 to 10 (or 100 for that matter) in exactly the same way that you treat ratings that are from 1 to 5. Second, as we'll see later, it gives you the opportunity to derive more elaborate similarity measures that account not only for the number of times that two users agreed on their ratings but also for the number of times and the extent to which they disagreed. Third, it's possible to generalize this matrix form into a more general object that may not be a simple two-dimensional array but a more complicated structure; this may be desirable in a situation where your assessment relies on more than a simple rating.

THE INNER WORKINGS OF DELPHI

Now, the code in listing 3.4 has been fully explained. The similarity value between user *A* and user *B*, in this case, is simply the ratio of the number of times that user *A* agreed with number *B* divided by the total number of times that both users rated a particular item. Thus, we're one step away from creating our recommendations.

Listing 3.6   Delphi: creating recommendations based on user similarity

```
public List<PredictedItemRating> recommend(User user, int topN) {

  List<PredictedItemRating> recommendations =
    new ArrayList<PredictedItemRating>();

  for (Item item : dataSet.getItems()) {      <── Loop through all items

      // only consider items that the user hasn't rated yet
      if (user.getItemRating(item.getId()) == null) {

        double predictedRating = predictRating(user, item);    <── Predict ratings
                                                                    for this user
    if (!Double.isNaN(predictedRating)) {
      recommendations.add(new PredictedItemRating(user.getId(),    <──
                  item.getId(), predictedRating));
    }
    }                                                   Add prediction as
  }                                           candidate recommendation
```

```
Collections.sort(recommendations);                    Sort candidate
                                                       recommendations
Collections.reverse(recommendations);

List<PredictedItemRating> topRecommendations =
⇒ new ArrayList<PredictedItemRating>();

for(PredictedItemRating r : recommendations) {         ⟵┐  Select top N
   if( topRecommendations.size() >= topN ) {               │  recommendations
         // had enough recommendations.
         break;
   }
    topRecommendations.add(r);
 }

 return recommendations;
}
```

Listing 3.6 shows the high-level method `recommend` of `Delphi`, which is invoked for providing recommendations, as we've seen in listing 3.3. This method omits from consideration the items that a user has already rated. This may or may not be desirable; consider your own requirements before using the code as-is. If you had to change it, you could change the behavior in this method; for example, you could provide an `else` clause in the first `if` statement.

The `recommend` method delegates the rating prediction of a `user` (the first argument) to the method `predictRating(user, item)` for each `item`, which in turn delegates the calculation of the weighted average to the method `estimateUserBasedRating`. Listing 3.7 presents the method `predictRating(user, item)`. The purpose of that method is to create a façade that hides all the possible implementations of evaluating similarity, such as user-based similarity, item-based similarity and so on. Some cases are suggested but not implemented, so that you can work on them!

Listing 3.7 Predicting the rating of an item for a user

```
public double predictRating(User user, Item item) {

    switch (type) {

        case USER_BASED:
           return estimateUserBasedRating(user, item);

        case ITEM_BASED:
           return estimateItemBasedRating(user, item);

        case USER_CONTENT_BASED:
           throw new IllegalStateException(
⇒ "Not implemented similarity type:" + type);

        case ITEM_CONTENT_BASED:
           throw new IllegalStateException(
⇒ "Not implemented similarity type:" + type);

        case USER_ITEM_CONTENT_BASED:
           return MAX_RATING * similarityMatrix
⇒ .getValue(user.getId(), item.getId());
```

```
        }

    throw new RuntimeException("Unknown type:" + type);
}
```

The method `estimateUserBasedRating` is the user-based implementation for predicting the rating of a user. If we know the rating of a user there's no reason for any calculation. This isn't possible in the execution flow that we described in listing 3.6 because we invoke the method call only for those items that the user hasn't yet rated. But the code was written in a way that handles independent calls to this method as well.

Listing 3.8   Evaluating user-based similarities

```
private double estimateUserBasedRating(User user, Item item) {

   double estimatedRating = Double.NaN;

   int itemId = item.getId();
   int userId = user.getId();

   double similaritySum = 0.0;

   double weightedRatingSum = 0.0;

   // check if user has already rated this item
   Rating existingRatingByUser = user.getItemRating(item.getId());

   if (existingRatingByUser != null) {                        // Get rating for
                                                              // same item
     estimatedRating = existingRatingByUser.getRating();

   } else {                                                   // Loop over all
                                                              // other users
      for (User anotherUser : dataSet.getUsers()) {   ←┘

         Rating itemRating = anotherUser.getItemRating(itemId);   ←

         // only consider users that rated this book
         if (itemRating != null) {                    // Get similarity
                                                       // between two users
            double similarityBetweenUsers =

              similarityMatrix.getValue(userId, anotherUser.getId());

            double ratingByNeighbor = itemRating.getRating();

            double weightedRating =                   // Scale rating according
 ➡  similarityBetweenUsers * ratingByNeighbor;        // to similarity

            weightedRatingSum += weightedRating;

            similaritySum += similarityBetweenUsers;
         }                                            // Estimate rating as ratio of
      }                                               // direct and scaled sum
      if (similaritySum > 0.0) {
         estimatedRating = weightedRatingSum / similaritySum;   ←
      }
   }

   return estimatedRating;
}
```

In the more interesting case where the user hasn't yet rated a specific item, we loop over all users and identify those who've rated the specific `item`. Each one of these users contributes to the weighted average rating in direct proportion to his similarity with our reference `user`. The `similaritySum` variable is introduced for normalization purposes—the weights must add up to 1.

As you can see in listings 3.4 through 3.6, this way of creating recommendations can become extremely difficult if the number of users in your system becomes large, which is often the case in large online stores. Opportunities for optimizing this code abound. We already mentioned storage optimization, but we can also implement another structural change that will result in both space and time efficiency during runtime. While calculating the similarity between users, we can store the top *N* similar users and create our weighted rating (prediction) based on the ratings of these users alone rather than taking into account the ratings of all users that have rated a given item; that's the version known as *kNN*, where *NN* stands for nearest neighbors and *k* denotes how many of them we should consider. Creating recommendations based on user similarity is a reliable technique, but it may not be efficient for large number of users; in this case, the use of item-based similarity is preferred.

3.2.2 Recommendations based on similar items

Collaborative filtering based on similar items works in much the same way as CF based on similar users, except that the similarity between users is replaced by the similarity between items. Let's configure `Delphi` to work based on the similarity between the items (music songs) and see what we get. Listing 3.9 shows the script that we use for that purpose. We load the data that we saved in listing 3.3 and request recommendations for the same user in order to compare the results. We also request the list of similar items for the song "La Bamba," which appears on both lists.

> **Listing 3.9   Creating recommendations based on similar items**

```
BaseDataset ds = BaseDataset                                      Load same data
 ➥ .load("C:/iWeb2/deploy/data/ch3_2_dataset.ser");   ◄─────────  as in listing 3.3

Delphi delphi = new Delphi(ds,RecommendationType.ITEM_BASED);   ◄──────
delphi.setVerbose(true);                                                 Create item-based
                                                                         recommendation
MusicUser mu1 = ds.pickUser("Bob");      │ Recommend a                   engine
delphi.recommend(mu1);                   │ few items to Bob

MusicItem mi = ds.pickItem("La Bamba");  │ Find items similar
delphi.findSimilarItems(mi);             │ to La Bamba
```

Figure 3.5 shows the results of execution for listing 3.9. If you compare these results with the results shown in figure 3.4, you'll see that the recommendations are the same but the order has changed. There's no guarantee that the recommendations based on user similarity will be identical to those based on item similarity. In addition, the scores will almost certainly be different. The interesting part in the specific example of our artificially generated data is that the ordering of the recommendations has been

```
bsh % MusicUser mu1 = ds.pickUser("Bob");
bsh % delphi.recommend(mu1);

Recommendations for user Bob:

    Item: Sunday, Bloody Sunday  , predicted rating: 4.483900
    Item: La Bamba               , predicted rating: 4.396600
    Item: I Love Rock And Roll   , predicted rating: 4.000000
    Item: Wind Beneath My Wings  , predicted rating: 4.000000

bsh % MusicItem mi = ds.pickItem("La Bamba");
bsh % delphi.findSimilarItems(mi);

Items like item La Bamba:

    name: Yesterday                   , similarity: 0.615385
name: Fiddler On The Roof            , similarity: 0.588235
name: Vivaldi: Four Seasons          , similarity: 0.555556
name: Singing In The Rain            , similarity: 0.529412
name: You've Lost That Lovin' Feelin' , similarity: 0.529412
```

Figure 3.5   Discovering similar items and providing recommendations with Delphi based on item similarity

inverted. That's not a general result; it just happened in this case. In other cases, and particularly in real datasets, the results can have any other ordering; run the scripts a few times to see how the results vary each time you generate a different dataset.

The code for creating recommendations based on item similarity is much the same, with the exception that we use items instead of users, of course. The calculation takes place in the method calculate of the class ItemBasedSimilarity.

Listing 3.10   Calculating the item-based similarity

```
protected void calculate(Dataset dataSet) {            Defines size of
                                                        similarity matrix
  int nItems = dataSet.getItemCount();        ◁

  int nRatingValues = 5;                              ◁   Defines size of rating
                                                          count matrix
  similarityValues = new double[nItems][nItems];

  if( keepRatingCountMatrix ) {
     ratingCountMatrix = new RatingCountMatrix[nItems][nItems];
  }
  // if mapping from itemId to index then generate index for every itemId
  if( useObjIdToIndexMapping ) {
    for(Item item : dataSet.getItems() ) {
       idMapping.getIndex(String.valueOf(item.getId()));
    }
  }

  for (int u = 0; u < nItems; u++) {

    int itemAId = getObjIdFromIndex(u);
```

```
   Item itemA = dataSet.getItem(itemAId);

   // we only need to calculate elements above the main diagonal.
   for (int v = u + 1; v < nItems; v++) {                          ❶

     int itemBId = getObjIdFromIndex(v);
     Item itemB = dataSet.getItem(itemBId);                           Agreement of
                                                                      ratings between
     RatingCountMatrix rcm =                                          two items
➡    new RatingCountMatrix(itemA, itemB, nRatingValues);       ◁───┘

     int totalCount     = rcm.getTotalCount();
     int agreementCount = rcm.getAgreementCount();

     if (agreementCount > 0) {                            ◁───┐ Calculate similarity
                                                                │ or set to zero
       similarityValues[u][v] =
➡     (double) agreementCount / (double) totalCount;

     } else {

       similarityValues[u][v] = 0.0;
     }

     if( keepRatingCountMatrix ) {
       ratingCountMatrix[u][v] = rcm;
     }
   }
   // for u == v assign 1
   similarityValues[u][u] = 1.0;          ❶
 }
}
```

This is the same code optimization ❶ that we've seen for the user-based similarity evaluation in listing 3.4.

The RatingCountMatrix class is used once again to keep track of the agreement versus disagreement in the ratings, although now, the agreement/disagreement is between the ratings of two different items rather than two different users. The code iterates through all the possible pairs of items and assigns similarity values based on the Jaccard metric. The code in the Delphi class for item-based recommendations closely follows the corresponding code for user-based recommendations. In listing 3.11, we show the evaluation of the similarity for item-based recommendations; compare it with the code in listing 3.8. The code in listings 3.6 and 3.7 is identical for all types of similarity evaluation.

Listing 3.11 Delphi: creating recommendations based on item similarity

```
private double estimateItemBasedRating(User user, Item item) {

  double estimatedRating = Double.NaN;

  int itemId = item.getId();
  int userId = user.getId();

  double similaritySum = 0.0;
  double weightedRatingSum = 0.0;
```

```
// check if the user has already rated the item
Rating existingRatingByUser = user.getItemRating(item.getId());

if (existingRatingByUser != null) {

  estimatedRating = existingRatingByUser.getRating();

} else {                                                    ┌─ Get rating for
                                                            │  same user
  double similarityBetweenItems = 0;
  double weightedRating = 0;                      ┌─ Loop over all
                                                  │  other items
  for (Item anotherItem : dataSet.getItems()) {  ◄─┘

    // only consider items that were rated by the user
    Rating anotherItemRating = anotherItem.getUserRating(userId);  ◄─

    if (anotherItemRating != null) {                        ┌─ Get similarity
                                                            │  between two
      similarityBetweenItems =                              │  items
⇒ similarityMatrix.getValue(itemId, anotherItem.getId());  ◄─┘

      if (similarityBetweenItems > similarityThreshold) {

        weightedRating =
⇒ similarityBetweenItems * anotherItemRating.getRating();  ◄─  ┌─ Scale rating
                                                              │  according to
        weightedRatingSum += weightedRating;                  │  similarity

        similaritySum += similarityBetweenItems;
      }
    }
  }

  if (similaritySum > 0.0) {

    estimatedRating = weightedRatingSum / similaritySum;  ◄─  ┌─ Estimate rating
  }                                                           │  as ratio of direct
}                                                             │  and scaled sum
  return estimatedRating;
}
```

These listings complete our initial coverage of collaborative filtering, or creating rec-ommendations based on users and items. Typically, CF based on item similarity is pre-ferred because the number of customers is large (millions or even tens of millions), but sometimes in the pursuit of better recommendations, the two CF methods are combined. In the following sections, we'll present the examples of customizing a site like Amazon.com (http://www.amazon.com), which employs an item-to-item collab-orative approach, and providing recommendations on a site like Netflix.com (http://www.netflix.com), which will demonstrate the combination of the two methods.

3.2.3 *Recommendations based on content*

Creating recommendations based on content relies on the similarity of content between users, between items, or between users and items. Instead of ratings, we now have a measure of how "close" two documents are. The notion of distance between doc-uments is a generalization of the relevance score between a query and a document, something that we discussed in chapter 2. You can always think of one document as the query and the other document as reference. Of course, you'd have to compare only the significant parts of each document; otherwise the information that each document carries may be lost by obfuscation.

CASE STUDY SETUP

We'll use the documents from chapter 2 as sources of content and assign a number of these web pages to each user, in a way that resembles the assignment of songs to users in our earlier example. For each user, we'll randomly pick a set of pages that corresponds to 80% of all the eligible pages from our collection. Eligible documents for each user are introduced with a strong bias as follows:

- If the username starts with the letters A through D (inclusive), we assign 80% of the documents that belong to either the Business or the Sports category.
- Otherwise, we assign 80% of the documents that belong to either the USA or the World category

Thus, we establish two large groups of users with similar (although somewhat artificial) preferences, which will allow us to quickly assess our results. Let's see the steps of creating content-based instances of our `Delphi` recommender. Listing 3.12 shows the code that prepares the data and then identifies similar users and similar items. We also provide the recommendation of items based on a hybrid user-item content-based similarity.

Listing 3.12   Creating recommendations based on content similarities

```
BaseDataset ds = NewsData.createDataset();

Delphi delphiUC = new Delphi(ds,RecommendationType.USER_CONTENT_BASED);
delphiUC.setVerbose(true);                          Create user-content-
                                                           based engine
NewsUser nu1 = ds.pickUser("Bob");
delphiUC.findSimilarUsers(nu1);

NewsUser nu2 = ds.pickUser("John");
delphiUC.findSimilarUsers(nu2);

Delphi delphiIC = new Delphi(ds,RecommendationType.ITEM_CONTENT_BASED);
delphiIC.setVerbose(true);                          Create item-content-
                                                           based engine
ContentItem i = ds.pickContentItem("biz-05.html");
delphiIC.findSimilarItems(i);

Delphi delphiUIC =
    new Delphi(ds,RecommendationType.USER_ITEM_CONTENT_BASED);
delphiUIC.setVerbose(true);                         Create user-item-
                                                    content-based engine
delphiUIC.recommend(nu1);
```

The first line of the script creates the dataset in the way that we described earlier. Once we get the dataset, we create a `Delphi` instance that's based on a user-to-user similarity matrix that we calculate in the class `UserContentBasedSimilarity`. Since each user has more than one document, we must compare each document of each user with each document of every other user. There are many ways to do this. In our code, as shown in listing 3.13, for each user-pair combination—user *A* and user *B*—we loop over each document of *A* and find the document of *B* with the highest similarity. Then we average the best similarities for each document of *A* and assign the average value as the similarity between *A* and *B*.

Listing 3.13 Calculating the similarity of users based on their content

```
protected void calculate(Dataset dataSet) {

  int nUsers = dataSet.getUserCount();

  similarityValues = new double[nUsers][nUsers];

  // if mapping from userId to index then generate index for every userId
  if( useObjIdToIndexMapping ) {
    for(User u : dataSet.getUsers() ) {
       idMapping.getIndex(String.valueOf(u.getId()));
    }
  }

  CosineSimilarityMeasure cosineMeasure =
➥ new CosineSimilarityMeasure();

  for (int u = 0; u < nUsers; u++ ) {

    int userAId = getObjIdFromIndex(u);
    User userA = dataSet.getUser(userAId);

    for (int v = u + 1; v < nUsers; v++) {          ❶

      int userBId = getObjIdFromIndex(v);
      User userB = dataSet.getUser(userBId);

      double similarity = 0.0;

      for(Content userAContent : userA.getUserContent() ) {

        double bestCosineSimValue = 0.0;

        for(Content userBContent : userB.getUserContent() ) {

          double cosineSimValue = cosineMeasure
➥ .calculate(userAContent.getTFMap(), userBContent.getTFMap());

          bestCosineSimValue =
➥ Math.max(bestCosineSimValue, cosineSimValue);
        }

        similarity += bestCosineSimValue;
      }

      similarityValues[u][v] = similarity /
➥ userA.getUserContent().size();
    }

    // for u == v assign 1.
    similarityValues[u][u] = 1.0;          ❶
  }
}
```

Create cosine similarity measure

Iterate over all rated items of user A

Iterate over all rated items of user B

Aggregate best similarities from all documents

Calculate similarity as simple average

This is the same code optimization ❶ that we've seen for the user-based similarity evaluation in listing 3.4.

THE KEY IDEAS BEHIND CONTENT-BASED SIMILARITIES

The key element to all content-based methods is representing the textual information as a numerical quantity. An easy way to achieve this is to identify the *N* most frequent terms in each document and use the set of most frequent terms across all documents as a coordinate space. We can take advantage of Lucene's `StandardAnalyzer` class to eliminate stop words and stem the terms to their roots, thus amplifying the importance of the meaningful terms while reducing the noise significantly. For that purpose, we've created a `CustomAnalyzer` class, which extends the `StandardAnalyzer`, in order to remove some words that are common and, if present, would add a significant level of noise to our vectors.

Let's digress for awhile here to make these important ideas more concrete. For argument's sake, let's say that *N = 4* and that you have three documents and the following (high frequency) terms:

- D1 = {Google, shares, advertisement, president}
- D2 = {Google, advertisement, stock, expansion}
- D3 = {NVidia, stock, semiconductor, graphics}

Each of these documents can be represented mathematically by a nine-dimensional vector that reflects whether a specific document contains one of the nine unique terms—{Google, shares, advertisement, president, stock, expansion, Nvidia, semiconductor, graphics}. So, these three documents would be represented by the following three vectors:

- D1 = {1,1,1,1,0,0,0,0,0}
- D2 = {1,0,1,0,1,1,0,0,0}
- D3 = {0,0,0,0,1,0,1,1,1}

Voilà! We constructed three purely mathematical quantities that we can use to compare our documents quantitatively. The similarity that we're going to use is called the *cosine similarity*. We've seen many similarity formulas so far, and this isn't much different. Instead of bothering you with a mathematical formula, we'll list the class that encapsulates its definition. Listing 3.14 shows the code from the `CosineSimilarity-Measure` class.

Listing 3.14 Calculating the cosine similarity between term vectors

```
public class CosineSimilarityMeasure {

    public double calculate(double[] v1, double[] v2) {

        double a = getDotProduct(v1, v2);                    ⊲┐

        double b = getNorm(v1) * getNorm(v2);   ⊲─┐  Normalize two      Find dot
                                                    vectors and      product
        return a / b;    ⊲── Get cosine similarity  calculate product
    }

    private double getDotProduct(double[] v1, double[] v2) {   ⊲─┘
```

```
        double sum = 0.0;

        for(int i = 0, n = v1.length; i < n; i++) {
            sum += v1[i] * v2[i];
        }

        return sum;

    }
    private double getNorm(double[] v) {          Calculate Euclidean
                                                   norm of a vector
        double sum = 0.0;

        for( int i = 0, n = v.length; i < n; i++) {
            sum += v[i] * v[i];
        }

        return Math.sqrt(sum);

    }
}
```

As you can see, first we form what's called the *dot (inner) product* between the two vectors—the double variable a. Then we calculate the norm (magnitude) of each vector and store their product in the double variable b. The cosine similarity is simply the ratio *a/b*. If we denote the cosine similarity between document *X* and document *Y* as CosSim(X,Y), for our simple example, we have the following similarities:

- *CosSim(D1,D2) = 2 / (2*2) = 0.5*
- *CosSim(D1,D3) = 0 / (2*2) = 0*
- *CosSim(D2,D3) = 1 / (2*2) = 0.25*

The technique of representing documents based on their terms is fundamental in information retrieval. We should point out that identifying the terms is a crucial step, and it's difficult to get it right for a general corpus of documents. For example, modify our code to use the StandardAnalyzer instead of our own CustomAnalyzer. What do you observe? The results can be altered significantly, even though at first sight, there's not much in our custom class. This small experiment should convince you that the content-based approach is very sensitive to the lexical analysis stage.

THREE TYPES OF CONTENT-BASED RECOMMENDATIONS

Coming back to our example, let's have a look at the results. Figure 3.6 shows a part of the results from executing the code in listing 3.12, which is responsible for finding similar users.

The algorithm is successful because it correctly identifies the two distinct groups as similar—users whose names start with *A* through *D* and users whose names start with *E* through *Z*. Note that the values of similarity don't vary much. The content-based approach doesn't seem to produce a good separation between the users when they're compared with each other. Figure 3.7 shows the execution of the code that's responsible for finding similar items. As you can see, a number of relevant items have been identified, but so were a number of items that a human user wouldn't find very similar.

```
bsh % BaseDataset ds = NewsData.createDataset();
bsh % Delphi delphiUC =
new Delphi(ds,RecommendationType.USER_CONTENT_BASED);

bsh % delphiUC.setVerbose(true);
bsh % NewsUser nu1 = ds.pickUser("Bob");
bsh % delphiUC.findSimilarUsers(nu1);

Top Friends for user Bob:

    name: Albert        , similarity: 0.950000
    name: Catherine     , similarity: 0.937500
    name: Carl          , similarity: 0.937500
    name: Alexandra     , similarity: 0.925000
    name: Constantine   , similarity: 0.925000

bsh % NewsUser nu2 = ds.pickUser("John");
bsh % delphiUC.findSimilarUsers(nu2);

Top Friends for user John:

    name: George        , similarity: 0.928571
    name: Lukas         , similarity: 0.914286
    name: Eric          , similarity: 0.900000
    name: Nick          , similarity: 0.900000
    name: Frank         , similarity: 0.900000
```

Figure 3.6   Users who are similar to Bob have names that start with the letters A through D. The algorithm identified the two groups of similar users successfully!

Once again, you can see that the similarity values don't vary much; it would be difficult for the algorithm to provide excellent recommendations. The reason for that lack of disambiguation lies in the paucity of our lexical analysis. *Natural language processing* (NLP)) is a rich and difficult field. Nevertheless, much progress has been made in the last two decades; although we won't go in-depth on that fascinating subject in this book, we'll summarize the various components of a NLP system in appendix D.

In figure 3.8 we present recommendations based on user-item similarity. Although CF usually deals with user-user or item-item similarities, a content-based approach is advantageous for building recommendations on user-item similarities. Nevertheless, the problems of lexical analysis remain, and without tedious and specific work based on NLP, the results won't be satisfactory. If you enlarge the dataset and run the script several times for different users, a large number of the recommendations will have identical ratings and the predicted ratings won't vary significantly.

In summary, recommendation systems are built around user-user, item-item, and content-based similarities. Creating recommendations based on user similarity is a reliable technique but may not be efficient for a large number of users. In the latter case, collaborative filtering based on item similarity is preferred because the number of customers (millions or even tens of millions) is orders of magnitude larger than the

```
bsh % Delphi delphiIC =
new Delphi(ds,RecommendationType.ITEM_CONTENT_BASED);

bsh % delphiIC.setVerbose(true);
bsh % ContentItem biz1 = ds.pickContentItem("biz-01.html");
bsh % delphiIC.findSimilarItems(biz1);

Items like item biz-01.html:

    name: biz-03.html     , similarity: 0.600000
    name: biz-02.html     , similarity: 0.600000
    name: biz-04.html     , similarity: 0.100000
    name: biz-07.html     , similarity: 0.100000

bsh % ContentItem usa1 = ds.pickContentItem("usa-01.html");
bsh % delphiIC.findSimilarItems(usa1);

Items like item usa-01.html:

    name: usa-02.html     , similarity: 0.300000
    name: usa-03.html     , similarity: 0.300000
    name: world-03.html   , similarity: 0.100000
    name: world-05.html   , similarity: 0.100000
    name: usa-04.html     , similarity: 0.100000

bsh % ContentItem sport1 = ds.pickContentItem("sport-01.html");
bsh % delphiIC.findSimilarItems(sport1);

Items like item sport-01.html:

    name: sport-03.html   , similarity: 0.400000
    name: sport-02.html   , similarity: 0.300000
```

Figure 3.7   Items that belong in the same category as the query item are correctly identified as similar.

```
bsh % Delphi delphiUIC = new Delphi(
➥    ds,RecommendationType.USER_ITEM_CONTENT_BASED);
bsh % delphiUIC.setVerbose(true);
bsh % delphiUIC.recommend(nu1);

Recommendations for user Bob:

    Item: biz-06.html     , predicted rating: 2.500000
    Item: biz-04.html     , predicted rating: 1.500000
    Item: usa-02.html     , predicted rating: 0.500000
    Item: world-03.html   , predicted rating: 0.500000
    Item: world-05.html   , predicted rating: 0.500000
```

Figure 3.8   We obtain item recommendations based on the content that's associated with the user Bob.

number of items. The content-based approach isn't widely used, but it does have certain advantages and can be used in combination with collaborative filtering to improve the quality of the recommendations. Usually, production systems employ a combination of these techniques. Let's look at the concept of combining recommendation engines.

3.3 Recommending friends, articles, and news stories

In this section, we present a more realistic example that'll help us illustrate combining the techniques that we've discussed so far. We'll work with a hypothetical website whose purpose is to identify individuals with similar opinions, articles with similar comments, and news stories with similar content. Let's call our website MyDiggSpace.com. As the name suggests, the site would use the Digg API to retrieve the articles that you submitted through your Digg account (information about your Digg account could be provided upon registration). Then it would identify and present to you stories similar to the ones that you "dug." In addition, it would allow you to rate the stories that you read, so that in the future the system can sharpen its selection of recommended stories based on your feedback. As if that weren't enough, the site would present you with groups of common interest that you can join if you'd like, thus facilitating social interaction with similar minded individuals.

3.3.1 Introducing MyDiggSpace.com

Let's take the steps of building such a site one by one. True to our promise in the introduction, we won't address issues such as the design of the UI, persistence, and other important engineering components. To keep things interesting, we'll use the Digg API to retrieve data and make our example more realistic. First, we need to explain that Digg is a website (http://digg.com/) where users share content that they've discovered anywhere on the Web. The idea is that content isn't aggregated by editors who know what's best for you (or not), but from the users themselves. Whether the item that you want to talk about comes from a high-profile commercial news outlet or an obscure blog, Digg will let you post your selections and let the best content be revealed through the votes of the participating users.

The Digg API allows third parties to interact programmatically with Digg. Most of the data that lives in the Digg website is available through the API. You can get lists of stories based on popularity, time, or category (topic of discussion). We've written a set of wrapper classes that use the Digg API, and you can later extend them for your own purposes.

We'll build the dataset of MyDiggSpace.com by executing several simple steps. First, we'll collect the top stories from each category in Digg. This will create a list of users and a list of stories (items) for each user.

For each story of each user, we'll identify 10 stories that were submitted by other users, based on the content similarity between the stories. In other words, we'll create a content-based item-item recommendation engine and we'll find the top 10 similar stories.

To complete our dataset, we pretend that the users provide ratings for these stories and therefore we assign a random rating for each story. The assigned rating follows the same convention that we used in our earlier examples—the users whose names start with the letters *A* through *D* assign ratings that are equal to either 4 or 5; the rest of the users assign ratings that are equal to 1, 2, or 3.

The purpose of this example is to introduce you to the concept of combining the results of different recommendation engines in order to get better results than any one engine alone could give you. This appears to be a wise practice across an area of applications that's much wider than recommendation engines. Later in the book, we'll talk about combining the results of classification engines. This example is the prelude to a broad and promising field. It also contains a bigger message that we want to convey in this book—the importance of the synergy of various elements of intelligence in delivering high-quality results for real applications.

3.3.2   *Finding friends*

Let's run our script, as shown in listing 3.15, and get in action with the hypothetical MyDiggSpace.com data.[2]

> **Listing 3.15   MyDiggSpace.com: an example of combining recommendation engines**

```
BaseDataset ds = DiggData
    .loadDataFromDigg("C:/iWeb2/data/ch03/digg_stories.csv");    ⟵┐ Save data
                                                                   │ from Digg
// BaseDataset ds = DiggData
[CA].loadData("C:/iWeb2/data/ch03/digg_stories.csv");    ⟵ Or load local data

iweb2.ch3.collaborative.model.User user = ds.getUser(1);    ⟵ Pick user

DiggDelphi delphi = new DiggDelphi(ds);    ⟵ Create instance of recommender

delphi.findSimilarUsers(user);    ⟵ Find similar users

delphi.recommend(user);    ⟵ Recommend stories
```

Similar users could be presented on a side panel, for example, as the user is reviewing her stories. The recommended stories could also be presented in a special panel and, in order to improve our recommendations for each user, we could use a click-based approach similar to the one described in chapter 2. We could also offer the ability to rate each recommended story in order to achieve an even higher level of confidence in the user's preferences. We'll discuss these improvements in a bit, but first, let's look at the results that our script produced while we were writing the book.

We collected 146 items (stories) from 7 categories, for 33 users; you can control the number and the content of categories in the class `iweb2.ch3.content.digg.Digg-Category`. For these users, we've assigned 811 item ratings. For each user, the selection of items and the ratings are random, except that we follow the same convention that we used before in terms of clustering the ratings based on the initial letter of the user-name. The minimum number of ratings that a user has made on that set is 7, the maximum is 31, and the median is 26.

---

[2] Disclaimer: The data that the script enables you to collect is publicly available. Obviously, we can't be responsible for the content that may be retrieved when you run our example. Our goal is to provide a working example of using the Digg API and demonstrate how you can do something useful with it.

THE TRIANGULATION EFFECT

Figure 3.9 presents the set of similar users for the first user (adamfishercox) on our list, then the similar users for his most similar user (adrian67), then the similar users for a user who's similar to adrian67 (although not the most similar), whose username is DetroitThang1. An interesting observation can be made about the data in figure 3.9, which may or may not be obvious. User amipress is in the top five similar users of adamfishercox but isn't in the top five similar users of adrian67. And yet, amipress is in the top five similar users of DetroitThang1 with a similarity score 0.7, which is almost equal to the similarity score that we found between amipress and adamfishercox. Interesting, isn't it? We call this the *triangulation effect* and it shows us that there are *second-order effects* that can be leveraged and improve the accuracy—and thereby effectiveness—of our recommendations.

Let's further clarify this point by using the data from figure 3.9. The user adamfishercox is related to adrian67 by rank 1 and a similarity score equal to 1; the user amipress is related to adamfishercox by rank 2 and a similarity score (approximately)

```
bsh % delphi.findSimilarUsers(user);
Top Friends for user adamfishercox:

    name: adrian67        , similarity: 1.000000
    name: amipress        , similarity: 0.666667
    name: dvallone        , similarity: 0.500000
    name: cosmikdebris    , similarity: 0.500000
    name: cruelsommer     , similarity: 0.500000

bsh % iweb2.ch3.collaborative.model.User u2 =
ds.findUserByName("adrian67");

bsh % delphi.findSimilarUsers(u2);

Top Friends for user adrian67:

    name: adamfishercox   , similarity: 1.000000
    name: dvallone        , similarity: 1.000000
    name: ambermacbook    , similarity: 1.000000
    name: DetroitThang1   , similarity: 0.800000
    name: cruelsommer     , similarity: 0.750000

bsh % iweb2.ch3.collaborative.model.User u3 =
ds.findUserByName("DetroitThang1");

bsh % delphi.findSimilarUsers(u3);

Top Friends for user DetroitThang1:

    name: adrian67        , similarity: 0.800000
    name: cosmikdebris    , similarity: 0.750000
    name: amipress        , similarity: 0.700000
```

Figure 3.9 Finding similar users and the triangulation effect on a random Digg dataset

equal to 0.67. The rank of user amipress in relation to adrian67 is 7 and their similarity is equal to 0.57. We show these relationships graphically in figure 3.10, where adamfishercox is User 1, amipress is User 2, and adrian67 is User 3.

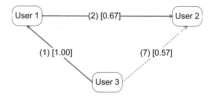

Figure 3.10 The triangulation effect and the opportunity for improvement of the relative ranking

The number inside the parentheses is the relative ranking, and the number inside the brackets is our similarity score; the base of the arrow refers to the user for whom we seek to find similar users. The arrow that connects User 3 with User 2 has a dotted line to depict the relationship that we can improve based on the information of the other relationships (arrows drawn with solid lines).

3.3.3 The inner workings of DiggDelphi

Now, let's look at the code that created these recommendations. Listing 3.16 presents the code from the class DiggDelphi.

Listing 3.16 Combining recommendation systems for the MyDiggSpace.com site

```
public class DiggDelphi {

  private Dataset ds;

  private Delphi delphiUC;
  private Delphi delphiUIC;
  private Delphi delphiUR;
  private Delphi delphiIR;

  private boolean verbose = true;

  public DiggDelphi(Dataset ds) {        Initialize various
    this.ds = ds;                        recommendation engines

    delphiUC =
    new Delphi(ds,RecommendationType.USER_CONTENT_BASED);

    delphiUIC =
    new Delphi(ds,RecommendationType.USER_ITEM_CONTENT_BASED);

    delphiUR  = new Delphi(ds,RecommendationType.USER_BASED);

    delphiIR  = new Delphi(ds,RecommendationType.ITEM_BASED);
  }

  public SimilarUser[] findSimilarUsers(User user, int topN) {    ❶

    List<SimilarUser> similarUsers =
    new ArrayList<SimilarUser>();

    similarUsers.addAll(
    Arrays.asList(delphiUC.findSimilarUsers(user, topN)));

    similarUsers.addAll(
    Arrays.asList(delphiUR.findSimilarUsers(user, topN)));
```

```
        return SimilarUser.getTopNFriends(similarUsers, topN);
  }

  public List<PredictedItemRating> recommend(User user, int topN) {      ❷

    List<PredictedItemRating> recommendations =
➥   new ArrayList<PredictedItemRating>();

    recommendations.addAll(delphiUIC.recommend(user, topN));
    recommendations.addAll(delphiUR.recommend(user, topN));
    recommendations.addAll(delphiIR.recommend(user, topN));

    return PredictedItemRating
➥     .getTopNRecommendations(recommendations, topN);
  }
}
```

We want to find similar users based on user-based and user-content-based similarities ❶ and recommend stories based on user-item-content-based, user-based, and item-based similarities ❷.

As you can see, in the method findSimilarUsers, we take the simplest approach of combining the lists of similar users—we add all the results in a list and sort the entries based on their similarity score (that happens inside the getTopNFriends method). We use the content-based approach, through the delphiUC instance, and the user-to-user similarity based on rankings approach (collaborative filtering), through the delphiUR instance. Note that the similarities between these two recommendation engines aren't in any way normalized. This means that the results will be a bit mixed up, even though we ordered them.

To understand this point better, think of a list that's made up of 20 bank accounts. If 10 of the accounts are in U.S. dollars and the other 10 are in euros, sorting a list that contains both of them based on their total amount won't make perfect sense unless we express them all in U.S. dollars or in euros. Nevertheless, the accounts that contain little money would still be at the bottom of the list, while the accounts that contain a lot of money would be at the top; the ordering just won't be exact.

Our analogy with the currencies, although illuminating, oversimplifies a major difference between the two cases. The normalization between currencies is well understood and straightforward. If I want to convert 100 U.S. dollars into 100 euros then I'd use the exchange rate between these two currencies to get the nominal value of 100 U.S. dollars into euros. In reality, if you want to get euros in your hands (or in your bank account), you have to pay the bank a commission fee, but your normalization formula is still extremely easy. Unfortunately, user similarities and recommendation scores aren't as easily susceptible to normalization. Combining recommendation engine scores is as much an art as it is a science. Ingenious heuristics are often used, and machine learning algorithms play an important role in creating an information processing layer on top of the initial recommendations.

Figure 3.11 shows the results of naïvely combining the recommendations from three different approaches, for the three users that we've examined so far. As shown in the method recommend of listing 3.16, we create a list that contains recommendations that

```
bsh % delphi.recommend(user);

Recommendations for user adamfishercox:

Item: Lumeneo Smera: French Concept of Car and MotorCycle,
predicted rating: 5.0
Item: Bill Gates to Congress: Let us hire more foreigners -
CNET N, predicted rating: 5.0
Item: The Best Tools for Visualization, predicted rating: 5.0
Item: Coolest Cubicle Contest, Part Three, predicted rating: 5.0
Item: Bush: Telecoms Should Be Thanked For Their Patriotic
Service, predicted rating: 5.0

bsh % delphi.recommend(u2);

Recommendations for user adrian67:

Item: Can women parallel park on Mars?, predicted rating: 5.0
Item: Coast Guard loses a few flares and ..., predicted rating:
5.0
Item: 10.5.2 released, predicted rating: 5.0
Item: They are all hot!, predicted rating: 5.0
Item: 11 Greatest Basketball Commercials Ever Made, predicted
rating: 5.0

bsh % delphi.recommend(u3);

Recommendations for user DetroitThang1:

Item: The Best Tools for Visualization, predicted rating: 5.0
Item: Coolest Cubicle Contest, Part Three, predicted rating:
5.000000
Item: Stink Films comes correct with 3 Adidas Original Films,
predicted rating: 5.0
Item: The Power Rangers Meet The Teenage Mutant Ninja Turtles,
predicted rating: 5.0
```

Figure 3.11   A sample of the results from the combination of three different recommendation engines

stem from a user-item content-based recommender, a user-user collaborative filtering recommender, and an item-item collaborative filtering recommender.

These are good results, in the sense that the recommended ratings are all fives as we'd expect due to our artificial bias on the ratings—the users whose names start with letters *A* through *D* always give a rating of 5 or 4. Remember that we said it's possible that the lack of normalization among the similarities is favoring one recommender over the others. We need a mechanism that will allow us to consider the recommendations of the various engines on an equal footing.

Look at the implementation of the recommend method shown in listing 3.17, which takes these concerns into consideration. The first step is to normalize all the predicted ratings, taking as reference the maximum predicted rating for the user across all recommendation engines. We also introduce an ad hoc threshold that eliminates recommendations whose predicted ratings are below a certain value. Let this be your first exposure to the interesting subject of accounting for the cost of bad recommendations. In other words, our threshold value (however artificial) sets a barrier for the predicted ratings that our recommendations must exceed before they're seriously taken into consideration.

The last part of that implementation consists of averaging all the predicted ratings for a particular item in order to get a single predicted rating. This is a valid approach because we've normalized the ratings; without normalization, the averaging wouldn't make much sense. If a particular recommendation engine doesn't rate a particular item then the value of the rating would be zero, and therefore the particular item would be pushed further down in the list of recommendations. In other words, our approach combines averaging and voting between the predicted ratings of the recommenders. Once the combined score has been computed, the recommendations are added in a list and the results are sorted on the basis of the new predicted rating.

Listing 3.17 Improved implementation of recommending by combining recommenders

```
public List<PredictedItemRating> recommend(User user, int topN) {

    List<PredictedItemRating> recommendations =
  new ArrayList<PredictedItemRating>();

 double maxR=-1.0d;

 double maxRatingDelphiUIC =
  delphiUIC.getMaxPredictedRating(user.getId());

 double maxRatingDelphiUR  =                      Max predicted
  delphiUR.getMaxPredictedRating(user.getId());   ratings by
                                                  recommender
 double maxRatingDelphiIR  =
  delphiIR.getMaxPredictedRating(user.getId());

 double[] sortedMaxR =
  {maxRatingDelphiUIC, maxRatingDelphiUR, maxRatingDelphiIR};

 Arrays.sort(sortedMaxR);                          Max predicted rating
                                                   across recommenders
 maxR = sortedMaxR[2];            maxR is max
                                  predicted rating
 // auxiliary variable
 double scaledRating = 1.0d;

 // Recommender 1 -- User-to-Item content based
 double scaling = maxR/maxRatingDelphiUIC;         Create scaling factor
                                                   for each engine
 //Set an ad hoc threshold and scale it
 double scaledThreshold = 0.5 * scaling;

 List<PredictedItemRating> uicList =
  new ArrayList<PredictedItemRating>(topN);

 uicList = delphiUIC.recommend(user, topN);        Get recommendations
                                                   from each engine
 for (PredictedItemRating pR : uicList) {

   scaledRating = pR.getRating(6) * scaling;
```

```
    if (scaledRating < scaledThreshold) {
      uicList.remove(pR);
    } else {
      pR.setRating(scaledRating);
    }
  }
}

// Recommender 2 -- User based collaborative filtering
scaling = maxR/maxRatingDelphiUR;

scaledThreshold = 0.5 * scaling;

List<PredictedItemRating> urList =
  new ArrayList<PredictedItemRating>(topN);

urList = delphiUR.recommend(user, topN);

  for (PredictedItemRating pR : urList) {

    scaledRating = pR.getRating(6) * scaling;

        if (scaledRating < scaledThreshold) {
          urList.remove(pR);
        } else {
          pR.setRating(scaledRating);
        }
  }

  // Recommender 3 -- Item based collaborative filtering
  scaling = maxR/maxRatingDelphiIR;

  scaledThreshold = 0.5 * scaling;

  List<PredictedItemRating> irList =
  new ArrayList<PredictedItemRating>(topN);

  irList = delphiIR.recommend(user, topN);

  for (PredictedItemRating pR : irList) {

        scaledRating = pR.getRating(6) * scaling;

        if (scaledRating < scaledThreshold) {
          irList.remove(pR);
        } else {
          pR.setRating(scaledRating);
        }
  }

  double urRating=0;
  double irRating=0;
  double vote=0;

  for (PredictedItemRating uic : uicList) {

      //Initialize
      urRating=0; irRating=0; vote=0;

    for (PredictedItemRating ur : urList) {
      if (uic.getItemId() == ur.getItemId()) {
        urRating = ur.getRating(6);
      }
```

Scaled rating should be above threshold

Create scaling factor for each engine

Get recommendations from each engine

Get average value and scale properly

```
      }
    for (PredictedItemRating ir : irList) {
      if (uic.getItemId() == ir.getItemId()) {
        irRating = ir.getRating(6);
      }
    }

    vote = (uic.getRating(6)+urRating+irRating)/3.0d;

   recommendations.add(
➥ new PredictedItemRating(user.getId(), uic.getItemId(), vote));
   }

   rescale(recommendations,maxR);

   return PredictedItemRating
➥ .getTopNRecommendations(recommendations, topN);
}
```

You can further improve your recommendations by targeting the preferences of each individual user on MyDiggSpace.com by combining the results obtained in the `Digg-Delphi` class and the `NaiveBayes` classifier that we encountered in chapter 2. For more details on this approach, see the to-do list at the end of this chapter. Any learning mechanism (a number of them are presented in chapter 5) as well as optimization techniques can be employed to enhance the results of the base recommenders. This approach of combining techniques with an encapsulating learning layer is gaining popularity and support from both industry leaders and academics (see also chapter 6).

You should, by now, have a good idea about combining recommendation systems and the interplay of their capabilities in identifying friends and interesting articles for the users of your web application. The next section will focus on a different example: the recommendation of movies on a site such as Netflix. The main characteristic of such examples is the large size of their datasets.

3.4 Recommending movies on a site such as Netflix.com

In the introduction, we talked about Netflix, Inc., the world's largest online movie rental service, offering more than 7 million subscribers access to 90,000 DVD titles plus a growing library of more than 5,000 full-length movies and television episodes available for instant watching on their PCs. If you recall, part of Netflix's online success is its ability to provide users with an easy way to choose movies from an expansive selection of titles. At the core of that ability is a recommendation system called Cinematch. Its job is to predict whether someone will enjoy a movie based on how much he liked or disliked other movies.

3.4.1 An introduction of movie datasets and recommenders

In this section, we'll describe a recommendation system whose goal is the same as that of Cinematch. We'll work with publicly available data from the MovieLens project. The MovieLens project is a free service provided by the GroupLens research lab at the University of Minnesota. The project hosts a website that offers movie recommendations.

You can try it out at http://www.movielens.org/quickpick. There are two MovieLens datasets available on the website of the GroupLens lab.

The first dataset[3] consists of 100,000 ratings by 943 users for 1,682 movies. The second dataset[4] has one million ratings by 6,040 users for 3,900 movies. The first dataset is provided with the distribution of this book; please make sure that you read the license and terms of use. The format of the data is different between the two datasets. We find the format of the second (1M ratings) dataset more appropriate and convenient; it contains just three files, movies.dat, ratings.dat, and users.dat. However, we want to use the smaller dataset for efficiency. So, we've transformed the original format of the small dataset (100K ratings) into the format of the larger dataset, for convenience. The original data and the large dataset can be retrieved from the GroupLens website. You should extract the data inside the `C:/iWeb2/data/ch03/MovieLens/` directory; if you don't then, in listing 3.18, you should alter the `createDataset` method so that it takes the path of the data directory as an argument.

Large recommendation systems such as those of Netflix and Amazon.com rely heavily on item-based collaborative filtering (see Linden, Smith, and York). This approach, which we described in sections 3.2.1 and 3.2.2, is improved by three major components.

The first is *data normalization*. This is a fancy term for something that's intuitively easy to grasp. If a user tends to rate all movies with a high score (a rating pattern that we adopted for our artificial rating of items in the earlier sections) it makes sense to consider the relative ratings of the user as opposed to their absolute values.

The second major component is the *neighbor selection*. In collaborative filtering, we identify a set of items (or users) whose ratings we'll use to infer the rating of nonrated items. So naturally, two questions arise from this mandate: how many neighbors do we need? How do we choose the "best" neighbors—the neighbors that will provide the most accurate prediction of a rating?

The third major component of collaborative filtering is determining the *neighbor weights*—how important is the rating of each neighbor? Bell and Koren showed that data normalization and neighbor weight selection are the two most important components in improving the accuracy of the collaborative filtering approach.

Let's begin by describing our Bean Shell script for this example. Listing 3.18 demonstrates how to load the data, create an instance of our recommender (called Movie-LensDelphi), pick users, and get recommendations for each one of them.

> **Listing 3.18   MovieLensDelphi: Recommendations for the MovieLens datasets**

```
MovieLensDataset ds = MovieLensData.createDataset();    ⟵— Load MovieLens dataset

MovieLensDelphi delphi = new MovieLensDelphi(ds);    ⟵— Create recommender

iweb2.ch3.collaborative.model.User u1 = ds.getUser(1);    ⟵⎤ Pick users and create
delphi.recommend(u1);                                       ⎦ recommendations
```

---

[3]   The URL for the original data is http://www.grouplens.org/system/files/ml-data.tar__0.gz
[4]   The URL for the original data is http://www.grouplens.org/system/files/million-ml-data.tar__0.gz

```
iweb2.ch3.collaborative.model.User u155 = ds.getUser(155);
delphi.recommend(u155);

iweb2.ch3.collaborative.model.User u876 = ds.getUser(876);
delphi.recommend(u876);
```

The first user could've been any user, so we picked the user whose ID is equal to 1. The other two users were identified by executing the command `Delphi.findSimilarUsers(u1);`. We did this so that we can quickly check whether our recommendations make sense. It's reasonable to expect that if two users are similar and neither has seen a movie, then if a movie is recommended to one of them, there's a good chance that it'll be recommended to the other user too. Figure 3.12 shows the results that we get when we run the script and corroborates this sanity check.

These datasets aren't as large as the ones that can be found in the Amazon.com or the Netflix applications, but they're certainly much larger than everything else that

```
bsh % iweb2.ch3.collaborative.model.User u1 = ds.getUser(1);
bsh % delphi.recommend(u1);

Recommendations for user 1:

Item: Yojimbo (1961)              , predicted rating: 5.000000
Item: Loves of Carmen, The (1948) , predicted rating: 4.303400
Item: Voyage to
the Beginning of the World (1997) , predicted rating: 4.303400
Item: Baby, The (1973)            , predicted rating: 4.303400
Item: Cat from Outer Space,
The (1978)                        , predicted rating: 4.123200

bsh % iweb2.ch3.collaborative.model.User u155 = ds.getUser(155);
bsh % delphi.recommend(u155);

Recommendations for user 155:

Item: Persuasion (1995)              , predicted rating: 5.000000
Item: Close Shave, A (1995)          , predicted rating: 4.373000
Item: Notorious (1946)               , predicted rating: 4.181900
Item: Shadow of a Doubt (1943)       , predicted rating: 4.101800
Item: Crimes and Misdemeanors (1989) , predicted rating: 4.061700

bsh % iweb2.ch3.collaborative.model.User u876 = ds.getUser(876);
bsh % delphi.recommend(u876);

Recommendations for user 876:

Item: Third Man, The (1949)       , predicted rating: 5.000000
Item: Bicycle Thief,
The (Ladri di biciclette)(1948)  , predicted rating: 4.841200
Item: Thin Blue Line, The (1988)  , predicted rating: 4.685600
Item: Loves of Carmen, The (1948), , predicted rating: 4.600200
Item: Heaven's Burning (1997)     , predicted rating: 4.600200
```

Figure 3.12 Recommendations from the MovieLensDelphi recommender based on the MovieLens dataset

we've presented so far, and large enough to be realistic. Running the script for the small MovieLens dataset (100K ratings) will take anywhere between 30 seconds to a minute simply to create the recommender. During that time, the recommender does a lot of processing, as we'll see. The recommendations themselves are relatively fast, typically under one second.

3.4.2   *Data normalization and correlation coefficients*

As promised, in the example for this section, we enriched our collaborative filtering approach by introducing two new tools. The first is data normalization and the second a new similarity measure for capturing the correlation between items. The new similarity measure is called the *linear correlation coefficient* (also known as the *product-moment correlation coefficient*, or *Pearson's r*). Calculating that coefficient for two arrays *x* and *y* is fairly straightforward. Listing 3.19 shows the three methods responsible for that calculation.

Listing 3.19   The calculation of the linear correlation coefficient (Pearson's r)

```
public double calculate() {

    if( n == 0) {
        return 0.0;
    }
    double rho=0.0d;
    double avgX = getAverage(x);        |  Calculate average
    double avgY = getAverage(y);        |  values for each vector

    double sX = getStdDev(avgX,x);      |  Calculate standard
    double sY = getStdDev(avgY,y);      |  deviations for each vector

    double xy=0;

    for (int i=0; i < n; i++) {

        xy += (x[i]-avgX)*(y[i]-avgY);      ❶
    }

     if( sX == ZERO || sY == ZERO) {        ❷

        double indX = ZERO;
        double indY = ZERO;

     for (int i=1; i < n; i++) {

       indX += (x[0]-x[i]);
       indY += (y[0]-y[i]);
     }

        if (indX == ZERO && indY == ZERO) {
        // All points refer to the same value
        // This is a degenerate case of correlation
        return 1.0;
     } else {
        //Either the values of the X vary or the values of Y
        if (sX == ZERO) {
            sX = sY;
```

```
            } else {
            sY = sX;
            }
        }
    }
}
    rho = xy / ((double)n*(sX*sY));     ◄───┐ The value of
    return rho;                              │ Pearson's r
}
private double getAverage(double[] v) {
    double avg=0;

    for (double xi : v ) {
        avg += xi;
    }
    return (avg/(double)v.length);
}
private double getStdDev(double m, double[] v) {
    double sigma=0;

    for (double xi : v ) {
        sigma += (xi - m)*(xi - m);
    }

    return Math.sqrt(sigma / (double)v.length);
}
```

❶ is the cross product calculation of the pointwise deviations from the mean value. ❷ is a special (singular) case, where all the points have the exact same values for either *X* or *Y*, or both. This case must be treated separately because it leads to division by zero.

The method getAverage is self-explanatory; it calculates the average of the vector that's provided as an argument. The getStdDev method calculates the *standard deviation* for the data of the vector that's passed as the second argument; the first argument of the method ought to be the average. There's a smarter way to do this that avoids a plague of numerical calculations called the *roundoff error,* read the article on the corrected two-pass algorithm by Chan, Golub, and LeVeque.

Calculating similarity based on Pearson's correlation is a widely used metric that has the following properties:

- Whenever it's equal to zero, the two items are (statistically) *uncorrelated.*
- Whenever it's equal to 1, the ratings of the two items fit exactly onto a straight line with positive slope; for example, (1,2), (3,4), (4,5), (4,5), where the first number in parentheses denotes the rating of the first item while the second number denotes the rating of the second item. This is called *complete positive correlation.* In other words, if we know the ratings of one item, we can infer the ratings of the other with high probability.
- Whenever it's equal to -1, the ratings of the two items fit exactly onto a straight line but with negative slope; for example (1,5), (2,4), (3,3), (4,2). This is called *complete negative correlation.* In this case too, we can infer the ratings of one item based on those of the other item, but now whenever the ratings for the first item increase, the ratings for the second item will decrease.

If the items are correlated linearly, the linear correlation coefficient is a good measure for the strength of that correlation. In fact, if you fit a straight line to your dataset then the linear correlation coefficient reflects the extent to which your ratings lie away from that line. But not everything fits that rosy picture. Unfortunately, this metric is a rather poor measure of correlation if no correlation exists! Say what? Yes, that's right.

A celebrated counterexample is known as the *Anscombe's quartet*. Figure 3.13 depicts Anscombe's quartet for four different pairs of values; this plot is available on Wikipedia, in SVG format, at http://en.wikipedia.org/wiki/Image:Anscombe.svg.

In plain terms, if you plot the ratings between two items against each other, and the plot is similar to the upper-left graph of figure 3.13, the linear correlation coefficient is a meaningful metric. In the other graphs, Pearson's correlation has the same value but its significance is questionable; the datasets are carefully crafted so that they also have the same mean, the same standard deviation, and the same linear fit ($y = 3 + 0.5 * x$). This inability to determine the significance of the linear (Pearson) correlation coefficient led people to a different kind of similarity metric called *nonparametric correlation*. There are two popular nonparametric correlation coefficients: the Spearman rank-order correlation coefficient (rs) and the Kendall's tau (τ). These metrics trade some loss of information for the assurance that a detected correlation is truly present in the data when the values of the metrics indicate so. We discuss nonparametric correlation in the to-do

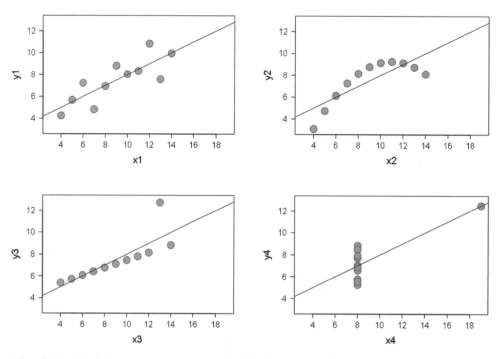

Figure 3.13 Anscombe's quartet: Four datasets that have the same Pearson's correlation but different distributions

section because in many cases the distribution of ratings will look like the graph in the lower-right corner. Nevertheless, from now on, we'll assume that whenever the item ratings are correlated, they're linearly correlated and we can safely use Pearson's correlation. You can find more information about the nonparametric correlations in the references section.

Having discussed the new possibilities that the linear coefficient (Pearson's r) and the nonparametric correlations offer for evaluating similarities, we'll proceed by showing you one way of achieving data normalization. Listing 3.20 shows code that does just that; it's one of the constructors for the class `PearsonCorrelation`. The first argument provides a reference to the original dataset, and the other two are references to the items whose correlation we want to calculate. As you can see, the arrays that are constructed for calculating the Pearson correlation don't refer to the ratings of each user, as they were recorded, but rather to a new set of data in which we've subtracted the average rating of an item from the user's ratings. Clearly, this isn't the only way of achieving data normalization. Bell and Koren describe sophisticated data normalization techniques as applied to the Netflix prize dataset.

> **Listing 3.20   Data normalization around the average rating of items**

```
public PearsonCorrelation(Dataset ds, Item iA, Item iB) {

  double aAvgR = iA.getAverageRating();
  double bAvgR = iB.getAverageRating();

  Integer[] uid = Item.getSharedUserIds(iA, iB);

  n = uid.length;

  x = new double[n];
  y = new double[n];

  User u;

  double urA=0;
  double urB=0;

  for (int i=0; i<n; i++) {

    u = ds.getUser(uid[i]);

    urA = (double) u.getItemRating(iA.getId()).getRating();
    urB = (double) u.getItemRating(iB.getId()).getRating();

    x[i] = urA - aAvgR;
    y[i] = urB - bAvgR;
  }
}
```

Data normalization and the use of Pearson's correlation are incorporated in the `PearsonCorrelation` class, and their use is encapsulated by the `MovieLensItemSimilarity` class. For that reason, the `MovieLensDelphi` class is slightly different from the other `Delphi`-type classes. The code in listing 3.21 highlights these differences.

Listing 3.21   Calculation of a rating involves data renormalization and rescaling

```
private double estimateItemBasedRating(User user, Item item) {

  double itemRating = item.getAverageRating();

  int itemId = item.getId();
  int userId = user.getId();

  double itemAvgRating = item.getAverageRating();
  double weightedDeltaSum = 0.0;

  int sumN=0;

  // check if the user has already rated the item
  Rating existingRatingByUser = user.getItemRating(item.getId());

  if (existingRatingByUser != null) {

    itemRating = existingRatingByUser.getRating();

  } else {

        double similarityBetweenItems = 0;

        double weightedDelta = 0;
        double delta = 0;

        for (Item anotherItem : dataSet.getItems()) {          ◁——— Iterate through
                                                                     all items
    // only consider items that were rated by the user
      Rating anotherItemRating =
    anotherItem.getUserRating(userId);

        if (anotherItemRating != null) {                      Perform data
                                                              renormalization
          delta = itemAvgRating - anotherItemRating.getRating();   ◁—

          similarityBetweenItems =
    itemSimilarityMatrix.getValue(itemId, anotherItem.getId());    ◁——

          if (Math.abs(similarityBetweenItems) >
    similarityThreshold) {                              ❶      Get similarity
                                                               between two
          weightedDelta = similarityBetweenItems * delta;          items

          weightedDeltaSum += weightedDelta;

          sumN++;
          }
        }
      }

    if (sumN > 0) {
      itemRating = itemAvgRating -
    (weightedDeltaSum/(double) sumN)            ❷
      }
  }

  return itemRating;
}

public List<PredictedItemRating> getTopNRecommendations(
    List<PredictedItemRating> recommendations, int topN) {
```

```
PredictedItemRating.sort(recommendations);

double maxR = recommendations.get(0).getRating();
double scaledR;

List<PredictedItemRating> topRecommendations =
  new ArrayList<PredictedItemRating>();

  for(PredictedItemRating r : recommendations) {

   if( topRecommendations.size() >= topN ) {
    // have enough recommendations.
    break;
   }

   scaledR = r.getRating() * (5/maxR);
   r.setRating(scaledR);

   topRecommendations.add(r);
  }

 return topRecommendations;
}
```

We weigh the deviation ❶ from the mean value based on the similarity of the two items and assign ❷ a rating based on the item's mean value and the sum of weighted deviations.

Data renormalization refers to the fact that our similarities were built around the item's average rating, so in order to calculate the predicted item rating, we need to renormalize from differences (delta) to actual ratings. One drawback of this kind of data normalization is that the maximum value of the predicted rating can fall outside the range of the acceptable values. Thus, a rescaling of the predicted ratings is required, as shown inside the method getTopNRecommendations.

3.5   *Large-scale implementation and evaluation issues*

Commercial recommendation systems operate under demanding conditions. The number of users is typically on the order of millions, and the number of items on the order of hundreds of thousands. An additional requirement is the capability to provide recommendations in real-time (typically, subsecond response times) without sacrificing the quality of the recommendations. As we've seen, by accumulating ratings from each user, it's possible to enhance the accuracy of our predictions over time. But in real life, it's imperative that we give excellent recommendations to new users for which, by definition, we don't have a lot of ratings. Another stringent requirement for state-of-the-art recommendation systems is the ability to update their predictions based on incoming ratings. In large commercial sites, there may be thousands of ratings and purchases that take place in a few hours, and perhaps tens of thousands in the course of a single day. The ability to update the recommendation system with that additional information is important and must happen online—without downtime.

Let's say that you wrote a recommender and you're satisfied with its speed and the amount of data that it can handle. Is this a good recommender? It's not useful to have a fast and scalable recommender that produces bad recommendations! So, let's talk about evaluating the accuracy of a recommendation system. If you search the related literature, you'll find that there are dozens of quantitative metrics and several qualitative methods for evaluating the results of recommendation systems. The plethora of metrics and methods reflects the challenges of conducting a meaningful, fair, and accurate evaluation for recommendations. The review article by Herlocker, Konstan, Terveen, and Riedl contains a wealth of information if you're interested in this topic.

We've written a class that evaluates our recommendations on the MovieLens data by calculating the *root mean square error (RMSE)* of the predicted ratings. The RMSE is a simple but robust technique of evaluating the accuracy of your recommendations. This metric has two main features: (1) it always increases (you don't get kudos for predicting a rating accurately) and (2) by taking the square of the differences, the large differences (>1) are amplified, and it doesn't matter if you undershoot or you overshoot the rating.

We can argue that the RMSE is probably too naïve. Let's consider two cases. In the first case, we recommend to a user a movie with four stars and he really doesn't like it (he'd rate it two stars); in the second case, we recommend a movie with three stars but the user loves it (he'd rate it five stars). In both cases, the contribution to the RMSE is the same, but it's likely that the user's dissatisfaction would probably be larger in the first case than in the second case; we know that our dissatisfaction would be!

You can find the code that calculates the RMSE in the class `RMSEEstimator`. Listing 3.22 shows you how you can evaluate the accuracy of our `MovieLensDelphi` recommender.

Listing 3.22 Calculating the root mean squared error for a recommender

```
MovieLensDataset ds = MovieLensData.createDataset(100000);        ⬅━┐  Create the
                                                                     dataset but
MovieLensDelphi delphi = new MovieLensDelphi(ds);                    reserve
                                                                     100,000
RMSEEstimator rmseEstimator = new RMSEEstimator();                   ratings for
                                                                  ❶ testing
rmseEstimator.calculateRMSE(delphi);
```

We create a dataset that excludes 100K ratings from the one million ratings that are available in the large MovieLens dataset ❶. The recommender will train on the remaining 900K ratings and be evaluated on the 100K ratings; the rest of the script is self-explanatory. If you run this with the code that we've described in this section then your RMSE should be equal to 1.0256. This isn't a bad RMSE but it's not very good either. We highly recommend that you improve on that result and set as your goal an RMSE that's below 1. As a relative measure of success, we should mention that the best teams that compete for the Netflix prize have an RMSE that is between 0.86 and 0.88. So, even though the dataset is different, don't be disappointed if your improvements bring your RMSE to be approximately equal to 0.9—it would be a great success for you and for us!

3.6   *Summary*

In this chapter, you've learned about the concepts of distance and similarity between users and items. We've seen that one size doesn't fit all, and we need to be careful in our selection of a similarity metric. Throughout the chapter we encountered several metrics: the Jaccard metric, the Pearson correlation, and variants of these metrics that we introduced. Similarity formulas must produce results that are consistent with a few basic rules, but otherwise we're free to choose the ones that produce the best results for our purposes.

We discussed the two broad categories of techniques for creating recommendations—collaborative filtering and the content-based approach. We walked through the construction of an online music store that demonstrated the underlying principles, in detail but with clarity. In the process of building these examples, we've created the infrastructure that you need for writing a general recommendation system for your own application.

Finally, we tackled two more general examples. The first example was a hypothetical website that used the Digg API and retrieved the content of our users for further analysis of similarity between them, and in order to provide unseen article recommendations to them. In this example, we pointed out the existence of second-order effects, and by extension of *higher-order effects*, and we suggested a way to leverage them in order to improve the accuracy of our recommendations. Our second example dealt with movie recommendations and introduced the concept of data normalization, as well as the popular linear (Pearson) correlation coefficient. In the latter context, we also introduced a class that evaluates the accuracy of our recommendations based on the root mean squared error.

In both examples, we demonstrated that as the complexity and the size of the problem increase, it becomes imperative to leverage the combination of techniques for improving the efficiency and quality of our recommendations. Thus, we discussed the possibility of reusing what you learning from user clicks in the example of MyDiggSpace.com. This is a theme that we'll encounter throughout this book—the combination of techniques that capture different aspects of our problem can, and often does, result in recommendations of higher accuracy.

In the next chapter, we'll encounter another family of intelligent algorithms: clustering algorithms. Nevertheless, if you haven't worked on the to-do topics yet then you might want to have a look at them now, while all the recommendation related material still reverberates in your mind.

3.7   *To Do*

1   *Similarity metrics.*   Implement the Jaccard similarity for the `MusicUsers`. What differences do you observe? A variation of the Jaccard metric is the *Tanimoto metric*, which is more appropriate for continuous values. The Tanimoto metric is equal to the ratio of the intersection of two sets ($Ni = |X \cap Y|$) over the union ($Nu = |X| + |Y|$) minus the intersection—$T = Ni/(Nu\text{-}Ni)$.

For example, if X = {baseball, basketball, volleyball, tennis, golf} and Y = {baseball, basketball, cricket, running} then the Tanimoto metric has a value equal to *2/((5+4)–2)*, which is approximately equal to 0.2857. Work out the formula in the case of vectors (Java arrays `double[] x` and `double[] y`). Hint: the intersection corresponds to the inner product of the two vectors and the union to the sum of their magnitudes.

Another interesting similarity measure is the *city block* metric. Its name stems from the fact that the values of the vectors, X and Y, are assumed to be coordinates on a multidimensional orthogonal grid. When the vectors are two-dimensional, it resembles the way that a taxi driver would give you instructions in a city: "the Empire State Building is two blocks south and three blocks east from here." If you like that metric or want to study the cases where it's most applicable, *Taxicab Geometry: An Adventure in Non-Euclidean Geometry* by Eugene F. Krause provides a detailed exposition.

2   *Varying the range of prediction.*   Did you ever wonder why various websites want you to rate movies, songs, and other products by assigning one integer value between 1 and 5 (inclusive)? Why not pick a value between 1 and 10? Or even between 1 and 100? Wouldn't that give you more flexibility to express the degree of your satisfaction with the product? To take this one step further, why not rate different aspects about a product? In the case of a movie, we could rate the plot, the performance of the actors, the soundtrack, and the visual effects. You can extend the code that we presented in this chapter and experiment along these lines. Can you identify any potential issues?

3   *Improving recommendations through ensemble methods.*   A technique that's becoming increasingly popular consists of combining independent techniques in order to improve the combined recommendation accuracy. There are many good theoretical reasons for pursuing ensemble methods; if you're interested in that topic, you could read the article by Dietterich. In addition to theory, there's empirical evidence that ensemble methods may produce better results than individual techniques. Bell and Korren are leading the Netflix prize competition (at the time of this writing), and their assessment was the following: "We found no perfect model. Instead, our best results came from combining predictions of models that complemented each other."

How about combining some of the recommenders that we've given you in this chapter, as well as those that you may invent, and comparing their results to the results of each individual recommender? If the results are better, your "soup" worked! If not, investigate what recommenders you used and to what extent they capture a different aspect of the problem.

4   *Minimizing the roundoff error.*   As you may know, the typical numerical types in Java and most other languages store the values with finite precision. The representation of an `integer` or `long` number is exact, even though the range of their values is finite and determined by the number of bits associated with each type.

But enter floating-point arithmetic (`float` and `double`) and a number of issues crop up due to the inexactness of the numerical representations. At best, you don't have to worry about them, and at worst, you can use `double` throughout.

Nevertheless, in intelligent applications, the heavy use of numerical calculations requires that you be aware of the implications that the finite precision of real numbers has on the result of computations, especially the results that are produced as a result of accumulations or multiplications with very small or large numbers. Let's consider the roundoff error mentioned in the evaluation of the standard deviation of the class `PearsonCorrelation`. The smallest floating-point number that gives a result other than 1.0, when added to 1.0, is called the *machine accuracy* (ϵ). Nearly every arithmetic operation between floating numbers introduces a fractional error on the order of magnitude of ϵ. That error is called the *roundoff error.*

Read the article on the corrected two-pass algorithm of Chan, Golub, and LeVeque, and implement the computation of the standard deviation accordingly. You can also find a brief description of this algorithm in the monumental *Numerical Recipes: The Art of Scientific Computing.* Do you see a perceptible difference in the outcome? What do you think will happen if you use sets that are even larger than the ones considered in this book? Note that the main points of the algorithm apply equally well in the computation of the RMSE that we conducted for evaluating the accuracy of our recommendations.

5   *Nonparametric or rank correlation.*   Correlations that belong in this category are useful if you have reason to question the validity of the linearity assumption underlying the Pearson correlation metric. You can create new similarity classes based on this type of metric, which trade off some information about the data for an assurance about the presence of a true correlation between two sets of data—in our case, two sets of ratings. The main idea behind nonparametric correlation is substituting the values of a variable with the rank of that value in the dataset. The best-known nonparametric correlation coefficients are the *Spearman rank-order correlation coefficient (rs)* and the *Kendall's tau* (τ). You can read all about these coefficients in the masterly written book *Numerical Recipes: The Art of Scientific Computing.*

In the case of movie ratings from 1 to 5, you'll get a lot of conflicts in the rank of values; for example, there will be a lot of movies whose value will be exactly 4. But this presents an opportunity to be creative about using these correlations. What if you use the time of the rating to break the tie of the values? Implement such an approach and compare with the results that you get from using the plain vanilla Pearson's correlation.

3.8   *References*

Bell, R.M., and Y. Koren. "Scalable Collaborative Filtering with Jointly Derived Neighborhood Interpolation Weights." IEEE International Conference on Data Mining (ICDM'07), 2007. http://www.research.att.com/~yehuda/pubs/BellKorIcdm07.pdf.

Chan, T.F., G.H. Golub, and R.J. LeVeque. "Algorithms for computing the sample variance: Algorithms and recommendations." *American Statistician*, vol. 37, pp. 242-247, 1983.

Dieterich, T.G., "Ensemble methods in machine learning." *Multiple Classifier Systems*, (Editors: J. Kittler and F.Roli) volume 1857 of *Lecture Notes in Computer Science*, Cagliari, Italy. Springer, pp.1-15, 2000. http://citeseer.ist.psu.edu/dietterich00ensemble.html.

Estes, W.K. *Classification and Cognition.* Oxford University Press, 1996.

Herlocker, J.L., J.A. Konstan, L.G. Terveen, and J.T. Riedl (2004). "Evaluating Collaborative Filtering Recommender Systems." *ACM Transactions on Information Systems,* Vol 22, 5-53. ACM Press, 2004. http://web.engr.oregonstate.edu/~herlock/papers/eval_tois.pdf.

James, W. *The Principles of Psychology.* Henry Holt and Company, 1918.

Krause, E.F. *Taxicab Geometry: An Adventure in Non-Euclidean Geometry.* Dover Publications, Inc. 1986.

Linden, G., B. Smith, and J. York. "Amazon.com recommendations: Item-to-item collaborative filtering." *IEEE Internet Computing*, January-February 2003, pp.76-80.

Press, W.H., S.A. Teukolsky, W.T. Vetterling, and B.P. Flannery. *Numerical Recipes: The Art of Scientific Computing* (3rd Edition). Cambridge University Press, 1997.

Clustering: grouping things together

Our ability as humans to accumulate and retain information relies greatly on our ability to structure the abundance of information that we receive through means, such as sensory perception, reason, language, and emotion. The profusion of available information would be overwhelming without some reference structures. Mental constructs that put order to all the data that we receive help us retain the essence of the data and understand the world around us.

Typically, we organize our perceptions into groups or categories. Intelligent applications follow the same principles and achieve the same results by means of two broad categories of algorithms—*clustering* and *classification*. This chapter is devoted to clustering algorithms; the next chapter is devoted to classification.

121

Broadly speaking, the term *clustering* refers to the process of grouping similar things together. Let's say that you have a set of records in a database that contains book information. In particular, let's say that you have an identity (ID) for each book, a title, an ISBN, a foreign key to the author's table (say, author_ID), and other pertinent fields. If you execute a SQL SELECT query with an ORDER BY author_ID clause, you'll retrieve the list of books ordered by the author's ID. If you navigate through the list, you'll start with books by the first author, followed by the second author, and so on. In effect, the books have been grouped on the basis of authorship. In the context of clustering, the groups of books are called *book clusters*, and what we just described is a straightforward, but limited, clustering algorithm for your books.

Clustering is useful in many situations, but it's not always possible to achieve a desired objective by issuing simple SQL queries. In many cases, the elements that we need to use for identifying the desired groups aren't unique identifiers, so we need to develop techniques that work well with arbitrary data.

In the preceding chapters, we saw that it's possible to define the notion of distance and the related notion of similarity for a large variety of objects. Our ability to define the distance between two arbitrary objects will come in handy again in this chapter, since any two objects will belong to the same cluster only if they're sufficiently "close" to each other and sufficiently "apart" from members of other clusters.

We'll begin with an example that illustrates some reasons for using clustering. Since the subject of clustering is vast, and we can't cover it in its entirety, we offer an overview of clustering algorithms according to cluster structure, cluster data type, and data size. The rest of the chapter will deal with a number of specific algorithms in great detail. We'll also devote one section on advanced clustering topics such as their computational complexity and the issue of high dimensionality.

4.1   *The need for clustering*

This section demonstrates the identification of user groups in a web application—a common use case. You could use it to perform targeted advertisement, enhance the user experience by displaying posts by like-minded individuals to each user, facilitate the creation of social networks in your site, and so on. The problem of identifying groups of users lends itself naturally to the use of clustering methods.

Our goal is to show that if you didn't know what clustering is, you'd have to invent it in order to solve this and similar problems in a satisfactory manner. In other words, we want to present a series of simple approaches that you may have taken to solve this kind of problem, had you never before read about clustering. We present clustering as a generalization of sorting in the case of records with many attributes, as well as arbitrary metrics of ordering based on these attributes.

To begin, we show that a straightforward approach based on SQL statements is limited to a few cases and explain why, in general, a solution based on plain SQL queries is deficient and impractical. We resort to sorting and show that although we do gain flexibility in terms of using arbitrary metrics of ordering, we're still unable to handle cases with many attributes effectively. Thus, we arrive at general-purpose clustering techniques.

4.1.1 User groups on a website: a case study

We'll now introduce a simple case study that we'll use throughout this section to illustrate clustering. Let's assume that we work for a large open source community software platform, such as SourceForge.net, and we want to know why people participate in open source projects. We could identify groups of users on the basis of their profiles by performing a cluster analysis. For argument's sake, let us take the following attributes into consideration:

- The *age* of the users, which we'll measure in years.
- Their *income*, which we'll measure with brackets or ranges; for example, an income of $65,000–$80,000 corresponds to income range 0, the range $80,000–$95,000 corresponds to income range 1, and so on. You can find all the details about the ranges and their values in the README file located in the data/ch04 directory.
- Their *education level*; high school, college, graduate school, and so on.
- The degree to which they consider their participation to be a good way of honing their *professional skills*; say, on a scale from 1 to 5.
- The degree to which they consider their participation to be a good way of building *social relationships* with people who have the same interests as they do; once again, we could measure that on a scale from 1 to 5.
- An indicator of *paid participation*, by which we mean whether an individual is getting paid to participate in the project. We could use a Boolean variable or we could create a finer-grained representation of paid participation by capturing the percentage of contribution time that's paid by a third party.

You can extend this example to any web application that involves a social networking structure by introducing the attributes that are most appropriate to your case. In order to make our example more concrete, we've created the artificial data in table 4.1. In the headers, you can see the six attributes that we just described. In each row, you'll find the values of these attributes for each of the 20 users that we'll consider.

Table 4.1 Artificial data for cluster analysis of users that participate in an online community

Username	Age	Income range	Education	Skills	Social	Paid work
Albert	23	0	0	3	3	0
Alexandra	25	1	2	4	2	0
Athena	24	0	1	3	4	0
Aurora	23	1	2	5	2	0
Babis	21	0	0	3	4	0
Bill	31	1	2	4	2	0
Bob	32	1	1	3	1	1

Table 4.1   **Artificial data for cluster analysis of users that participate in an online community** *(continued)*

Username	Age	Income range	Education	Skills	Social	Paid work
Carl	30	0	2	4	2	0
Catherine	31	1	1	3	3	0
Charlie	30	1	2	3	2	0
Constantine	37	1	1	3	2	0
Dmitry	35	2	2	1	1	1
Elena	38	1	1	3	2	0
Eric	37	2	2	2	2	0
Frank	39	3	1	3	1	1
George	42	2	2	2	1	1
Jack	43	3	1	1	1	1
John	45	4	2	1	1	1
Maria	43	2	1	3	1	0
Lukas	45	3	2	1	1	1

Our objective is straightforward: identify, if possible, groups of individuals that participate in open source projects based on the values of these attributes. In the next two
sections, we'll present two naïve approaches that can help us achieve our objective in
order of increasing complexity and effectiveness.

4.1.2 *Finding groups with a SQL order by clause*

The simplest approach to achieving our objective would be to load our data in a
table—if it isn't already in a database table—and write a SQL query to find possible
user groups (clusters) of interest. We loaded the data in MySQL, but you can use the
database of your choice to reproduce our results; the README.txt file in the folder
`data/ch04` contains the SQL statements for loading the data in MySQL.

Figure 4.1 shows the results of executing the following query: `select * from`
`sf_users` `order by IncomeRange, Education;`. As you can see, the plain SQL works great
for a single attribute. We can easily identify five groups based on the attribute `Income-`
`Range`; the clusters are (Albert, Babis, Athena, Bill, Carl), (Elena, Constantine, Catherine, Bob, Charlie, Aurora, Alexandra), (Maria, Dmitry, Eric, George), and so on. We
can obtain similar results for any other attribute. But note that as we add more attributes
to the `order` `by` clause, we can't easily identify other groups. The first attribute dominates the results of the query, and additional attributes result in further segmentation
of the clusters that were discovered based on previous attributes in the SQL clause.

If we assume that we can identify useful clusters merely by visual examination we
need to answer the following question: what's the most appropriate attribute ordering

```
mysql> select * from sf_users order by IncomeRange, Education;
+-------------+-----+--------+-----+--------+--------+--------+
| Name        | Age | Income | Edu | Skills | Social | isPaid |
|             |     | Range  |     |        |        |        |
+-------------+-----+--------+-----+--------+--------+--------+
| Albert      | 23  |   0    |  0  |   3    |   3    |   0    |
| Babis       | 21  |   0    |  0  |   3    |   4    |   0    |
| Athena      | 24  |   0    |  1  |   3    |   4    |   0    |
| Carl        | 30  |   0    |  2  |   4    |   2    |   0    |
| Elena       | 38  |   1    |  1  |   3    |   2    |   0    |
| Constantine | 37  |   1    |  1  |   3    |   2    |   0    |
| Catherine   | 31  |   1    |  1  |   3    |   3    |   0    |
| Bob         | 32  |   1    |  1  |   3    |   1    |   1    |
| Bill        | 31  |   1    |  2  |   4    |   2    |   0    |
| Charlie     | 30  |   1    |  2  |   3    |   2    |   0    |
| Aurora      | 23  |   1    |  2  |   5    |   2    |   0    |
| Alexandra   | 25  |   1    |  2  |   4    |   2    |   0    |
| Maria       | 43  |   2    |  1  |   3    |   1    |   0    |
| Dmitry      | 35  |   2    |  2  |   1    |   1    |   1    |
| George      | 42  |   2    |  2  |   2    |   1    |   1    |
| Eric        | 37  |   2    |  2  |   2    |   2    |   0    |
| Frank       | 39  |   3    |  1  |   3    |   1    |   1    |
| Jack        | 43  |   3    |  1  |   1    |   1    |   1    |
| Lukas       | 45  |   3    |  2  |   1    |   1    |   1    |
| John        | 45  |   4    |  2  |   1    |   1    |   1    |
+-------------+-----+--------+-----+--------+--------+--------+
20 rows in set (0.03 sec)
```

Figure 4.1 Using SQL queries to identify clusters

that'll allow us to identify useful clusters? There's no simple answer. What if the data contains thousands of records? And what happens if we need to consider a dozen or more attributes, not just two or three? In these cases, unless we have a priori knowledge about the data, our task will become arduous, if not impossible. If you think about it, it should become clear that using SQL queries can't take us very far.

The fundamental problem with the SQL approach is that discovering the clusters is difficult to automate and impractical to implement for more than a couple of attributes. Identifying clusters is easier with enumerated data, but it becomes more complicated with continuous variables and almost impossible for text data that hasn't been cleansed. More importantly, it's not easy to identify groups using more than one attribute, because the results will vary greatly depending on the ordering of the attributes in the query. The plain SQL approach is quite limited for clustering.

Nonetheless, the combination of SQL with more advanced algorithms can lead to viable implementations of clustering, because a number of operations can be done efficiently in SQL for large datasets. See the description and the references about the SQLEM algorithm in our "To do" section.

4.1.3 *Finding groups with array sorting*

You might be thinking that the problems of the SQL approach may go away if we load the data in our Java code and use a custom comparator to create a meaningful ordering of the raw multidimensional data. If our data is in some kind of an array equipped with our custom comparator, then we should be able to sort it and reveal any clusters that may be present, right? Let's do that and see what happens. Figure 4.2 shows the results that we get from an array with custom sorting.

These results look great, but defining the boundaries between the clusters remains an exercise for the user of the algorithm. We could have added a few lines of code that create one cluster for every four names, but that could be deceiving. People who belong to the same age group tend to be similar to each other, but it would be presumptuous to think that these results are reflective of what will happen in the general case. Listing 4.1 shows the two lines of code that create the output shown in figure 4.2. The first command loads the data from table 4.1. The second command uses the class SortedArrayClustering for identifying clusters in our data.

Listing 4.1 Identifying clusters by sorting an array of DataPoints

```
SFDataset ds = SFData.createDataset();

SortedArrayClustering.cluster(ds.getData());
```

Listing 4.2 shows the content of the class SortedArrayClustering. In principle, this is similar to the SQL statement approach, because all we do is sort the data and print it on the screen. But we've transferred the responsibility of ordering the set of points from the SQL order by statement to our custom Comparator definition. So, there's something fundamental that these two approaches don't capture.

Sorting is an efficient and appropriate technique for clustering when we deal with a single dimension. The multidimensional nature of our data was suppressed in the

```
bsh % SortedArrayClustering.cluster(ds.getData());
John        ([45.0, 4.0, 2.0, 1.0, 1.0, 1.0])
Lukas       ([45.0, 3.0, 2.0, 1.0, 1.0, 1.0])
Maria       ([43.0, 2.0, 1.0, 3.0, 1.0, 0.0])
Jack        ([43.0, 3.0, 1.0, 1.0, 1.0, 1.0])
George      ([42.0, 2.0, 2.0, 2.0, 1.0, 1.0])
Frank       ([39.0, 3.0, 1.0, 3.0, 1.0, 1.0])
Elena       ([38.0, 1.0, 1.0, 3.0, 2.0, 0.0])
Eric        ([37.0, 2.0, 2.0, 2.0, 2.0, 0.0])
Constantine ([37.0, 1.0, 1.0, 3.0, 2.0, 0.0])
Dmitry      ([35.0, 2.0, 2.0, 1.0, 1.0, 1.0])
Bob         ([32.0, 1.0, 1.0, 3.0, 1.0, 1.0])
Bill        ([31.0, 1.0, 2.0, 4.0, 2.0, 0.0])
Catherine   ([31.0, 1.0, 1.0, 3.0, 3.0, 0.0])
Carl        ([30.0, 0.0, 2.0, 4.0, 2.0, 0.0])
Charlie     ([30.0, 1.0, 2.0, 3.0, 2.0, 0.0])
Alexandra   ([25.0, 1.0, 2.0, 4.0, 2.0, 0.0])
Athena      ([24.0, 0.0, 1.0, 3.0, 4.0, 0.0])
Aurora      ([23.0, 1.0, 2.0, 5.0, 2.0, 0.0])
Albert      ([23.0, 0.0, 0.0, 3.0, 3.0, 0.0])
Babis       ([21.0, 0.0, 0.0, 3.0, 4.0, 0.0])
```

Figure 4.2 Clustering data by sorting the elements of an array with a custom Comparator class

method call getR(). This method calculates the distance of every element from the origin of all the attribute values. Think of it as an arrow from the center of our coordinates (whose attribute values are all zero) to each data point. The actual value is obtained by using the class EuclideanDistance, which, as the name suggests, implements the Euclidean distance that we introduced in chapter 3.

Listing 4.2 `SortedArrayClustering` : **sort an array of data points and print them**

```
public class SortedArrayClustering {

  public static void cluster(DataPoint[] points) {              Sort in
                                                                descending order
    Arrays.sort(points, new Comparator<DataPoint>() {    ◁────┘

    public int compare(DataPoint p1, DataPoint p2) {

        int result = 0;
      // sort based on score value
      if (p1.getR() < p2.getR()) {
        result = 1;
      } else if (p1.getR() > p2.getR()) {
        result = -1;
      } else {
        result = 0;
      }
      return result;
    }
    });

    for (int i=0; i < points.length; i++) {
      System.out.println(points[i].toString());
    }
  }
}
```

Since our attributes evaporated and we're left with all the elements on a line, we must deal with two main issues. First, we still have to decide how many clusters exist and what they are. Second, the lack of normalization of the data causes the value of age to dominate over all the other values in the calculation of the Euclidean distance. This undesirable effect can be ameliorated by normalizing the value of the attributes in the dataset, but it would be hard to do this well for an arbitrary dataset.

We're looking for clustering algorithms that could be characterized as intelligent. Assuming that humans are intelligent, what would a human think after looking at that dataset? What clusters would a human identify in it? In particular, let's focus on the group of people over 40. George, Jack, John, Maria, and Lukas are all in their early 40s and most of their attribute values are identical or very similar. But, everybody except Maria is paid to contribute in their open source projects and Maria's main motivation for participating in open source projects seems to be a desire to improve her skills, and thereby increase her income. Maria should probably not be included in the same cluster as George, Jack, John, and Lukas, but that's impossible based on our sorting results!

You could go back and manipulate the distance that we used so that you achieve the desirable effect of excluding Maria from that cluster. If you did that, you'd destroy the simplicity of the approach, and in all likelihood, you wouldn't be able to use the algorithm successfully in a different set.

Deciding what are the "right" clusters for a given set of data is a difficult problem to solve and is an area of active research. The two naïve approaches—SQL and array sorting—as well as all the algorithms that we'll present in the following sections have certain advantages and disadvantages. In the end, it's the nature of the data that determines the success of the algorithms.

This isn't a conclusion that applies specifically to clustering, and you should always keep it in mind when designing intelligent applications. Clustering is the hardest case, because there's no direct measure of success that the machine can use. Clusters aren't known a priori; if they were you wouldn't need a clustering algorithm to begin with! This is why clustering belongs in the category of machine learning known as *unsupervised learning*.

The next section will provide an overview of clustering and a categorization of the algorithms based on a number of criteria, such as the resulting structure of the clusters, the structure and type of data considered, and the size of the data that need to be clustered.

4.2   *An overview of clustering algorithms*

We presented the SQL approach and sorted arrays as a prelude to clustering so you can consider clustering to be a generalization of sorting. Yes, that's right! When we sort a list of objects, in effect, we line up all the objects and use the comparator to pick the first object on the line, the second, and so on. As a result of that process, we identify the immediate neighbors of every object on that line.

When we cluster a set of objects, we also identify the immediate neighborhood of an object, but our objects can retain their multidimensional nature. They could be points on a plane or in 3D space, or they could be points in a more general geometric construct depending on the number of attributes that we want to consider and the notion of distance that we want to adopt.

The goal of clustering algorithms is identifying groups in a way that doesn't suffer from the drawbacks of the SQL approach or the simple array-sorting approach, and can thus extend to many dimensions and arbitrary object spaces. Members of a cluster should be very similar to each other (their neighbors) and very dissimilar to the members of any other cluster in the entire set. Clustering is applicable in a wide range of problems, ranging from biology and medicine to finance and marketing.

Clustering algorithms come in a lot of shapes and forms, and it's difficult to create a categorization for them on the basis of a single criterion. For that reason we'll provide an overview of clustering algorithms before we proceed to specific implementations and lose track of the big picture. The first categorization of clustering algorithms that we present is based on the nature of the cluster structure. Is the algorithm looking for hierarchical relations between the points or simply dividing regions of space into different groups? The second categorization of clustering algorithms is based on the type and structure of the data. Some clustering algorithms perform best on numerical data and others specialize on categorical data. The third categorization is based on whether the algorithm was built to deal with large datasets from the outset. So, let's now give an overview of clustering algorithms from these perspectives.

4.2.1 *Clustering algorithms based on cluster structure*

Figure 4.3 shows the categorization of the various clustering algorithms based on the resulting structure of the clusters.

Hierarchical algorithms result in the identification of clusters within clusters. A hierarchical algorithm for news articles could come up with four large groups that represent broad topics, such

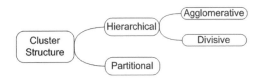

Figure 4.3 Categorizing clustering algorithms based on cluster structure

as politics, sports, business, and technology, and have within each group subgroups; for example, inside sports news, you could have basketball news, baseball news, and so on. In our example for this section, a hierarchical algorithm could divide users of open source projects into two large groups: those who get paid to participate and those who don't. It could further break down these two major groups on the basis of age or income range.

Most hierarchical clustering algorithms admit a *threshold parameter* that indicates at what depth the algorithm should stop seeking smaller subgroups. Aside from being a reasonable thing to do with respect to the final structure of the data clusters, these parameters eliminate a certain amount of unnecessary computational effort. Of course, the final number of clusters isn't known a priori but depends on the configuration parameters of the algorithm that determine the termination criteria for the hierarchy of clusters.

The category of *agglomerative hierarchical* algorithms follows a bottom-up approach—starting with individual elements and forming clusters by associating them with other elements from the bottom up toward the global (super) cluster. The category of *divisive hierarchical* algorithms follows a top-down approach—it starts with the global (super) cluster and proceeds by dividing the data into smaller clusters.

Partitional algorithms create a fixed number of clusters. The so-called k-means clustering algorithm belongs in this category; we'll use this algorithm later in the chapter. The *minimum spanning tree (MST)* and the *nearest neighbor* algorithms also have partitional versions. There are two basic approaches within this category: the *conceptual modeling* approach and the *iterative optimization* approach. Typical representatives of the first approach are based on probabilistic models; a typical representative of the second approach is the k-means algorithm.

4.2.2 *Clustering algorithms based on data type and structure*

In figure 4.4, we show the categorization of clustering algorithms based on data types and the data structure. If you deal exclusively with numerical data—for example, the geographic coordinates on a map or the historic data of stock prices—grid-based algorithms may be more appropriate for your work. In this category, algorithms that are based on *spectral* and *wavelet* methods can provide significant advantages. The algorithm WaveCluster by Gholamhosein Sheikholeslami et al. results in high-quality of clusters with minimum computational complexity.

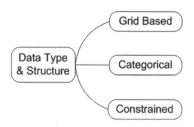

Figure 4.4 Categorizing the clustering algorithms based on data type and data structure

Another category of clustering algorithms specializes in handling categorical data. The main characteristic of these algorithms is that they use metrics based on set membership, such as the Jaccard coefficient. Typically, categorical data lacks ordering, and it's often hard to find a numerical representation that would be appropriate. How do you numerically represent a list of names? Whatever way you come up with will depend on your context rather than a magic algorithm that'll work well in all cases. In the case of people's names, lexicographic ordering may be good enough, but for the names for corporate entities, lexicographic ordering may mix up companies that aren't related in any way. As a result, a lot of clustering algorithms that work great with data that is inherently numeric fail to perform well with categorical data.

To further clarify this point, let's revisit the approach we used in section 2.5. There, we ranked a number of news articles by using a set of words that characterized the articles rather than the hyperlinks between them. The natural representation of our data was categorical (not numeric), and we took the number of shared terms as a measure of the strength by which any two documents can be linked. One of the clustering algorithms that we'll present in this chapter is similar to the technique of section 2.5, and works well with categorical data. It's called *ROCK* and it's a hierarchical agglomerative algorithm that employs the Jaccard similarity measure (see section 3.1.3) in order to define the notion of neighborhood among news articles.

Constrained clustering algorithms are used when clusters must satisfy certain constraints. The typical case here is clustering points on a two-dimensional surface, in the presence of obstacles. Clearly, the clusters that we form should avoid the obstacles. In these cases, the typical Euclidean distance won't work well, and more meaningful metrics are needed for measuring the distance between two points. One good candidate is the length of the shortest path between two points; the shortest path calculation incorporates the avoidance of the obstacles. Tung et al. present an algorithm that deals with that problem satisfactorily. We won't cover constrained clustering algorithms in this book.

4.2.3 *Clustering algorithms based on data size*

Figure 4.5 depicts the categorization of clustering algorithms that are designed for large datasets. We treat this category of clustering algorithms in somewhat special ways. The space and time complexity of many clustering algorithms increases as the square of the number of data points that you want to cluster. If you aren't careful, you may run out of memory quickly or wait forever for your clustering to complete!

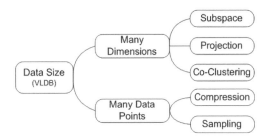

Figure 4.5   The categorization of clustering algorithms based on the size of the data

For that reason, Paul S. Bradley, Usama M. Fayyad, and Cory A. Reina proposed a framework that required the following properties from algorithms that deal with large databases for online applications:

- If possible, you should scan the database only once.
- You should allow for online behavior—a good answer is available at any time.
- The algorithm should be able to suspend, stop, and resume its activity.
- You should support incremental updates to account for new data.
- You should respect RAM limitations, if any.
- You should utilize various scan modes, such as sequential, index-based, and sampling, if they're available.
- You should prefer algorithms that can work with the forward-only cursor over a view of the database, because these views are typically the result of computationally expensive joins.

These requirements result in different kinds of algorithms that tend to mix the conceptually cleaner versions of basic algorithms with heuristics and other techniques (such as compression and sampling), thus trading complexity for efficiency and performance.

As you can imagine, an algorithm could satisfy more than one criterion; a single algorithm can belong in more than one category. For example, the *BIRCH* algorithm *(balanced iterative reducing and clustering using hierarchies)* can be categorized as both a clustering algorithm for very large databases (VLDB) and a hierarchical clustering algorithm.

This was a lengthy overview, but it turns out that what seemed to be a fairly straightforward problem—identifying groups of similar objects—is a fascinating subject of great depth. We have many clustering algorithms to choose from and our choices depend on many factors, such as the nature of our data, the type of desired output, and computational limitations. In the following sections, we'll present a number of clustering algorithms that cover a good portion of what we discussed here and we'll also address, in more detail, clustering very large datasets. So, let's roll up our sleeves and get to work!

4.3   Link-based algorithms

In this section, we'll continue using the data that we described in section 4.1 and try to find what kind of user groups can be identified on that fictitious open source repository. We'll start with the description of the *dendrogram* data structure, which is helpful when it comes to clustering and is used throughout the code of this chapter. We'll describe the core ideas behind link-based algorithms and will present three of them in detail. In particular, we'll cover the single link, the average link, and the minimum spanning tree algorithms.

4.3.1   The dendrogram: a basic clustering data structure

The basic structure that we will use throughout clustering is encapsulated by the class `Dendrogram`. The structure of a dendrogram is shown in figure 4.6. It's a tree data structure[1] that helps us capture the hierarchical formation of clusters. You can think of it as a set of ordered triples—[*d*, *k*, {...}], where the first element is the proximity threshold (*d*), the second element is the number of clusters (*k*), and the third element is the set of clusters.

Figure 4.6 gives a visual representation of a dendrogram that has four levels; as an ordered set it could be represented by the following set: *{[0,5,{ {A},{B},{C},{D},{E}}], [1, 3, {{A,B},{C}, {D,E}}], [2, 2, {{A,B,C}, {D,E}}], [3,1,{A, B,C,D,E}]}*. Thus, the dendrogram is equipped to capture a set of clusters, not just one cluster. In turn, this allows us to capture the formation of the clusters, as they emerge from the single elements, in a single structure. All hierarchical agglomerative algorithms would do the following:

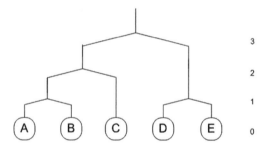

Figure 4.6   Visualizing hierarchical clusters: A simple dendrogram.

1   Define an initial dendrogram for which all elements are single element clusters.
2   Increase the distance threshold by a notch and decide what elements should form new clusters.
3   Take all the new clusters and add a level to the dendrogram.
4   Continue the execution of steps 2 and 3 until all elements belong to one big cluster.

From an implementation perspective, we capture the structure of the dendrogram with two linked hash maps, as shown in listing 4.3; we omitted two auxiliary printing methods from this listing.

---

[1]   *Dendro* means "tree" in Greek.

Listing 4.3   Dendrogram: an essential class for encapsulating hierarchical clusters

```java
public class Dendrogram {

  private Map<Integer, ClusterSet> entryMap;
  private Map<Integer, String> levelLabels;
  private Integer nextLevel;
  private String levelLabelName;

  public Dendrogram(String levelLabelName) {
    entryMap = new LinkedHashMap<Integer, ClusterSet>();
    levelLabels = new LinkedHashMap<Integer, String>();
    nextLevel = 1;
    this.levelLabelName = levelLabelName;
  }

  public int addLevel(String label, Cluster cluster) {
    List<Cluster> values = new ArrayList<Cluster>();
    values.add(cluster);
    return addLevel(label, values);
  }

  public int addLevel(String label, Collection<Cluster> clusters) {

    ClusterSet clusterSet = new ClusterSet();

    for(Cluster c : clusters) {
      // copy cluster before adding - over time cluster elements may change
      // but for dendrogram we want to keep current state.
      clusterSet.add(c.copy());
    }

    int level = nextLevel;

    entryMap.put(level, clusterSet);
    levelLabels.put(level, label);

    nextLevel++;
    return level;
  }

public void setLevel(int level, String label,
➥ Collection<Cluster> clusters) {

  ClusterSet clusterSet = new ClusterSet();

  for(Cluster c : clusters) {
    clusterSet.add(c.copy());
  }

  System.out.println("Setting cluster level: "+level);

  entryMap.put(level, clusterSet);
  levelLabels.put(level, label);

  if( level >= nextLevel ) {
    nextLevel = level + 1;
  }
}
}
```

In summary, the dendrogram data structure can capture all possible cluster configurations of a dataset, whether or not hierarchical. It's the data structure of choice for representing the clustering results. Let's proceed and look at the family of link-based algorithms.

4.3.2   *A first look at link-based algorithms*

In listing 4.4, we show the script for loading the SourceForge-like data and invoking the algorithms successively.

Listing 4.4   Hierarchical agglomerative clustering algorithms

```
SFDataset ds = SFData.createDataset();

DataPoint[] dps = ds.getData();                              Load data

double[][] adjMatrix = ds.getAdjacencyMatrix();

SingleLinkAlgorithm sla = new SingleLinkAlgorithm(dps,adjMatrix);   Single link
                                                                    clustering
Dendrogram dendroSLA = sla.cluster();

dendroSLA.print(4);

MSTSingleLinkAlgorithm sla2 =
➥ new MSTSingleLinkAlgorithm(dps,adjMatrix);     Single link
                                                 clustering with MST
Dendrogram dendroSLA2 = sla2.cluster();

dendroSLA2.print(4);

AverageLinkAlgorithm ala = new AverageLinkAlgorithm(dps,adjMatrix);   Average
                                                                     link
Dendrogram dendroALA = ala.cluster();                                clustering

dendroALA.print(4);
```

The class `SFDataset` represents our dataset from section 4.1. The three classes that contain the respective algorithms, in order of appearance, are `SingleLinkAlgorithm`, `MSTSingleLinkAlgorithm`, and `AverageLinkAlgorithm`. In order to remove effects related to the representation of the data and the lack of normalization, all the algorithms use the same information as a starting point—the raw data of table 4.1 (in the form of the array `Datapoint[]` dps) and the adjacency matrix (in the form of the `double[][]` adjMatrix) that captures the relative proximity of each user with every other user in the dataset.

All our link-based algorithms initialize their dendrogram by assigning the triplet *[0, N, {{X1}, {X2}, …, {XN}}]*. When the proximity threshold (the first element of the triplet) is set to 0, the only element that can be close to any other element is the element itself, and therefore all elements are loaded as individual clusters.

As we mentioned, all algorithms use a two-dimensional array of `doubles` to represent the *adjacency matrix*. This matrix contains the distance between any two elements of the set; you can think of it as being analogous to the similarity matrix that we saw for users and items in chapter 3. The values of the adjacency matrix allow us to use a threshold of proximity and determine whether two elements should merge and form a new cluster or remain in disjoined individual clusters. These comparisons take place iteratively by increasing the threshold value of proximity. After a finite number of steps, all elements will belong in a single cluster and the algorithm stops.

Figure 4.7 depicts this process by showing three of these iterations; for illustration purposes, we restrict ourselves to two dimensions. The principle is identical in higher dimensions; it's just harder to visualize high-dimensional spaces. The black circles are data points that we want to cluster; the circles with dashed lines are the proximity thresholds for each data point and iteration level.

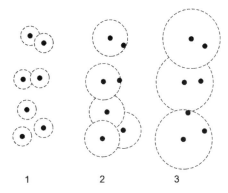

Figure 4.7 A depiction of the single-link algorithm in action (three iterations)

In the first iteration, every data point belongs to its own cluster and we have a total of seven clusters. In the second iteration, two clusters formed at the top and we have five clusters. In the third iteration, the three data points in the bottom of the figure merged and we have three clusters in total. As the iterations succeed one another, the circles become larger and larger until the first proximity circle drawn with the first data point at the center has such a large radius that it includes the entire dataset. At that point, the iterations stop.

The agglomerative algorithms differ with respect to two things:

- The approach that they use for merging clusters at each step of the iteration
- The definition of the adjacency matrix

The single link, average link, and minimum spanning tree algorithms are three well-known versions of agglomerative hierarchical clustering that are based on graph theoretic concepts. We'll examine each one of them in the following three subsections.

4.3.3 *The single-link algorithm*

The single-link algorithm (depicted in figure 4.5) tries to find the largest number of connected components in a graph. This algorithm merges two clusters if at least one edge connects the two clusters; hence the name *single link*. In other words, if the minimum distance between any two points is less than or equal to the *proximity threshold*, which means that the data points are inside the circle with the dashed line, then the clusters are merged. Algorithmically, this is shown in the methods `cluster` and `buildClusters` of listing 4.5.

Listing 4.5 Merge clusters even with a single link between them

```
public Dendrogram cluster() {
  Dendrogram dnd = new Dendrogram("Distance");
  double d = 0;

  List<Cluster> initialClusters = new ArrayList<Cluster>();
  for(DataPoint e : elements) {                              ❶
```

```
    Cluster c = new Cluster(e);
    initialClusters.add(c);
  }

  dnd.addLevel(String.valueOf(d), initialClusters);
  d = 1.0;
  int k = initialClusters.size();

  while( k > 1 ) {          ❷
    int oldK = k;
    List<Cluster> clusters = buildClusters(d);
    k = clusters.size();
    if( oldK != k ) {
      dnd.addLevel(String.valueOf(d), clusters);
    }
    d = d + 1;
  }
  return dnd;
}

private List<Cluster> buildClusters(double distanceThreshold) {

  boolean[] usedElementFlags = new boolean[elements.length];

  List<Cluster> clusters = new ArrayList<Cluster>();

  for(int i = 0, n = a.length; i < n; i++) {

    List<DataPoint> clusterPoints = new ArrayList<DataPoint>();

    for(int j = i, k = a.length; j < k; j++) {                    ❸

      if( a[i][j] <= distanceThreshold && usedElementFlags[j] == false ) {
        clusterPoints.add(elements[j]);
        usedElementFlags[j] = true;
      }
    }

    if( clusterPoints.size() > 0 ) {
      Cluster c = new Cluster(clusterPoints);
      clusters.add(c);
    }
  }
  return clusters;
}
```

Initially, we load every data point to its own cluster ❶. We iterate until there's only one cluster that contains all data points ❷. At every iteration, the clustering is happening inside the buildClusters method, and the distance threshold increases by one unit.

Note that even though we leverage the symmetry of the adjacency matrix (the second loop starts from the index i, rather than zero) ❸, the algorithm requires a number of operations that grow as the square of the number of elements that we want to cluster. We say that the computational complexity of the algorithm, in space and time, is $O(N^2)$. This isn't important for small datasets, but it's vital when we cluster real-world datasets. We'll talk more about these real-world aspects of clustering in section 4.4. Figure 4.8

shows the results that we obtain from the single-link algorithm when we use the sample dataset from table 4.1; the output is set to print the clusters for the value level that's equal to 4.

{Dmitry}　　{Frank}　　{Alexandra, Aurora}
{John, Lukas}　　　{George, Jack, Maria}
{Albert, Athena, Babis}
{Constantine, Elena, Eric}
{Bill, Bob, Carl, Catherine, Charlie}

Figure 4.8   Clustering results based on the single link algorithm for level 4

4.3.4   The average-link algorithm

The average-link algorithm, shown in listing 4.6, is similar to the single-link algorithm, but it merges two clusters on a different condition. In particular, it checks whether the *average distance* between any two points in the two target clusters is below the proximity threshold. Note that in this algorithm, we increase the threshold proximity by half a point (0.5) rather than a whole point. This is an arbitrary increment; you can vary its value and observe the effect that this has on the results.

Listing 4.6   Merge clusters based on the average distance

```
public Dendrogram cluster() {

  Dendrogram dnd = new Dendrogram("Distance");      <-- Initialization
  double d = 0.0;

  for(DataPoint e : elements) {
    Cluster c = new Cluster(e);
    allClusters.add(c);
  }

  dnd.addLevel(String.valueOf(d), allClusters.getAllClusters());
  d = 1.0;

  while( allClusters.size() > 1 ) {        <-- Top-level loop for
                                               building hierarchy
    int K = allClusters.size();

    mergeClusters(d);

    // it's possible that there were no clusters to merge for current d.

    if( K > allClusters.size() ) {
      dnd.addLevel(String.valueOf(d),
  allClusters.getAllClusters());
      K = allClusters.size();
    }
    d = d + 0.5;
  }
  return dnd;
}

private void mergeClusters(double distanceThreshold) {

  int nClusters = allClusters.size();

  ObjectToIndexMapping<Cluster> idxMapping =
  new ObjectToIndexMapping<Cluster>();

  double[][] clusterDistances = new double[nClusters][nClusters];
```

```
for(int i = 0, n = a.length; i < n; i++) {                    ⟵┐ Adding distances of all
    for(int j = i + 1, k = a.length; j < k; j++) {              │ links for all clusters

        double d = a[i][j];

        if( d > 0 ) {
            DataPoint e1 = elements[i];
            DataPoint e2 = elements[j];

            Cluster c1 = allClusters.findClusterByElement(e1);
            Cluster c2 = allClusters.findClusterByElement(e2);

            if( !c1.equals(c2) ) {
                int ci = idxMapping.getIndex(c1);
                int cj = idxMapping.getIndex(c2);

                clusterDistances[ci][cj] += d;
                clusterDistances[cj][ci] += d;
            }
        }
    }
}

boolean[] merged = new boolean[clusterDistances.length];

for(int i = 0, n = clusterDistances.length; i < n; i++) {

    for(int j = i+1, k = clusterDistances.length; j < k; j++) {

        Cluster ci = idxMapping.getObject(i);
        Cluster cj = idxMapping.getObject(j);
        int ni = ci.size();
        int nj = cj.size();

        clusterDistances[i][j] =                      ⟵┐ Average distance
➡   clusterDistances[i][j] / (ni * nj);                │ between clusters

        clusterDistances[j][i] = clusterDistances[i][j];

        // merge clusters if distance is below the threshold
        if( merged[i] == false && merged[j] == false ) {
            if( clusterDistances[i][j] <= distanceThreshold) {
                allClusters.remove(ci);
                allClusters.remove(cj);
                Cluster mergedCluster = new Cluster(ci, cj);
                allClusters.add(mergedCluster);
                merged[i] = true;
                merged[j] = true;
            }
        }
    }
}
```

As before, the dendrogram is initialized by setting every element of the set in its own cluster, and new clusters are formed until all elements belong to a single cluster. Unlike with the single-link algorithm, we need to find the distance of all the links between two clusters. The average-link algorithm requires more computations. The first loop of the method `mergeClusters` in listing 4.6 adds the distance between any two elements of the set to the total distance of the clusters that they happen to belong to. The second loop, from the same method, divides the total sum by the number of links and compares the average distance to the threshold. If the average distance is below the threshold value, the clusters are merged. Upon completion of all mergers and acquisitions for the given level, the algorithm proceeds with the next level of the dendrogram just as the single-link algorithm did.

Figure 4.9 shows the results that we obtain from the average-link algorithm when we use the sample dataset from table 4.1; the output is set to print the clusters for the value level equal to 4, as we did in figure 4.8. Note that there are fewer clusters now. What do you think happened? Why is there such a clear difference in the results? Even though we kept the level constant, the way that each algorithm proceeds to calculate the distance is different. Thus, the proximity threshold is different at the same level. In other words, after four iterations, the single-link algorithm has expanded its proximity circles (see figure 4.5) far more than the average-link algorithm did. So naturally, the results of clustering for the average-link algorithm show fewer clusters. The moral of the story is that you should compare algorithms of that kind by the size of the proximity circles, rather than the level of iteration.

Figure 4.9 Clustering results based on the average-link algorithm

4.3.5   *The minimum-spanning-tree algorithm*

In order to understand our third agglomerative algorithm, we'll need to talk about the concept of a *minimum spanning tree*. In general, given a set of elements, we can construct a tree by connecting any two vertices with exactly one edge (link). A *spanning tree* would connect all vertices of the given set, and clearly there are many ways to do this. But the MST connects the vertices in such a way as to *minimize the sum of the adjacency values* for the connected vertices. Given the adjacency matrix, our implementation employs the Prim-Jarník algorithm for identifying the minimum spanning tree, and this involves $O(N^2)$ operations. There are other algorithms with nearly linear performance—$O(N log(N))$. If you'd like to read more on graph theoretic algorithms related to the minimum spanning tree and more advanced topics, consult the "To do" section and the references section.

The MST single-link algorithm, as the name suggests, is a variant of the single-link algorithm that's based on the minimum spanning tree. The latter is derived from the adjacency matrix, and it produces a natural ordering between the elements of the set. If the adjacency matrix is a 5x5 array, the MST is also represented by a two-dimensional array that's 5x5, and it must also be symmetrical. For both matrices, we set the diagonal elements equal to –1 to indicate that we're not interested in self-links. This is the only part that differs from the other two agglomerative clustering algorithms that we've seen. The algorithm uses the information in the MST to merge the clusters based on the increasing order of their elements in the tree.

Let's look at the results that we get when we run the script of listing 4.4. The single-link algorithm, at level four, produces the clusters that were shown in figure 4.5. Figure 4.10 shows the results that we obtain from the MST single-link algorithm when we use the example dataset from table 4.1. The output is set to print the clusters for the value level equal to 4, like we did before in figures 4.8 and 4.9 for the single- and average-link algorithms, respectively.

The MST single-link algorithm results in fewer clusters than the single-link algorithm because, similar to the case of the average-link algorithm, the proximity circles at level four haven't expanded as much as they did for the single-link algorithm. If you increase the level progressively you can observe the merging of the various *singletons* and clusters into bigger cluster formations. As before, the algorithm terminates when all elements of the dataset belong to one cluster. So, let's look at the code. Listing 4.7 shows the auxiliary class MST, which is used to create the minimum spanning tree for a given adjacency matrix.

{Alexandra}   {Aurora}   {Babis}   {Bob}

{Dmitry}   {Frank}   {George}   {Jack}

{Maria}   {Albert, Athena}   {John, Lukas}

{Constantine, Elena, Eric}

{Bill, Carl, Charlie, Catherine}

Figure 4.10   Clustering results based on the MST link algorithm

Listing 4.7   Creating the minimum spanning tree based on the adjacency matrix

```
public class MST {

  public double[][] buildMST(double[][] adjM) {          ← Initialize vector to hold MST nodes

    boolean[] allV = new boolean[a.length];
    allV[0] = true;
                                                          ← Initialize MST matrix
    double[][] mst = new double[adjM.length][adjM.length];
    for(int i = 0, n = mst.length; i < n; i++) {
      for(int j = 0; j < n; j++) {
        mst[i][j] = -1;
      }
    }

    Edge e = null;                                        ← Iterate until you find minimum
    while( (e = findMinimumEdge(allV, adjM)) != null ) {
      allV[e.getJ()] = true;
      mst[e.getI()][e.getJ()] = e.getW();
      mst[e.getJ()][e.getI()] = e.getW();
    }
    return mst;
  }

  private Edge findMinimumEdge(boolean[] mstV, double[][] a) {
    Edge e = null;
    double minW = Double.POSITIVE_INFINITY;
    int minI = -1;
```

```
    int minJ = -1;
    for( int i = 0, n = a.length; i < n; i++ ) {
      if ( mstV[i] == true ) {
        for(int j = 0, k = a.length; j < k; j++) {
          if ( mstV[j] == false ) {
            if ( minW > a[i][j]) {
                minW = a[i][j];
                minI = i;
                minJ = j;
            }
          }
        }
      }
    }
    if ( minI > -1 ) {
      e = new Edge(minI, minJ, minW);
    }
    return e;
  }
}
```

To shorten the listing, we didn't include an inner class called Edge, which is a rudimentary class that encapsulates the edges of the graph and their weight; see the complete source code for the details. As you can see, this is a simple algorithm for finding the minimum spanning tree and it's known as the Prim-Jarník algorithm. The algorithm can be summarized in the following steps:

1 Initialize a vector that indicates whether an element belongs to the MST (allV).
2 Initialize the MST matrix (variable mst) to some default negative value (such as −1).
3 Start from any node and find the edge that emanates from that node and has the minimum length compared to all other edges that emanate from that node.
4 The node that's on the other end of the edge with minimum length is added to the MST nodes.
5 Repeat steps 3 and 4 until all nodes have been included; the tree must span the graph.

In other words, Prim's algorithm augments a spanning tree from an arbitrary starting node, iteratively adding an edge of least weight between a node that's already part of the MST and a node that's not yet part of the MST, and it finishes when all nodes are part of the MST. The MST resulting from one execution of Prim's algorithm may vary from the MST resulting from another execution. There is a way to consistently obtain the same MST regardless of what node you considered to be first. Can you figure out under what conditions that's possible? Of course, this isn't the only algorithm available for identifying a minimum spanning tree. Two more algorithms are well-known—*Kruskal's algorithm* and *Borůvka's algorithm*.

The time complexity of the MST link algorithm is $O(N^2)$ because that's the order of magnitude of computations that we need to make to get the MST. To convince yourself, look at the method `findMinimumEdge` and note the double loop of size N. This number of operations dominates the rest of the algorithm. This can be improved by using a hash table and storing the smallest edge for each one of the nodes that we've already examined.

Finally, we should mention that all the single-link algorithms are notorious due to the so-called *chain effect*, which can result in two clusters merging just because they happened to have two points close to each other while most of their other points are far apart. Single-link algorithms have no cure for this problem, but the rest of the algorithms that we'll discuss don't suffer from this shortcoming.

4.4   The k-means algorithm

The three link-based algorithms of the previous section were all hierarchical agglomerative clustering algorithms. The k-means algorithm is the first partitional algorithm that we'll examine, and we should mention that it's the most widely used in practice due to its excellent performance characteristics.

4.4.1   A first look at the k-means algorithm

Let's begin by running the k-means algorithm to obtain some clusters. Listing 4.8 shows the steps needed to load the data from table 4.1 and execute the k-means implementation that we provide. In order to compare the results of the k-means algorithm with those of the single-link algorithm, where we identified eight clusters at level four, we chose $k = 8$.

Listing 4.8   The k-means algorithm in action

```
SFDataset ds = SFData.createDataset();              Load data

DataPoint[] dps = ds.getData();                                    Initialize k-means
                                                                   algorithm
KMeansAlgorithm kMeans = new KMeansAlgorithm(8, dps);   ◁

kMeans.cluster();      ◁── Begin clustering

kMeans.print();
```

Figure 4.11 illustrates candidate clusters based on the k-means algorithm; compare these clusters with the clusters that were identified by the other (hierarchical) algorithms, and especially the clusters in figure 4.8, where the number of clusters is again equal to eight. Central to the idea of the k-means algorithm is the idea of the cluster's *centroid*, which is also called the *center* or *mean value*. Think of

> {Jack}   {Frank}   {Catherine, Bob}
>
> {John, Lukas}   {Maria, George}
>
> {Charlie, Carl, Bill}
>
> {Elena, Eric, Dmitry, Constantine}
>
> {Athena, Babis, Albert, Aurora, Alexandra}

Figure 4.11   Clustering results based on the k-means algorithm, with k = 8

the elements that make up a cluster as bodies with mass: the cluster's centroid would be the equivalent of the center of mass for that system of bodies.

Figure 4.12 illustrates the idea of the centroid for a cluster whose points (shown as black circles) lie on the vertices of a hexagon. The centroid of that cluster (due to symmetry) is located at the center of the hexagon, and is shown as a dashed circle. The centroid itself doesn't have to be one of the data points that we want to cluster. In fact, as illustrated in figure 4.12, most of the time it won't be. Its role is to create a representative point of reference for the set of points that form the cluster.

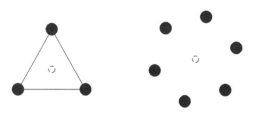

It's possible that the candidate clusters that you'll get when you execute the script from listing 4.8 may differ from what's shown in figure 4.11. The reason for any differences lies in the initialization of the locations of the centroids; this will become clear in the next section.

Figure 4.12 The centroids (dashed circles) for a triangular and hexagonal cluster of points (black circles)

4.4.2 The inner workings of k-means

To better understand the inner workings of the k-means algorithm, let's look at its implementation, which is provided in the listing 4.9.

Listing 4.9 `KMeansAlgorithm`: the core method of the k-means algorithm

```
public void cluster() {

  boolean centroidsChanged = true;

  while (centroidsChanged == true) {
    List<Set<DataPoint>> clusters =
    new ArrayList<Set<DataPoint>>(k);

      for (int i = 0; i < k; i++) {                          Create set of points
        clusters.add(new HashSet<DataPoint>());             for each cluster
      }

      for (DataPoint p : allDataPoints) {                    Assign points
        int i = findClosestCentroid(allCentroids, p);       based on distance
        clusters.get(i).add(p);
      }

      for (int i = 0; i < k; i++) {                          Create
        allClusters[i] = new Cluster(clusters.get(i));      clusters
      }

    centroidsChanged = false;

    for (int i = 0; i < allClusters.length; i++) {          Calculate new
                                                            centroids
      if (clusters.get(i).size() > 0) {
```

```
        double[] newCentroidValues = findCentroid(allClusters[i]);

        double[] oldCentroidValues =
    allCentroids[i].getNumericAttrValues();

        if (!Arrays.equals(oldCentroidValues, newCentroidValues)) {

          allCentroids[i] =
    new DataPoint(allCentroids[i].getLabel(), newCentroidValues);

          centroidsChanged = true;
        }

      } else {
        // keep centroid unchanged if cluster has no elements.
      }
    }
  }
}

public static DataPoint[] pickInitialCentroids(int k,
    DataPoint[] data) {

  Random randGen = new Random();

  DataPoint[] centroids = new DataPoint[k];

  Set<Integer> previouslyUsedIds = new HashSet<Integer>();

  for (int i = 0; i < k; i++) {

    // pick point index that we haven't used yet
    int centroidId;
    do {
      centroidId = randGen.nextInt(data.length);
    }
    while( previouslyUsedIds.add(centroidId) == false );

    String label = "Mean-"+i+"("+data[centroidId].getLabel()+")";

    double[] values = data[centroidId].getNumericAttrValues();

    String[] attrNames = data[centroidId].getAttributeNames();

    centroids[i] = new DataPoint(label,
    Attributes.createAttributes(attrNames, values));
  }
  return centroids;
}
```

The k-means algorithm randomly picks (see method pickInitialMeanValues) *k* points that represent the initial centroids of the candidate clusters. Subsequently the distances between these centroids and each point of the set are calculated, and each point is assigned to the cluster with the minimum distance between the cluster centroid and the point. As a result of these assignments, the locations of the centroids for each cluster have now changed, so we reevaluate the new centroids until their locations stop changing. This particular algorithm for k-means is attributed to E.W. Forgy and to S.P. Lloyd, and has the following advantages:

- It works well with many metrics.
- It's easy to derive versions of the algorithm that are executed in parallel—when the data are divided into, say, N sets and each separate data set is clustered, in parallel, on N different computational units.
- It's insensitive with respect to data ordering.

At this point you may wonder, what happens if the algorithm doesn't stop? Don't worry! It's guaranteed that the iterations will stop in a finite number of steps. In practice, the algorithm *converges* quickly (that's the mathematical jargon). Of course, we should always be careful with variations of the algorithm. If your metric isn't the Euclidean distance, you may run into problems; see, for example, the article on clustering very large document collections by Inderjit S. Dhillon, James Fan, and Yuqiang Guan, where the use of cosine similarity is inferior to the Euclidean distance. In a different case, some of the same authors reported some advantage in using Kullback-Leibler divergences (these things aren't even distances!) instead of squared Euclidean distances.

The k-means algorithm is fast, especially compared to other clustering algorithms. Its computational complexity is typically $O(N)$, where N is the number of data points that we want to cluster. It suffices to say that the name of the procedure for k-means, in the commercial package SAS, is FASTCLUS (for fast clustering).

Note that, unlike with agglomerative algorithms, the k-means algorithm requires the number of clusters that must be formed as an input. The question that arises naturally is: what should be the value of k? The answer depends on your data (again): you should run k-means with different values of k and examine the resulting clusters. Sometimes, as with very large data or when hierarchical clustering is required, it's useful to first run the k-means algorithm with a low value and subsequently run a hierarchical clustering algorithm inside the large partitions that were formed by k-means. This approach lends itself naturally to parallelization, and you can take advantage of additional computational bandwidth if you have it!

Note also that the k-means algorithm is appropriate for data points whose attributes are numeric. The challenge for using the k-means algorithm in the case of categorical data (such as string values) is reduced to finding an appropriate numerical representation for the nonnumeric attribute values. In the latter case, the choice of metric is also important.

You should know that the selection of the initial centroids is crucial for quickly terminating the iterations as well as producing good quality clusters. From a mathematical perspective, the k-means algorithm tries to minimize the average squared distance between points in the same cluster. So, if you select your initial centroids in regions with a high concentration of data points, it seems reasonable that you may get your results faster and achieve high-quality clusters. That's exactly what David Arthur and Sergei Vassilvitskii proposed in a recent article that describes what they called k-means++.

In summary, the previous sections provided a number of algorithms that allow you to identify groups of users on a website. Of course, by being creative, you can apply the same algorithms in different circumstances. Combining algorithms is also possible, and sometimes it's recommended. The algorithm of choice in the industry is k-means and its variants. The k-means algorithm is preferred due to its simplicity (in implementation), its speed, and its ability to run on a parallel computational platform.

4.5   Robust Clustering Using Links (ROCK)

In this section, we continue our coverage of clustering with an algorithm that differs from what we've seen so far in two ways. First, the algorithm is particularly well-suited for categorical data, such as keywords, Boolean attributes, enumerations, and so forth. Second, this algorithm is designed to work well on very large datasets. Our example will be a collection of data from Digg.com.

For illustration purposes, we'll use a fixed dataset that you can find in the directory data/ch4 called ch4_digg_stories.csv. The data was collected using the Digg API, from chapter 3. The data contains 49 Digg stories, with several attributes, submitted by 10 random users. In the data, we've fabricated 8 clusters that are easily identifiable by a human; you can open the file with your favorite text editor and have a look. Is it possible to identify these clusters with our algorithms rather than our eyes? Let's see!

4.5.1   Introducing ROCK

Listing 4.10 loads the data, initializes `ROCKAlgorithm`, and uses the by-now familiar `Dendrogram` class to capture the structure of the clusters.

Listing 4.10   Clustering large collections of web stories with ROCK

```
MyDiggSpaceDataset ds = MyDiggSpaceData.createDataset(15);        ⊲── Load Digg stories,
                                                                      use only top 15
DataPoint[] dps = ds.getData();                                       terms

ROCKAlgorithm rock = new ROCKAlgorithm(dps, 5, 0.2);    ⊲──

Dendrogram dnd = rock.cluster();                        Initialize ROCK to seek
                                                        5 desired clusters
dnd.print(21);
```

In the `print` method of the `Dendrogram` class, we've restricted the output to clusters that have more than one element. In other words, we don't show the single elements, also known as *singletons* in the industry, in order to improve the visual quality of the groupings. Figure 4.13 shows the results of the execution for listing 4.10.

Note that the text used by the algorithm for identifying similar stories from our forum isn't just the titles, but rather the titles and the descriptions. The descriptions can be significantly different from a syntax point of view (see for example the stories related to blood donors and Facebook), which would rule out a direct string comparison between their content. The key is that the Jaccard coefficient doesn't depend on the syntax of the words in the text, but it rather compares the number of common terms between the descriptions. As you can see, at level 21, six out of the eight clusters have been correctly identified. You can use your own data and see what kind of clusters you'd get with your documents, stories, articles, and so on—the list is long! As long as you place your data in an array of the `DataPoint` class, you should be good to go.

```
bsh % dnd.print(21);
Clusters for: level=21, Goodness=1.044451296741812
─────────────────────────────────────────────────
{5619782:Lack Of Democracy on Digg and Wikipedia?,
 5611165:Lack Of Democracy on Digg and Wikipedia?}
─────────────────────────────────────────────────
{5571841:Lack Of Democracy on Digg and Wikipedia?,
 5543643:Lack Of Democracy on Digg and Wikipedia?}
─────────────────────────────────────────────────
{5142233:The Confederacy's Special Agent,
 5620839:The Confederacy's Special Agent,
 5586183:The Confederacy's Special Agent,
 5610584:The Confederacy's Special Agent,
 5598008:The Confederacy's Special Agent,
 5613383:The Confederacy's Special Agent,
 5613380:The Confederacy's Special Agent}
─────────────────────────────────────────────────
{5585930:Microsoft, The Jekyll And Hyde Of Companies,
 5524441:Microsoft, The Jekyll And Hyde Of Companies,
 5609070:Microsoft, The Jekyll And Hyde Of Companies,
 5618201:Microsoft, The Jekyll And Hyde Of Companies,
 5620878:Microsoft, The Jekyll And Hyde Of Companies,
 5609797:Microsoft, The Jekyll And Hyde Of Companies}
─────────────────────────────────────────────────
{5607788:Recycle or go to Hell, warns Vatican -- part I,
 5592940:Recycle or go to Hell, warns Vatican -- part II,
 5618262:Recycle or go to Hell, warns Vatican -- part III,
 5595841:Recycle or go to Hell, warns Vatican --- part IV}
─────────────────────────────────────────────────
{5608052:Contract Free on AT&T,
 5620493:Contract Free on AT&T,
 5621623:Contract Free on AT&T,
 4955184:Contract Free on AT&T,
 5594161:Contract Free on AT&T}
```

Figure 4.13   **The clustering results of listing 4.10**

4.5.2   *Why does ROCK rock?*

Let's have a closer look at the inner workings of the ROCK algorithm. Listing 4.11 shows the constructor and the core method `cluster` of the `ROCKAlgorithm` class. The key idea of ROCK is to use links as a similarity measure, rather than a measure that's based only on distances. Of course, in order to determine the points that "link" to any given point, we'll still have to use our familiar distance metrics. The objective will be to cluster together points that have many common links.

Listing 4.11   `ROCKAlgorithm`: the `cluster` method of Robust clustering using links

```
public ROCKAlgorithm(DataPoint[] points, int k, double th) {

  this.points = points;    ◁── Data points to cluster

  this.k = k;    ◁── Minimum number of clusters
```

```
    this.th = th;    ←── Link creation threshold

    this.similarityMeasure = new JaccardCoefficient();    ←── Similarity matrix

    this.linkMatrix =
➥ new LinkMatrix(points, similarityMeasure, th);    ←── Link matrix
}
public Dendrogram cluster() {

  List<Cluster> initialClusters = new ArrayList<Cluster>();
  for(int i = 0, n = points.length; i < n; i++) {                    ❶
     Cluster cluster = new Cluster(points[i]);
     initialClusters.add(cluster);
  }

  double g = Double.POSITIVE_INFINITY;

  Dendrogram dnd = new Dendrogram("Goodness");

  dnd.addLevel(String.valueOf(g), initialClusters);

  MergeGoodnessMeasure goodnessMeasure =
➥ new MergeGoodnessMeasure(th);                    ❷

  ROCKClusters allClusters = new ROCKClusters(initialClusters,
➥ linkMatrix, goodnessMeasure);                    ❸

  int nClusters = allClusters.size();

while( nClusters > k ) {                    ❹

     int nClustersBeforeMerge = nClusters;

     g = allClusters.mergeBestCandidates();

     nClusters = allClusters.size();

     if( nClusters == nClustersBeforeMerge ) {
       // there are no linked clusters to merge
       break;
     }
     dnd.addLevel(String.valueOf(g),
➥ allClusters.getAllClusters());
  }
  return dnd;
}
```

The arguments of the constructor are the following:

- The data points that we want to cluster.
- The minimum number of clusters that we want to have; ROCK is a bottom-up hierarchical agglomerative algorithm—we start with every point on its own cluster and keep merging until all points belong to a single cluster. This parameter allows us to stop before all points are grouped into a single cluster by providing a minimum number of clusters that we want to have.
- A parameter that determines the proximity that's required between two points in order to form a link between them.

In the constructor, we create an instance of the Jaccard similarity (`JaccardCoeffi-cient`) and an instance of a new class (`LinkMatrix`) whose purpose is to encapsulate the structure of the links between the data points. You can use a different distance measure, such as the `CosineSimilarity`, and examine whether you get better, worse, or about the same clusters. Can you explain the similarities and the differences in the results? Through experimentation, you'll soon realize that the value of the threshold will be different for each distance measure, but in the end, your results will agree to a large extent; that's why we call this algorithm "robust."

Of course, this class can't do all the heavy lifting for ROCK. It delegates to various other classes that we'll examine shortly. The following are the steps involved in the method `cluster` in listing 4.11:

❶ This is the initialization stage, where we create a new cluster for every data point.

❷ This step creates a "goodness measure" that will be used to evaluate whether or not we should merge two clusters. In every clustering algorithm, an essential question to answer is: "What are the best clusters?" If we can define the "best" clusters, we can devise algorithms that aim to produce them. ROCK adopts the position that the best clusters are those that maximize the value of the goodness measure.

❸ The `ROCKClusters` class encapsulates all the relevant data and algorithms that are required to identify the best clusters that must be formed, based on the goodness measure.

❹ This step iterates the process of identifying best clusters and enforces two termination criteria. First, if the number of clusters already formed is equal to the desired minimum number of clusters the algorithm stops. Recall that if we let the algorithm run without such a criterion, we'll end up with all the data points inside a single cluster, which isn't very informative. Second, if the number of clusters doesn't change between two iterations there's no reason to proceed and the algorithm terminates.

Let's more closely examine the class `MergeGoodnessMeasure`. As we already mentioned, this class encapsulates our criterion for evaluating how good a cluster is. Algorithms that are based on similarity distance alone can't easily distinguish between two clusters that aren't "well separated" because it's possible for data points that belong in different clusters to be near neighbors. Thus, other algorithms may merge two clusters because two of their elements (one on each side) are close to each other, even though these two points may not have a large number of common neighbors.

So, the first thing that we want to do is make sure that our criterion for good clusters can help us deal effectively with these cases. To accomplish that goal, the ROCK algorithm uses links, as its name suggests. What's a link? We say that there's a link between two data points if a common neighbor between these two data points exists. When we consider whether to merge cluster X and Y, our interest is in the number of links between all pairs of points between X and Y, one point of the pair taken from cluster X, and the other point of the pair taken from cluster Y. A large number of links should indicate a higher probability that two points belong in the same cluster, and should give us the best clusters. Let's look at the mechanics; listing 4.12 shows the relevant code.

Listing 4.12 MergeGoodnessMeasure: a criterion for identifying the best clusters

```
public class MergeGoodnessMeasure {

    private double th;

    private double p;

    public MergeGoodnessMeasure(double th) {
        this.th = th;
        this.p = 1.0 + 2.0 * f(th);
    }

    public double g(int nLinks, int nX, int nY) {
        double a = Math.pow(nX + nY, p);
        double b = Math.pow(nX, p);
        double c = Math.pow(nY, p);

        return (double)nLinks / (a - b - c);
    }

    private double f(double th) {

        return (1.0 - th) / (1.0 + th);
    }
}
```

The essential method call is g(int nLinks, int nX, int nY), where nLinks is the number of links between the cluster X and the cluster Y. You should've expected (based on what we said about common neighbors and links) that the value of the g method will depend on the number of links between any two points from two clusters. But what do the other arguments stand for? Why is the formula so complicated? Let's answer the first question. The parameters nX and nY are the number of data points contained in clusters X and Y, respectively. The answer to the second question is a bit more elaborate but far more interesting.

You may think that maximizing the number of links for all pairs of points between two clusters should be a sufficiently good criterion for deciding whether to merge the clusters. Remember, though, that our objective in clustering is twofold. We need to group together points that belong in the same cluster and separate those that don't. Even though the maximization of the number of links would ensure that points with a large number of links are assigned to the same cluster, it doesn't prohibit the algorithm from assigning all points to a single cluster. In other words, using only the number of links won't help points with few links between them to separate into different clusters.

The ROCK formula estimates the total number of links in cluster X with the variable b, and the total number of links in cluster Y with the variable c. The method f represents a simple function with the following important property: each point that belongs in cluster X has approximately Math.pow(nX,f(th)) neighbors in X. Hence, the calculation of this goodness measure divides the number of links between each pair of points with the *expected* number of links, which is represented as (a - b - c). This property of the goodness measure prohibits the data points that have few links between them from being assigned to the same cluster. The variable th is specific to this choice of implementation for f, and its value is larger or equal to zero and smaller or equal to one. If it's zero then the value of f is equal to one and all data points are neighbors. If it's equal to one then the value of f is equal to zero and the only neighbor of a point is itself. This implementation of f has been found to work well with market basket data, but may not be appropriate in other cases. The conditions that can lead to such a choice would be attribute values that are more or less uniform across the data points. You should experiment with the implementation of the f method on our data or your own data. You can find out more details on this in the "To do" section.

4.6 DBSCAN

This section describes an advanced clustering algorithm, Density-Based Spatial Clustering of Applications with Noise, (DBSCAN) that's not based on the notion of links or the direct distance of the points from each other, but rather on the newly introduced idea of *point density*. To illustrate the idea, let's say that you have a shallow dish of water and you let a few drops of ink fall into the initially clear water dish. You wouldn't have any problem identifying the region that contains the ink immediately after the impact of the drops. That's because light reflects differently for ink than it does for water due to their different densities. What does this have to do with clustering?

4.6.1 A first look at density-based algorithms

There's an entire class of clustering algorithms that attempts to take advantage of that simple, everyday experience. In particular, *density-based algorithms* stem from the intuitive idea that visual pattern recognition is based on the density gradients for identifying the boundaries of objects. Thus, by extending the same principle to arbitrary two-, three-, or even multidimensional spaces, we may be able to identify clusters (objects) based on the notion of density of points within a certain region of space. Most people who look at the left side of figure 4.14 will visually identify the three clusters that are shown on the right side of figure 4.14. We'd typically consider the points that don't belong in the clusters (seven white circles) to be noise.

The DBSCAN algorithm, proposed by Martin Ester and others, is designed to discover the clusters and the noise in a dataset. Before we dive into the details, let's run the script in listing 4.13 to obtain clustering results for the same data that we used in the previous section with ROCK.

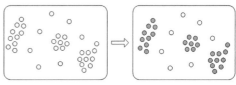

Figure 4.14   Density-based clustering is inspired by our ability to visually recognize shapes and forms.

Listing 4.13   Using the DBSCAN algorithm

```
MyDiggSpaceDataset ds = MyDiggSpaceData.createDataset(15);        ⟵┐ Load Digg
                                                                     stories and
DataPoint[] dps = ds.getData();                                      use only top 15

CosineDistance cosD = new CosineDistance();

DBSCANAlgorithm dbscan = new DBSCANAlgorithm(dps,cosD,0.8,2,true); ⟵
                                                     Initialize DBSCAN algorithm
dbscan.cluster();
```

As you can see, using the DBSCAN algorithm is as easy as using any of the other algorithms that we've presented. The only step that precedes the instantiation of the class DBSCANAlgorithm, aside from loading our data, is the definition of an appropriate distance metric. In this case, we used the CosineDistance, but any class that implements the distance interface would do.

Of course, we could've integrated the distance metric into the implementation of the algorithm, but the choice of the distance metric turns out to be important. So, it's better to define it explicitly as an argument in the constructor. The choice of the distance metric defines the shape (surface or volume) of a "neighborhood" and, in turn, the neighborhood defines various density-related parameters, which we'll examine shortly. But, first, let's look at the results. Executing the script from listing 4.13 will produce the output shown in figures 4.15(a) and 4.15(b).

These are fairly good results! Note that the algorithm correctly identified the obvious clusters, but it has also discovered a not-so-obvious cluster of articles (cluster 8). The algorithm has also identified the data points that don't belong to any given cluster as

```
bsh % dbscan.cluster();
DBSCAN Clustering with NeighborThreshold=0.8 minPoints=2
Clusters:
1:
{5605887:A Facebook Application To Find Blood Donors Fast,
5611687:A Facebook Application To Find Blood Donors Fast,
5608576:A Facebook Application To Find Blood Donors Fast}

2:
{5142233:The Confederacy's Special Agent,
5613383:The Confederacy's Special Agent,
5620839:The Confederacy's Special Agent,
5598008:The Confederacy's Special Agent,
5586183:The Confederacy's Special Agent,
5610584:The Confederacy's Special Agent,
5613380:The Confederacy's Special Agent}

3:
{5620878:Microsoft, The Jekyll And Hyde Of Companies,
5618201:Microsoft, The Jekyll And Hyde Of Companies,
5585930:Microsoft, The Jekyll And Hyde Of Companies,
5609797:Microsoft, The Jekyll And Hyde Of Companies,
5609070:Microsoft, The Jekyll And Hyde Of Companies,
5524441:Microsoft, The Jekyll And Hyde Of Companies}

4:
{5594161:Contract Free on AT&T,
4955184:Contract Free on AT&T,
5608052:Contract Free on AT&T,
5621623:Contract Free on AT&T,
5579109:Contract Free on AT&T,
5620493:Contract Free on AT&T}
```

Figure 4.15(a) The clustering results from the execution of listing 4.13

```
5:
{5607863:Lack Of Democracy on Digg and Wikipedia?,
 5571841:Lack Of Democracy on Digg and Wikipedia?,
 5619782:Lack Of Democracy on Digg and Wikipedia?,
 5611165:Lack Of Democracy on Digg and Wikipedia?,
 5543643:Lack Of Democracy on Digg and Wikipedia?}
─────────────────────────────────────────────────
6:
{5481876:How Traffic Jams Occur : Simulation,
 5613023:How Traffic Jams Occur : Simulation}
─────────────────────────────────────────────────
7:
{5617459:Robotic drumstick keeps novices on the beat,
 5619693:Robotic drumstick keeps novices on the beat}
─────────────────────────────────────────────────
8:
{5617998:Obama: ""I Am NOT Running for Vice President"",
 5625315:Obama Accuses Clinton of Using ""Republican Tactics""}
─────────────────────────────────────────────────
9:
{5607788:Recycle or go to Hell, warns Vatican -- part I,
 5595841:Recycle or go to Hell, warns Vatican --- part IV,
 5618262:Recycle or go to Hell, warns Vatican -- part III,
 5592940:Recycle or go to Hell, warns Vatican -- part II}
─────────────────────────────────────────────────

Noise Elements:
 {5610213:Senate panel critiques prewar claims by White House,
  5619818:A Facebook Application To Find Blood Donors Fast,
  5612810:Super Mario Bros Inspired Wii with USB base [ Pics ],
  5522983:Smoking Monkey[flash],
  5609833:NSA's Domestic Spying Grows As Agency Sweeps Up Data,
  5625339:Lawmaker's Attempt to Criminalize Anonymous Posting
Doomed,
  5610081:Digg's Algo Change Cut Promotions by 38%,
  5604438:Archaeologists Unveil Finds in Rome Digs,
  5614085:House Files Contempt Lawsuit Against Bush Officials,
  5592473:Maryland police officers refuse to pay speeding
tickets,
  5622802:House Democrats Defy White House on Spying Program}
```

Figure 4.15(b)   The clustering results from the execution of listing 4.13 (continued)

noise. But note also that there's one more cluster that could be extracted from the noise elements, and that the story with ID=5619818 could be assigned to the first cluster.

4.6.2   *The inner workings of DBSCAN*

Now, the details! First, we need to define the arguments that construct the DBSCANAl-gorithm class. The signature of the constructor is:

```
public DBSCANAlgorithm(DataPoint[] points,
                Distance distance,
                double eps,
                int minPoints,
                boolean useTermFrequencies)
```

You must be familiar with the `DataPoint` array by now; that's where we store the data. The `Distance` interface allows us to pass whatever distance we think is more appropriate for our data. The fun begins with the eps variable, which probably stands for epsilon, the Greek letter that usually denotes a small positive number. The epsilon value helps us define an *epsilon neighborhood* for any given `DataPoint` *p* as the set of `Data-Points` (q) whose distance from p is less than or equal to epsilon. So, the definition of an epsilon neighborhood is quite straightforward and exactly what you'd expect. Things get more complicated for the next few definitions, so let's resort to figure 4.16, which is similar to the figure in the original paper by Ester et al.

The large circles in figure 4.16 are the epsilon neighborhoods for the data points *p* and *q*; one circle has its center at *p* and the other at *q*. The radius of the circle is equal to epsilon (eps) and the `minPoints` variable designates the minimum number of points that must be inside the circle for a data point to be considered a *core point*. The points that belong in a cluster but aren't core points are called *border points*. According to that nomenclature, the data point *p* is a core point, and the data point *q* is a border point. We say that a data point *p* is *directly density-reachable* from a data point *q*, with respect to eps and min-Points, if the following two conditions are met:

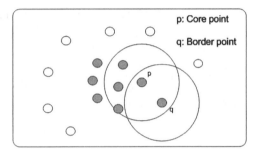

Figure 4.16   Core points and border points in DBSCAN

- *p* is inside the epsilon neighborhood of *q*.
- There are more than `minPoints` data points inside the epsilon neighborhood of *q*.

In figure 4.16, *q* is directly density reachable from *p*, but *p* isn't directly density reachable from *q*. These are the basic concepts that you need in order to understand the code in the `DBSCANAlgorithm`, whose core methods are shown in listing 4.14.

Listing 4.14   DBSCANAlgorithm: the two core methods of the our implementation

```
public List<Cluster> cluster() {
  int clusterId = getNextClusterId();

  for(DataPoint p : points) {
    if( isUnclassified(p) ) {

      boolean isClusterCreated = createCluster(p, clusterId);    ❶

      if( isClusterCreated ) {
        clusterId = getNextClusterId();
      }
    }
  }

  List<Cluster> allClusters = new ArrayList<Cluster>();
```

```
  for(Map.Entry<Integer, Set<DataPoint>> e : clusters.entrySet()) {
    String label = String.valueOf(e.getKey());
    Set<DataPoint> points = e.getValue();
    if( points != null && !points.isEmpty() ) {
      Cluster cluster = new Cluster(label, e.getValue());
      allClusters.add(cluster);
    }
  }

  return allClusters;
}

private boolean createCluster(DataPoint p, Integer clusterId) {

  boolean isClusterCreated = false;

  Set<DataPoint> nPoints = findNeighbors(p, eps);          ❷

  if( nPoints.size() < minPoints ) {                       ❸
    assignPointToCluster(p, CLUSTER_ID_NOISE);
    isClusterCreated = false;
  } else {

    assignPointToCluster(nPoints, clusterId);              ❹

    nPoints.remove(p);

    while( nPoints.size() > 0 ) {          ❺

      DataPoint nPoint = nPoints.iterator().next();

      Set<DataPoint> nnPoints = findNeighbors(nPoint, eps);     ❻

      if( nnPoints.size() >= minPoints ) {

        for(DataPoint nnPoint : nnPoints ) {

            if( isNoise(nnPoint) ) {

              assignPointToCluster(nnPoint, clusterId);      ❼

            } else if( isUnclassified(nnPoint) ){

              nPoints.add(nnPoint);          ❽

              assignPointToCluster(nnPoint, clusterId);
            }
        }
      }

    nPoints.remove(nPoint);          ❾
    }

    isClusterCreated = true;
  }

  return isClusterCreated;
}
```

❶ For each point in the dataset that hasn't been clustered, create a cluster that contains it; everything else in the cluster method is mere mechanics.

❷ Find the epsilon neighborhood of the data point p, given the parameter eps.

❸ If there aren't enough data points in the epsilon neighborhood of p then it's either noise or a border point. Treat it temporarily as noise and if it's a border point we'll change its label later. At this stage, no cluster has been created for p.

❹ If the number of data points in the epsilon neighborhood is greater than or equal to the minimum number of data points `minPoints`, we can proceed. But first, we need to remove the given data point (p) from its own set of cluster points.

❺ Iterate through all the data points other than p.

❻ Find its epsilon neighborhood and determine whether it's directly density reachable.

❼ If it's a border point, we should assign it to the cluster.

❽ This point isn't noise but we must examine whether it's a core point, so we add it to the original list to find its epsilon neighborhood, and we assign it to the cluster that we examine

❾ Before we continue with the next data point from the neighborhood of p, we remove the data point that we just examined

As you might expect from this description, the choice of `eps` and `minPoints` is important. The best way to identify good values for these two parameters is to experiment with your data for some known cluster formations. If you deal with a two-dimensional dataset (the data points have two attributes), a reasonable choice for `minPoints` is 4. You can use that value as your starting point and then take a few more values to examine whether the results of the clustering are improving. The case of multidimensional datasets is harder because the properties of multidimensional spaces are quite different from those of the lower-dimensional spaces; we'll discuss that in appendix C. The choice of `eps` will be easier if you can leverage the following factors:

- Data normalization. You should use normalized data whenever possible, especially for more than two dimensions.
- Availability of statistics about the intrapoint distances.
- Dataset dimensionality—how many attributes do your data points have?

Provide an initial value for `eps` such that you'd consider the distance between two points in the set to be "close." Then create a few increments in geometric progression, say, factors of 2 and cluster again. How do the results change as the `eps` value changes? If the results don't change significantly then you're done; select the average value as your `eps`. If the results do change, there are two possibilities:

- The results get better, or worse, as the value increases.
- The results don't show a consistent behavior—for example, you double the value of `eps` and the results get worse; you double it again and the results get better!

The first case is easy. If the clustering results are better as the value increases then select the maximum value, or keep increasing the value—provided that you have time and resources—until you don't get good results.

The second case is rare; it typically arises in high-dimensional clustering and is usually associated with a bad distance metric. So, the first thing that you want to do is to examine whether you really need all the attributes. The second solution that you can try is to use a different distance metric that may be more appropriate for your data. These are the core ideas and the basic steps of an actual implementation for DBSCAN. The original article by Ester et al. provides a lot more details of the algorithm, and it should be easier to understand after reading this section.

All the algorithms that we described so far will work well with most datasets. Some will perform better than others depending on the nature of your data, as we discussed. Nevertheless, the quality of the results isn't the single factor that we need to worry about, and it's certainly not the only one. In the next section, we'll take a closer look at some clustering issues that are ubiquitous when we deal with very large datasets.

4.7 Clustering issues in very large datasets

There are two broad categories of issues that appear in very large datasets. The first issue is the number of data points that we want to cluster. This leads us to consider the *computational complexity* of the clustering algorithms and its effect on their performance. In other words, we want to know the number of computations that we need to make as a function of the number of data points that we need to cluster. The second issue is the number of attributes (dimensions) that may be significant for our clustering. The world that we're familiar with has three dimensions, so our intuition is developed for three or fewer dimensions. In higher dimensions, the nature of geometrical objects and the notion of proximity are different. The implications of that fact are twofold. First, with more dimensions, you need to do more computations and that, in turn, will slow you down. Second, there are a number of issues that appear and are related with the special nature of high-dimensional spaces, which are summarily referred to as the *curse of dimensionality*. Let's look at each of these topics separately.

4.7.1 Computational complexity

It's important to know the performance characteristics of a clustering algorithm as a function of the number of data points that we want to cluster. There's a huge difference between trying to find clusters of users in MySpace (with $O(10^8)$ registered users) versus clusters in the database of some local newspaper (with a few hundred registered users) or a community college (with a few thousand students). If we want to quantify the impact of the number of data points (n), then it's important to understand the *computational complexity* of the algorithms in space and time. This means the size of memory and the number of operations that are required, respectively, in order to execute a particular clustering algorithm. Table 4.2 shows both of these metrics for the algorithms that we've implemented in this chapter; here k denotes the number of clusters and t the number of iterations (in the case of k-means).

Notice the prominence of the n^2 factor. It's exactly that quadratic dependency on the number of data points that causes a problem with many clustering algorithms.

Table 4.2   The space and time complexity of our clustering algorithms

Algorithm name	Space complexity	Time complexity
Single link	$O(n^2)$	$O(k\,n^2)$
Average link	$O(n^2)$	$O(k\,n^2)$
MST single link	$O(n^2)$	$O(n^2)$
k-means	$O(n)$	$O(t\,k\,n)$
ROCK	$O(n^2)$	$O(n^2 \log(n))$ or $O(n \log(n))$ with spatial indices
DBSCAN	$O(n^2)$	$O(n^2)$

Data Mining by Margaret Dunham (see references) offers a more detailed comparison of clustering algorithms in that form. From an efficiency perspective, the k-means algorithm is a clear winner, and in practice, it's used widely, probably due to its efficiency. But remember that it doesn't handle categorical data. The time complexity of DBSCAN can be improved, as indicated, by using spatial indices on the data points; since we're dealing with density on metric spaces, it's natural to view the values of the attributes as coordinates for the data points. Typically, R-trees are used for the spatial indices, and most commercial databases offer R-tree implementations for spatial data. Nevertheless, you should be aware of the difficulties involved in indexing spatial data in high dimensions. That's an active area of research and although many good ideas have been published, the last word on this problem (efficiently indexing high-dimensional data) hasn't been said.

Of course, a wealth of other clustering algorithms has been devised to address these efficiency issues. BIRCH is a well-studied and quite popular clustering algorithm that's designed specifically for large data sets. Its space and time complexity are both linear—$O(n)$—and it requires only one scan of the database. This algorithm belongs in a category of algorithms that are based on *data squashing*. That is, they create data structures that store compressed information about the data. A description of such algorithms would lead us outside the scope of this book. If you want to learn more about data squashing algorithms, please consult the references.

4.7.2   *High dimensionality*

The second broad category of issues for very large datasets is the high dimensionality of the data. In very large datasets, it's possible that our data points have many attributes, and unless we neglect a number of them from the outset, our metric space can span several dimensions—sometimes even hundreds of dimensions! We alerted you about high dimensionality earlier, but we didn't specify what "high" means. Typically, high dimensionality implies that we're dealing with more than 16 attributes—we favor base 2 here—so, for our problem to be affected by high dimensionality, the number of dimensions required is O (10). You may wonder, though, why is this such a big deal? The formulae that we've seen so far didn't restrict us to low-dimensional spaces. So, what's going on?

There are two fundamental problems with high dimensions that are particularly important for clustering—although most of what we'll discuss will be pertinent for classification algorithms as well. The first problem is that the large number of dimensions increases the amount of space that's available for "spreading" our data points. That is, if you keep the number of your data points fixed and you increase the number of attributes that you want to use to describe them, the density of the points in your space decreases exponentially! So, you can wander around for a long time without being able to identify a formation (cluster) that's preferable to another one.

The second fundamental problem has a frightening name. It's called the *curse of dimensionality*. In simple terms, it means that if you have *any* set of points in high dimensions and you use *any* metric to measure the distance between these points, they'll all come out to be roughly the same distance apart! In order to illustrate this important effect of dimensionality, let's consider the following simple case, which is illustrated in figure 4.17.

If you look at figure 4.17 from left to right, the dimensionality increases by 1 for each drawing. We start with eight points in one dimension (x axis) distributed in a uniform fashion, say, between 0 and 1. It follows that the minimum distance that we need to traverse from any given point until we meet another point is $min(D) = 0.125$, whereas the maximum distance is $max(D) = 1$. Thus, the ratio of min(D) over max(D) is equal to 0.125. In two dimensions, the eight data points are again distributed uniformly, but now we have $min(D) = 0.5$ and $max(D) = 1.414$ (along the main diagonal); thus, the ratio of min(D) over max(D) is equal to 0.354. In three dimensions, we have $min(D) = 1$ and max $(D) = 1.732$; thus, the ratio of min(D) over

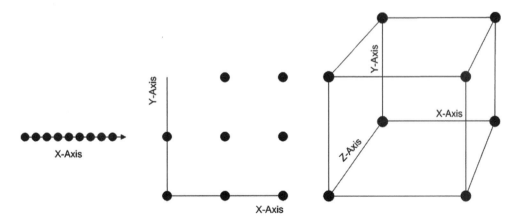

Figure 4.17 The curse of dimensionality: every point tends to have the same distance with any other point.

max(D) is equal to 0.577. In other words, as the dimensionality increases, the ratio of the minimum distance over the maximum distance approaches the value of 1. This means that no matter which direction you look at, and what distance you measure, it all looks the same!

As a result, all the algorithms that rely on distance calculations will run into trouble rather quickly as the number of dimensions increases. In this example, we used the standard Euclidean distance, but you can use whatever (proper) distance metric you like and convince yourself that the problem persists. Some people (Kevin Beyer et al.) have even questioned whether it's meaningful to talk about the concept of nearest neighbors in high-dimensional data. For an interesting approach to tackling this problem, refer to the paper by C.C. Aggarwal.

4.8   Summary

Clustering algorithms are valuable as a data exploration tool. We can construct a hierarchical structure that contains many levels of clusters or we can build a predetermined number of clusters for our data. There are many application areas for which clustering can be applied. In theory, any dataset that consists of objects that can be defined in terms of attribute values is eligible for clustering. But attention is required in the choice of measuring distances between our objects and the selection of an appropriate algorithm.

In this chapter, we covered grouping forum postings and identifying similar website users. The complexity of these algorithms varies from simple SQL statements to fairly advanced mathematical techniques. We presented a general overview of clustering types and full implementations for six algorithms: single link, average link, MST single link, k-means, ROCK, and DBSCAN.

The single-link, average-link, and MST single-link algorithms are agglomerative hierarchical algorithms and assume that all data is present at the time of computation. The computational complexity, in both space and time, isn't very good because it varies as the square of the number of data points. Thus, although they're easily implemented, these algorithms won't perform well on large data sets. One caveat here is the MST-based single-link algorithm. We can improve the time complexity of the MST single-link algorithm and make it almost proportional to the number of data objects.

The *k*-means algorithm is an iterative partitional algorithm that's very efficient and often results in good results. But it doesn't handle categorical data well because it relies on the geometric notion of a centroid, which may not be readily applicable when we deal with categorical data. Another disadvantage is its inability to handle *outliers*—points that are far away from the main clusters.

The ROCK algorithm is particularly well-suited for Boolean and categorical data because it relies on the number of links rather than a distance. It's a hierarchical agglomerative algorithm whose space complexity isn't good—$O\ (n^2)$—and its time complexity is even worse—$O\ (log(n)\ n2)$.

The DBSCAN algorithm introduced the notion of density, and implicitly distinguishes between core points and border points in a cluster. It handles outliers well, and although its space and time complexity are $O(n2)$, it can be used in combination with the k-means algorithm to provide a good and fast clustering approach; see the corresponding to-do item in the next section.

Our coverage is neither exhaustive nor complete. There are many more algorithms in the literature and many variations of the algorithms that we already discussed. It would be impossible to fit them all in a single section of this book. But you've now learned all the fundamentals, and you have solid implementations for a number of clustering algorithms that you can experiment with and extend to fit your purpose.

4.9   To Do

1 *The SQLEM algorithm*   This is a SQL-based version of the Expectation-Maximization (EM) algorithm. This is a well-known algorithm in statistics that uses two steps, an *E-step* and an *M-step*. The theory behind the algorithm involves advanced mathematical knowledge, which we don't assume that you have. But without complicating things, you can think of the k-means clustering (described in section 4.4) as an EM algorithm; the E-step is the assignment, whereas the M-step is the update of the centroid values.

Since the vast majority of applications rely, one way or another, on a relational database, you can implement this algorithm and compare its results with what we presented in this chapter. A detailed description of the algorithm can be found in the original paper by Carlos Ordonez and Paul Cereghini.

2 *Minimum spanning tree (MST) algorithms*   We've provided an implementation of the Prim-Jarník algorithm. Minimum spanning trees aren't relevant only for clustering; they also apply to network organization and touring problems. In 1926, Otakar Borůvka presented the first known algorithm for calculating the MST, in the context of evaluating efficient electrical coverage of Moravia!

In a tutorial that's freely available on the internet (see the references section), Jason Eisner explains the classical algorithms and also presents the improved approach of Harold Gabow, Zvi Galil, and Thomas H. Spencer, as well as the randomized algorithm of David R. Karger, Philip N. Klein, and Robert E. Tarjan. The last one performs only $O(m)$ computations, where (m) is the number of the edges. Read the tutorial discussion by Eisner and extend the MST class to support the more efficient algorithms that he presents.

3 *ROCK: Evaluating the expected number of links*   As we mentioned earlier, the ROCK algorithm is particularly good at dealing with categorical and Boolean attribute values by using the notion of links instead of direct distance comparisons. It finds the "best" clusters by maximizing the value of the *goodness measure*. The goodness measure is arbitrary; the main idea is that we use the links for our comparison of best clusters, but the specific choice of implementation can vary. The heuristic that's used in our implementation is the one that was originally proposed by Ramanathan V. Guha et al. It calculates the goodness measure as the ratio of the number of cross links between two clusters divided by the expected number of cross links between those clusters.

What do you think is the rationale behind that choice? What other estimates can we construct for the expected number of links between two clusters? Investigate various ideas and compare the results. What happens if we simply consider the goodness measure to be proportional to the number of cross links between two clusters?

4   *Large dataset clustering*   In the case of large datasets, it's often desirable to combine the methods that we discussed in this section in order to balance efficiency with good clustering quality. One possible hybrid scheme would be combining the k-means algorithm with either the ROCK algorithm (if your data is dominated by categorical or Boolean attributes), or the DBSCAN algorithm (if your data refer to spatial or other metric coordinates where metric distance is meaningful and effective).

How would you go about it? Recall that k-means has the best performance in terms of space and time. So, if you have a lot of processing power available, you could take a parallelization approach. That is, you could use the k-means for a few iterations and for a small number of high-level clusters, which would then be processed by the ROCK or the DBSCAN algorithms. Write an implementation for that purpose and use a large dataset (hundreds of thousands of data points) to test your results. You could use the documents on your personal computer or a copy of a large database from work.

Consider the alternative of sampling the large dataset and clustering the sample with a powerful algorithm such as ROCK or DBSCAN. Subsequently, use the number of clusters identified as the value of k, and select the centroids of the sample clusters to seed the iterations of the k-means algorithm. Compare the two approaches: which one gives you better clusters (judged empirically by you looking at the data)? Which approach is more efficient? Can you analytically justify your findings?

4.10   *References*

Aggarwal, C.C. "Towards Meaningful High-Dimensional Nearest Neighbor Search by Human-Computer Interaction." *ICDE*, 2002. http://citeseer.ist.psu.edu/aggarwal02towards.html.

Arthur, D. and S. Vassilvitskii. "k-Means++: The advantages of careful seeding." *Symposium on Discrete Algorithms* (SODA), 2007. http://www.stanford.edu/~darthur/kMeansPlusPlus.pdf.

Beyer, K., R. Ramakrishnan, U. Shaft, J. Goldstein. "When is nearest neighbor meaningful?" ICDT Conference 1999.

Bradley, P.S., U. Fayyad, and C. Reina. "Scaling clustering algorithms to large databases." Proc. 4th International Conference on *Knowledge Discovery and Data Mining* (KDD-98). AAAI Press, pp. 9 – 15.

Dhillon, I.S., J. Fan, and Y. Guan. "Efficient clustering of very large document collections." *Data Mining for Scientific and Engineering Applications*, 2001. Kluwer Academic Publishers.

Dhillon, I.S., S. Mallela, and R. Kumar. "A Divisive Information-Theoretic Feature Clustering Algorithm for Text Classification." *Journal of Machine Learning Research* 3 (March 2003).

Eisner, J. "State-of-the-art algorithms for minimum spanning trees – A tutorial discussion." 1997. http://citeseer.ist.psu.edu/eisner97stateart.html.

Kruskal, J.B. "On the Shortest Spanning Subtree of a Graph and the Traveling Salesman Problem." Proceedings of the American Mathematical Society, Vol 7 (1), pp. 48–50. 1956.

Ordonez, C. and Cereghini, P. "SQLEM: Fast clustering in SQL using the EM algorithm." *ACM SIGMOD* Rec. 29 (2), pp.559 – 570. 2000.

Prim, R.C. "Shortest connection networks and some generalizations." *Bell System Tech. J.* 1957.

Sheikholeslami, G., S. Chatterjee, and A. Zhang. "WaveCluster: A Multi-Resolution Clustering Approach for Very Large Spatial Databases." *Proceedings of the 24th VLDB Conference.* 1998.

Tung, A.K.H., J. Hou, and J. Han. "Spatial clustering in the presence of obstacles." In *Proceedings of the 17th ICDE*, 359-367, Heidelberg, Germany. 2001.

Classification: placing things where they belong

This chapter covers:

- Understanding classification techniques based on probabilities and rules
- Automatically categorizing email messages
- Detecting fraudulent financial transactions with neural networks

"What is this?" is the question children perhaps ask most frequently. The popularity of that question among children—whose inquisitive nature is as wonderful as it is persistent—shouldn't be surprising. In order to understand the world around us, we organize our perceptions into groups and categories (labeled groups, possibly structured). In the previous chapter, we presented a number of *clustering* algorithms that can help us group data points together. In this chapter, we'll present a number of *classification* algorithms that'll help us assign each data point to an appropriate category, also referred to as a *class* (hence the term *classification*). The act of classification would answer a child's question by providing a statement in the form "This is a boat," "This is a tree," "This is a house," and so on. Classification relies on a priori reference structures that divide the space of all possible data points into a set of classes that are usually, but not necessarily, nonoverlapping. Contrast this with the arbitrary nature of the clusters that we described in the previous chapter.

We could argue that, as part of our mental processing, clustering precedes classification because the reference structures that we need for classification are much richer representations of knowledge than a statement of the sort "*X* belongs in the same group as *Y*." The term *ontology* is typically used for a reference structure that constitutes a knowledge representation of the world or a part of the world that's of interest in our application. A practical aspect of classification that's usually not discussed is the maintenance of an ontology. There are many books that exclusively address aspects of *ontology engineering* and *ontology management* (see Staab and Studer; Gómez-Pérez, Fernández-López, and Corcho).

In section 5.1, we provide a number of real-world examples where classification is important. We also provide the definition of an abstract ontology structure and present an analogy between ontology structures and the structure of Java code! Sufficiently motivated, we proceed to section 5.2, where we present an overview of classifiers. We clearly can't cover all known classifiers in this book, so the overview should help you orient yourself in the related literature.

In section 5.3, you'll learn the naïve Bayes classification algorithm, one of the most celebrated and well-known classification algorithms of all time. We'll discuss both the specific case of filtering spam messages and a more general case of placing email messages in several appropriate folders. This is a good example of classifying freeform text with a statistical classification algorithm.

But the most common classification algorithms for email messages are based on rules. Section 5.3.2 covers email classification from the perspective of a *rules engine*. We introduce all the relevant concepts and demonstrate the use of rules by employing the Drools (JBoss) rules engine. In section 5.4, we tackle fraud detection as a classification problem. In that context, we introduce another broadly used classification approach—classification through *neural networks*.

How can we tell whether we assigned the most appropriate class to a data point? How can we tell whether classifier A is better than classifier B? If you ever read brochures of business intelligence tools you may be familiar with statements such as "our classifier is 75% accurate." What's the meaning of such a statement? Is it useful? These questions will be addressed in section 5.5. We'll discuss classifying large volumes of data points, classifying with respect to very large ontology structures, and doing efficient online classification. Each of these three mutually nonexclusive categories requires special attention, and is common in real-world applications.

Let's now begin by discussing the potential applications of classification and present of technical terms that we'll encounter repeatedly along the way. So, what's classification good for? What practical problems can it solve for us?

5.1 The need for classification

Whether we realize it or not, we encounter classification on a daily basis. In our everyday experiences, we can list the food items on a restaurant's menu, which are classified according to menu categories—salads, appetizers, specialties, pastas, seafood, and so on. The articles in a newspaper or a newsgroup on the internet are classified based on their subject—politics, sports, business, world, entertainment, and so on.

The books in a library carry a *call number*, which consists of two numbers: the *Dewey classification number* and the *Cutter number*. The top categories of that system are things such as generalities, religion, natural science and mathematics, and so forth. The Library of Congress in the United States has its own classification system that was first developed in the late nineteenth and early twentieth centuries to organize and arrange its book collections.

Over the course of the twentieth century, the Library of Congress system was adopted for use by other libraries as well, especially large academic libraries in the United States. We mention two systems of classifying books because the Library of Congress classification system isn't strictly hierarchical as the Dewey classification system is, where the hierarchical relationships between the topics are reflected in the numbers of the classification. As we'll see, it's important to distinguish between reference structures that are hierarchical and those that aren't.

In medicine, a plethora of classification systems are used to diagnose injuries or diseases. For example, the Schatzker classification system is used by radiologists and orthopedic surgeons to classify tibial plateau fractures (a complex knee injury). Similarly, there are classification systems for spinal cord injuries; for coma, concussion, and traumatic brain injuries; and so on.

The Occupational Injury and Illness Classification (OIIC) manual provides a classification system for coding the characteristics of injuries, illnesses, and fatalities in the Survey of Occupational Injuries and Illnesses (SOII) and the Census of Fatal Occupational Injuries (CFOI), according to the U.S. government. The ICD-10, by the World Health Organization (WHO), was endorsed by the 43rd World Health Assembly in May 1990, and came into use in member states as of 1994. It's used to classify diseases and other health problems recorded on many types of health and vital records including death certificates and hospital records. After your visit to the doctor's office, that's what your insurance company consults to determine the amount of coverage. Top-level categories include certain infectious and parasitic diseases; neoplasms; endocrine, nutritional, and metabolic diseases; and so on. In biological sciences, the Linnaean classification system uses two attributes for classifying all living things—*genus* and *species*. You must have heard of the term *Homo sapiens*, of which *Homo* is our genus and *sapiens* is our species. This classification can, and typically is, extended to include other attributes such as *family, order, class, phylum*, and so forth.

Let's digress to alarm you about the number of attributes. Generally speaking, the more attributes you use, the finer the degree of classification is going to be. A "large" number of attributes is usually a good thing, but there are caveats to this general principle. One notorious symptom of dealing with many attributes is the *curse of dimensionality*, which was discussed in section 4.6.2. Typically, a large number of attributes means that we're dealing with more than sixteen.

As you may recall, the curse of dimensionality refers to the fact that our space becomes more and more homogenous as the number of attributes increases. In other words, the distance between any two points will be roughly the same no matter which points you select and what metric you apply to measure the distances. If that's the case, it becomes increasingly difficult to distinguish which category is "closer" to a given data point, since no matter where you "stand" in our space, everything seems to be the same distance apart! You can always add attributes to your ontology, so that you can have all your domain knowledge in one place and later select the attributes that should be used for classification.

It should be clear from these examples that *flat reference structures* aren't as "rich" as *hierarchical reference structures*. In turn, the hierarchical reference structures are less rich than those that are hierarchical *and* semantically enriched. This observation falls again under our discussion of ontologies. We didn't provide a clear definition of the term *ontology* because it doesn't seem that there's consensus on that matter.

For the purposes of this book, an ontology consists of three things: *concepts*, *instances*, and *attributes*.

In figure 5.1, we depict a minute segment of a (rudimentary) general ontology by focusing on the concepts of "vehicle." Concepts are depicted as ellipses, instances are depicted as rectangles, and attributes are depicted as rounded rectangles. Note the hereditary property of attribute assignment. If attribute 1 is assigned to the root of the concept tree then it cascades to the concept leaf nodes. Thus, values for attribute 1 can be assigned to instances of a boat and an automobile. Only an automobile instance can have values for attribute 2. Attribute 1 could be the attribute Name, which for practical reasons you always want to have, whereas attribute 2 could be the attribute Number of wheels. Attributes are defined at the level of the concepts, but only instances have concrete and unique values because only instances represent real "things."

Think of concepts as analogous to Java classes, instances as analogous to instances of Java classes, and attributes as variables of Java classes. Clearly, a source code base that uses packages to group together classes by functionality or component, that uses inheritance to abstract common structure and behavior, and that properly uses encapsulation, is superior to a source code base that doesn't have these qualities. Similar to attributes, in our definition of an ontology, when you define a class, you define the data type of the variables but you don't assign a value to a variable (unless it's a constant). This is a good working definition that'll serve you well 80% to 90% of the time. If you're ever in doubt, you can consult this analogy to obtain some insight into your structure.

We could obviously go on with more classification systems; they're everywhere. The point is that classifying data is equivalent to structuring or organizing it. Classification systems improve communication by reducing errors due to ambiguities. They also help us organize our thoughts and plan our actions. The reference structure, which is used for organizing our data, can be as simple as a set of labels or as advanced as a *semantic ontology*. Have you heard of the *semantic Web*? At the heart of the semantic Web

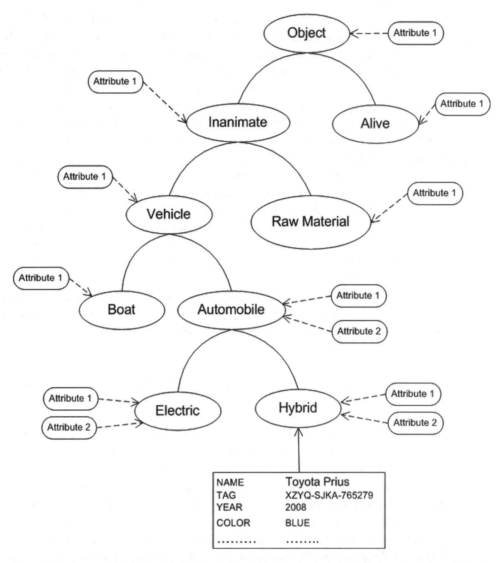

Figure 5.1   An example that depicts the basic elements of a reference structure (a rudimentary ontology)

(see Antoniou and van Harmelen) lie a number of technologies and formal specifications related to creating, using, and maintaining semantic ontologies. Ontologies are
also useful in model-driven architectures (see Gasevic, Djuric, and Devedzic), which is
a software design initiative of the Object Management Group (OMG) (http://
www.omg.org/).

Look at your database. Your application could be an online store, an intranet
document management system, an internet mashup, or any other kind of web application. When you think about your data and the ways it could be organized, you'll realize
the value of a classification system for your application. Starting with section 5.3 and

continuing through most of chapter 6, we'll introduce classification mechanisms in some fictitious web applications in order to demonstrate the use of classification algorithms and the issues that may arise. But first, let's give an overview of classification systems. If you want to jump into action quickly, you can skip the next section.

5.2 An overview of classifiers

One way that we could view the set of all classification systems is with respect to the reference structure that they use. At the top level of such a perspective, we can divide all classification systems into two broad categories—*binary* and *multiclass*. Binary classification systems, as the name suggests, provide a yes/no answer to the question: Does this data point belong to class X? A medical diagnosis system could answer the question of whether a patient has cancer. Or an immigration classification system could answer whether a person is a terrorist. Multiclass classification systems assign a data point to a specific class, out of many, such as the assignment of a news article in a news category.

Within the set of multiclass classification systems, we can further group classification systems on the basis of two criteria: whether the multiple classes are discrete or continuous, and whether the multiple classes are "flat" (just a list of labels) or have a hierarchical structure. The Dewey classification scheme and the ICD-10 catalogue from the previous section are examples of a classification system that has multiple discrete and finite classes. The result of classification may be a continuous variable such as when classification is used for predictions, also known as *forecasting*. If you provide the value of a stock on Monday, Tuesday, Wednesday, and Thursday as input, and want to find the value of a stock on Friday, you can cast that problem as a multiclass classification that's discrete or continuous. The discrete version could predict whether the stock price will increase, remain unchanged, or decrease on Friday. The continuous version could provide a prediction for the actual stock price.

Categorization of classification systems, with respect to the underlying technique, isn't quite as clear or widely accepted. But we could say that there are two broad categories that have gained a significant level of adoption in the industry. The first category includes *statistical algorithms* and the second *structural algorithms*, as shown in figure 5.2.

Statistical algorithms come in three flavors. *Regression algorithms* are particularly good at forecasting—predicting the value of a continuous variable. Regression algorithms are based on the assumption that it's sufficient to fit our data to a particular model; quite often that model is a linear function of the variables at hand. Another kind of statistical classification algorithms stems from the Bayes theorem, which we encountered briefly in chapter 2. A fairly successful and modern statistical approach combines Bayes theorem with a probabilistic network structure that depicts the dependency between the various attributes of the classification problem.

Structural algorithms have three main branches: *rule-based* algorithms, which include if-then rules and decision trees; *distance-based* algorithms, which are generally separated into functional and nearest neighbor schemes; and *neural networks (NN)*. Neural networks form a category on their own—although we should mention that

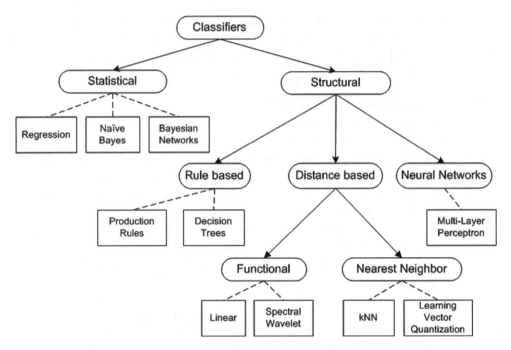

Figure 5.2   **An overview of the classification algorithms based on their design**

equivalency between certain neural networks and some advanced statistical algorithms (Gaussian processes) has been established and studied extensively. In the following subsections, we'll give a brief summary of each of these classifier categories.

5.2.1   Structural classification algorithms

As shown in figure 5.2, the branch of rule-based structural algorithms consists of *production rules* (if-then clauses) and *decision tree (DT)*–based algorithms. The production rules can be collected manually by human experts or deduced by decision trees. Rule-based algorithms are typically implemented as *forward-chaining* production systems—a frightening term, if you ask me! The best algorithm in this category is called *Rete* (see Russell and Norvig); *rete* means "network" in Latin. It's the basis for well-known libraries such as CLIPS, Jess, and Soar.

In this book, we'll be using an object-oriented implementation of Rete, which is offered by the JBoss project. It's the JBoss Rules library, also known as *Drools* (the original project name for this rule engine). This project is stable, it has ample documentation, and the code base is appropriate for study and development alike. Incidentally, we should mention that we enjoy working with the Drools APIs as much as we enjoy working with the Lucene APIs, which we encountered in chapter 2. These two projects are truly production-ready.

The decision tree-based algorithms are based on a simple but powerful idea. Did you ever read Charles Dickens's *A Christmas Carol*? In that book, Dickens describes a game (Yes and No) in which Scrooge's nephew had to think of something and the rest had to figure out what it was, while he would answer only yes or no, depending on their question. Versions of this game exist in many cultures—it's fairly popular in Spanish-speaking countries among children, where it's known as *veo, veo*. Similar to these familiar games, the idea behind most DT algorithms is to ask questions whose answers will eliminate as many candidates as possible based on the provided information. Decision-tree algorithms have several advantages, such as ease of use and computational efficiency. Their disadvantages are usually prominent when we deal with continuous variables, because we're forced to perform a discretization—the continuum of the values must be divided into a finite number of bins in order to construct the tree. In general, decision-tree algorithms don't have good generalization properties, and as a result, they don't perform well with unseen data. A commonly used algorithm in this category is C5.0 (on Unix machines) or See5 (on Microsoft Windows machines). It can be found in a number of commercial products, such as Clementine (http://www.spss.com/clementine/) and RuleQuest (http://www.rulequest.com/).

The second branch of structural algorithms is composed of distance-based algorithms. In the previous chapters, we introduced and extensively used the notions of similarity measure and generalized distance. These algorithms are fairly intuitive, but it's easy to misuse them and end up with bad classification results because a lot of the data point attributes aren't directly related to each other. A single similarity measure can't expediently capture the differences in the way that the attributes should be measured; careful normalization and analysis of the attribute space is crucial to the success of distance-based algorithms. Nevertheless, in many low-dimensional cases, with low complexity, these algorithms perform well and are fairly simple to implement. We can further divide distance-based algorithms into functional and nearest neighbor-type algorithms.

Functional classifiers approximate the data by function, as the name suggests. This is similar to regression, but we differentiate between them on the basis of the rationale behind the use of the function. In regression, we use a function as a model of the probability distribution (Dunham); in the case of functional classifiers, we're merely interested in the numerical approximation of the data. In practice, it's hard (and perhaps pointless) to distinguish between linear regression and linear approximation through the minimization of the squared error.

Nearest-neighbor algorithms attempt to find the nearest class for each data point. By using the same formulas that we've seen earlier about generalized distances, we can calculate the distance of each data point from each available class. The class that's closest to the object is assigned to that object. Perhaps the most common classification algorithm of that type is K nearest neighbors (kNN), although another algorithm known as learning vector quantization (LVQ) is also well studied and broadly adopted.

Neural network (NN) algorithms belong in a subcategory of structural algorithms by themselves. These algorithms require a good deal of mathematical background to be presented properly. We'll do our best to present them from a computational perspective without resorting to mathematics. The main idea behind this family of classification algorithms is the construction of an artificial network of computational nodes that's analogous to the biological structure of the human brain, which is basically made of *neurons* and *synapses* that connect them.

Neural network algorithms have been shown to perform well on a variety of problems. There are two major disadvantages of neural networks: we don't have a design methodology that would be applicable in a large number of problems, and it's difficult to interpret the results of neural network classification; the classifier may commit few errors but we're unable to understand why. This is why we consider neural networks to be a "black box" technique, as opposed to a decision tree or a rule-based algorithm— where the result of a classification for a particular data point can be easily interpreted.

5.2.2 *Statistical classification algorithms*

Regression algorithms are based on the idea of finding the best fit of the data to a formula; the most common formula is a linear function of the input values (see Hastie, Tibshirani, and Friedman). Regression algorithms are usually employed when the data points are inherently numerical variables (such as the dimensions of an object, the weight of a person, or the temperature in the atmosphere) but, unlike Bayesian algorithms, they're not very good for categorical data (such as employee status or credit score description). In addition, if the model about the data is linear then it's not easy to justify the adjective "statistical"; in essence, linear regression isn't different from the good old high school exercise of fitting a line to a bunch of x-y points.

Things get more interesting and obtain the flavor of a statistical approach in the case of so-called *logistic regression*. In this case, the model (the logistic function) takes values between 0 and 1, which can be interpreted as the probability of class membership and works well in the case of binary classification (see Dunham).

Most of the techniques in the statistical algorithms category use a probability theorem known as the *Bayes rule* or *Bayes theorem* (see Papoulis and Pillai). We encountered the Bayes rule in chapter 2, in the context of learning from user clicks. In this kind of statistical classification algorithms, the least common denominator is the assumption that the attributes of the problem are independent of each other, in a fairly quantitatively explicit form. The fascinating aspect of Bayesian algorithms is that they seem to work well even when that independence assumption is clearly violated! In section 5.3, we'll study the most celebrated algorithm of this approach—the naïve Bayes classification algorithm.

Bayesian networks are a relatively modern approach to machine learning that attempts to combine the power of the Bayes theorem with the advantages of structural approaches, such as decision trees. Naïve Bayes classifiers and their siblings can represent simple probability distributions, but fall short in capturing the probabilistic structure of the data, if there is one. By leveraging the powerful representation of *directed acyclic graphs (DAG)*, the probabilistic relations of the attributes can be depicted graphically. We won't cover Bayesian networks in this book; if you're interested in learning more about this subject then you should look at *Learning Bayesian Networks* by Richard E. Neapolitan.

5.2.3   *The lifecycle of a classifier*

No matter what type of classifier you choose for your application, the lifecycle of your classifier will fit in the general diagram of figure 5.3. There are three stages in the lifecycle of a classifier: training, testing, and production.

In the training stage, we provide the classifier with data points for which we've already assigned an appropriate class. Every classifier contains a number of parameters that must be determined before it's used. The purpose of that stage is to determine the various parameters; we used a question mark inside a star to indicate that the primary goal is determining these parameters. In the validation stage, we want to validate the classifier and ensure that before we roll it out to a production system, we've achieved a certain level of credibility for our results. We've used an *E* in a circle to indicate that the primary goal is determining the classification error, but the quality standard can and should be measured by various metrics (see section 5.6 for a discussion on the credibility and cost of classification). The data that we use in the validation stage (test data) must be different than the data that we used in the training stage (training data).

The training and validation stages may be repeated many times before the classifier transitions into the production stage, because there may be configuration parameters that aren't identified by the training process but are given as input during the design of a classifier. This important point means that we can write software that wraps the classifier and its configuration parameters for the purpose of automatically testing and validating a large number of classifier designs. Even classifiers that are fundamentally different in nature, such as naïve Bayes, neural network, and decision trees, could participate in the testing. We can either pick the best classifier, as determined by the quality metrics of the validation stages, or combine all the classifiers into what could

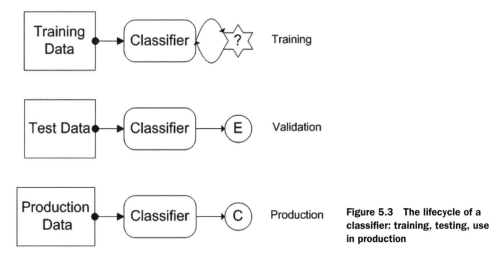

Figure 5.3   The lifecycle of a classifier: training, testing, use in production

be called a *metaclassifier* scheme. This approach is gaining ground in the industry and has provided consistently better results in a wide range of applications. We'll discuss combining classifiers in chapter 6.

In the production stage we're using our classifier in a live system to produce classifications on-the-fly. Typically, the parameters of the classifier don't change during the production stage. But it's possible to enhance the results of the classifier by embedding (into the production stage) a short-lived training stage that's based on human-in-the-loop feedback. These three steps are repeated as we get more data from our production system and as we come up with better ideas for our classifier.

We've now seen the big picture about classification algorithms. In the literature, you can find many different overviews of classification algorithms (such as Holmström et al.). In the following section, we'll introduce one of the most celebrated statistical classification algorithms: the naïve Bayes classifier. In particular, we'll demonstrate the use of classification for categorizing legitimate email messages and filtering out spam.

5.3   *Automatic categorization of emails and spam filtering*

In this section, we want to achieve two objectives. Our first objective is coarse in its scope—we want to be able to distinguish between legitimate email messages and spam, which is an example of *binary classification*. Our second objective is to achieve a finer granularity of sorting email messages. we want to refine our classification results and be able to categorize nonspam email messages into one of the following categories: business, world, usa, and sports. This is an example of a *multiclass classification*.

Email doesn't require special introduction. It was one of the first applications that became available with the advent of the internet, and it's perhaps the most common application in use today. For most users, all messages go straight to the inbox. Wouldn't it be nice if you could define your own folders and have your emails (automatically) distributed in the appropriate folders? You could have a folder with an icon that depicts hell and send all your spam email (also known as *unsolicited bulk email*) straight to that folder!

Your email client probably already does that. Most email clients today implement at least some form of a rule-based classification. Due to this, most of these clients aren't very good at learning, in the sense that they don't generalize from previously "seen" and manually categorized email messages. Web email clients offer unprecedented opportunities in that respect, because algorithms that can generalize can quickly cover a much broader range of emails messages such as brand new spam messages.

The algorithms that we'll discuss here are applicable for an arbitrary collection of documents. You could use them in an application that allows users to upload their Word or PDF files and offers automatic categorization (another marketing term for classification) of the documents into a list of user-provided categories.

In our example for this section, the email collection is generated from the same files that we used in chapter 2 for searching through web pages. For each web page from chapter 2, we've created an email that corresponds to it. If you read that chapter then you're already familiar with the content. If you didn't read it yet, we should tell you that our emails include the following (the choice of content was random and the temporal context was November 2006):

- Seven emails that are related to business news. Three are related to Google's expansion into newspaper advertisement, another three primarily discuss NVidia stock, and one talks more generally about stock price and index movements.
- Three emails that are related to Lance Armstrong's attempt to run the marathon in New York.
- Four emails that are related to U.S. politics and, in particular, the congressional elections.
- Five emails that are related to world news; four of them are about Ortega winning the elections in Nicaragua and one about global warming.
- Four emails that are spam.

Email classification is interesting in many respects. One peculiarity is there's "someone out there" trying to beat your classifier. In fact, the spammers may use the same techniques that we describe here to beat your email classification scheme, so keep an eye on the competition! We use the term *scheme* intentionally. You'd hardly ever use only a classifier to write an email-filtering application or an email organizer. Here's a list of things that complement the classifiers:

- Header tests
- Automatic email address white- and blacklists
- Manual email address white- and blacklists
- Collaborative spam identification databases
- Real-time blackhole lists (RBLs)
- Character set and locale identification

Our focus is on the intelligent aspects of email classification systems, so we won't cover the other techniques that we mentioned. For an example of a useful module, look at the Apache project Spam Assassin (http://spamassassin.apache.org/). We'll present two classification methods that you'd use to create such systems. The first classification method will be based on the naïve Bayes classifier that we introduced in chapter 2. The second classification method will be based on rules and we'll use the Drools rules engine.

5.3.1 NaïveBayes classification

In this section, we'll use a statistical classifier that's encapsulated in the `EmailClassifier` class. As we mentioned earlier, it employs what's known as the naïve Bayes algorithm by extending the `NaiveBayes` class, which is a general-purpose implementation of the naïve Bayes algorithm. In general, classifiers are agnostic with respect to the objects of classification; they're only concerned with `Concepts`, `Instances`, and `Attributes`. A classifier's job is to assign a `Concept` to an `Instance`; that's all it does. In order to know what Concept should be assigned to a particular Instance, a classifier reads a TrainingSet—a set of Instances that already have Concepts assigned to them. Upon loading those Instances, the classifier *trains* itself; put another way it *learns* how to map a Concept to an Instance based on the assignments in the TrainingSet. The way that each classifier trains depends on the classifier. In this chapter, we'll use the terms concept, class, and category interchangeably.

SAMPLING EMAIL MESSAGES AND TRAINING THE CLASSIFIER

Let's start by demonstrating how to load the emails and train our email classifier. Listing 5.1 shows the BeanShell script that you can run to accomplish the loading of the emails and the training of the classifier.

Listing 5.1   Loading the email training set and training the NaiveBayes classifier

```
EmailDataset trainEmailDS = EmailData.createTrainingDataset();       ❶

trainEmailDS.printEmail("biz-04.html");
trainEmailDS.printEmail("spam-biz-03.html");                         ❷

EmailClassifier emailFilter = new EmailClassifier(trainEmailDS, 10); ❸

emailFilter.train();       ❹
```

❶ The class EmailData is responsible for loading the HTML files that we used in chapter 2 and translating them into instances of the Email class, which is a simple class that encapsulates an email message based on the attributes from, to, subject, and text-Body. The method createTrainingDataset() loads the list of documents that we want to use for training our classifier. That list is given by the two-dimensional String array TRAINING_DATA; the testing dataset is determined by the two-dimensional String array TEST_DATA. You can change the content of these lists and observe the effect on the results of classification. An honest evaluation should use different sets of files for training and testing.

❷ This step prints the content of two emails—one legitimate and one spam—just to make sure that our data loaded properly before we proceed, and gauge the kind of content that we're working with.

❸ We instantiate EmailClassifier by passing the EmailDataset reference and the number of terms that should be taken into consideration in the analysis of the emails. For each email, we analyze the content and retain the top 10 (in this example) most frequent terms.

❹ We train the classifier. This is a sanity check to ensure that we have instances to train on; it sets the attributes on which we want to train the classifier, calls the train() method of the NaiveBayes parent class, and sets an ad hoc level of probability for attribute values that we haven't seen before.

THE EMAIL CLASSIFIER IN ACTION

Once we have our classifier trained we're ready to test it. Listing 5.2 is the continuation of listing 5.1; so, you need to execute it within the same shell. Note how easy it is to use the classifier at this level. It's literally two lines of code!

Listing 5.2   Using the naïve Bayes classifier for detecting spam emails

```
EmailDataset testEmailDS = EmailData.createTestDataset();        ⟵┐  Load
                                                                 │  emails
email = testEmailDS.findEmailById("biz-01.html");          ⟵─────┤  from
emailFilter.classify(email);                                     │  testing
                                                   Classify      │  dataset
email = testEmailDS.findEmailById("sport-01.html");  ⟵─ legitimate
emailFilter.classify(email);                            email

email = testEmailDS.findEmailById("usa-01.html");               Retrieve
emailFilter.classify(email);                                    email by
                                                                filename
email = testEmailDS.findEmailById("world-01.html");
emailFilter.classify(email);

email = testEmailDS.findEmailById("spam-biz-01.html");
emailFilter.classify(email);
```

The results are shown in figure 5.4. Note that all emails are classified properly. This provides a baseline for experimenting with the settings. It also allows you to compare the change in the accuracy of the classifier as you augment or reduce the training set.

Note that it's not hard to be successful in classifying our emails if all the unseen emails are similar to the ones that we have in our training set. In general, if our training set is

```
*** Classifying instance: biz-01.html
P(NOT SPAM|biz-01.html) = 0.944444444444445
P(SPAM|biz-01.html) = 0.055555555555556

Classified biz-01.html as NOT SPAM

*** Classifying instance: sport-01.html
P(NOT SPAM|sport-01.html) = 0.894736842105263
P(SPAM|sport-01.html) = 0.105263157894737

Classified sport-01.html as NOT SPAM

*** Classifying instance: usa-01.html
P(NOT SPAM|usa-01.html) = 0.882352941176471
P(SPAM|usa-01.html) = 0.117647058823529

Classified usa-01.html as NOT SPAM

*** Classifying instance: world-01.html
P(NOT SPAM|world-01.html) = 0.962264150943396
P(SPAM|world-01.html) = 0.037735849056604

Classified world-01.html as NOT SPAM

*** Classifying instance: spam-biz-01.html
P(NOT SPAM|spam-biz-01.html) = 0.468750000000000
P(SPAM|spam-biz-01.html) = 0.531250000000000

Classified spam-biz-01.html as SPAM
```

Figure 5.4   Email spam filtering results (binary classification) for the classifier that's based on the naïve Bayes algorithm

very similar to our testing set, it's not difficult to achieve high levels of accuracy. That's typically due to *overfitting*; see to-do item 3 for more details on the tradeoff between specialization and generalization.

At this point, it may be helpful to repeat these steps by changing the number of frequent terms (listing 5.1, step 3), retrain the classifier, and observe the impact that this change has on the results of the classification. You could execute the classification steps of listing 5.2 at once, by calling the method `sample()` of the `EmailClassifier`.

As we mentioned, a classifier's job is to assign a `Concept` to an `Instance`; for the `EmailClassifier`, the concepts are SPAM and NOT SPAM in the case of email filtering (binary classification), and the names of the email categories in the case of email categorization (multiclass classification). The email instances are encapsulated by the class `EmailInstance`, which extends the `BaseInstance` class. This example demonstrates the specialization of the general base classes that we provide in order to meet specific needs (emails).

The `EmailClassifier` obtains its `TrainingSet` through the method `getTrainingSet` of the `EmailDataset` instance. Upon loading those `Instances`, the classifier *trains* itself (*learns* how) to map a `Concept` to an `Instance` based on the assignments in the `TrainingSet`. The `EmailClassifier` doesn't use all the email information for its training. It uses a single attribute whose value is evaluated during the construction of an `EmailInstance` as shown in listing 5.3.

Listing 5.3   Creating an `EmailInstance`

```
public EmailInstance(String emailCategory, Email email, int topNTerms) {
  super();
  this.id = email.getId();
  this.setConcept(new BaseConcept(emailCategory));

  String text = email.getSubject()+" "+email.getTextBody();
  Content content = new Content(email.getId(), text, topNTerms);

  Map<String, Integer> tfMap = content.getTFMap();

  attributes = new StringAttribute[1];
  String attrName = "Email_Text_Attribute";
  String attrValue = "";

  for(Map.Entry<String, Integer> tfEntry : tfMap.entrySet()) {
     attrValue = attrValue + " " + tfEntry.getKey();
  }

  attributes[0] = new StringAttribute(attrName, attrValue);
}
```

First, we concatenate the text of the subject line and the email's body. Then we use the `Content` class (which we encountered in chapter 3) to analyze the result of the text concatenation and create the list of the top *N* frequent terms. The textual analysis is based on a custom analyzer that extends Lucene's `StandardAnalyzer` class and uses the `PorterStemFilter` class for tokenizing strings. Both Lucene classes can be found in the package `org.apache.lucene.analysis`.

As you can see, the only attribute of our instance (`Email_Text_Attribute`) takes as a value the concatenation of the top N frequent terms. This is a simplifying modeling assumption, of course. Despite its simplicity, this approach can provide good results in many cases. Remember that when you design (or select) an intelligent algorithm for a real application, you should always start with the simplest possible design that can work. This is equivalent to the maxim of avoiding premature code optimization, if you like to think in those terms.

Even though the simple solution may not be the one that you'll end up using, it'll allow you to understand the nature of your data and the difficulties related to your problem, without complicating matters from the outset. Other choices abound. You could select two attributes, one attribute value for the subject and one attribute value for body of the email. You could also include the `from` attribute. If your email had a timestamp, you could include whether the email was sent during normal business hours or late at night. In the "To do" section, we invite you to explore these and other alternatives (feel free to be creative) and compare the results, and the complexity involved, as you consider more information from your emails for the training of the classifier.

A CLOSER LOOK AT THE NAÏVE BAYES CLASSIFIER

Now, it's time to have a closer look at the implementation of the naïve Bayes algorithm. Listing 5.4 shows the `NaiveBayes` class deprived of its straightforward constructor, its Javadoc comments, some logging output, and a couple of trivial getters. Other than that, it's all here, in just two pages of code: one of the most robust, successful, and widely used classification algorithms of all time!

Recall that a classifier learns the association between instances and classes from the training instances, and it provides the class that a given instance is associated with. Naturally, the interface of a `Classifier` demands that every classifier implement the method `boolean train()` and the method `Concept classify(Instance instance)`. Of course, every classifier implements these methods in their own way, so let's see how it works for `NaiveBayes`.

Listing 5.4 `NaiveBayes`: a general Bayesian classifier

```
public class NaiveBayes implements Classifier {

  private String name;

  protected TrainingSet tSet;

  protected Map<Concept,Double> conceptPriors;              ❶

  protected Map<Concept, Map<Attribute, AttributeValue>> p;   ❷

  protected ArrayList<String> attributeList;       ❸

  public boolean train() {          ❹
    boolean hasTrained = false;

    if ( attributeList == null || attributeList.size() == 0) {
      System.out.print("Can't train the classifier
      without attributes for training!");
```

```
      System.out.print("Use the method -->
      trainOnAttribute(Attribute a)");
    } else {
     calculateConceptPriors();

     calculateConditionalProbabilities();

     hasTrained = true;
    }
    return hasTrained;
  }

  public void trainOnAttribute(String aName) {

    if (attributeList ==null) {
      attributeList = new ArrayList<String>();
    }
    attributeList.add(aName);
  }

  private void calculateConceptPriors() {        ❺

    for (Concept c : tSet.getConceptSet()) {

      int totalConceptCount=0;

      for (Instance i : tSet.getInstances().values()) {

        if (i.getConcept().equals(c)) {
          totalConceptCount++;
        }
      }
      conceptPriors.put(c, new Double(totalConceptCount));
    }
  }

  protected void calculateConditionalProbabilities() {        ❻
    p = new HashMap<Concept, Map<Attribute, AttributeValue>>();

    for (Instance i : tSet.getInstances().values()) {

      for (Attribute a: i.getAtrributes()) {

        if (a != null && attributeList.contains(a.getName())) {

          if ( p.get(i.getConcept())== null ) {

            p.put(i.getConcept(), new HashMap<Attribute,
    AttributeValue>());
          }
          Map<Attribute, AttributeValue> aMap = p.get(i.getConcept());
          AttributeValue aV = aMap.get(a);
          if ( aV == null ) {

            aV = new AttributeValue(a.getValue());
            aMap.put(a, aV);
          } else {
            aV.count();
          }
        }
      }
    }
```

```
    }
  }
  public double getProbability(Instance i, Concept c) {        ❼
    double cP=1;

    for (Attribute a : i.getAtrributes()) {

      if ( a != null && attributeList.contains(a.getName()) ) {

        Map<Attribute, AttributeValue> aMap = p.get(c);
        AttributeValue aV = aMap.get(a);
        if ( aV == null) {
          cP *= ((double) 1 / (tSet.getSize()+1));
        } else {
          cP *= (double)(aV.getCount()/conceptPriors.get(c));
        }
      }
    }
    return (cP == 1) ? (double)1/tSet.getNumberOfConcepts() : cP;
  }
public double getProbability(Concept c, Instance i) {        ❽
    double cP=0;

    if (tSet.getConceptSet().contains(c)) {

      cP = (getProbability(i,c)*getProbability(c))/getProbability(i);

    } else {
      cP = 1/(tSet.getNumberOfConcepts()+1.0);
    }
    return cP;
  }
  public double getProbability(Instance i) {
    double cP=0;

    for (Concept c : getTset().getConceptSet()) {

      cP += getProbability(i,c)*getProbability(c);
    }
    return (cP == 0) ? (double)1/tSet.getSize() : cP;
  }

  public double getProbability(Concept c) {        ❾
      Double trInstanceCount = conceptPriors.get(c);
      if( trInstanceCount == null ) {
         trInstanceCount = 0.0;
      }
      return trInstanceCount/tSet.getSize();
  }

  public Concept classify(Instance instance) {        ❿
    Concept bestConcept = null;
    double bestP = 0.0;

    for (Concept c : tSet.getConceptSet()) {
       double p = getProbability(c, instance);
       if( p >= bestP ) {
          bestConcept = c;
```

```
            bestP = p;
        }
    }
    return bestConcept;
    }
}
```

This is a long listing. So, before we go into its details, let's recap what we've seen in chapter 2. The naïve Bayes algorithm evaluates what's called the *conditional probability* of X given Y. That is, the probability that tells us how likely it is to observe Concept X provided that we already observed Instance Y. In particular, this classifier uses as input the following:

- The probability of observing Concept X in general, also known as the *prior* probability and denoted by $p(X)$.
- The probability of observing Instance Y provided that we randomly select an Instance from Concept X, also known as the *likelihood* and denoted by $p(Y|X)$.
- The probability of observing Instance Y in general, also known as the *evidence* and denoted by $p(Y)$.

The output of the classifier is the calculation of the probability that an observed Instance Y belongs in Concept X, which is also known as the *posterior probability* and denoted by $p(X|Y)$. The calculation is performed based on the following formula (known as Bayes theorem):

$$p(X|Y) = \frac{p(Y|X)p(X)}{p(Y)}$$

Until now we've systematically avoided presenting explicit mathematical formulas. But despite its simple appearance, this formula is very powerful and is the basis of a large number of classifiers, ranging from implementations that use the naïve Bayes algorithm to implementations based on Gaussian processes and Bayesian belief networks (see McKay). If you're going to remember one formula, learn this one well!

As far as we're concerned with the classification per se, the evaluation of the evidence $p(Y)$ isn't required because its value doesn't change for the various classes. The classifier works by calculating the posterior probabilities $p(X|Y)$ for all classes and selecting the class with the highest posterior probability. Whether or not we divide by $p(Y)$, the ordering won't be affected. Since it's computationally cheaper not to perform the division, the implementation can avoid the division by $p(Y)$.

Now, let's examine one-by-one the main points of listing 5.4. First we set a name for this instance of the NaiveBayes classifier. If you use a single classifier this is redundant. But as you'll see in chapter 6, quite often we want to create ensembles of classifiers and combine them in order to improve our results. Keeping an identifier for the classifier will be useful later on. Of course, every classifier needs a training set. The name of the classifier and its training set are intentionally set during the construction phase. Once you've created an instance of the NaiveBayes classifier, you can't reset its TrainingSet, but you can always get the reference to it and add instances.

❶ The `conceptPriors` map stores the counts for each of the concepts in our training set. We could have used it to store the prior probabilities, not just the counts. But we want to reuse these counts, so in the name of computational efficiency, we store the counts; the priors can be obtained by a simple division.

❷ The variable p stores the conditional probabilities—the probability of observing concept X given that we observed instance Y, or in the case of the user clicks, the probability that user A wants to see URL *X* provided that he submitted query Q.

❸ This is the list of attributes that should be considered by the classifier for training. The instances of a training set may have many attributes, and it's possible that only a few are relevant, so we keep track of what attributes should be used. The method `train-OnAttribute(String)` is used to populate this list.

❹ The `train()` method is responsible for training the classifier. After a quick check that we have at least one attribute to train on, this method calculates the concept priors and the conditional probabilities as dictated by the formula of the Bayes theorem. If all goes well, it'll return a `true` value; otherwise it'll return `false`.

❺ This is the first part of the training, where we calculate the prior probabilities *p(X)*. For all the instances in the training set, we calculate how many times we've seen each concept. We keep track of the count in this implementation. The real concept priors are the counts divided by the total number of instances in the training set.

❻ This is the second part of the training, where we count the number of times that a specific attribute value appears in a concept. This number is needed for the calculation of the conditional probabilities *p(Y|X)*, which occurs in `getProbability(Instance I, Concept c)`. For each instance in the training set and for each attribute that belongs in the training attributes list, we count the number of times we've encountered a particular value for a given concept.

❼ This is the calculation of the conditional probabilities *p(Y|X)*. The term *naïve* has its origin in this method. Note that we're seeking the probability of occurrence for a particular instance, given a particular concept. But each instance is uniquely determined by the unique values of its attributes. The conditional probability of the instance is, in essence, the joint probability of all the attribute value conditional probabilities. Each attribute value conditional probability is given by the term `(aV.getCount()/concept-Priors.get(c))`. In the preceding implementation, it's assumed that all these attribute values are statistically independent, so the joint probability is simply the product of the individual probabilities for each attribute value. That's the "naïve" part. In general, without the statistical independence of the attributes, the joint probability wouldn't be equal to that product.

We use quotes around the word naïve because it turns out that the naïve Bayes algorithm is very robust and widely applicable, even in problems where the attribute independence assumption is clearly violated. In fact, it can be shown that the naïve Bayes algorithm is optimal in the exact opposite case—when there's a completely deterministic dependency among the attributes (see Rish).

In the case of attribute values that haven't been encountered before, we assign an arbitrary conditional probability that's equal to the inverse of the number of instances in the training set plus one. This is an arbitrary approximation; you could add the value of two or three, or calculate the missing attribute value probability in some entirely different manner. Don't underestimate the impact of this approximation in the classification results, especially when the training set isn't large. What do you think should that value be for a small training set?

❽ This method calculates the posterior probability of a class. This is the output of the Bayes theorem formula. The classification of a given instance is based on calling this method repeatedly, once for each class. A possible optimization here is to avoid the method call `getProbability(i)` and the subsequent division, since as we already mentioned, the evaluation of the evidence (the term *p(Y)* in the Bayes theorem formula) isn't required for classification. The method itself—`getProbability(Instance)`—could be ignored; we included it here for completeness.

   In the method `getProbability(Concept, Instance)` we check whether we've seen the particular concept. If we used the `NaiveBayes` class for classifying with respect to a fixed set of concepts, this step wouldn't be necessary. But recall that we used the same class in chapter 2 in the context of learning from the user's clicks, where it was possible to pass a concept that wasn't included in the training set.

❾ This method calculates the prior probability *p(X)* of class X, as the ratio of instances that correspond in that class over the total number of instances in the training set.

❿ The `classify(Instance)` method classifies the given instance by returning the class with the highest probability of occurrence. You could use an array to store the values of the probability for each class. Then you could sort them and return the best three (or five) classes in the case of multiclass classification. In a real-world system, this would be preferable, because the probabilities may be very close to each other and the application may show the end-user a range of choices for selection, rather than assign automatically one.

A GENERAL-PURPOSE EMAIL CLASSIFIER

Now, let's take a closer look at the `EmailClassifier` class itself. Listing 5.5 shows the code, except for the definition of instance variables, the constructor, and the classify methods, which are trivial. Since we've just explained the `NaiveBayes` classifier in detail, we'll focus on the overriding methods of that class.

> **Listing 5.5 An email classifier based on the general-purpose `NaiveBayes` class**

```
public class EmailClassifier extends NaiveBayes {

    public boolean train() {                           ❶
        if( emailDataset.getSize() == 0) {
            System.out.println("Can't train classifier –
            training dataset is empty.");
            return false;
        }
        for(String attrName : getTset().getAttributeNameSet()) {
```

```
            trainOnAttribute(attrName);
        }
        super.train();

        return true;
    }

    protected void calculateConditionalProbabilities() {

        p = new HashMap<Concept, Map<Attribute, AttributeValue>>();

        for (Instance i : tSet.getInstances().values()) {

            Attribute a = i.getAtrributes()[0];                    ❷

            Map<Attribute, AttributeValue> aMap = p.get(i.getConcept());
            if ( aMap == null ) {
                aMap = new HashMap<Attribute, AttributeValue>();
                p.put(i.getConcept(), aMap);
            }

            AttributeValue bestAttributeValue =
➡   findBestAttributeValue(aMap, a)                    ❸

            if (bestAttributeValue != null ) {
                bestAttributeValue.count();
            } else {
                AttributeValue aV = new AttributeValue(a.getValue());
                aMap.put(a, aV);
            }
        }
    }

public double getProbability(Instance i, Concept c) {
    double cP=1;
    for (Attribute a : i.getAtrributes()) {

      if ( a != null && attributeList.contains(a.getName()) ) {

        Map<Attribute, AttributeValue> aMap = p.get(c);
        Attribute bestAttributeValue = findBestAttributeValue (aMap, a);
        if (bestAttributeValue == null) {
          cP *= ((double) 1 / (tSet.getSize()+1));           ❹
        } else {
          cP *= (double)(bestAttributeValue.getCount()/conceptPriors.get(c));
        }
      }
    }
    return (cP == 1) ? (double)1/tSet.getNumberOfConcepts() : cP;
}
private Attribute findBestAttributeValue(Map<Attribute,
➡  AttributeValue> aMap, Attribute a) {

    JaccardCoefficient jaccardCoeff = new JaccardCoefficient();        ❺

    String aValue = (String)a.getValue();
    String[] aTerms = aValue.split(" ");
    Attribute bestMatch = null;
    double bestSim = 0.0;
```

```
    for(Attribute attr : aMap.keySet()) {
      String attrValue = (String)attr.getValue();
      String[] attrTerms = attrValue.split(" ");
      double sim = jaccardCoeff.similarity(aTerms, attrTerms);
      if( sim > jaccardThreshold && sim > bestSim) {          ❻
          bestSim = sim;
          bestMatch = attr;
      }
    }
  }
  return bestMatch;
 }
}
```

❶ The purpose of this method is to make sure that we loaded some training data, to set the appropriate training attributes from the training dataset, and to invoke the `train()` method of the `NaiveBayes` class for the actual training of the classifier.

❷ This statement is true only for this specific implementation. In general, you'd have more than one attribute. One of the to-do items asks you to explore the email classification case by introducing more attributes. If you work on that, you must revisit this part of the implementation.

❸ This step is needed because we're using a pure-text representation for our emails. It's a general technique that you can employ when you deal with text. In our implementation, the only attribute that we use takes its value from the string concatenation of the email's subject and body; don't forget that this was processed by our custom analyzer in order to reduce the noise and extract as much information as possible. If we consider strict string equality between attribute values, every email from our sample dataset will have its own attribute value. Instead, we consider two attribute values to be equivalent if they match according to the algorithm of the `findBestAttribute-Value` method

❹ Our estimate, in the case of attribute values that haven't been encountered before, is the same as in the `NaiveBayes` class. We assign an arbitrary conditional probability that's equal to the inverse of the number of instances in the training set plus one. Don't underestimate the impact of this approximation in the classification results, especially when the training set isn't large. Remember that this is the conditional probability of encountering a particular attribute value. In certain cases, these values are provided by human domain experts who use their experience to create an estimate that can be larger (or smaller) than the estimate that's produced based on the size of the training set. You could substitute this estimate with a small, constant number (typically a small number such as 10^{-4} or 10^{-5} would serve you well) and observe its impact on the results of the classification.

❺ You may recall the Jaccard coefficient from chapter 3 (the "To do" section) or chapter 4 (it's used in the ROCK implementation). It's a similarity metric based on the ratio of the size of the intersection over the size of the union between two sets. In this case, the two sets are the tokens that result from splitting the attribute values into individual terms. You could use one of the many other similarity metrics that we've encountered so far. It would be instructive to use the `CosineSimilarity` class instead of the `JaccardCoefficient` class and compare the results of classification.

6 The `jaccardThreshold` is an instance variable, and it has associated get and set methods. Its default value is set to 0.25, but you can change it to whatever value you like on the fly. To set it equal to 0.3 from the BeanShell environment, you can execute the following command: `emailFilter.setJaccardCoefficient(0.3);`. This is the minimum value of similarity that we want the two attribute values to have before we consider them equivalent.

That's it! We've covered the implementation of a probabilistic email classifier. We've demonstrated the capabilities of our classifier only for filtering spam email. So, let's present its use for the general (multiclass) case. Listing 5.6 shows the necessary steps. The only difference is the invocation of the method `setBinary(false)` of the `Email-Dataset` class. That's because the different classes (or email categories, if you prefer) are assigned during the construction of our dataset. The classifier doesn't treat the binary and the multiclass cases differently.

> **Listing 5.6 Loading the email training set and classifying the emails**

```
EmailDataset trainEmailDS = EmailData.createTrainingDataset();

trainEmailDS.setBinary(false);    ←── Use all email categories

EmailClassifier emailFilter = new EmailClassifier(trainEmailDS, 10);

emailFilter.train();              Test by classifying
                                  a few emails
emailFilter.sample();         ←──┘
```

The results are shown in figure 5.5, where you can see that only one of the emails (usa-01) has been misclassified. You can interpret the probabilities as a measure of confidence that the email belongs in a particular class. In a real application of multiclass classification, if the confidence level is below a certain level (say, 0.7) the system would select the top three or five classes and present them as candidates to the end user. These kinds of human-in-the-loop workflow designs are common in intelligent applications, and are actually required in order to continuously improve the performance of the classifier.

As we mentioned, a real email filter involves much more than a probabilistic classifier. The next section will provide a rule engine implementation, which is a good complementary technique to a probabilistic classifier. Many features of good spam filters rely on rules, such as whitelists, blacklists, collaborative spam identification databases, and so forth.

In summary, the `NaiveBayes` classifier can be used to filter out spam emails from your legitimate emails, and it can also be used to categorize your emails into several categories of your choice. Of course, everything that we said about emails can be applied to any other document from which you can obtain its textual representation—Microsoft Word documents, XML documents, HTML documents from websites, PDF documents, and so on.

```
*** Classifying instance: biz-01.html
P(WORLD|biz-01.html) = 0.085106382978723
P(BIZ|biz-01.html) = 0.765957446808511
P(USA|biz-01.html) = 0.063829787234043
P(SPAM|biz-01.html) = 0.042553191489362
P(SPORT|biz-01.html) = 0.042553191489362
Classified biz-01.html as BIZ

*** Classifying instance: sport-01.html
P(WORLD|sport-01.html) = 0.121212121212121
P(BIZ|sport-01.html) = 0.181818181818182
P(USA|sport-01.html) = 0.090909090909091
P(SPAM|sport-01.html) = 0.060606060606061
P(SPORT|sport-01.html) = 0.545454545454546
Classified sport-01.html as SPORT

*** Classifying instance: usa-01.html
P(WORLD|usa-01.html) = 0.235294117647059
P(BIZ|usa-01.html) = 0.352941176470588
P(USA|usa-01.html) = 0.176470588235294
P(SPAM|usa-01.html) = 0.117647058823529
P(SPORT|usa-01.html) = 0.117647058823529
Classified usa-01.html as BIZ

*** Classifying instance: world-01.html
P(WORLD|world-01.html) = 0.805970149253731
P(BIZ|world-01.html) = 0.089552238805970
P(USA|world-01.html) = 0.044776119402985
P(SPAM|world-01.html) = 0.029850746268657
P(SPORT|world-01.html) = 0.029850746268657
Classified world-01.html as WORLD

*** Classifying instance: spam-biz-01.html
P(WORLD|spam-biz-01.html) = 0.121212121212121
P(BIZ|spam-biz-01.html) = 0.181818181818182
P(USA|spam-biz-01.html) = 0.090909090909091
```

Figure 5.5   Using the `EmailClassifier` for multiclass classification of emails

5.3.2   *Rule-based classification*

In this section, we'll examine a different approach to classification: *rule-based classification*. So what are rules? And how are they different from a Bayesian classifier? To answer these two questions, let's look at the larger picture of programming paradigms. There are many programming paradigms in use today. A typical Java/J2EE application is characterized by elements of imperative programming, object-oriented programming, and perhaps aspect-oriented programming. In particular, imperative programming means that we tell the computer *what* to do and *how* to do it. This is the predominant paradigm that we use to write our software. But there's another programming paradigm called *declarative* programming that puts more emphasis on what to do and delegates the "how" to a runtime engine.

Rule-based reasoning is an example of declarative programming. A rule-based system consists of *facts*, a *rule engine*, and (of course) *rules*. The facts are merely data about the world. The rules are conditional statements that tell us what to do when the data satisfies certain conditions; in other words they're equivalent to if-then programming clauses. The rule engine is responsible for executing the rules according to the facts. A rule engine, when compared to probabilistic classifiers, differs significantly in the way that it captures and represents knowledge. In the case of a probabilistic classifier, such as the naïve Bayes classifier that we examined in the previous section, knowledge is represented in terms of the prior probabilities of the concepts and the conditional probabilities of occurrence that we obtain from the training set. There's no manual intervention for accumulating that knowledge (the probabilities); given an arbitrary, well-formed training set, the classifier will extract the information content that it needs (knowledge) in order to perform its classification tasks. A rule-based classifier captures the knowledge in the form of the rules, so the rules are the knowledge of the system, which begets the question of how do we get these rules? The rules are entered into the system manually or semiannually by providing convenient workflow screens that human experts can use to capture rules.

There are two basic modes of operation for a rule-based system. The first is *forward chaining* and is data-driven, in the sense that we're given the data and want to find what rules we should apply to them. The second is *backward chaining* and is goal-driven, in the sense that we start with a goal that the engine tries to satisfy (if possible). We won't cover backward chaining in this book; we'll only say that programming languages such as Prolog and ECLiPSe support backward chaining (for details see Russell and Norvig).

THE DROOLS RULE ENGINE

There are two Java-based rule engine implementations that are production ready. The first is called *Jess* and was written in the Sandia National Laboratories. At the time of this writing (Spring 2008), it's in its seventh release (7.1) so it's fairly stable. It's free for academic use but not free for commercial use. (For details on the Jess rule engine see Friedman-Hill.) The second rule engine implementation is called *Drools* (http://www.jboss.org/drools/) but you may also hear people referring to it as *JBoss Rules*. JBoss is a well-known middleware open source project, now under the auspices of Red Hat. Drools is a robust rule engine with ample documentation and a fairly liberal open source license (Apache 2.0), which means that you can use it in your application for free. We've used Drools with great success over the past four years. In our opinion, in the Java world, Drools is the rule engine of choice.

The Drools rule engine consists of two main modules: a pattern-matching module and an agenda module. The pattern-matching module is responsible for identifying what rules are matched by the facts. Once these rules have been identified, they're placed in the agenda module. Figure 5.6 shows the basic elements of the Drools engine. In order to perform the pattern matching, Drools implements and extends the Rete algorithm—the word *rete* means "network" in Latin and is pronounced "re-tay" in

Europe and "ree-tee" in the USA. The
Rete algorithm was designed by Charles
Forgy in 1974; it was and remains, in its
many incarnations, one of the most efficient and successful pattern-matching
algorithms. The Drools implementation of Rete is called *ReteOO*, to indicate
that Drools has an improved implementation of the Rete algorithm that's most
suitable for object-oriented software.

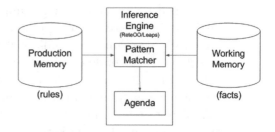

**Figure 5.6   The basic elements of the Drools rule
engine system (source: Drools online)**

The Rete algorithm exchanges memory consumption for processing speed; its theoretical performance is independent of the number of rules in the system. But in practice,
as the number of rules increases, we're bound to encounter a well-known problem of
AI systems, the so-called *utility problem*. We'll discuss more about this in section 5.7. We
won't go into the details of the Rete algorithm itself; if you're interested in its implementation then the Drools source code and documentation, along with the references
at the end of this chapter, should suffice for a thorough understanding of its inner workings. In addition, *Jess in Action* by Dr. Ernest J. Friedman-Hill and published by Manning
Publications provides a detailed explanation of how the Rete algorithm works (in particular, see chapter 8).

After this brief introduction to rule engines, we're ready to describe the use of the
Drools library in our task of filtering the emails that are spam. In particular, let's see
how we can write rules. The Drools engine comes with a scripting (non-XML) language that's easy to learn; it's so easy to learn that you could expose it directly to the
end users of your application! Let's take a look.

Listing 5.7   A simple set of rules for email spam filtering

```
package demo;
import iweb2.ch5.classification.data.Email;
import iweb2.ch5.classification.rules.ClassificationResult;

global ClassificationResult classificationResult;

rule "Tests for viagra in subject"
when
   Email( $s : subject )
   eval( classificationResult.isSimilar($s, "viagra" ) )
then
   classificationResult.setSpamEmail(true);
end

rule "Tests for 'drugs' in subject"
when
  Email( $s : subject )
    eval( classificationResult.isSimilar($s, "drugs" ) )
then
   classificationResult.setSpamEmail(true);
end
```

**Rule for identifying
"Viagra" in email
subject**

**Rule for identifying
"drugs" in email
subject**

Listing 5.7 shows the content of spamRules.drl, which contains two simple rules. The content is almost self-explanatory; you can find this file in the subdirectory `C:\iWeb2\data\ch05`. As we'll see shortly, rules are provided to Drools in packages, so the first thing we do is give the name of the package that these rules belong to—demo. The `import` statements inform the rule execution engine about the class definitions of the objects that we're going to use in our rules—the classes `Email` and `ClassificationResult`. The `global` statement allows us to access the object identified by `classificationResult`. This is equivalent to declaring the `classification-Result` as a global variable within our rules. So what do the rules mean?

Our first rule is called Tests for "viagra" in subject. As promised, it checks whether the variable `subject` of an `Email` object contains the word *viagra*. If that condition is met it sets the `isSpamEmail` variable of the `ClassificationResult` to `true`. Similarly our second rule, which is called Tests for 'drugs' in subject, checks whether the variable `subject` of an `Email` object contains the word *drugs*. If that condition is met it sets the `isSpamEmail` variable of the `ClassificationResult` to `true`.

We don't insinuate that these conditions are totally appropriate to characterize an email as spam; we're merely using them to illustrate the structure of the Drools file. As you can see, the general structure of defining a rule in Drools is straightforward:

```
rule "Put the name of your rule here"
when
    <Put here your conditions>
then
    <Put here the actions that must be taken
      when the above conditions are satisfied>
end
```

You can include more than one condition, and you can include more than one action. We don't think it can get simpler than that! Notwithstanding the simplicity, and ensuing beauty, of the Drools rule language, we believe that the real strength of the engine is its support for objects. Note that the real evaluation of the condition in both rules happens inside the method `isSimilar` of the class `ClassificationResult`. We can invoke quite complicated evaluations in an objected-oriented fashion.

Now, let's see these rules in action. The first line of listing 5.8 loads the emails from the testing dataset; we used it before in listing 5.2. So, let's look at each one of the other steps in this listing.

Listing 5.8 Employing the email spam rules on a set of data

```
EmailDataset ds = EmailData.createTestDataset();

EmailRuleClassifier classifier =
    new EmailRuleClassifier("c:/iWeb2/data/ch05/spamRules.drl");   ❶

classifier.train();        ❷

classifier.run(ds,"Expecting one spam email.  :-(");        ❸
```

① We construct an email classifier that uses rules and is aptly encapsulated in the `Email-RuleClassifier` class. Note that the only argument in the constructor of that class is the Drools file that we described in listing 5.7.

② We ask the classifier to "train" itself. Unlike the script in listing 5.1, where we trained our probabilistic classifier, here we didn't create a training dataset. We never passed the reference of the dataset in the constructor of the classifier; we only passed the name of the Drools file. Why? In the probabilistic approach, we're trying to infer the knowledge that's contained in the training set. In the case of rule-based systems, the rules are the knowledge. The "training" part for the rule-based system involves merely loading the rules from the file.

③ We "apply" the rules on the test dataset by passing the dataset information and a descriptive message. Although the prevailing expression among business people and end users of rule-based systems is "applying the rules," in reality, the execution of the Rete algorithm more resembles the filtering of data (the facts) through a funnel. That funnel is made of a net (hence the term *rete*) of nodes. As each fact trickles down this funnel, it passes a number of tests (the conditions of the rules), and when it reaches the bottom, we know exactly what rule should be triggered by that fact. For a detailed description of the Rete structure, see Doorenbos.

The results of executing listing 5.8 are shown in figure 5.7. The spam email entry that corresponds to the spam-biz-01.html file triggered the classifier because its subject contains the word "drugs" as the spam rule in listing 5.7 required. The rule is fired because its conditions have been met.

```
bsh % classifier.run(ds,"Expecting one spam email.  :-(");

Expecting one spam email.  :-(
_____

Classifying email: world-01.html ...
Rules classified email: world-01.html as: NOT-SPAM

Classifying email: spam-biz-01.html ...
Invoked ClassificationResult.setSpamEmail(true)
Rules classified email: spam-biz-01.html as: SPAM

Classifying email: sport-01.html ...
Rules classified email: sport-01.html as: NOT-SPAM

Classifying email: usa-01.html ...
Rules classified email: usa-01.html as: NOT-SPAM

Classifying email: biz-01.html ...
Rules classified email: biz-01.html as: NOT-SPAM
_____
```

Figure 5.7   Identifying spam email spam-biz-01 based on the rules of listing 5.7

A CLOSER LOOK AT THE IMPLEMENTATION

Now that you're familiar with the use of the Drools engine, let's take a closer look at the wrapper classes we used in listings 5.7 (the rule definition file) and 5.8. If you think about it, we were able to pack an enormous amount of functional capability in just a few lines of code. Let's see what code allowed us to abstract the use of a rules engine into just three simple steps. We'll start from the centerpiece of that implementation, the class `RuleEngine`, shown in listing 5.9.

Listing 5.9   `RuleEngine`: building a rule engine based on the Drools library

```java
public class RuleEngine {

  private RuleBase rules;

  public RuleEngine(String rulesFile) throws RuleEngineException {
    try {
      Reader source = new InputStreamReader(
          new BufferedInputStream(new FileInputStream(rulesFile)));

      Properties properties = new Properties();
      properties.setProperty("drools.dialect.java.compiler", "JANINO" );

      PackageBuilderConfiguration cfg =
      new PackageBuilderConfiguration( properties );

      PackageBuilder builder = new PackageBuilder(cfg);

      builder.addPackageFromDrl(source);

      Package pkg = builder.getPackage();

      rules = RuleBaseFactory.newRuleBase();

      rules.addPackage(pkg);

    } catch (Exception e) {
      throw new RuleEngineException(e);
    }
  }

  public void executeRules(ClassificationResult classificationResult,
  Email email ) {

    WorkingMemory workingMemory = rules.newStatefulSession();

    workingMemory.setGlobal("classificationResult",
      classificationResult);

    workingMemory.insert(email);

    workingMemory.fireAllRules();
  }
}
```

- **❶** Determine runtime compiler
- **❷** Contains our rules
- **❸** Runtime container for rules
- **❹** Stateful Working-Memory
- **❺** Insert fact in working memory
- **❻** Execute all rules

The creation of a Drools rule engine has two parts: *authoring* and *runtime*. The authoring part begins with the parsing of the Drools file—the file with the .drl extension. The parser checks the grammatical consistency of the Drools file and creates an intermediate *abstract syntax tree (AST)*. For this, Drools uses the lexical parser provided by the open source project ANTLR—Another Tool for Language Recognition (http://www.antlr.org/). Valid rules are loaded in serialized objects of the class `Package`; a `Package` instance is a self-contained deployable unit that contains one or more rules. The runtime part of a Drools engine is based on the class `RuleBase`. `Package` instances can be added to or removed from a `RuleBase` instance at any time.

Let's examine each step to create and use a Drools rule engine, as shown in listing 5.9:

❶ After creating a reference to the file that contains the rules, we create a `Properties` instance and give a value to the property `drools.dialect.java.compiler`. What's this property? And what does the value `JANINO` mean? You can incorporate Java code straight into the Drools rule files. This property determines the runtime compiler that we want Drools to use in order to compile Java code. Janino is the name of an embedded Java compiler that's included in the Drools distribution under the BSD license (http://www.janino.net/).

To complete the authoring part, we need to create an instance of the `Package-Builder` class, which in turn will create instances of the class `Package`. We use the auxiliary `PackageBuilderConfiguration` class for the configuration of our package builder. This class has default values, which you can change through the appropriate `set` methods or, as we do here, on first use via property settings. In this case, we pass only a single property, but we could've provided much more information. At the heart of the settings is the `ChainedProperties` class, which searches a number of locations looking for `drools.packagebuilder.conf` files. In order of precedence, those locations are system properties, a user-defined file in system properties, the user's home directory, the working directory, and various META-INF locations. The `PackageBuilderConfiguration` handles the registry of `AccumulateFunctions`, registry of `Dialects`, and the main `ClassLoader`. For more details, consult the Drools online documentation at http://downloads.jboss.com/drools/docs/4.0.7.19894.GA/html_single/index.html-d0e766.

❷ With the `PackageBuilder` in our disposal, we can build packages that contain the rules. We pass the reference of the file to the `addPackageFromDrl` method and immediately call the `getPackage` method of our builder. Our rules are ready to use now!

❸ This is our first step in building the runtime part of the engine. A `RuleBase` can have one or more `Packages`. A `RuleBase` can instantiate one or more `WorkingMemory` instances at any time; a weak reference is maintained unless configured otherwise. The `WorkingMemory` class consists of a number of subcomponents; for details, consult the Drools online documentation.

❹ The class `StatefulSession` extends the `WorkingMemory` class. It adds asynchronous methods for inserting, updating, and firing rules, as well as a `dispose()` method. The `RuleBase` retains a reference to each `StatefulSession` instance that it creates, in order to update them when new rules are added. The `dispose()` method is needed to release the `StatefulSession` reference from the `RuleBase` in order to avoid memory leaks.

In the Drools file, shown in listing 5.7, we used the `global` statement in order to access the object identified by `classificationResult`. This is equivalent to declaring the `classificationResult` as a global variable within our rules. But that won't work unless we also call the `setGlobal` method on the `WorkingMemory` instance. The argument of this method must match exactly the entry in the Drools rules file.

❺ We use the `insert` method to add facts into the `WorkingMemory` instance. When we insert a fact, the Drools engine will match it against all the rules. This means that all the work is done during insertion, but no rules are executed until you call `fireAll-Rules()`, which we do in the next step.

❻ This invokes the rule execution. You shouldn't call `fireAllRules()` before you've finished inserting all your facts. The crucial matching phase happens during the insertion of the facts, as mentioned previously. So, you don't want to execute the rules without matching all the facts against the rules first.

That's pretty much everything that you need to do in order to build a rule engine with Drools. Now let's see how the `EmailRuleClassifier` class delegates its actions to the `RuleEngine` in order to classify the emails. Our implementation of the `RuleEngine` is specific to emails; we invite you to create a generalization that uses the `Instance` interface in one of our to-do items for this chapter. Listing 5.10 shows the code from the `EmailRuleClassifier` class, except for the `main` method, which contains more or less the same code as listing 5.8.

Listing 5.10 A Drools-based rule engine that detects spam email

```
public class EmailRuleClassifier {

    private String ruleFilename;
    private RuleEngine re;
    private Concept spam;
    private Concept notSpam;

    public EmailRuleClassifier(String ruleFilename) {
        this.ruleFilename = ruleFilename;
    }

    public void train() {
        re = new RuleEngine(ruleFilename);           ❶

        spam = new BaseConcept("SPAM");              ❷
        notSpam = new BaseConcept("NOT-SPAM");
    }

    public Concept classify(Email email) {
        ClassificationResult result = new ClassificationResult();     ❸

        re.executeRules(result, email);       ❹

        if( result.isSpamEmail() ) {       ❺
            return spam;
        } else {
            return notSpam;
        }
    }

    public void run(EmailDataset ds, String msg) {
        System.out.println("\n");
        System.out.println(msg);
```

```
      System.out.println("_____");
        for(Email email : ds.getEmails() ) {      ⑥

          Concept c = classify(email);

          System.out.println("Email: "+
➡      email.getId()+" classified as: "+c.getName());
        }

        System.out.println("_____");
      }
  }
```

❶ First we need to create a RuleEngine instance, so that we can delegate the application of the rules. We pass the name of the file that contains the rules and let the Rule-Engine do the heavy lifting.

❷ These are two auxiliary variables used by the classify method. Since they're constant in our case, no matter what the rules or the emails are, we treat them as instance variables. It's possible that your implementation of the ClassificationResult class is responsible for identifying the right concept from a more elaborate data structure of concepts (for example, an ontology).

❸ This class encapsulates two important things. It includes the tests of the rule conditions (through the isSimilar method) as well as the actions of the rules (through the setSpamEmail method). We could have created different objects to encapsulate the conditions and the actions. If your conditions or actions involve algorithmically difficult implementations, it's better to separate the implementations and create a clean separation of these two parts.

❹ This is where we delegate the application of the rules to the RuleEngine. We reviewed this method in listing 5.9.

❺ We again use the ClassificationResult instance to obtain the information that was created as a result of the (fired) rules actions. That information could have been recorded in a persistent medium (such as a database record or a file); in our simple case, we use the ClassificationResult class as the carrier of all related activity.

❻ This method helps us classify all the emails in our dataset at once. Note that we could have passed the dataset itself to the classify method and overridden the executeRule method in the RuleEngine class, so that we load into the working memory all the emails at once. But note that, in the context of a rule-based system, the classification of an email as spam doesn't depend on whether other emails are spam.

CONFLICT RESOLUTION

The last point is related to (but distinct from) another interesting subject. What happens if the action of rule A modifies fact X, which activates rule B, which then modifies fact Y and triggers rule A again? You can fall into infinite loops unless there's a way to stop recursion. What if you have a rule that classifies an email as spam and another one that classifies the same email as not spam? In other words, what happens when there is conflict between two or more rules? In the end of the executeRule method, we must have an answer, so what's it going to be?

Fortunately for us, Drools provides answers to these problems, as well as many others, through rule attributes. The solution to the first problem is provided by the rule attribute *no-loop*; the solution to the second problem is provided by the rule attribute *salience*. Rule attributes allow us to influence the behavior of the rules in a declarative way—in the Drools rule file. Some are quite simple, such as salience, while others are rather elaborate, such as *ruleflow-group*. Consult the official Drools documentation, as well as the source code, to obtain a thorough understanding of each attribute.

Let's see now how we can employ salience to provide *conflict resolution*. Listing 5.11 shows a Drools rule file that contains three rules. This time there's going to be a conflict between the rules for certain emails, because the conditions of more than one rule will be satisfied simultaneously. The file looks much the same as the first Drools rule file that we showed in listing 5.7, but now we've introduced the attribute salience, with an integer value, for each rule.

> **Listing 5.11 A simple set of email spam rules for filtering (with conflicts)**

```
package demo;

import iweb2.ch5.classification.data.Email;
import iweb2.ch5.classification.rules.ClassificationResult;

global ClassificationResult classificationResult;

rule "Rule 1: Tests for viagra in subject"          ◁── Rule for identifying
salience 100                                              "Viagra" in email subject
when
   email: Email( $s : subject )
   eval( classificationResult.isSimilar($s, "viagra" ) )
then
   email.setRuleFired(1);
   classificationResult.setSpamEmail(true);
end

rule "Rule 2: Tests for 'drugs' in subject"         ◁── Rule for identifying
salience 100                                              "drugs" in email subject
when
   email: Email( $s : subject )
   eval( classificationResult.isSimilar($s, "drugs" ) )
then
    email.setRuleFired(2);
    classificationResult.setSpamEmail(true);
end                                                      Could conflict
                                                         with A or B
rule "Rule 3: Tests for known sender address"       ◁──
salience 10
when
   email: Email( $sender : from )
   eval( classificationResult.isSimilar($sender, "friend@senderhost" ) )
then
   email.setRuleFired(3);
   classificationResult.setSpamEmail(false);
end
```

The email that we're going to create from the document spam-biz-01.html contains the word "drugs" in its subject, so it fires rule 2. At the same time, it was sent by user friend@senderhost, so we must fire rule 3. According to rule 2, this is a spam email; according to rule 3, this is a legitimate email. In other words, rule 2 and rule 3 are in conflict for that specific email (our fact) and we need a conflict resolution. The attribute salience comes to our rescue!

The term *salience* in the context of the rule-based systems originated probably from *semiotics*, which is the study of signs—the Greek word σημειωση means a sign, a symbol, or a note depending on the context. In semiotics, salience refers to the relative importance of a sign with respect to the plethora of signs that a person receives at any given moment. Similarly, in the context of our rules, the salience attribute refers to the prominence of a rule over other rules, when all rules apply on a particular fact or set of facts. The lower the salience of a rule is, the higher the prominence of the rule. In essence, the prominence of a rule is reflected in the order of execution. If rule X has lower salience than rule Y, rule Y will execute first and rule X last. Wherever and whenever there's a conflict between the actions of Y and X, the actions of X will override the actions of Y.

Let's see all this in action. Listing 5.12 shows a script that's almost identical to the one in listing 5.8, except that we now use the rules with the conflicts.

Listing 5.12   Resolving a conflict of email rules using attribute salience

```
EmailDataset ds = EmailData.createTestDataset();

EmailRuleClassifier classifier = new EmailRuleClassifier(
➥   "c:/iWeb2/data/ch05/spamRulesWithConflict.drl");

classifier.train();

classifier.run(ds," Hurray! No spam emails here.");
```

Figure 5.8 present the results of the execution. As you can see, both rule 2 and rule 3 fired for the email spam-biz-01.html. But rule 2 (salience=100) fired first and rule 3 (salience=10) fired second and reset the email's flag to NOT-SPAM.

This is a simple example that allows you to see every step and understand the exact effect of introducing the salience rule attribute. The real value of rule-based systems is that they can do this efficiently with thousands of complicated rules and millions of facts, while allowing you to experiment with various conditions in a declarative manner rather than having to change your code. The mere idea of having to go through thousands of possibly nested if-then statements makes me shiver!

Now, we've completed our coverage of email classification. So far, you've learned how to classify a general text document using the probabilistic naïve Bayes algorithm and the Drools rule engine, the rule-based system of choice for Java. In the next section, we'll present additional classification algorithms, and to keep things interesting, we'll work in the context of a new example: *fraud detection*.

```
bsh % EmailDataset ds = EmailData.createTestDataset();
bsh % EmailRuleClassifier classifier = new EmailRuleClassifier(
å    "c:/iWeb2/data/ch05/spamRulesWithConflict.drl");

bsh % classifier.train();
bsh % classifier.run(ds," Hurray! No spam emails here.");

Hurray! No spam emails here.
```

```
Classifying email: world-01.html ...
Rules classified email: world-01.html as: NOT-SPAM

Classifying email: spam-biz-01.html ...
Invoked Email.setRuleFired(2), current value ruleFired=0,
emailId: spam-biz-01.html
Invoked ClassificationResult.setSpamEmail(true)
Invoked Email.setRuleFired(3), current value ruleFired=2,
emailId: spam-biz-01.html
Invoked ClassificationResult.setSpamEmail(false)
Rules classified email: spam-biz-01.html as: NOT-SPAM

Classifying email: sport-01.html ...
Rules classified email: sport-01.html as: NOT-SPAM

Classifying email: usa-01.html ...
Rules classified email: usa-01.html as: NOT-SPAM

Classifying email: biz-01.html ...
Rules classified email: biz-01.html as: NOT-SPAM
```

Figure 5.8   Resolving rule conflicts by using the salience rule attributes

5.4   *Fraud detection with neural networks*

Fraud is prevalent in our electronic world. It ranges from insurance fraud to internet auction fraud and from fraudulent benefit application forms to telecommunications fraud. If you do anything over the internet that engages more than one person or legal entity, the ability to identify when someone didn't play by the rules is valuable. In this section, we'll consider the use case of fraudulent purchasing transactions. We'll see that we can employ classification algorithms to distinguish the fraudulent transactions from the legitimate purchases.

5.4.1   *A use case of fraud detection in transactional data*

Our sample data will be artificial—you wouldn't want to see your transactions printed in a technical book, would you? Nonetheless, we provide facilities to make the data somewhat realistic and we do account for effects that you'd see on real data. The scenario should be familiar to everyone. You work for a large bank that issues credit cards and you want to ensure that your system will be able to detect fraudulent behavior quickly, if not in real-time, so that the proper mechanisms of protecting your client can be activated. We'll consider the following typical attributes that can be associated with a transaction:

- The description of the transaction
- The amount of transaction
- The location of the transaction

We've created a set of legitimate transaction descriptions, which we included in a file called descriptions.txt, and a set of what we'll consider to be fraudulent transaction descriptions, which we included in a file called fraud-descriptions.txt. You can find both files in the directory data\ch05\fraud. We have five different profiles of users, because spending habits vary on the basis of many factors; a transaction of 3,000 USD in one account can be suspect of fraud but it could be legitimate for another account. Five profiles are sufficient to make the point, but of course, in the real world there are many more spending profiles. The transaction amount is drawn from a Gaussian distribution and it's determined on the basis of the average value of transaction amounts for that profile and its standard deviation. If you don't know what Gaussian distribution is or the standard deviations are, see appendix A.

Now is a good time to let you know about an intriguing property of large aggregates of transactional data. If you aggregate transactional data from various sources and look at how frequently the first significant digit of these numbers will be equal to 1, you'll realize that it's much higher than you would've anticipated. Every normal person (that means not a mathematician) will tell you that since I have nine digits, the likelihood of seeing the digit 1 is 11.1%, the digit 2 is 11.1%, and so on. Right? Wrong! *Benford's law* tells us that the probability should be logarithmic rather than uniform. It turns out that the probability for the first significant digit to be equal to 1 is about 30%. There's an interesting story behind this powerful statistical fact, which in 1995 was successfully employed by the district attorney's office in Brooklyn to detect fraud in seven New York companies (see Hill).

Back to the description of our transactional data: we simplify the location of a transaction by providing Euclidean (x,y) coordinates. A real system would probably use GPS data to precisely describe the locations of the transactions. In our case, plain (x,y) coordinates will serve us equally well without complicating the use case unnecessarily. The (x,y) coordinates of a transaction are drawn from a uniform distribution between a minimum and a maximum value. In other words, for each profile, we set a minimum and a maximum value for both X and Y, and a given transaction is assigned a random location that falls anywhere between these ranges of (x,y) coordinates with equal probability.

You can experiment with the code and generate your own data; you could add more profiles or more users and more transactions per user. The class TenUsers-Sample is the right place to start for that; you can find it in the package iweb2.ch5.usecase.fraud.util together with other auxiliary classes. The execution of the `main` method in that class generates two files; the first is called generated-training-txns.txt and the other is called generated-test-txns.txt. These files contain the training and the testing data, respectively, as you may have guessed. In the folder `data\ch05\fraud` you'll find the data that we used to write this section; we called the files training-txns.txt and test-txns.txt. There are about 10,000 transactions available for training and about 1,000 transactions available for testing. Each transaction is specified by the following attribute values (in the listed order):

- The ID of the user
- The ID of the transaction
- The description of the transaction
- The amount of the transaction
- The x coordinate of the transaction
- The y coordinate of the transaction
- A Boolean variable that determines whether the transaction is fraudulent (true) or not (false)

Our goal is fairly straightforward. We want to build a classifier that can learn how to identify a fraudulent transaction based on the transactions in the training dataset. Once we've built (trained) our classifier, we want to test it against the testing data, which was drawn from the same statistical distributions. In the following sections, we're going to achieve our goal by utilizing two different classification systems. The first will be based on a neural network algorithm; the second will be based on a decision tree. We briefly discussed both of these classification approaches in our introductory overview of section 5.2, and it's time to have a closer look at them.

5.4.2 *Neural networks overview*

In this section, we'll present the central ideas behind neural networks in a nutshell. The subject of neural networks is vast. We'll present what's known as *computational neural networks*—we avoid the term *artificial* intentionally since there've been implementations of neural networks that are hardware-based (such as Maier et al.). Our focus will be on software implementations of neural networks.

Generally speaking, a neural network consists of neuron nodes, or simply *neurons*, and links between neurons that are called *synapses* or *links*. Some nodes are responsible for simply transmitting the data into and out of the network, while others are responsible for processing the data. The former nodes provide the I/O capabilities of the network. They're aptly called the *input* and *output* layers depending on whether they insert data into the network or export the processed data out of the network, respectively. All other nodes are called *hidden* nodes and don't interact with the "outside" world.

A typical neural network is shown in figure 5.9. For a given input, denoted here with the vector {x1, x2, x3}, a neural network produces output that's a function of the input and the network parameters. The output of the network in the figure is denoted as y;

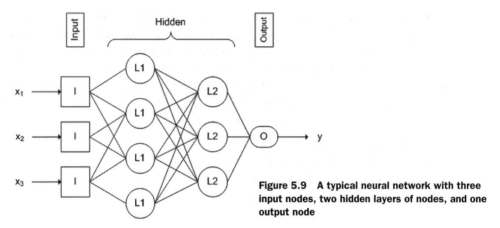

Figure 5.9   A typical neural network with three input nodes, two hidden layers of nodes, and one output node

in general, the output could be a vector itself, not just a single value. You can think of the initial values {x1, x2, x3} propagating from left to right. Each node collects its input values and calculates its output values. The final value (y) depends on the initial values {x1, x2, x3} and the way that these values propagate through the network.

The synapses connect the nodes, in the sense that information can be exchanged between any two nodes that are shown as linked with a synapse. The exchange of information is regulated by a parameter called the *weight* of the synapse, which, roughly speaking, indicates the importance of the connection between the two nodes. During the training phase of a neural network, the weights of the synapses are continuously evaluated and modified according the values of the training dataset.

The graphical representation of a neural network is common. A lot can be said about a neural network by looking at such a graphical representation.

First, note that we've placed an arrow only in the links that place the variables in the input nodes and the one that provides us with the "answer"—the y value. If the nodes and the synapses form a *directed acyclic graph (DAG)*—a rule of thumb for this condition would be to check whether all the arrows point from left to right—then we say that we have a *feedforward* neural network. Otherwise, we say that we have a *feedback* neural network.

Second, note that we've arranged the nodes as vertical stacks, going from left to right. That's not necessary but is customary. We say that the nodes that belong to a given vertical stack belong to a given *layer*. Following this customary convention, we denoted the nodes of the first hidden layer as L1 nodes and the nodes of the second hidden layer as L2 nodes. The input layer nodes are denoted by I while the single node in the output layer is denoted by O.

Third, note that the input nodes don't connect to all the nodes of the first hidden layer. But every node in the first hidden layer connects to every node in the second hidden layer. When all the nodes of one layer connect to every node of the next layer, we say that the layers are *fully connected*.

These observations are a psychological preparation for the following mantra: We can fully define a neural network by identifying three essential elements (see McKay):

- The *neural network architecture*, which dictates the number of nodes in the network, the number of input and output nodes, and the synapses and their directionality
- The *activation rule*, which dictates the laws of direct interaction between the nodes
- The *learning rule*, which dictates the laws of indirect interaction between the nodes and the information that propagates through the network

All this flexibility in defining a neural network provides enormous potential, but at the same time renders the identification of the ideal neural network difficult in practice. We don't intend to provide a comprehensive introduction to neural networks in a few pages; it would be presumptuous on our part. In appendix E, you can find more references to the neural networks literature.

5.4.3 A neural network fraud detector at work

Let's now take the first steps toward using a neural network that can help us identify fraudulent transactions. Listing 5.13 shows you how to:

- Load a transaction dataset and calculate user statistics from it.
- Build the NNFraudClassifier, train it, and store it on the disk.
- Load an instance of the NNFraudClassifier from the disk and use it to classify transactions.
- Load a set of new transactions for testing our classifier with an instance of the class FraudErrorEstimator.

Listing 5.13 NNFraudClassifier: a neural network classifier for fraud detection

```
TransactionDataset ds = TransactionLoader.loadTrainingDataset();        ❶

ds.calculateUserStats();        ❷

NNFraudClassifier nnFraudClassifier = new NNFraudClassifier(ds);        ❸

nnFraudClassifier.setName("MyNeuralClassifier");

nnFraudClassifier.useDefaultAttributes();        ❹

nnFraudClassifier.setNTrainingIterations(10);        ❺

nnFraudClassifier.train();        ❻

nnFraudClassifier.save();        ❼

NNFraudClassifier nnClone = NNFraudClassifier
➥ .load(nnFraudClassifier.getName());        ❽

nnClone.classify("1");        ❾

nnClone.classify("305");

TransactionDataset testDS = TransactionLoader.loadTestDataset();        ❿

FraudErrorEstimator auditor = new FraudErrorEstimator(testDS, nnClone);        ⓫

auditor.run();
```

As you can see, by using our code, building and using a neural network based classifier is simple. Everything can be written down in a few steps. Let's examine the steps one by one:

❶ The transaction dataset from the file training-txns.txt is encapsulated by the class `TransactionDataset`. The code in the packages `iweb2.ch5.usecase.fraud.*` allows you to build your own dataset. We could have presented the transaction file itself and left the rest of the details out. But this is a practical book and going through the process of building your own dataset (and possibly extending what we give you) is what will help you model the data of your own application. Using the right data and using data properly is extremely important in intelligent applications.

❷ Once we obtain the raw transactions we collect statistical information about the spending habits of each user. Remember that in the real world you'll be collecting the data from some back-end or data warehouse system. We need to mine the data for information that'll help us set a baseline for each user. If user A limits her spending within the range of $20 to $200, while user B within the range of $100 to $5,000, a transaction of $2,000 means something completely different for these two users. This process belongs in the general category of data preprocessing that goes by the name *data normalization*.

Look at the class `UserStatistics`, which encapsulates the baseline of spending for each user. Three things are worth noticing. The first, which we already mentioned, is the bracketing of the spending. We identify the minimum and maximum amount for the *legitimate* transactions that we get from the training set. Second, pay attention to the collection of terms found in the descriptions of legitimate transactions. Third, notice that aside from the minimum and maximum coordinate locations, we also calculate the centroid of locations. The argument here is that most transactions take place around the area of residence, so if a new transaction comes in and its location is far away from the baseline—the location centroid that we have for that user—we should take that into account, although its contribution shouldn't be dominant since people do travel occasionally.

❸ The `NNFraudClassifier` is the main class for classifying transactions. This class isn't itself a neural network; it delegates the learning aspects of its function to the class `TransactionNN`. We'll examine both of these classes later in this section. We give a name to our classifier, so that we can refer to it later on. This name will be used for the construction of its file name (during serialization), so you should give a name that's descriptive of what you are doing.

❹ If you recall from our earlier examples (specifically the user clicks example in chapter 2), we need to identify which attributes of the transactions should be used for the classification. This is important in the real world because you typically have dozens of attributes in your transactions, if not hundreds. A certain amount of careful consideration is required in selecting the attributes that will be used for training. Irrelevant attributes can overwhelm the classifier and significantly hinder its ability to identify fraudulent transactions. This method automatically selects the three attributes of the transactions that we discussed: the amount, the location, and the description.

❺ This step determines how many times the data will propagate through the network. How large should the value be? It depends on your data and your network. As you'll see, 10 times works great in our example.

❻ Once we set up all the parameters of our neural network, we're ready to start the training process. At the end of this method call, our classifier is ready to be used and it has learned everything that it could learn from the given training dataset.

❼ We save our instance of the trained classifier on the disk. This is important because you may want to distribute the classifier to several systems or because the system that builds the classifier is different from the system that uses it. In addition, it's a safeguard against system failures. Imagine that you spent two hours training your classifier on 10 attributes and over a set of several million transactions, but all of a sudden, for whatever reason, the system goes down! What do you do? Trained classifiers should be treated like every other electronic document whose content can change—when additional training occurs over the period of its usage, copies of the classifier should be persisted; for example, they could be stored on the disk.

❽ This is how you can load a trained classifier. All you need to know is the filename of the classifier. Our implementation saves all serialized classifiers in the same location on the disk, which is determined by the constant `NNFraudClassifier.` `SERIALIZATION_PATH`. If that isn't convenient you can change that variable or change the related code and add more flexibility in your classifier storage capabilities.

❾ Here we go! We're ready to classify a couple of instances. The first transaction ID (1) corresponds to a legitimate transaction, the second transaction ID (305) corresponds to a fraudulent transaction. This is a sanity check, not a thorough evaluation of our classifier, because we selected transactions that the classifier has already encountered during its training.

❿ Let's create a dataset that contains transactions never before seen by the classifier. We call this the *testing dataset* and denote it as `testDS`.

⓫ `FraudErrorEstimator` is an auxiliary class that can help us assess the accuracy of our classifier. The assessment begins by invoking the method `run()`. At the end, it summarizes the number of transactions that were correctly classified and the number of transactions that were misclassified. In particular, it reports separately the number of valid transactions that the classifier thought were fraud, and the number of fraudulent transactions that the classifier thought were legitimate. There's a difference between these two types of misclassification, which we'll discuss in the next section.

Now, let's look at the results before we look deeper into the neural network code. Figure 5.10 shows the outcome from the execution of listing 5.13. Wow! How about that? The classifier seems to be perfect! Is it possible? Let's say that it's very unlikely. This is a classic trap for people who use black box libraries and don't grasp the inner working of classification algorithms. To understand this, open the test-txns.txt file with the text editor of your choice and replace every occurrence of the entry BLACK DIAMOND COFFEE with SOME DUDE.

```
bsh % nnClone.classify("1");
Transaction:
  >> 1:1:EXPEDIA TRAVEL:63.29:856.0:717.0:false

Assessment:
  >> This is a VALID_TXN
bsh % nnClone.classify("305");
Transaction:
  >> 1:305:CANADIAN PHARMACY:3978.57:52.0:70.0:true

Assessment:
  >> This is a FRAUD_TXN
bsh % TransactionDataset testDS =
å   TransactionLoader.loadTestDataset();

bsh % FraudErrorEstimator auditor =
å   new FraudErrorEstimator(testDS, nnClone);

bsh % auditor.run();
Total test dataset txns: 1100, Number of fraud txns:100
Classified correctly: 1100,
Misclassified valid txns: 0,
Misclassified fraud txns: 0
```

Figure 5.10   Results of classification from the neural network classifier `NNFraudClassifier` **(listing 5.12)**

If you rerun the last three steps of listing 5.13 you should see the results shown in figure 5.11; your results will also include the normalized values of the transactions, which we ignored here to improve legibility. The only transactions associated with the replaced description were legitimate—their value for the last attribute was `false`. The output indicates that there were four legitimate transactions (`VALID_TXN`) that were misclassified as fraud. Our impeccable score has been marred because the replacement has introduced *noise* in our data. In other words, we're now dealing with data that we never before encountered.

The first set of test transactions (used in the results of figure 5.10) didn't include even one transaction from the training set. But in that case, all the test transactions were created from the same statistical distributions. In particular, the transactional descriptions were introduced from a fixed set of descriptions without any variations. Even though each test transaction had never before been encountered,[1] they all belonged in exactly the same data space. Nearly all classification algorithms can do well in that case, but they all generate errors on data that's significantly different than the training dataset. The ability of a classifier to gracefully handle data that it hasn't encountered before is a measure of its generalization capability.

---

[1] In the sense that if we were to compare all the attribute values, one by one, between a test transaction and all training transactions, we wouldn't have found a single training transaction that was identical to the test transaction.

```
bsh % TransactionDataset testDS =
å  TransactionLoader.loadTestDataset();

bsh % FraudErrorEstimator auditor =
å  new FraudErrorEstimator(testDS, nnClone);

bsh % auditor.run();

userid = 25.0 - txnid = 500523 - txnamt = 63.79 -
å  location_x = 533.0 - location_y = 503.0 -
å  description = SOME DUDE -->  VALID_TXN

userid = 26.0 - txnid = 500574 - txnamt = 127.97 -
å  location_x = 734.0 - location_y = 507.0 -
å  description = SOME DUDE -->  VALID_TXN

userid = 23.0 -  txnid = 500273 -  txnamt = 47.76 -
location_x = 966.0 -  location_y = 991.0 -
description = SOME DUDE -->  VALID_TXN

userid = 21.0 -  txnid = 500025 -  txnamt = 50.47 -
location_x = 980.0 -  location_y = 996.0 -
description = SOME DUDE -->  VALID_TXN

Total test dataset txns: 1100, Number of fraud txns:100
Classified correctly: 1096,
Misclassified valid txns: 4,
Misclassified fraud txns: 0
```

Figure 5.11 Introducing noise in the data by replacing the description of valid transactions

The moral of the story is that a good understanding of the data is extremely important. In particular, it's important to know the degree to which your data is representative of all possible data for your application. Typically, collecting a lot of data helps us obtain a lot of relevant data.

In practice, this isn't as easy as it sounds because the same data can mean different things in different contexts. Moreover, a small number of attributes result in greater ambiguity about the meaning of the data but a large number of attributes can obfuscate the essential classification features with unimportant information. There's a fine balance between making our classifier accurate on what we already know and concomitantly endowing the classifier with the power of generalization.

It's important to know the *sensitivity* that your classifier shows when you introduce noise. In the preceding example, we changed the description of 39 transactions in a total set of 1,100 test transactions, and our neural network classifier was inaccurate in 4 out of the 39 "polluted" transactions. What would happen if you change the substitution string to something else? How many of the polluted transactions become misclassified as the number of polluted transactions increases? Use your own name as the substitution string and study the results.

5.4.4   *The anatomy of the fraud detector neural network*

Now, it's time to take a close look at the `NNFraudClassifier` class, shown in listing 5.14. At its core lies the class `TransactionNN`, which is a neural network specifically built to meet the needs of our fraud detection use case. In turn, `TransactionNN` extends a general neural network class called `BaseNN`, which you can use as the basis for writing your own neural network; we'll examine the `BaseNN` class in listing 5.16.

Listing 5.14   A classifier for fraud detection based on a special neural network

```
public class NNFraudClassifier
   implements Classifier, java.io.Serializable {

private String name;
private TransactionNN nn;
private TransactionDataset ds;
private transient TrainingSet ts;
private TransactionInstanceBuilder instanceBuilder;
private List<String> availableAttributeNames;

public NNFraudClassifier(TransactionDataset ds) {          ❶
  this.ds = ds;
  this.ts = ds.createTrainingDataset();
  this.instanceBuilder = ds.getInstanceBuilder();
  this.availableAttributeNames = new ArrayList<String>();

  nn = createNeuralNetwork();
}

public Concept classify(String transactionId) {            ❷
  setVerbose(true);
  Transaction t = ds.findTransactionById(transactionId);
  return classify(t);
}

public Concept classify(Transaction t) {
  return classify(instanceBuilder.createInstance(t));
}

public Concept classify(Instance instance) {               ❸

  double[] x = createNNInputs(instance);

  double[] y = nn.classify(x);

  Concept c = createConceptFromNNOutput(y);

  return c;
}

public boolean train() {                                   ❹

  if( ts == null ) {
    throw new RuntimeException("Can't train classifier -
      training dataset is NULL.");
  }
  if( nn == null ) {
    throw new RuntimeException("No Neural Network found.");
  }
```

```
  if( nn.getInputNodeCount() != availableAttributeNames.size()) {
    throw new RuntimeException("Number of attributes doesn't match");
  }
  if( nn.getOutputNodeCount() != 1) {
    throw new RuntimeException("Classifier expects network
    with only one output node.");
  }

  trainNeuralNetwork(nTrainingIterations);

  return true;
}
private void trainNeuralNetwork(int nIterations) {      ❺

  for(int i = 1; i <= nIterations; i++) {

    for(Instance instance : ts.getInstances().values()) {

        double[] nnInput = createNNInputs(instance);

        double[] nnExpectedOutput = createNNOutputs(instance);

        nn.train(nnInput, nnExpectedOutput);
    }
  }
}

public double[] createNNInputs(Instance instance) {      ❻

  int nInputNodes = nn.getInputNodeCount();

  double[] x = new double[nInputNodes];

  for(int i = 0; i < nInputNodes; i++) {

    String attrName = this.availableAttributeNames.get(i);
    Attribute a = instance.getAttributeByName(attrName);

    if( a instanceof DoubleAttribute ) {

      x[i] = (Double)a.getValue();

    } else {

      if( a == null ) {
        throw new RuntimeException("Failed to find attribute with name:
      '"+attrName);
      } else {
        throw new RuntimeException("Invalid attribute type.");
      }
    }
  }
  return x;
}

public double[] createNNOutputs(Instance i) {      ❼

  int nOutputNodes = nn.getOutputNodeCount();

  double[] y = new double[nOutputNodes];

  if( TransactionConcept.CONCEPT_LABEL_FRAUD.equals(i.getConcept().getName()) ) {
```

```
      y[0] = 1;
  } else {
      y[0] = 0;
  }
  return y;
}

private Concept createConceptFromNNOutput(double[] y) {        ❽

  double threshold = 0.5;

  Concept c = null;

  if( y[0] >= threshold ) {

    c = new TransactionConcept(TransactionConcept.CONCEPT_LABEL_FRAUD);

  } else {

    c = new TransactionConcept(TransactionConcept.CONCEPT_LABEL_VALID);
  }

  return c;
}

public void useDefaultAttributes() {                           ❾
    trainOnAttribute(TransactionInstance.ATTR_NAME_N_TXN_AMT);
    trainOnAttribute(TransactionInstance.ATTR_NAME_N_LOCATION);
    trainOnAttribute(TransactionInstance.ATTR_NAME_N_DESCRIPTION);
    }
}
```

Listing 5.13 shows the essential methods of the NNFraudClassifier class; for brevity we've eliminated Javadoc, getters and setters, and so forth. As you can see, the classifier is a wrapper around more elementary classes that allow us to map the use case of transaction fraud onto the standard "instance to concept" framework. Let's comment on these methods in order of appearance:

❶ Our constructor takes a reference to the transaction dataset and constructs the objects that will be needed for classification. Recall that our data is transactions, so we need to create instances from them in order to use the classification algorithms. That's the role of the TransactionInstanceBuilder class. The invocation of the method create-NeuralNetwork() creates an instance of the TransactionNN class, which we describe in listing 5.14.

❷ The method classify is overloaded for the specific usage of this classifier. According to our iweb2.ch5.classification.core.intf.Classifier interface, a classifier is obligated to provide an implementation that takes an Instance as its single argument and returns a Concept. We facilitate the use of our classifier by providing additional classify methods, which eventually delegate to the main classify method.

❸ This is the essential method of the classifier and its implementation involves three steps. Our neural networks accept an array of double values as input, and provide an array of double values as output. The first step is to translate the data of a transaction instance into an array of double values. The second step loads the input values into the network and obtains the result of the neural network's classification (a single double value). Since we aren't interested in the precise `double` value that the neural network returns, but want the classifier to tell us whether that instance is fraudulent, we need to translate that `double` value into one of the two `Concepts`—either `CONCEPT_LABEL_FRAUD` or `CONCEPT_LABEL_VALID`. That's what the method `createConceptFromNNOutput` does.

❹ This is the training method that you need to call for the `NNFraudClassifier` and it results in the training of the neural network. First, this method performs a number of checks before it delegates to the main training method. In particular, it tests for the following conditions:

- The existence of a training set
- The existence of a `TransactionNN` instance
- The conformity of the input to the specifications of the `TransactionNN` instance
- The conformity of the output to the specifications of the `TransactionNN` instance

❺ This is the main training method. It requires a single argument that specifies the number of times that the instances of the training set should propagate through the neural network. Each instance results in changing the weights of the synapses of the neural network in order to optimize the classification of the neural network for all the instances that have been seen so far. In other words, you keep telling the neural network what the answer for a given input should be and it tries to adjust itself so that it can "remember" the answer without forgetting all the other answers that it's seen so far.

❻ This is the auxiliary method that takes as argument an `Instance` and creates the input values for the neural network.

❼ This is the auxiliary method that takes an `Instance` as argument and creates the output values of the neural network. This is used only in the training phase.

❽ This is the auxiliary method that takes the output value of the neural network as argument and translates it into one of the two `Concepts`—either `CONCEPT_LABEL_FRAUD` or `CONCEPT_LABEL_VALID`.

❾ This is the auxiliary method that defines the attributes of the transaction instance that we want to use in the classification. In our case, we don't have many attributes, but this wrapper simplifies our scripts. In general, it's convenient and prudent to define the list of training attributes in a single place in the code. You could also add a getter for the `availableAttributeNames` variable.

At this point, you probably have a good understanding of the high-level definition of our fraud classifier based on a neural network. But, how do we define a neural network? What steps should you take if you want to write your own fraud detection classifier with a different neural network? Listing 5.15 shows the code from the class `TransactionNN`. This is the neural network that we use in the fraud classifier, but as you can see, there's nothing special about fraud or transactions in the definition of that class. It only carries the signature of how we decided to cast our fraud detection problem in our neural network framework.

Listing 5.15   A special neural network for the fraud detection use case

```java
public class TransactionNN extends BaseNN {          ❶

    public TransactionNN(String name) {             ❷
        super(name);

        createNN351();
    }

    private void createNN351() {

        Layer inputLayer = createInputLayer(        ❸
            0, // layer id
            3  // number of nodes
            );

        Layer hiddenLayer = createHiddenLayer(      ❹
            1, // layer id
            5, // number of nodes
            new double[] {1, 1.5, 1, 0.5, 1} // node biases
            );

        Layer outputLayer = createOutputLayer(      ❺
            2, // layer id
            1, // number of nodes
            new double[] {1.5} // node biases
            );

        setInputLayer(inputLayer);                  ❻
        setOutputLayer(outputLayer);
        addHiddenLayer(hiddenLayer);

        setLink("0:0", "1:0", 0.25);                ❼
        setLink("0:0", "1:1", -0.5);
        setLink("0:0", "1:2", 0.25);
        setLink("0:0", "1:3", 0.25);
        setLink("0:0", "1:4", -0.5);

        setLink("0:1", "1:0", 0.25);
        setLink("0:1", "1:1", -0.5);
        setLink("0:1", "1:2", 0.25);
        setLink("0:1", "1:3", 0.25);
        setLink("0:1", "1:4", -0.5);

        setLink("0:2", "1:0", 0.25);
        setLink("0:2", "1:1", -0.5);
        setLink("0:2", "1:2", 0.25);
        setLink("0:2", "1:3", 0.25);
        setLink("0:2", "1:4", -0.5);

        setLink("1:0", "2:0", -0.5);
        setLink("1:1", "2:0", 0.5);
        setLink("1:2", "2:0", -0.5);
```

```
        setLink("1:3", "2:0", -0.5);
        setLink("1:4", "2:0", 0.5);

        System.out.println("NN created");
    }
}
```

Based on the listing, the steps involved in the definition of our fraud detection neural network are the following:

❶ The `TransactionNN` class is an extension of the `BaseNN` class, which we'll describe in greater depth later. You can build general neural networks by extending the `BaseNN` class. In the code that comes with this book, you can also find a neural network that replicates an XOR gate, which means that it takes two `double` values as input and creates one `double` value as output. If both values are approximately equally to one or zero, the output is zero. If one value is approximately equal to one and the other is approximately equal to zero, the output is equal to one. The class is called `XORNetwork`, and it's even simpler than the `TransactionNN` class. Read it and run it to reinforce your understanding of how you can build a neural network.

❷ The constructor delegates to the `BaseNN` constructor for all basic initialization steps and creates the specific network topology with three input nodes, five hidden layer nodes, and one output layer node. Wait a second! Three input nodes? Our transactional data that we described earlier had a lot more attribute values. In particular, we included the user ID, the transaction amount, the transaction location in terms of two coordinates, and a transaction description string. The description string isn't numeric and can be translated into a number in many ways, but it's reasonable to expect that it would contribute in the input data in at least one node. That adds up to five input data (minimum), so why do we use only three?

The data values that we pass as input to the neural network are all normalized values; to convince yourself, look at the method `createInstance(Transaction t)` of the class `TransactionInstanceBuilder`. The transaction amount is normalized, based on the minimum and maximum value of the legitimate transactions, so that it's always a value within the interval 0 and 1. We use the `JaccardCoefficient` in order to achieve the same result for the description of a transaction. For the transaction locations, we do something more elaborate. We normalize both the location of the user's centroid and the location of the transactions (based on the minimum and maximum values of the x and y coordinates), and subsequently calculate the distance between these two normalized locations. That distance is one of our three input values in the neural network `TransactionNN`. That's why we have only three input nodes. This is clearly a design choice, and as is often the case in neural network design, it's more or less an arbitrary choice. But it's not a bad choice and it can be justified; in fact, we ask you to do that in one of to-do items.

The overall network topology (3/5/1 nodes, only one hidden layer, full connectivity) is also a design decision that isn't set in stone but can be optimized based on experimentation. You could try different topologies that would result in different classifiers.

In the same to-do item as the data normalization, we urge you to implement your own network topology and compare the results of the resulting classifiers. The best network topology depends on the nature of the input data and the nature of your problem. The fraud detection use case and the `TransacticnNN` base implementation provide a baseline that can help you investigate this dependency.

3 We create the input layer by providing an ID and specifying that the input layer should have three nodes.

4 We create the hidden layer of the network. Note that now we've introduced an array of new parameters (each value in the array corresponds to one node in the layer) called *biases*. We talked about the weights of the synapse earlier. For now, consider these to be additional constant weights that denote a bias that should be added to the output value from a node.

Note also that the method uses the prefix *add* instead of *set*. That's intentional because we want to indicate that you can have more than one hidden layer. We recommend that you study the effect of the number of hidden layers as one aspect of designing your neural networks.

5 This is the last of our three layers. We define a bias value for the output layer as well, but you can opt not to have a bias in the output node. In the latter case, simply set the bias equal to zero.

6 We assign the references of the three layers to the network. At this point, we have all our nodes ready. The only thing that we have left to do is create the connectivity (the edges) of our network.

7 We build all the links (synapses) between the nodes one by one. The first argument determines the origin of the link in the form LayerID:NodeID. The second argument determines the destination of the link in the form LayerID:NodeID. The third argument determines the weight of the link upon initialization. As we discussed, the values of the weights change continuously during the training phase.

5.4.5   *A base class for building general neural networks*

The material that we presented in the previous sections was tied to the specific use case of fraud detection. In order to create the neural network, as well as every time that we needed to access the inner workings of the neural network, we delegated the calls to the general implementation that we provided—the class `BaseNN`. Due to its importance and general applicability, this section will provide a dissection of that class.

For better exposition, we'll present this class in two listings. Listing 5.16 will address the structural aspects of the class (setting up the neural network), listing 5.17 will present the operational aspects (the training and classification related code).

Listing 5.16   BaseNN (structural aspects): excerpt from the base class of a general NN

```
public Layer createInputLayer(int layerId, int nNodes) {    1

    BaseLayer baseLayer = new BaseLayer(layerId);
```

```
      for(int i = 0; i < nNodes; i++) {
         Node node = createInputNode(layerId + ":" + i);
         Link inlink = new BaseLink();
         inlink.setFromNode(node);
         inlink.setWeight(1.0);
         node.addInlink(inlink);
         baseLayer.addNode(node);
      }

      return baseLayer;
   }
   public Layer createHiddenLayer(int layerId,
      int nNodes, double[] bias) {                    ❷

      if( bias.length != nNodes ) {
         throw new RuntimeException("Each node should have bias.");
      }
      BaseLayer baseLayer = new BaseLayer(layerId);
      for(int i = 0; i < nNodes; i++) {
         Node node = createHiddenNode(layerId + ":" + i);
         node.setBias(bias[i]);
         baseLayer.addNode(node);
      }
      return baseLayer;
   }
   public Layer createOutputLayer(int layerId,
      int nNodes, double[] bias) {                    ❸

      if( bias.length != nNodes ) {
         throw new RuntimeException("Each node should have bias.");
      }
      BaseLayer baseLayer = new BaseLayer(layerId);
      for(int i = 0; i < nNodes; i++) {
         Node node = createOutputNode(layerId + ":" + i);
         node.setBias(bias[i]);
         baseLayer.addNode(node);
      }
      return baseLayer;
   }
   public void setLink(String fromNodeId, String toNodeId, double w) {    ❹
      Link link = new BaseLink();
      Node fromNode = allNodes.get(fromNodeId);
      if( fromNode == null ) {
         throw new RuntimeException("Unknown node id: " + fromNodeId);
      }
      Node toNode = allNodes.get(toNodeId);
      if( toNode == null ) {
         throw new RuntimeException("Unknown node id: " + toNodeId);
      }
      link.setFromNode(fromNode);
      link.setToNode(toNode);
      link.setWeight(w);

      fromNode.addOutlink(link);
```

```
        toNode.addInlink(link);
    }

    protected Node createInputNode(String nodeId) {        ❺
        Node node = new LinearNode(nodeId);
        node.setLearningRate(learningRate);
        return node;
    }

    protected Node createHiddenNode(String nodeId) {
        Node node = new SigmoidNode(nodeId);
        node.setLearningRate(learningRate);
        return node;
    }

    protected Node createOutputNode(String nodeId) {
        Node node = new LinearNode(nodeId);
        node.setLearningRate(learningRate);
        return node;
    }

    public abstract double fireNeuron();

    public abstract double fireNeuronDerivative();
}
```

Let's start with the structural aspects as shown in listing 5.16. This is not the entire implementation. We've kept the minimum methods required to describe the structure of a neural network.

❶ This method creates the input layer of the network; it takes as arguments the layer ID and the number of nodes that this layer should have. It instantiates a BaseLayer, which is the base neural network layer implementation in our framework. This class consists of a layer ID and a list of nodes. The loop iterates nNodes times in order to create all the nodes of the input layer. Each node of the input layer is assigned a link (synapse), which we call inlink to indicate that it's responsible for transferring the data into the network. The weight of that link is set equal to one and doesn't change during training because we don't want to distort the original values of the data. For that reason, many authors don't consider the input layer to be part of the neural network per se.

❷ This method creates the hidden layer of the network; it takes as arguments the layer ID, the number of nodes that this layer should have, and the bias that each one of these nodes should have. After validating that there are as many bias values as there are nodes, it instantiates a BaseLayer. The loop iterates nNodes times, in order to create all the nodes of the hidden layer. Each node of the input layer is assigned the bias that corresponds to the enumeration of the loop; since this is the creation stage, we assume that this is the intended ordering. Unlike the case of input layer nodes, a link (synapse) isn't created at this stage and therefore a weight isn't provided either. This is done separately, via the method setLink, as we'll see shortly.

❸ We conclude the creation of the neural network's layers by constructing the output layer. This is similar to the construction of the hidden layer. But there's implicitly a difference related to the fact that the nodes of the output layer are instances of the LinearNode class, while the hidden layer nodes are instances of the SigmoidNode class.

❹ The previous methods were responsible for creating neural network nodes. This method is responsible for creating the neural network links (synapses). The only layer nodes for which we created a link were the input layer nodes. The rest of the nodes are connected using this method. Its arguments are the IDs of the two nodes that the link should connect and the weight that should be attributed to the link. You can also define other methods such as `connectFully(Layer x, Layer y)`, which would create a link for all the possible combinations of nodes between these two layers. You can experiment and explore the possibilities according to your needs.

❺ The remainder of the methods in listing 5.16 are responsible for creating the instances of the specific implementations of neural network nodes. We've written two specific implementations of a `BaseNode`; the `BaseNode` is an abstract class. The first implementation is given by the class `LinearNode` and is used by the input and output layers. The second implementation is given by the class `SigmoidNode` and is used by the hidden layer nodes. Once the nodes have been created, we set the *learning rate.*

Nearly all the functionality of a node is provided by the base class. The `LinearNode` and the `SigmoidNode` offer implementations for only two methods—the `fireNeuron()` and the `fireNeuronDerivative()`. If you recall our design mantra in section 5.4.2, we can fully determine a neural network by defining the network architecture, the activation rule, and the learning rule. Creating the layers of the network, their nodes, and their connections establishes the network architecture, but doesn't tell us how the nodes will respond to a given input (activation rule) or how the network will learn. The `fire-Neuron()` method defines the response of a neuron node to the given input, which is the crux of the activation rule, while the `fireNeuronDerivative()` (which must provide the numerical derivative of the `fireNeuron()` method) is directly related to the learning rule. The parameter `learningRate` doesn't depend on the specific implementation of the node and is typically a value between 0 and 1.

The preceding methods adequately define the neural network as a structure. So, let's move on to listing 5.17, which describes the operational aspects of our network.

> **Listing 5.17 `BaseNN` (operational aspects): excerpt from the base class of a general NN**

```
public void train(double[] tX, double[] tY) {
  double lastError = 0.0;
  int i = 0;

  while( true ) {        ❶
    i++;
    double[] y = classify(tX);

    double err = error(tY, y);

    if( Double.isInfinite(err) || Double.isNaN(err) ) {        ❷
      throw new RuntimeException("Training failed.");
    }

    double convergence = Math.abs(err - lastError);

    if(err <= ERROR_THRESHOLD ) {        ❸
      lastError = err;
```

```
            break;
        }
        if( convergence <= CONVERGENCE_THRESHOLD ) {        ❹
            break;
        }
        lastError = err;

        outputLayer.setExpectedOutputValues(tY);            ❺

        outputLayer.calculateWeightAdjustments();

        for(Layer hLayer : hiddenLayers) {
            hLayer.calculateWeightAdjustments();
        }

        outputLayer.updateWeights();          ❻

        for(Layer hLayer : hiddenLayers) {
            hLayer.updateWeights();
        }
    }
  }
}
public double[] classify(double[] x) {        ❼

  inputLayer.setInputValues(x);

  inputLayer.calculate();
  inputLayer.propagate();

  for(Layer hLayer : hiddenLayers) {
    hLayer.calculate();
    hLayer.propagate();
  }

  outputLayer.calculate();
  double[] y = outputLayer.getValues();

  return y;
}
```

Every neural network has two main operational characteristics. It should be able to train itself, and it should be able to classify its input—create the expected output values. The algorithm that we adopt in our implementation is called the *back propagation* algorithm; it's an online gradient-descent learning algorithm. In practical terms, this algorithm examines each training instance and adjusts the weights of its links (synapses) so that the difference of the output value from the expected value is minimized. Minimization relies on examining the slope of the error. For each instance we enter an infinite loop, which breaks under three conditions.

❶ Enter an open loop, during which we try to improve the accuracy of the classifier. The termination conditions are described in points 2–4.

❷ The first termination condition is that we're able to calculate the error. If we can't there's no point in iterating. This is simply a sanity check. If that condition happens to be true then it usually indicates a bad neural network design or some other error in the way that you're trying to cast your problem as a classification task for neural networks.

❸ The second termination condition is related to the magnitude of the error. If the error of classifying this instance is less than a predefined threshold we can stop.

❹ The third termination condition checks whether the difference that we get in the errors improves significantly over time. We're trying to reduce the error, so we keep varying the weights and try to get a better value for our output value. It is possible that we may not achieve the error threshold that we've set. In other words, we may have set the bar too high for our classifier. Look at the way that we implemented that condition. Can you come up with a better convergence criterion?

❺ At this point, we haven't yet met any of our termination criteria. So, we set the value of the output node to the expected value and begin our reevaluation of the network's weights. This is done by calling `calculateWeightAdjustments()` for all the nodes starting with the nodes of the output layer.

❻ In the previous step we evaluated the adjustments of the weights but we didn't take any action. In this step, upon completion of the weight adjustment calculations for all the nodes, we update the values of the weights by calling the method `update-Weights()`. That's it! Our cycle completed and we're ready to repeat it until one of our three termination conditions is met.

❼ This method is the top-level wrapper of the classification process. As we stated earlier, when the neural network operates, think of the information traveling through the nodes from the input nodes to the output nodes. This is captured succinctly in this method. We begin with the nodes of the input layer, we move on to the hidden layers, and we close by calculating the output value of the network. Each node makes its own calculations, based on the weights and the biases that it has; this is taken care of by the `calculate()` method. The node will pass on its output to the nodes that it connects to by using the method `propagate()`. Once the neural network has been trained, operating it is quite straightforward.

A lot of this material relies on mathematical prerequisites that aren't a requirement for the general audience of this book. We've focused on the mechanics of neural network classifiers rather than their fundamentals. If you're interested in learning more about the inner workings of neural networks, there's a vast amount of literature that you can consult. In appendix E, we list many good books from the literature of neural networks that can help you expand your knowledge in this field.

The previous section focused on the definition and description of the classification algorithms that are needed in order to build a classifier. From the perspective of a product, there's a set of important issues such as the credibility of classification, the consistency of the results on large datasets, as well as the computational requirements of classification that must be taken into account. We'll tackle some of these issues in the following sections.

5.5 *Are your results credible?*

Let's say that you've built your classifier based on Bayes theorem or neural networks, or something else. How do you know whether you did a good job? How do you know that you're ready to use your intelligent module in production and reap the awe of your colleagues and the accolades of your boss? Evaluating your classifier is as important as building it. On the "street" (also known as "sales meetings"), you're going to hear things that range from exaggerations to outright nonsense. The goal of this section is to help you evaluate your own classifier, if you're a developer, and help you understand the legitimacy (or otherwise) of third-party products, whether you're a developer or a product manager.

Let's start by stating that there's not a single classifier that will perform classification well on every problem and every dataset. Think of it as the computational version of "nobody knows everything" and "everybody makes mistakes." The learning techniques that we discussed in the context of classification belong to the category of supervised learning (for an example of an unsupervised learning algorithm, see the related to-do item). The learning is "supervised" because the classifier undergoes a process of training, based on known classifications, and through supervision it attempts to learn the information contained in the training dataset. As you can imagine, the relation of the training data to the actual data in your deployment will be crucial for the success of classification.

For the purpose of clarity, let's introduce a few terms. To make things simple, we'll consider a standard binary classification problem such as identifying email spam or fraud. For example, let's pretend that we're trying to discern whether a particular email message should be characterized as spam. A basic tool in assessing the credibility of a classifier, and typically the starting point of such an investigation, is the *confusion matrix*. It's a simple matrix, where the rows refer to the category that the classifier assigns a particular instance, and the columns refer to the category that an instance of a description belongs to. In the case of binary classification, there are only four cells in that matrix. The general case (multiclass classification) doesn't differ conceptually from the binary case, but it results in more complicated analysis.

Table 5.1 presents the confusion matrix for a binary classification such as email spam filtering or fraud detection. The table captures the possible outcomes of binary classification. If the classification assigns a particular email message to the spam category then we say that the classification is *positive*. Otherwise, we say that the classification is *negative*. Of course, the classification itself could be correct (true) or incorrect (false). Thus, the matrix contains four possible outcomes—the possible combinations between positive/negative and true/false. This also leads to the realization that there are two types of error. The first type of error consists of false positive classifications; an error of this type is called a *type I error*. The other type of error consists of false negative classifications; an error otf this type is called *type II error*. In plain terms, when you commit a

	Positive	Negative
True	True Positive (TP)	True Negative (TN)
False	False Positive (FP)	False Negative (FN)

Table 5.1 A typical confusion matrix for a simple binary classification problem

type I error, you convict the innocent, and when you commit a type II error, you free the guilty! This analogy is particularly good in pointing out the importance of *classification cost*. Voltaire would prefer to release 100 guilty people than convict one innocent person; that sensitivity remains in the European courts. The moral of this anecdote is that decisions have consequences, and the degree of the consequences isn't uniform. This is particularly true in the case of multiclass classification. We'll revisit this point.

Based on the values of table 5.1, let's introduce the following definitions:

- *FP rate = FP / N, where N = TN + FP*
- *Specificity = 1 − FP rate = TN / N*
- *Recall = TP / P, where P = TP + FN*
- *Precision = TP / (TP + FP)*
- *Accuracy = (TP + TN) / (P + N)*
- *F-score = Precision * Recall*

Suppose that we find out about a classifier whose accuracy, as defined earlier, is 75%. How close to the true accuracy of the classifier is our estimate? In other words, if you repeat the classification task with different data, how likely is it that your accuracy will be 75%? To answer that question, we'll resort to something that's known in statistics as a *Bernoulli process*. This is described as a sequence of independent events whose outcome is considered either as success or as failure. That's an excellent example for our email spam filtering use case or our fraud detection use case, and in general for any binary classification. If we denote the true accuracy as A*, and the measured accuracy as A, then we want to know if A is a good estimate of A*.

You may recall from your statistics courses the notion of a *confidence interval*. That's a measure for the certainty that we assign to a specific statement. If our accuracy is 75%, in a set of 100 email messages, our confidence may not be very high. But if our accuracy is 75%, in a set of 100,000 email messages, our confidence will probably be much higher. Intuitively, we understand that, as the size of the set increases, the confidence interval must become smaller and we feel more certain about our results. In particular, it can be shown that, for a Bernoulli process with 100 samples, the true accuracy is located between 69.1% and 80.1%, with 80% confidence (see Witten & Frank). If we increase the size of the set that we use to measure the accuracy of the classifier 10 times then the new interval ranges from 73.2% to 76.7%, for the same confidence level (80%). Every good statistics textbook has formulas for calculating these intervals. In theory, these results are valid when your sample size is greater than 30 instances. In practice, you should use as many instances as you can.

Unfortunately, in practice, you may not have as many instances as you would have liked. To face that challenge, machine learning folks have devised a number of techniques that can help us evaluate the credibility of classification results when data are scarce. The standard method of evaluation is called *10-fold cross-validation*. This is a simple procedure that's best illustrated by an example. Let's say that we have 1,000 emails that we've already classified manually. In order to evaluate our classifier, we need to use some of them as a training set and some as the testing set. The 10-fold cross-validation tells us to divide the 1,000 emails into 10 groups of 100 emails; each batch of 100 emails should contain roughly the same proportion of legitimate to spam emails as the 1,000 emails set does. Subsequently, we take 9 of these groups of emails and we train the classifier. Once the training is completed, we test the classifier against the group of 100 emails that we didn't include in our training. We can measure metrics, some of which we mentioned earlier, and typically people will measure the accuracy of the classifier. This is repeated 10 times, and each time we leave out a different group of 100 emails. In the end of these trials, we have 10 values of accuracy that we can now use to obtain an average value of accuracy.

You may wonder whether your accuracy will change if you divide your original set into 8 or 12 parts. Yes, of course, it's unlikely that you'll obtain an identical answer. Nevertheless, the new averaged value of accuracy should be close enough to what you obtained before. Results from a large number of tests, on various datasets and with many different classifiers, suggest that the 10-fold cross-validation will produce fairly representative measurements for your classifier.

Taking the 10-fold cross-validation to its extreme case, you can always use as a training set all the email instances except for one, and use the one that you left out for testing. Naturally, this technique is called *leave-one-out*. It has certain theoretical advantages, but on real datasets (with hundreds of thousands, if not millions, of instances) the computational cost is often prohibitive. You could opt to leave one instance out but not do it for all instances in your dataset. This leads to a technique called *bootstrap*. The basic idea of bootstrap is that we can create a training set by sampling the original dataset with replacements. In other words, we can use an instance from the original dataset more than once and create a training set of 1,000 emails in which a particular email instance may appear more than once. If you do that then you'll end up with a testing set of about 368 email instances that weren't used in the training set. The size of your training set remains equal to 1,000 email instances because some of the remaining 632 email instances are repeated in the training set; for more mathematical explanation of these numbers, see Witten & Frank.

It's been found that plotting the TP rate (TPR) versus the FP rate (FPR) can be useful in analyzing the credibility of a classifier. These plots are called *ROC curves* and originated in signal detection theory in the '70s. In recent years, there's been a large amount of work in machine learning that utilizes ROC graphs for analyzing the performance of one or more classifiers. The basic idea is that the ROC curve should be as far away from the diagonal of a TPR/FPR plot as possible. We'll defer the analysis of ROC graphs to the excellent technical report by Tom Fawcett, which includes pseudoalgorithms and many tips about issues that appear in practice.

In the real world, classification systems are used often as decision support systems; mistakes of classification can lead to wrong decisions. In some cases, making wrong decisions, although undesirable, can be relatively harmless. But in other cases, it may be the difference between life and death; think of a physician who misses a cancer diagnosis or an emergency situation for an astronaut in deep space relying on the result of your classifier. The evaluation of classification systems should examine both the degree of credibility and the associated cost of making classifications. In the case of binary classification, the idea is to assign a *cost function* that's a function of the FP and FN rates. For assigning cost in the multiclass classification cases, see the related to-do item.

In summary, one of the most important aspects of a classifier is the credibility of its results. In this section, we described a number of metrics that can help us evaluate the credibility of classifiers such as the precision, the accuracy, the recall, and the specificity. Combinations of these metrics can yield new metrics, such as the F-score. We also discussed the idea of crossvalidating the results by splitting the training set in different ways and looking at the variation of these classifier metrics as the datasets change. We discussed the concept of a ROC curve, which is a simple plot between TPR and FPR. In the following section, we'll discuss a number of issues that are related to large datasets.

5.6   *Classification with very large datasets*

Many datasets used for academic and research purposes are quite small when compared to real-world implementations. Transactional datasets of large corporations are anywhere between 10 million to 100 million records, if not larger; insurance claims, telecommunications log files, recordings of stock prices, click trace logs, audit logs, and so on (the list is long) are on the same order of magnitude. So, dealing with large datasets is the rule rather than the exception in production applications, whether or not they are web-based. The classification of very large datasets deserves special attention for (at least) three reasons: (1) the proper representation of the dataset in the training set; (2) the computational complexity of the training phase; (3) the runtime performance of the classifier on a very large dataset.

Regardless of the specific domain of your application and the functionality that your classifier supports, you must ensure that your training data is representative of the data that will be seen in production. You shouldn't expect that a classifier will perform as well as the validation stage measurements suggest, unless your training data is very representative of your production data. We repeat ourselves to stress that point! In many cases, early excitement quickly turns to disappointment simply because this condition isn't met. So, you wonder, in that case, how can I ensure that my training data is representative?

The case of binary classification is easier to address because there are only two classes—an email message is either spam or it isn't, a transaction is fraudulent or it isn't, and so on. In that case, assuming that you have a reasonable number of training instances from both classes, our focus should be on the coverage of the attribute values among the training instances. Your assessment can be purely empirical ("Yeah, that's good enough. We have enough values; let's roll it to production!"), utterly scientific (sampling your data over time and testing whether the samples come from the same statistical distribution as the training data), or somewhere in between these extremes. In practice, the latter scenario is more likely; we could call it the semiempirical approach to supervised learning. The empirical aspect of it is that, along the way to assessing the completeness of your training set, you make a number of reasonable assumptions that reflect your understanding and experience of the data that your application is using. The scientific aspect of it is that you should collect some basic statistical information about your data, such as minimum and maximum values, mean values, median values, valid outliers, percentage of missing data in attribute values, and so on. You can use that information to sample previously unseen data from your application and include it in your training set.

The case of multiclass classification is similar in principle to the case of binary classification. But in addition to the guidelines that we mentioned previously, we're now faced with an additional complexity . Our new challenge is that we need to select our training instances so that all classes are represented equivalently in the training set. Discriminating between 1,000 different classes is a much harder problem to solve compared to binary selection. The case of multidimensional (many attributes) multiclass classification has the additional drawbacks that result from the curse of dimensionality (see chapter 4).

If your database contains 100 million records you'd naturally want to take advantage of all the data and leverage the information contained there. In the design phase of your classifier, you should consider the scaling characteristics of the training and validation stages for your classifier. If you double the size of your training data then ask yourself:

- How much longer does it take me to train the classifier?
- What's the accuracy of my classifier on the new (larger) set?

You probably want to include more quality metrics than just accuracy, and you probably want to take a few more data sizes (four times the original size, eight times the original, and so on) but you get the idea. It's possible that your classifier works great (it's trained quickly and provides good accuracy) in a small sample dataset but its performance degrades significantly when it's trained over a substantially larger dataset. This is important because time to market is always important, and the "intelligent" modules of your application should obey the same production rules as the other parts of your software.

The same principle holds for the runtime performance of the classifier during the third stage of its lifecycle—in production. It's possible that your classifier was trained quickly and provides good accuracy, but it's all for naught if it doesn't scale well in production! In the validation stage of the classifier, you should measure its performance and its dependency on the size of the data. Let's say that you use a classifier whose dependence on the size of the data is quadratic—if the data doubles in size then the time that it takes to process the data is four times larger. Let's further assume that your intelligent module will use the classifier in the background to detect fraudulent transactions. If you used 10,000 records for your validation and all records were classified in 10 minutes, then you'd process 10 million records in about 10 million minutes! You probably wouldn't have that much time available, so you should either pick a different classifier or improve the performance of the one that you have. Frequently, in production systems, people have to trade classifier accuracy for speed; if a classifier is extremely accurate and extremely slow, it's most likely useless!

Pay attention to the idiosyncrasies of your classification system. If you use a rule-based system, you may encounter what's known as the *utility problem*. The learning process—the accumulation of rules—can result in the overall slowdown of the system in production. There are ways to avoid or at least mitigate the utility problem (see Doorenbos) but you need to be aware of them and ensure that your implementation is compatible with these techniques. Of course, the degradation of performance isn't the only problem in that case. You'd also need to provide ways to manage and organize these rules, which is an engineering problem with a solution that'll depend strongly on the specific domain of your application. In general, the more complicated the classifier implementation, the more careful you should be to understand the performance characteristics (both speed and quality) of your classifier.

5.7   *Summary*

Classification is one of the essential components of intelligent applications. We started this chapter by presenting a number of cases in which some form of classification is used. We discussed reference schemes that are relevant in diverse application areas, from library catalogs to medical insurance manuals, and thereby established that classification is ubiquitous and valuable. We also introduced the three building blocks of classification—concepts, instances, and attributes. These three blocks define an ontology—a complete description of a particular area of expertise. If semantic information is also available then we speak of a semantic ontology. Classification can always be cast as the problem of assigning the "best" concept to a given instance. Classifiers differ from each other in the way that they represent and measure that optimal assignment. Nevertheless, they all share a similar lifecycle that consists of three stages: training, validation, and the production stage.

You've learned that, broadly speaking, all classifiers fall into two categories—binary and multiclass—depending on whether the decision that the classifier has to make is between two or multiple choices, respectively. You also learned that, with respect to the underlying technique, classifiers are either statistical or structural. We provided what seems to be the greatest common denominator in the literature, and proceeded with a high-level presentation of regression algorithms, Bayesian algorithms, rule-based algorithms, functional algorithms, nearest neighbor algorithms, and neural networks.

You've also learned two powerful algorithms for performing text classification. The first algorithm was the naïve Bayes algorithm as applied to a single string attribute. The second was the Drools rule engine, an object-oriented implementation of the Rete algorithm, which allows us to declare and apply rules for the purpose of classification. It's likely that your email client already contains some form of a rule engine;

when you declare that an email with a particular word in its subject sent from the domain *.foo.com should be considered spam, in essence, you're defining a rule. Now, you should be ready to apply our algorithms to many other freeform or semi-structured text classification tasks.

In addition, we introduced the construction of *computational neural networks* and presented a basic but robust implementation that can be used to build general neural networks. We provided designing guidelines as well as observations about the structure of the data and the importance of using training and validation data sets that are representative of the production data.

Although the benefits of classification are numerous, we pointed out that it's also important to investigate known issues related to the credibility and computational requirements of classification, before we introduce it in our application.

In conclusion, we can say that:

- Classification algorithms are important for building an intelligent application because they help us leverage (automatically) and augment (systematically) our knowledge about the world.
- We classify always with respect to a reference structure, which could be as simple as a binary set (true and false classes) or a large ontology.
- At the highest level, classifiers can be viewed as statistical versus structural.
- The choice of the classifier depends strongly on your data and the nature of the classification problem.
- Special attention is required with regard to the credibility and cost of classification.
- Very large datasets, very large ontologies, online requirements, or any combination of these three may cause trouble.
- Each one of the classification algorithms that we described will do its job well. But no single classifier can provide infallible decision-making capability. In fact, if you're looking for infallibility, you're out of luck!

In the next chapter, we're going to look at several techniques of combining classifiers in order to improve the results of any one of the single classifiers that we described so far.

5.8   To do

1   *The tradeoff between specialization and generalization*   Every classification algorithm that you can think of uses a number of variables as input and produces a number of variables as output. The input consists of two kinds of variables. The first kind are variables associated with the attribute values of our instances; the second kind are associated with a number of model variables that are specific to the classifier at hand. During the training stage, we estimate the model variables based on the input and output variables of the training set. In other words, we calibrate these arbitrary model parameters in such a way that, provided the input of the training set, the output variables take on the desired values.

Clearly, you can "cheat" and introduce as many model parameters as your data points, thus achieving very high, if not perfect, accuracy of classification for your training set. That is called *overfitting* and makes your classifier a specialist on your training set but probably a poor performer on a dataset that's quite different from your training set. In general, overfitting (we could also call it *specialization*) isn't good and should be avoided. Conversely, you may have too few model parameters and be unable to capture the *information content* of your training set. That is called *underfitting*. Using fewer parameters, but still enough of them to represent the information content of the training set, might increase your accuracy for unseen data—data points that weren't included in your training set. The ability to do so is generally referred to as *generalization*.

It becomes clear that a good classifier should aim to reach a fine balance between specialization and generalization. Experiment with the datasets that we provided in this chapter and introduce new testing instances in your data. Plot the error of your classifier as a function of the number of instances in the training set. Plot two curves. The first should plot the error for instances that belong in the training set, and the second should plot the error for instances that weren't included in the training set. Do you see the tradeoff between specialization and generalization for a given classifier? You could also introduce a third dimension that captures the model's complexity. Expressing the model complexity for rules and decision trees may be straightforward (for example, number of rules), but how would you express the model complexity in the case of a classifier based on Bayes theorem such as our own `NaiveBayes` class? How about the case of a neural network?

2 *Occam's razor and the number of training attributes*   In the same spirit as item 1, we can argue that the more training attributes we include in our model, the better results we'll get. There are two problems with that approach. First, from a real-world implementation perspective, we typically have a finite amount of resources and a small amount of time available for classification. Thus, our classification schemes should be easy to maintain, easy to test, and they should produce results rather quickly; you don't want to wait five minutes for your email to be classified as spam or not. Of course, there are cases that call for long-running calculations, such as discovering a location that may be rich in petroleum or creating reports that help your users make critical (strategic) business decisions.

The second problem with using as many training attributes as possible is related to the fact that "more data" doesn't necessarily mean more *information content*. There are many metrics that we can use to define information content, but let's bypass the mathematical jargon and think of it in the following way. We're typically interested in the value of some variables that are relevant in our application; it could be the value of one or more stocks in NASDAQ, the appropriate category of an email message, a Boolean variable describing whether we should purchase an item on eBay, and so on. We usually assume that there's an underlying model that describes the problem at hand and whose solution consists of the variables that we want to evaluate. By providing a set of data and a classifier, we're attempting to approximate that physical model as best we can. If we use data that isn't relevant to the physical model or if we overwhelm the classifier with redundant information, we might end up with a distorted representation of that physical model. By referring to *information content,* we mean data that can help us improve the representation of the underlying physical model. If we add a training attribute that has no effect in the accuracy of the classifier we can safely say that the new training attribute didn't carry significant information content in it.

Of course, we need to be careful in our selection of training attributes because different classifiers might be able to exploit more or less the data of a particular training attribute. In general, we can use the principle of Occam's razor: if two approaches produce the same results, the simplest approach is preferable. So, consider the email filtering example of section 5.3 and add more training attributes to your classifier. You could start by splitting the single attribute that we used in 5.3.1 into two attributes, one for the subject of the email and one for the main body. Are the results of your classification substantially different? In the context of information content, how do you interpret the applicability of rules in classifying email messages?

3 *A general-purpose RuleEngine class*   Our implementation of the `RuleEngine` class is using the `Email` class as an argument in the `executeRules` method. That's okay for classifying a single email message but isn't sufficient for a general implementation. In the general case, you'd insert all the facts into your working memory before you fire the rules. Modify the existing `RuleEngine` class so that it can be used under more general conditions.

Moreover, build a use case for a rule engine that deals with more complicated rules, conditions, and actions. The `ClassificationResult` class can guide you in customizing your conditions and your actions. Note that due to the objected-oriented nature of the Drools engine, you can build complicated rules with involved conditions and quite elaborate actions. It's a good practice to use auxiliary classes such as the `ClassificationResult` and put all your Java code in them; avoid writing code inside the Drools rule file itself.

How would you proceed to build a general-purpose classification system based on rules? Imagine a system that can classify an arbitrary text into many classes; it could be an email, a Word document, a PDF document, and so on. What rules do you need? What conditions do you need? And how would you express them in code?

4 *The importance of data normalization and effects of the neural network topology*   Note that the data values that we pass as input to the neural network are all normalized values. The transaction amount is normalized, based on the minimum and maximum value of the legitimate transactions, so that it's always a value within

the interval 0 and 1. We also use the `JaccardCoefficient` in order to achieve the same result for the description of a transaction. For the transaction locations we do something a bit more elaborate. We normalize the location of the user's centroid and the location of the transactions, and subsequently calculate the distance between these two locations. That distance is one of our three input values in the neural network `TransactionNN`. Why do we do that? Does it matter? Experiment by using the same code but switching to input that's not normalized. Use identical training and test data, so that you can compare the effect of the algorithms only. You probably want to change one thing at a time so you can relate the effect of your changes to their cause.

A second type of experiment that can be fairly instructive is the effect of the network topology on the results of your classifier. The best network topology depends on the nature of the input data and the nature of your problem. The fraud detection use case and the `TransactionNN` base implementation provide a baseline that can help you investigate this dependency. Implement your own network topology and compare the results of the resulting classifiers. For example, you could try to explicitly provide the x and y coordinates as input to the network, rather than provide only the distance of each location from the user's location centroid. You could also provide the description in more than one node. One way to do this would be to tokenize the description and use the similarity of each token with the top five description tokens, which would result in five input nodes related to the description; or more generally, the similarity of each token with the top N description tokens, which would result in N input nodes related to the description. How do your results vary as you increase N? How do the results of these neural networks compare with respect to the base `TransactionNN` implementation?

5 *Unsupervised learning: Hebbian learning and self-organizing maps (SOM)* In this chapter, we covered only supervised learning techniques, which are very common as well as useful. But unsupervised learning techniques are also useful and deserve your attention. In supervised learning, you always have that feeling that you entered the answer from the "back door"— mathematicians call that *interpolation*, which is a less conspicuous and more honorable term. In any case, the fact is that we tell the classifier what it should know and it tries to assimilate that knowledge by modifying its parameters, whether by calculating prior and conditional probabilities, in the case of Bayesian methods, or by adjusting the various weights, in the case of neural networks, or by shamelessly "writing down" everything, in the case of a rule-based systems. The amazing thing with unsupervised learning is that it can "remember" what it saw without feedback from a human.

In 1949, in his book *The Organization of Behavior*, Donald Hebb introduced a simple model that nicely illustrates the ability to learn without supervision. If you don't tell the classifier what's correct, how does it work? Consider a neural network whose nodes are fully connected through symmetrical bidirectional links (synapses); *symmetrical* here means that the weight of the link from node i to node j is equal to the weight of the link from node j to node i. What kind of activation rules and learning rules can help us build an unsupervised neural network?

6   *Counting the cost of classification errors*   In the real world, classification systems are used often as decision support systems, hence the mistakes of classification can lead to wrong decisions. In some cases, making wrong decisions, although undesirable, can be relatively harmless. But in other cases, it may be the difference between life and death; think of a physician who misses a cancer diagnosis or an emergency situation for an astronaut in deep space relying on the result of your classifier. So, the evaluation of classification systems should examine both the degree of credibility and the associated cost of making classifications. In the case of binary classification, the idea is to assign a *cost function* that's a function of the FP and FN rates. How would you generalize that idea in the case of multiclass classification?

In the case of multiclass classification, if you have N classes and you make an error, there are *N-1* possibilities. So, we need a way to assign the cost for *N x (N-1)* cases. Naturally, a matrix would be the most appropriate tool to achieve this goal. In multiclass classification, the confusion matrix is an *N x N* matrix, and we can also define a *cost matrix* that's also *N x N* but has the value 0 along its diagonal (you shouldn't penalize the classifier for the right answers). Work out the details and evaluate, for example, the `NaiveBayes` classifier with different cost matrices.

5.9   References

Classification schemes

The dewey Decimal classification (DDC) system. http://www.oclc.org/dewey/

International Classification of Diseases (ICD). World Health Organization (WHO). http://www.who.int/classifications/icd/en/.

The Library of Congress: Cataloging Distribution Service. http://www.loc.gov/cds/

Myhre, A.P., and M. L. Richardson, "A Web-based Tutorial for Teaching the Schatzker Classification for Tibial Plateau Fractures." http://uwmsk.org/schatzker/.

Occupational Injury and Illness Classification Manual. Bureau of Labor Statistics, U.S. Department of Labor. http://www.bls.gov/iif/oshoiics.htm.

Books and articles

Antoniou, G., and F. van Harmelen. *A Semantic Web Primer.* The MIT Press, 2004.

Doorenbos, R.B. *Production Matching for Large Learning Systems.* Ph.D. Thesis, Carnegie Mellon University, 1995.

Dunham, M.H. *Data Mining: Introductory and Advanced Topics.* Prentice Hall, Pearson Education Inc. 2003.

Fawcett, T. "ROC Graphs: Notes and practical considerations for researchers." 2004. http://home.comcast.net/~tom.fawcett/public_html/papers/ROC101.pdf.

Friedman-Hill, E. *Jess in Action.* Manning Publications, 2003.

Gasevic, D., D. Djuric, V. Devedzic. *Model Driven Architecture and Ontology Development*. Springer, 2006.

Gómez-Pérez, A., M. Fernández-López, and O. Corcho. *Ontological Engineering: with examples from the areas of Knowledge Management, e-Commerce and the Semantic Web*. Springer, 2004.

Hastie, T., R. Tibshirani, and J. Friedman. *The Elements of Statistical Learning: Data Mining, Inference, and Prediction*. Springer, 2001.

Hill, T. (1996). "A note on distributions of true versus fabricated data." *Perceptual and Motor Skills*. Vol 83, pp.776-778. http://www.math.gatech.edu/~hill/publications/cv.dir/truvsfab.pdf.

Holmström, L., P. Koistinen, J. Laaksonen, and E. Oja. "Neural and statistical classifiers—taxonomy and two case studies." *IEEE Transactions on Neural Networks*, Vol 8 (1), pp. 5-17, 1997.

Maier, K.D., C. Beckstein, R. Blickhan, W. Erhard, and D. Fey. "A multi-layer-perceptron neural network hardware based on 3D massively parallel optoelectronic circuits." Proceedings of the 6th International Conference on Parallel Interconnects, pp. 73-80, 1999.

MacKay, D.J.C.. *Information Theory, Inference, & Learning Algorithms*. Cambridge University Press, 2003.

Neapolitan, R.E. *Learning Bayesian Networks*. Prentice Hall, 2003.

Papoulis, A., and S.U. Pillai. *Probability, Random Variables, and Stochastic Processes*, Fourth Edition. McGraw-Hill, 2002.

Rish, I. "An empirical study of the naïve Bayes classifier." *IBM Research Report*, RC22230 (W0111-014). http://www.cc.gatech.edu/~isbell/classes/reading/papers/Rish.pdf.

Russell, S., and P. Norvig. *Artificial Intelligence: A Modern Approach* (Second Edition). Prentice Hall, 2002.

Staab, S., and R. Studer. *Handbook on Ontologies*. Springer, 2004.

Combining classifiers 6

Epictetus, an ancient Greek philosopher, proclaimed "One must neither tie a ship to a single anchor, nor life to a single hope." Similarly, we don't have to rely on a single classifier. No single classifier can provide infallible decision-making capability. In fact, there are plenty of examples that demonstrate the great potential of combining classifiers, and this chapter will provide an introduction to that fascinating subject. In the context of recommendation systems (see chapter 3), Bell, Koren, and Volinsky have recently employed similar ideas with great success.

The main idea behind combining classifiers is achieving better classification results at the expense of computational complexity and higher computational cost (for example, longer computational times or additional computational resources). The combination of classifiers is divided into two general categories—*classifier fusion* and *classifier selection*. In the category of classifier fusion, all classifiers contribute to a given classification; so, every classifier must cover the entire domain of possible data points. In classifier selection, each classifier is responsible for a particular domain of data points and is supposed to perform well only within its region of influence.

This distinction between the types of classifier combination is helpful for orienting ourselves in the field but isn't absolute. We'll see (in to-do item #5) that the concepts of fusion and selection can't always be easily distinguished.

If you'd like to read the theoretical justifications about combining classifiers, look at Dietterich's report. He basically divides the reasons for combining classifiers into three types.

The first type is based on statistical considerations and its main argument is the combination of classifiers might not outperform the single best classifier of a collection of classifiers, but it'll significantly reduce the risk of using a classifier that will be inadequate on unseen data.

The second type is based on computational considerations, which point out that classifiers are often sensitive to training. Thus, Dietterich argues, combining classifiers may provide better results by smoothing out the sensitivities of each classifier in the collection during training.

The third type is representational. In order to understand this, let's say that we need to classify some brief textual descriptions that are written in French (for example, *porte*, *fenêtre*, and *guerre*). The catch is that we don't have a classifier that can understand French; we only have a classifier that understands English and Spanish. The idea of representational motivation is that the combination of English and Spanish will better represent the French language, even though neither of them alone can ever do a decent job. The English translation of *guerre* is "war" while the Spanish word is *guerra*; conversely, you can also find French words that are closer to the lexicographic string of their English counterpart than they are to their Spanish counterpart. You'll be able to identify these types of motivation throughout our discussion.

We'll start this chapter by introducing the case study of evaluating the credit worthiness of mortgage applicants. This is a hot topic, due to its connection with the economic downturn that we experience today (circa 2008). In particular, we'll consider the use case of evaluating the credit worthiness of an applicant for a mortgage; conversely, one could consider the credit risk. The use case data will be artificial—credit risk assessment data and models are proprietary—but realistic. Naturally, the first point to address is the application of single classifier for our use case. So, we build three classifiers to classify the applicants into five categories of credit worthiness. Specifically, we present a classifier that's based on the naïve Bayes algorithm, a neural network–based classifier, and a newly introduced decision tree classifier.

Our next step is to examine whether one classifier is better than another. To do that, we'll demonstrate how to compare two or more classifiers by using four statistical techniques. For comparing only two classifiers, we introduce McNemar's test and the *difference of proportions* test. For comparing more than two classifiers, we introduce Cochran's Q test and the F test. Don't worry about the somewhat intimidating names; we've reduced their practical use to a few method calls.

We present two categories of techniques for combining classifiers. First, we show how to implement the category of combinations referred to as *bagging*, which stands for "bootstrap aggregating." We'll use bagging to improve the accuracy of the decision tree classifier and study the results of classification as the number of classifiers that are combined is increased. The second approach of combining classifiers that we'll study is called *boosting*. We'll present an algorithm that goes under the rather cryptic name *arc-x4* and discuss its predecessor, which is called *AdaBoost*. Naturally, we'll use these combination techniques in the context of our credit worthiness identification problem.

6.1   *Credit worthiness: a case study for combining classifiers*

We start this section by introducing our case study: evaluating a user's credit worthiness for a mortgage application. We examine the application of three different classifiers, specifically designed for our problem. In particular, we present a classifier based on the naïve Bayes algorithm, a neural network–based classifier, and a newly introduced decision tree classifier. So, what's credit worthiness and why's it important to evaluate it? Here's some background that will provide some context and underline the (perhaps unexpected) impact that good intelligent applications can have on the global economy!

In 2007, a mortgage mess of historic proportions and global impact was revealed in the United States. People were allowed, if not encouraged, to buy homes they couldn't afford, with credit lines that they didn't deserve. When housing prices began to fall and the market cash flow tightened, the loans of people who didn't have the assumed buying power started to default. It's not clear how many foreclosures and forced sales this situation has created; at the time of this writing the crisis continues.

In order to avoid further economic woes and social unrest, U.S. government agencies scrambled and tried to find ways to keep many of the buyers in their homes. It's estimated that there are about 2 million homeowners with adjustable mortgages, many of whom had low initial "teaser" rates. Unless these people get direct pecuniary aid from somebody, they'll face higher payments no matter what the Federal Reserve funds rate is.[1] Inevitably, the foreclosures and the forced sales tend to depress overall housing prices and decrease the wealth and consumption for most households.

This issue can have global implications for two reasons. Experts believe that the same financial turbulence may erupt in Europe's mortgage markets as well and large exporting nations, especially developing countries such as China whose wares stock shelves of American stores, will need to find new customers, as cash-strapped Americans can no longer buy their products.

What, you might wonder, does this have to do with intelligent software applications? As it turns out, quite a lot! The whole financial problem is complicated and may be ongoing. Nevertheless, so far, one thing is clear: barring fraud and spurious schemes of mortgage financing that affect the input data, the ability to assess the

---

[1] The Federal Reserve funds rate is the interest rate at which depository institutions lend balances, at the Federal Reserve, to other depository institutions overnight.

credit worthiness (or credit risk) associated with a particular transaction played a cata-lytic role in the propagation speed of the crisis's consequences, and the breadth of the social fabric that was affected by it.

In this chapter, we'll study the assessment of credit worthiness for a particular indi-vidual based on a number of criteria. In other words, we'll look at the values of a num-ber of attributes that describe the financial standing, social status, and credit history of an individual in order to place him in one of the five categories of credit worthiness—excellent, very good, good, bad, and dangerous.

We'll consider credit worthiness as a function of eleven attributes. The choice of attributes is arbitrary. We provided a sufficient number of attributes to make things interesting and realistic, but you shouldn't consider this to be the most sophisticated model of credit worthiness. It would be instructive to examine which of these attri-butes you can exclude or what other attributes you can add. Our first item in this chapter's To do section will provide motivation and additional guidance about the important subject of attribute selection.

6.1.1   A brief description of the data

Let's examine the eleven attributes one-by-one, in alphabetic order. The first attribute is the *chronological age* of an individual (as opposed to the mental age, which is typically not available in official records). The age is clearly a continuous variable because time is a continuous variable. So, our first assumption is that we measure age in years. Our values will be integers between 0 and 100; if you look at the implementation you'll realize that the exact value for the end of the age range isn't significant per se. We divide the range of ages between 18 and 100 into 10 intervals as indicated in table 6.1.

The second attribute that we consider is whether an individual has declared *bank-ruptcy*. The significance of bankruptcy varies from country to country; declaring bank-ruptcy in the United States is completely different from declaring bankruptcy in

Attribute ID	From	To
1	18	25
2	26	30
3	31	35
4	36	40
5	41	50
6	51	60
7	61	70
8	71	75
9	76	80
10	81	100

Table 6.1   Ten ranges for the attribute Age. This partition is neither too fine nor too coarse; the objective is to adequately represent the various stages of financial developments and risks in a person's life.

Germany. In the former case, it could be considered a badge of entrepreneurial curiosity that you can proudly refer to. In the latter case, it might be a financial and social stigma that will mark you to the end of your life! Moreover, there are many kinds of bankruptcy. In making an assessment of credit worthiness, it's important to understand whether a bankruptcy was due to medical reasons or to an extravagant personal life. In our example, the bankruptcy attribute will be Boolean.

The third attribute is *ownership of a car.* Owning a Lamborghini is worlds apart from owning a car from KIA. Nevertheless, we'll consider car ownership as a Boolean attribute. Since we're concerned with credit worthiness, the mere fact that an individual owns a car is the strongest and simplest discriminating factor. When do you think it would be useful to assign an integer value to car ownership, such as specific ranges of the car's monetary worth? Consider, for example, the case where you need a finer classification of credit worthiness that entails assignment to one of 20 classes instead of 5. In addition, you should consider the case of outliers—people who don't own a car because they're unable to drive (they have a physical disability) or they don't need or want to own a car even though they could afford it.

The fourth attribute is an individual's *credit score.* There are three major companies that accumulate information related to credit card activity, mortgages, home equity lines of credit, and so on. These companies assign each individual a credit score, whose range varies based on the company but is generally a number between 0 and 800. We'll use eight different brackets for the credit score, as indicated in table 6.2.

The fifth attribute is an indicator as to whether an individual has a *criminal record.* A misdemeanor or a simple complaint against an individual is fundamentally different from armed robbery. But the use of a Boolean attribute value isn't as restrictive as it may seem initially; it's simply a matter of setting the threshold of "criminality" at an appropriate level. Felonies or some other detailed list of crimes would set the Boolean variable to true while "softer" crimes wouldn't alter the default value (false) for the criminal record variable.

Attribute ID	From	To
1	0	500
2	501	550
3	551	600
4	601	650
5	651	700
6	701	750
7	751	800
8	801	—

Table 6.2
The range of values for the credit score attribute

The sixth attribute is the *percentage of down payment* that the applicant is willing to pay at the time of closing. In table 6.3 we show four ranges for the value of down payment. If the applicant is able to pay more than 25% of the loan amount, it doesn't matter how much she can pay. The interesting discriminating area is between 0% and 25%.

Attribute ID	From	To
1	0	5
2	6	10
3	11	20
4	21	–

Table 6.3 The range of values for the down payment attribute (as percentage of the total loan amount)

The seventh attribute is the *amount of income*. Like the down payment attribute, when we consider the income values, we don't care if someone has $5 million or $100 million. We're more interested in the stratification of the income values at the low end of the spectrum. Moreover, the spread of income values can be any number between 0 and several billion. We'll use a larger number of income ranges to discriminate among the applicants. Table 6.4 shows the 10 values for this attribute and the associated ranges; the values are presented in thousands of dollars.

Attribute ID	From	To
1	0	25
2	26	35
3	36	45
4	46	60
5	61	80
6	81	100
7	101	125
8	126	150
9	151	200
10	201	–

Table 6.4
The range of values for the income attribute

The eighth attribute is determined by the *kind of work* that an individual performs. For the purpose of this example, we came up with five "job classes" but a finer division is possible. Table 6.5 shows the five possible values of the job class attribute.

The ninth attribute is related to the *ownership of a motorcycle* and it's a Boolean attribute. In certain countries, owning a motorcycle is a luxury, while in other countries it's the prevailing means of transportation (if not the only one). This attribute

Attribute ID	Job Class Name
1	C-level executive
2	Professional
3	Employee
4	Business owner
5	Contractor

Table 6.5
The range of values for the income attribute

shouldn't have much influence on the results, because when we generate our data, we assign motorcycle ownership to every class (except the dangerous class) with the same probability. Later on, we'll discuss the definition of each class of individuals based on the values of these attributes and elaborate further on this point.

The tenth attribute is related to the *ownership of property*—land property—and it's also a Boolean attribute. A natural extension would be a monetary representation of the land's value, but for our example we'll treat this attribute as a Boolean variable.

The eleventh attribute is related to the *amount of financial assets* that are *associated with retirement accounts*. It's, of course, a continuous variable that we discretize into specific ranges. Table 6.6 shows the eight values for this attribute and the associated ranges; the values are presented in thousands of dollars.

At this point, we should iterate that there's nothing magic about the number 11 or these specific attributes. In reality, you'll have many attributes to choose from and your attribute selections are part of formulating and solving the classification problem; see the first item in our To do section. The main point is the importance of understanding the nature of your data. You can learn all the algorithms known to man, but if you don't understand the nature of your data it will be difficult to provide a satisfactory solution to your problem.

Attribute ID	From	To
1	0	25
2	26	75
3	76	150
4	151	300
5	301	500
6	501	1000
7	1001	2000
8	2001	—

Table 6.6   The range of values for the retirement accounts attribute

6.1.2 Generating artificial data for real problems

Let's examine a number of decisions that must be made to define our data, so that you get an idea of what we mean by the nature of the data. As we discussed, each user will be represented by 11 attribute values. In order to define a class of users, we assign a set of eligible attribute values for each one of our classes. In other words, we "draw" five regions in the 11-dimensional space and give it one of the five class labels. If we want to create a user of a particular class then we select randomly one of the eligible tuples—for each attribute, we pick a value from the region of that class.

You can find the eligible attribute values for each class in the Java classes `ExcellentUserType`, `VeryGoodUserType`, `GoodUserType`, `BadUserType`, `Dangerous-UserType`—all of which extend the abstract class `UserType`, which contains the common functionality. Listing 6.1 shows the content of the `GoodUserType`, which is the majority class of credit worthiness. As you can see, according to this definition, users with good credit could be of any age, they shouldn't have declared bankruptcy, they should own a car, and so on.

Listing 6.1 `GoodUserType`: definition of the "good" class through attribute values

```
public class GoodUserType extends UserType {

  {
    setAge(new int[] { 2, 3, 4, 5, 6, 7, 8 });
    setBancruptcy(new int[] { 0 });
    setCarOwnership(new int[] { 1 });
    setCreditScore(new int[] { 3, 4, 5, 6 });
    setCriminalRecord(new int[] { 0 });
    setDownPayment(new int[] { 2, 3 });
    setIncome(new int[] { 5, 6, 7, 8 });
    setJobClass(new int[] {2, 3, 4, 5});
    setMotorcycleOwnership(new int[] { 0, 1});
    setPropertyOwnership(new int[] { 0, 1 });
    setRetirementAccounts(new int[] { 1, 2, 3, 4 });
  }

  @Override
  public String getUserType() {
    return UserType.GOOD;
  }
}
```

Look at the other `UserType` classes. What do you observe? There's a slight overlap between neighboring classes, as you'd expect. This fuzzy boundary makes the data more realistic. You may wonder, isn't it possible that a user who belongs to the "bad" class has attribute values that fall entirely within the domain that defines the "good" class? In real-life data, it would not only be possible but likely. That's exactly the problem that we're trying to solve! Provided a set of attribute values, we want an automated way to tell the credit worth of a user. If real-world data could fit some preconceived models then "learning" wouldn't be very useful; all the intelligence could be fed into an a priori model and put into action. In order to emulate that characteristic of real-world data, we introduce *noise levels*.

Noise levels define the likelihood that a user with attribute values from the domain of class X will truly belong to class Y. Noise levels allow us to mix the definition of classes to an arbitrary extent. Listing 6.2 shows the crucial steps found in the class `DataGenerator`.

Listing 6.2   `DataGenerator`: creating the sets of users for all classes

```
public List<User> generateUsers(List<UserType> userTypes) {

  List<User> allUsers = new ArrayList<User>();

  for(UserType userType : userTypes) {
    allUsers.addAll(
    generateUsers(userType, userType.getNUsers() ));
  }
  return allUsers;
}

public List<User> generateUsers(UserType userType, int n) {

  List<User> users = new ArrayList<User>();

  userTypeDistributions.put(userType, n);

  for(int i = 0; i < n; i++) {                      ❶
    User u = generateUser(userType);
    users.add(u);
  }
  return users;
}

public User generateUser(UserType userType) {

  User user = new User();

  long userId = generateNextUniqueUserId();

  String username;

  if (isNoiseOn) {                                  ❷
    username = userType.getNoisyType();
  } else {
    username = userType.getUserType();
  }

  username = username + String.valueOf(userId);

  user.setUsername(username);
  user.setAge(userType.pickAge());
  user.setCarOwnership(userType.pickCarOwnership());
  user.setCreditScore(userType.pickCreditScore());
  user.setIncome(userType.pickIncome());
  user.setJobClass(userType.pickJobClass());
  user.setDownPayment(userType.pickDownPayment());
  user.setBicycleOwnership(userType.pickMotorcycleOwnership());
  user.setPropertyOwnership(userType.pickPropertyOwnership());
  user.setCriminalRecord(userType.pickCriminalRecord());
```

```
user.setBankruptcy(userType.pickBancruptcy());
user.setRetirementAccount(userType.pickRetirementAccounts());

return user;
}
```

❶ For each user type, create a number of users according to the predefined distribution for that user type.

❷ If noise is present, mix up the user types as defined in the `getNoisyType` method. Otherwise, use only the predefined distributions of each user type.

Since the data for our example is artificial, the proportion of users in the various classes of credit worthiness is fully controlled. The default distribution of users per class is shown in table 6.7.

Class	Number of users (%)
Excellent	5
Very Good	15
Good	50
Bad	25
Dangerous	5

Table 6.7 The distribution of users, as a percentage of the total number of users, for each class of credit worthiness

Obviously, you could change the proportion of users for each class. You can do that by changing the implementation of the method `createUserTypes` in the class `UseCase-Data`. The important thing to note is that the distribution is hardly uniform. Most users belong to the good class, but for those users whose credit worthiness isn't good, it's more likely that their credit will be worse than good by the ratio 3 to 2. The two extreme classes are equally likely according to this distribution.

You can create your own artificial data by executing the commands shown in listing 6.3.

Listing 6.3 Creating artificial data for the credit worthiness use case

```
UseCaseData useCaseData = new UseCaseData(40000,20000);    ← Define new dataset
UserType.addNoiseLevel("EX",
    new Double[] {1.0d, 5.0d, 8.0d, 10.0d});
UserType.addNoiseLevel("VG",
    new Double[] {1.0d, 2.5d, 6.0d, 10.0d});
UserType.addNoiseLevel("GD",
    new Double[] {1.0d, 3.0d, 4.0d, 8.0d});        Define noise levels of each class
UserType.addNoiseLevel("BD",
    new Double[] {1.0d, 3.0d, 7.5d, 10.0d});
UserType.addNoiseLevel("DN",
    new Double[] {1.0d, 6.0d, 10.0d, 14.0d});

useCaseData.create(false);    ← InitializTrue value will override existing filesation
```

If you want to use the default noise levels you can skip the `UserType.addNoiseLevel` calls. Beware of the last method call. If you assign a true value to the Boolean argument, it will override the existing dataset and the results from the execution of the listings will be different from what you see in the book. You can always recover the original files by extracting them from the file clean_40k_20k.7z, which can be found in the `data/ch06/samples/clean` directory of the distribution.

Before we move on, let's take a closer look at the definition of noise levels. In listing 6.2, a crucial step was the call to the `getNoisyType` method. Listing 6.4 shows the related code for the "excellent" user type and it should help you interpret the semantics of the `UserType.addNoiseLevel` calls.

Listing 6.4 `UserType.getNoisyType`: adding noise to the user type "excellent"

```
public String getNoisyType() {
    double gaussian = rnd.nextGaussian();
    String noisyType=null;
    String userType= getUserType();
    Double[] nLevels = noiseLevels.get(userType);
    if (getUserType().equals(EXCELLENT)) {
        if (gaussian <= nLevels[0]) {
            noisyType = EXCELLENT;
        } else if (gaussian > nLevels[0] &&
            gaussian <= nLevels[1]) {
            noisyType = VERY_GOOD;
        } else if (gaussian > nLevels[1] &&
            gaussian <= nLevels[2]) {
            noisyType = GOOD;
        } else if (gaussian > nLevels[2] &&
            gaussian <= nLevels[3]) {
            noisyType = BAD;
        } else {
            noisyType = DANGEROUS;
        }
    }
}
```

The class `Random` from the `java.util` package is used to draw a double number according to a standard normal distribution. This means that the values drawn are centered around zero and about 68.2% of them are within the values −1 and 1, 95% of them are within the values −2 and 2, and 99.7% of them are within −3 and 3. When we create a dataset with noise levels as indicated in listing 6.3, the code in listing 6.4 tells us that a user from the excellent class of user types may end up being a user from the very good class of user types with probability about 16%. It also tells us that the probability that such a user will belong in the bad or dangerous classes of user types is practically equal to zero. The lower the noise level of your datasets, the higher the accuracy that a classifier can achieve.

6.2   *Credit evaluation with a single classifier*

Let's now apply each of our classifiers to the data of our case study and evaluate their accuracy. In subsection 6.2.1, we'll use a naïve Bayes classifier. In subsection 6.2.2, we'll introduce a new classifier based on a decision tree. In subsection 6.2.3, we'll use a classifier based on a neural network implementation. Here, the objective is to establish a baseline, so that we can evaluate whether we've achieved improvement by combining the classifiers.

6.2.1   *The naïve Bayes baseline*

In listing 6.5, we show the steps that you can follow to quickly load, train, and evaluate the naïve Bayes classifier. By default, these commands will load the training dataset from a file called c:/iWeb2/data/ch06/training-users.txt. If you want to load a different file then you can use the desired filename as an argument. For the testing dataset, these commands will load the dataset from a file called c:/iWeb2/data/ch06/test-users.txt.

Listing 6.5   Assessing credit worthiness with a naïve Bayes classifier

```
UserDataset ds = UserLoader.loadTrainingDataset();

NBCreditClassifier naiveBayes = new NBCreditClassifier(ds);   ⟵┐ Create
                                                               │ classifier
naiveBayes.useDefaultAttributes();                             │ based on
                                                               │ Naïve Bayes
naiveBayes.train();   ⟵ Train classifier

UserDataset testDS = UserLoader.loadTestDataset();

CreditErrorEstimator nb_err =
➥ new CreditErrorEstimator(testDS, naiveBayes);

nb_err.run();   ⟵ Estimate error
```

In figure 6.1, we show the results of executing the commands of listing 6.5, for a test set of 20,000 transactions. As you can see, the naïve Bayes classifier produces decent results with an accuracy of 0.826 on this specific dataset. Of the 20,000 credit worthiness evaluations performed; 16,520 were classified correctly while 3,480 were wrong. The *confusion matrix* helps us visualize how bad our misclassifications were. The numbers along the main diagonal of this matrix are the correct classifications. The numbers away from the main diagonal are the erroneous classifications. If a classification is attributed to the left of the diagonal (as you look at the matrix) the credit worthiness was inflated due to the misclassification. For an entry on the right side of the diagonal, the classifier underestimates the credit worthiness of a user.

The visualization of the confusion matrix for classification results is important because, as we discussed in chapter 5, the cost of misclassifications isn't uniform in

```
Classification completed in 1.575 seconds.

 Total test dataset txns: 20000
    Classified correctly: 16520, Misclassified: 3480
               Accuracy: 0.826


                     CONFUSION MATRIX


          EX      VG      GD      BD      DN
   EX    828      24      18       0       0
   VG    161    2149    1900       4       0
   GD      1     418    8482     800       0
   BD      0       0       0    4208     147
   DN      0       0       0       7     853
```

Figure 6.1 The results of credit worthiness classification for the naïve Bayes classifier

real-world problems. We can also build metrics that are based on the confusion matrices of two different classifiers in order to compare them; we'll say more on this subject in section 6.3. The `CreditErrorEstimator` keeps track of the classification results and is responsible for producing the output shown in figure 6.1

Listing 6.6 shows the code from the class `NBCreditClassifier`, without some auxiliary methods that are unimportant. The essence of this class is captured from the code present in the listing. Once again, we see that creating a custom classifier as an extension of the `NaiveBayes` class is a breeze; there's little code that you have to write. Let's have a closer look.

Listing 6.6 The `NaiveBayes` classifier for evaluating credit worthiness

```
public class NBCreditClassifier extends NaiveBayes {

  private UserInstanceBuilder instanceBuilder;          ①

  public NBCreditClassifier(String name, TrainingSet ts,
                  UserInstanceBuilder instanceBuilder) {    ②

      super(name, ts);
      this.instanceBuilder = instanceBuilder;
  }

  public Concept classify(Instance instance) {        ③
      return super.classify(instance);
  }

  public Concept classify(User user) {                  ④
      return classify(instanceBuilder.createInstance(user));
  }

  public void useDefaultAttributes() {                  ⑤
      trainOnAttribute(CreditInstance.ATTR_NAME_JOB_CLASS);
      trainOnAttribute(CreditInstance.ATTR_NAME_INCOME_TYPE);
```

```
          trainOnAttribute(CreditInstance.ATTR_NAME_AGE);
          trainOnAttribute(CreditInstance.ATTR_NAME_CAR_OWNERSHIP);
          trainOnAttribute(CreditInstance.ATTR_NAME_CREDIT_SCORE);
          trainOnAttribute(
➥    CreditInstance.ATTR_NAME_MORTGAGE_DOWN_PAYMENT);
          trainOnAttribute(
➥    CreditInstance.ATTR_NAME_MOTOR_BICYCLE_OWNERSHIP);
          trainOnAttribute(
➥    CreditInstance.ATTR_NAME_OTHER_PROPERTY_OWNERSHIP);
          trainOnAttribute(CreditInstance.ATTR_NAME_CRIMINAL_RECORD);
          trainOnAttribute(CreditInstance.ATTR_NAME_BANKRUPTCY);
          trainOnAttribute(
➥    CreditInstance.ATTR_NAME_RETIREMENT_ACCOUNT);
      }
}
```

❶ The class `UserInstanceBuilder` is responsible for translating a `User` into an `Instance`. If you were working on a different problem, say evaluating cars, your custom classifier would have a similar auxiliary class that would translate a `Car` into an `Instance`. That's because we extend the `NaiveBayes` classifier, which is unaware of general objects—it only deals with `Concepts` and `Instances`. The critical step of deciding whether to treat the various attributes as numerical or categorical variables is done by the `UserInstanceBuilder` class.

❷ The constructor requires a name, a training set, and an instance of the `UserInstanceBuilder`.

❸ We point out that eventually all implementations will delegate the classification to the base method of the `NaiveBayes` classifier.

❹ The value of the `UserInstanceBuilder` class. The overloaded `classify` method leverages that class to create an `Instance`, which it passes on to the base classification method.

❺ You can customize this method by commenting out some of the lines. By default, we use all 11 attributes for our classification purposes. If you comment out some of these lines the corresponding attributes won't be used during the classification.

You can trust the naïve Bayes classifier to give you reasonable results in many cases. It's also very stable, which means that if some instances of your training set aren't typical, or if some instances enter in your data erroneously, the results won't be significantly affected. But as we'll see, this isn't a desirable property when we combine classifiers. On the contrary, for the combination methods that we'll present, we want the base classifiers to be *unstable* (see section 6.4). We can build an unstable classifier by using a decision tree. So, let's move on and see how to build and use a decision tree for our problem.

6.2.2 *The decision tree baseline*

In listing 6.7, we show the steps to create, train, and evaluate a classifier based on a decision tree. We didn't present decision trees in chapter 5, but we include a brief description in our second to-do item in this chapter. For the purposes of this chapter, the specific algorithmic implementation doesn't really matter; we could have a classifier based on any classification algorithm. The important part is that the classification algorithms are different.

The steps in listing 6.7 are similar to those of listing 6.5. If you execute listing 6.7 within the same shell as you executed listing 6.5, you can ignore the loading of the training dataset and the loading of the testing dataset.

> **Listing 6.7 Assessing credit worthiness with a decision tree–based classifier**

```
UserDataset ds = UserLoader.loadTrainingDataset();

DTCreditClassifier decisionTree = new DTCreditClassifier(ds);    ◁──┐ Create
                                                                     │ classifier
decisionTree.useDefaultAttributes();                                 │ based on
                                                                     │ decision
decisionTree.train();    ◁── Train classifier                        │ tree
                                                                     │
UserDataset testDS = UserLoader.loadTestDataset();               ───┘

CreditErrorEstimator dt_err =
➥ new CreditErrorEstimator(testDS, decisionTree);

dt_err.run();    ◁── Estimate error
```

In figure 6.2, we show the results of executing the commands of listing 6.7. As you can see, the decision tree classifier is fast—faster than the naïve Bayes implementation by an order of magnitude. It produces results with an accuracy of 0.8262, which is nominally better than the accuracy that we got from the naïve Bayes implementation on the same dataset. In particular, a total of 20,000 credit worthiness evaluations were performed; 16,524 of those were classified correctly while 3,476 were wrong. As we'll see in the later sections, the difference between the results of the naïve Bayes classifier and the decision tree-based classifier isn't statistically significant.

```
Classification completed in 0.132 seconds.

Total test dataset txns: 20000
    Classified correctly: 16524, Misclassified: 3476
               Accuracy: 0.8262


               CONFUSION MATRIX


          EX     VG     GD     BD     DN
    EX    831    24     15     0      0
    VG    164    2321   1725   4      0
    GD    0      585    8319   797    0
    BD    0      0      8      4200   147
    DN    0      0      0      7      853
```

Figure 6.2 The results of credit worthiness classification for the classifier based on a decision tree

```
Node:attrName=priorCriminalRecord,isLeaf=false,concept=null
-> Branch: [priorCriminalRecord=1]
     Node:attrName=null,isLeaf=true,concept=DN
-> Branch: [priorCriminalRecord=0]
Node:attrName=priorDeclaredBankruptcy,isLeaf=false,concept=null
 -> Branch: [priorDeclaredBankruptcy=1]
      Node:attrName=null,isLeaf=true,concept=BD
-> Branch: [priorDeclaredBankruptcy=0]
   Node:attrName=carOwnership,isLeaf=false,concept=null
-> Branch: [carOwnership=1]
   Node:attrName=mortgageDownPayment,isLeaf=false,concept=null
-> Branch: [mortgageDownPayment=3]
   Node:attrName=otherPropertyOwnership,isLeaf=false,concept=null
-> Branch: [otherPropertyOwnership=1]
   Node:attrName=retirementAccount,isLeaf=false,concept=null
-> Branch: [retirementAccount=3]
   Node:attrName=creditScore,isLeaf=false,concept=null
-> Branch: [creditScore=3]
   Node:attrName=null,isLeaf=true,concept=GD
```

Figure 6.3   The top-level nodes of the decision tree for the credit worthiness data

If you execute the command `decisionTree.printTree()` in your shell, you'll see what the decision tree looks like. In figure 6.3, we show the first few lines from the output of `printTree()`. Make sure that the height of the screen buffer size for your shell is a few thousand lines long. Also note that, due to the format limitations of the book, the tree-like structure is suppressed in the figure. The first attribute that the classifier looks at is the prior criminal record attribute. According to the decision tree, you can forget about getting a mortgage if you've been identified as having a criminal record! If the instance refers to a user without a criminal record then the tree will look into whether this instance refers to a user who has declared bankruptcy in the past. If bankruptcy has been declared then the credit worthiness of that user will be classified as bad. Otherwise, the analysis continues as indicated by the output on your screen.

The simple interpretation of the classification with a decision tree is one of the main reasons why decision trees are popular. But the value of a direct interpretation is questionable when we deal with the combination of 10 or 100 classifiers. In that context, we're primarily interested in the fact that decision trees are inherently unstable. Of course, decision trees aren't the only classification algorithms that are unstable. Other typically unstable classifiers are those based on neural networks.

6.2.3   *The neural network baseline*

Let's add one more classifier to our collection, a classifier based on a neural network implementation. Listing 6.8 shows how to assess the credit worthiness of users by using our neural network-based credit classifier. If you execute listing 6.8 within the same shell as you executed listing 6.5 or listing 6.7, you can ignore the loading of the training dataset and the loading of the testing dataset.

Listing 6.8   Assessing credit worthiness with a neural network–based classifier

```
UserDataset ds = UserLoader.loadTrainingDataset();

NNCreditClassifier neuralNet = new NNCreditClassifier(ds);

neuralNet.setLearningRate(0.025);

neuralNet.useDefaultAttributes();

neuralNet.train();

UserDataset testDS = UserLoader.loadTestDataset();

CreditErrorEstimator nn_err =
    new CreditErrorEstimator(testDS, neuralNet);

nn_err.run();
```

Create classifier based on neural network

Set learning rate for back propagation

Train classifier

Estimate error

As you can see, the only difference between these listings is the setup of the classifier. That repetitiveness is both intentional and important. In the context of comparing classifiers (or anything else), you should strive to be as methodical and systematic as possible. As the number of classifiers increases, it may become difficult to ensure that you're comparing apples to apples. In figure 6.4, we show the results from the execution of listing 6.8.

```
Classification completed in 0.266 seconds.

Total test dataset txns: 20000
     Classified correctly: 14330, Misclassified: 5670
                 Accuracy: 0.7165


                CONFUSION MATRIX


          EX     VG     GD     BD     DN
   EX    498      0    372      0      0
   VG     91      0   4100     23      0
   GD      0      0   8804    897      0
   BD      0      0     33   4175    147
   DN      0      0      0      7    853
```

Figure 6.4   The results of credit worthiness classification for the classifier based on a neural network

The class `iweb2.ch6.usecase.credit.NNCreditClassifier` encapsulates the custom neural network classifier for our credit worthiness use case. The neural network itself is located in the class `iweb2.ch6.usecase.credit.UserCreditNN` and is shown in listing 6.9. Let's examine it; we don't show the definition of all the links or nonessential methods.

Listing 6.9   A custom neural network for the mortgage credit risk assessment

```
public class UserCreditNN extends BaseNN {

  public UserCreditNN(String name) {
```

```
      super(name);
      create();
   }

   public void create() {
      createNN_11_7_5();
   }

   private void createNN_11_7_5() {

      Layer inputLayer = createInputLayer(0, 11);

      Layer hiddenLayer = createHiddenLayer(1, 7,
   new double[] { 0.5, -1, 1.5, 0.5, 1, -0.2, 0.1 });

      Layer outputLayer = createOutputLayer(2, 5,
           new double[] {-1.5, 0.5, -1, 0.5, 1});

      setInputLayer(inputLayer);
      setOutputLayer(outputLayer);
      addHiddenLayer(hiddenLayer);

      setLink("0:0", "1:0", 0.25);
      setLink("0:0", "1:1", -0.7);
      setLink("0:0", "1:2", 0.25);
      setLink("0:0", "1:3", 0.25);
      setLink("0:0", "1:4", -0.3);
      setLink("0:0", "1:5", 0.25);
      setLink("0:0", "1:6", -0.5);

      setLink("0:1", "1:0", 0.25);
      setLink("0:1", "1:1", -0.5);
      setLink("0:1", "1:2", 0.25);
      setLink("0:1", "1:3", 0.25);
      setLink("0:1", "1:4", 0.50);
      setLink("0:1", "1:5", 0.25);
      setLink("0:1", "1:6", 0.50);

   [... Snip ...]

   }
}
```

Define input layer with 11 nodes

Define hidden layer with 7 nodes

Define output layer with 5 nodes

Define links between nodes

The choice of an 11-node input layer is dictated by our decision to use 11 attributes, but the choice of 7 nodes for the hidden layer and 5 nodes for the output layer is arbitrary. In fact, we could have two or more hidden layers in our network. Let this be a reminder of our discussion from chapter 5 about the overwhelming complexity involved in modeling a neural network. The enormous flexibility comes at the price of complexity. Although rules of thumb exist, following design principles for neural networks should be treated with caution, and its neural network should be validated within the context of its use. In one of the to-do items, we invite you to create your own neural network by defining your own architecture in the UserCreditNN class. Then you can use the methods of this chapter to compare the two or more neural networks and see the effect of your design decisions in action.

This subsection concludes the presentation of the three classifiers that we'll employ in the rest of the chapter. One last observation we want to make is based on the training time of the neural network. Aside from the quality assurance characteristics of a classifier, you should always consider two essential performance characteristics—the training time and the runtime. The training times are printed in the shell after the execution of the `train()` method call, which is invoked for all classifiers (see listings 6.5–6.8). For the naïve Bayes, decision tree, and neural network classifiers, they're 0.5, 5.6, and 265.6 seconds, respectively. Training time is usually not an issue; the runtime for classification is typically more precious. Nevertheless, several orders of magnitude in training time between two classifiers can practically eliminate the slower (in training) classifier from consideration, especially if training data growth is anticipated for a production system.

As we mentioned earlier, the classification with the decision tree classifier produces results with an accuracy of 0.8262, which is better than the accuracy that we got from the naïve Bayes implementation on the same dataset. Both the decision tree and the naïve Bayes classifiers appear to be better than the neural network classifier, but are they? Are the differences in these accuracies statistically significant? These are important questions that we need to answer before we move on to combining versions of any of the classifiers. In the next section, we develop tools that can help us answer these questions.

6.3   *Comparing multiple classifiers on the same data*

We'll present four tests that allow us to compare classifiers. *McNemar's test* and the *difference of proportions test* can be used to compare two classifiers. *Cochran's Q test* and the *F test* can be used to compare three or more classifiers. These are statistical tests and require an understanding of statistics that isn't required for this book; nevertheless, the general idea is easy to follow. All statistical tests have an initial premise (*null hypothesis* is the technical name) that's proved or disproved based on a numerical comparison between the value of a *statistic* and a *threshold value* that can be looked up in tables or be calculated from a known formula. So, in all the tests that we'll present, you'll see that we follow two steps. First, we evaluate a value for the relevant statistic. Second, we compare it with a hardcoded value—the threshold value. If you're interested in the mathematical details, *Combining Pattern Classifiers: Methods and Algorithms* by Ludmila Ilieva Kuncheva is a great place to start; in this section, we follow the layout of her presentation.

Whether we want to select a single classifier out of many or design a classifier based on many other classifiers, it's possible to use only pair-wise comparisons. There's a practical reason why we discuss tests that apply to three or more classifiers: the number of possible pairs grows quickly with the number of classifiers. In fact, it's equal to $N*(N-1)/2$ where N is the number of classifiers. So, we need a way to quickly tell whether a bunch of classifiers is different in a statistically significant manner. Eventually, we'd need to do pair-wise comparisons in order to find out which of the classifiers are the culprits!

The justification for these tests is beyond the scope of this book; the interested reader will find plenty of references to the literature at the end of this chapter and in appendix C. The important knowledge that you need, from a practical perspective, consists of three things:

- You need to understand that differences in accuracy between classifiers aren't always significant, and that there are tests for pair-wise comparisons, as well as tests for multiclassifier comparisons.
- You need to know how to calculate the appropriate statistic for each test; our code provides the implementation for the four tests that we consider, as well as a generic abstract class that you can extend to write your own test.
- You need to know how to look up the appropriate threshold value for each test. Typically, these can be found in publicly available tables for given level of significance and degrees of freedom (whenever applicable). You can also write your own classes that evaluate these values based on their mathematical definitions.

6.3.1 McNemar's test

Assuming that you've executed listings 6.5, 6.7, and 6.8 in the same shell, go ahead and run the script that's shown in listing 6.10 to compare the three possible pairs of classifiers. As you'd expect, McNemar's test is encapsulated in the class McNemarTest, which requires two arguments in its constructor—the ClassifierResults instance from each classifier.

> **Listing 6.10 McNemar's test for comparing two classifiers**

```
McNemarTest mnTest1 = new McNemarTest(nb_err.getResults(),
    nn_err.getResults());

McNemarTest mnTest2 = new McNemarTest(nb_err.getResults(),     One test for
    dt_err.getResults());                                      each pair of
                                                               classifiers
McNemarTest mnTest3 = new McNemarTest(dt_err.getResults(),
    nn_err.getResults());

mnTest1.evaluate();

mnTest2.evaluate();          Evaluating each test

mnTest3.evaluate();
```

The results are shown in figure 6.5 and are what you would've thought instinctively by looking at the test classification reports of each classifier. The neural network produces results of lower accuracy that are statistically significant according to this test. The variable Chi2 that you see in the output is called the χ^2 (chi-square) statistic) and its probability distribution can be defined for *n* degrees of freedom; in our case, we take *n=1*. For details on the χ^2 statistic, see the fourth to-do item in this chapter and the references mentioned in appendix C.

The χ^2 statistic can be used in many different ways. In our implementation, we followed Dietterich and Kuncheva, and calculated the χ^2 as shown in listing 6.11. The variable n01 stands for the number of times that the first classifier has performed a classification erroneously while the second classifier performed the same classification correctly, and the variable n10 stands for the number of times that the reverse is true.

```
bsh % mnTest1.evaluate();
      Evaluating classifiers
      NBCreditClassifier and NNCreditClassifier:

      NBCreditClassifier accuracy: 0.826
      NNCreditClassifier accuracy: 0.7165
      N = 20000, n00=3050, n10=2620, n01=430, n11=13900

      Confidence Interval              : 0.05
      Degrees of Freedom               : 1
      Statistic threshold (Chi-square) : 3.841

      Chi2 = 1571.0560655737704 > 3.841
      The two classifiers are different: TRUE

bsh % mnTest2.evaluate();
      Evaluating classifiers
      NBCreditClassifier and DTCreditClassifier:

      NBCreditClassifier accuracy: 0.826
      DTCreditClassifier accuracy: 0.8262
      N = 20000, n00=3252, n10=224, n01=228, n11=16296

      Confidence Interval              : 0.05
      Degrees of Freedom               : 1
      Statistic threshold (Chi-square) : 3.841

      Chi2 = 0.01991150442477876 <= 3.841
      The two classifiers are different: FALSE

bsh % mnTest3.evaluate();
      Evaluating classifiers
      DTCreditClassifier and NNCreditClassifier:

      DTCreditClassifier accuracy: 0.8262
      NNCreditClassifier accuracy: 0.7165
      N = 20000, n00=2872, n10=2798, n01=604, n11=13726

      Confidence Interval              : 0.05
      Degrees of Freedom               : 1
      Statistic threshold (Chi-square) : 3.841

      Chi2 = 1413.6534391534392 > 3.841
      The two classifiers are different: TRUE
```

Figure 6.5   The results of applying the McNemar test to the three pairs of classifiers

Listing 6.11   The evaluation of the χ^2 statistic in the McNemar test

```
protected void calculate() {
  int n = c1.getN();

  for(int i = 0; i < n; i++) {

    if( c1.getResult(i) && c2.getResult(i) ) {      Both classifiers
                                                    were correct
      n11++;
```

```
    } else if ( c1.getResult(i) && !c2.getResult(i) ) {        The first was correct,
                                                               the second wrong
        n10++;

    } else if ( !c1.getResult(i) && c2.getResult(i) ) {        The first was wrong,
                                                               the second correct
        n01++;
                                  Both classifiers
    } else {                      were wrong
        n00++;
    }
}

double a = Math.abs(n01 - n10) - 1;
chi2 = a * a / (n01 + n10);              Value of χ² statistic
}
```

Note that the absolute value ensures that the result of the difference between *n01* and *n10* is symmetrical. In addition, taking the square of the numerator ensures that the final result is symmetrical. In other words, the order that you pass the classifier results in the constructor of the McNemar class doesn't matter. Once the value of the statistic has been calculated, we compare it with the threshold value of 3.841, which is the value of the χ^2 probability distribution for *level of significance* 0.05; if you don't know what that means, see the references in appendix C for the definition of the level of significance of a statistical test. In other words, if the value of the χ^2 statistic is greater than 3.841 then we're fairly confident that the two classifiers are different in a statistically significant way.

In one of our to-do items, we invite you to apply the χ^2 statistic in a somewhat different manner. The basic idea is to interrogate whether the classification results that we get from two different classifiers are drawn from the same probability distribution. In problems similar to the one that we study here—credit worthiness of applicants distributed across five classes—our proposed approach may be a better comparison metric than the McNemar test. Read the to-do item to learn more!

6.3.2 *The difference of proportions test*

Once again, we assume that you've executed listings 6.5, 6.7, and 6.8 in the same shell. If you did then go ahead and run the script shown in listing 6.12 to compare the three possible pairs of classifiers based on the difference of proportions test. The difference of proportions test is encapsulated in the class Diff2PropTest, which requires two arguments in its constructor—just as the McNemarTest did.

Listing 6.12 The difference of proportions test for comparing two classifiers

```
Diff2PropTest d2pTest1 = new Diff2PropTest(nb_err.getResults(),
    nn_err.getResults());
                                                                One test for
Diff2PropTest d2pTest2 = new Diff2PropTest(nb_err.getResults(),  each pair of
    dt_err.getResults());                                        classifiers
Diff2PropTest d2pTest3 = new Diff2PropTest(dt_err.getResults(),
    nn_err.getResults());

d2pTest1.evaluate();
d2pTest2.evaluate();     Evaluating each test
d2pTest3.evaluate();
```

The results are shown in figure 6.6 and corroborate the results we got from McNemar's test. The neural network produces results of lower accuracy that are statistically significant according to this test as well. The variable z that you see in the output is a statistic whose probability distribution is supposed to be a standard normal distribution; so, its mean value is zero and its variance is one. For details on the standard normal distribution, see the references mentioned in appendix C.

Listing 6.13 shows the calculation of the z statistic, whose distribution is supposed to follow the standard normal distribution. This statistic is commonly used in machine learning literature, but the assumption of independence is questionable. Can you figure out why? (Hint: see Dietterich.)

```
bsh % d2pTest1.evaluate();
       Evaluating classifiers
       NBCreditClassifier and NNCreditClassifier:

       NBCreditClassifier accuracy: 0.826
       NNCreditClassifier accuracy: 0.7165

       Confidence Interval            : 0.05
       Statistic threshold (Std Normal): 1.96

       |z| = 26.069696745398772 > 1.96
       The classifiers are different: TRUE

bsh % d2pTest2.evaluate();
       Evaluating classifiers
       NBCreditClassifier and DTCreditClassifier:

       NBCreditClassifier accuracy: 0.826
       DTCreditClassifier accuracy: 0.8262

       Confidence Interval            : 0.05
       Statistic threshold (Std Normal): 1.96

       |z| = -0.05276718103090302 <= 1.96
       The classifiers are different: FALSE

bsh % d2pTest3.evaluate();
       Evaluating classifiers
       DTCreditClassifier and NNCreditClassifier:

       DTCreditClassifier accuracy: 0.8262
       NNCreditClassifier accuracy: 0.7165

       Confidence Interval            : 0.05
       Statistic threshold (Std Normal): 1.96

       |z| = 26.12132981820125 > 1.96
       The classifiers are different: TRUE
```

Figure 6.6 The results of applying the difference of proportions test to the three pairs of classifiers

---

Listing 6.13 The evaluation of the z statistic in the difference of proportions test

```
double diff = c1.getAccuracy() - c2.getAccuracy();

double mean = 0.5 * (c1.getAccuracy() + c2.getAccuracy());

double b = ( 2.0 * mean * ( 1 - mean ) ) / n;

z = diff / Math.sqrt(b);     <── Define z statistic
```

Evaluate difference between accuracies

Evaluate average accuracy

In listing 6.13, the variable n refers to the number of instances in the testing set, which is the same for both classifiers. Once the z statistic has been calculated, its absolute value is compared with the value of 1.96, which corresponds to a two-sided test (it shouldn't matter which classifier you used first) with a level of significance of 0.05.

6.3.3 Cochran's Q test and the F test

We now move on to the case of comparing three or more classifiers. As you'd expect, these tests are more complicated than the tests that compared two classifiers. But the general idea remains the same—we evaluate an appropriate statistic and compare it with the appropriate threshold value, which is obtained by the probability distribution of the statistic itself. Our statistic in these cases will involve the data of all classifiers, of course. Listing 6.14 shows the single-line commands that you need to execute at this point to compare the three classifiers based on Cochran's Q test and the F test—the *F* stands for *Fisher* because Ronald A. Fisher introduced this statistic in the 1920s. Once again, we assume that you've executed listings 6.5, 6.7, and 6.8 in the same shell.

Listing 6.14 Cochran's Q and F tests for comparing three or more classifiers

```
CochransQTest cqTest = new CochransQTest(
⮕ nb_err.getResults(),dt_err.getResults(), nn_err.getResults());

cqTest.evaluate();

FTest fTest = new FTest(nb_err.getResults(),
⮕ dt_err.getResults(), nn_err.getResults());
fTest.evaluate();
```

Cochran's test is based on the premise that if there's no difference between the classifiers then the statistic q, calculated as shown in listing 6.15, should be distributed as an χ^2 distribution with two degrees of freedom; in general, for *N* classifiers, the degrees of freedom would be *N-1*.

Listing 6.15 Evaluating Cochran's Q statistic

```
protected void calculate() {

  int n = c1.getN();

  double T = calculateT();
  double T2 = 0.0;
```

Total correct classifications

```
for(int i = 0; i < n; i++) {

  double x = 0.0;                        Number of classifiers that
  if( c1.getResult(i) ) {                correctly classified given entry
    x++;
  }
  if( c2.getResult(i) ) {
    x++;
  }
  if( c3.getResult(i) ) {
    x++;
  }
  T2 += (x * x);
}
double sum = 0.0;
sum =   (double)c1.getNCorrect() * c1.getNCorrect() +
        (double)c2.getNCorrect() * c2.getNCorrect() +
        (double)c3.getNCorrect() * c3.getNCorrect() ;

double a = L * sum;

q = (L - 1) * (a - T * T) / (L * T - T2);
}
```

In the context of comparing classifiers, the F test has been proposed by Looney. The calculation of the F statistic is elaborate. You can peruse it in the method `calculate()` of the class `FTest`; we defer to Looney for its mathematical explanation. From a practical perspective, it's important to know that the F statistic is compared with the value of the Fisher-Snedecor distribution. For our purposes, the latter can be considered the ratio of two χ^2 distributions, where each χ^2 distribution is first divided by its degrees of freedom. One χ^2 distribution has *(N-1)* degrees of freedom, and the other χ^2 distribution has *(N-1) x (M-1)*, where *N* is the number of classifiers and *M* is the number of instances in the testing set. The threshold values for the Fisher-Snedecor distribution, or simply called the F distribution, can be found online at the Engineering Statistics Handbook for various levels of statistical significance and pairs of degrees of freedom (http://www.itl.nist.gov/div898/handbook/).

The results for Cochran's Q test and the F test are shown in figure 6.7. The tests fail—the classifiers are different—because the value of each statistic is greater than the value of the respective threshold value. This was expected, since we found earlier that the differences between the accuracy of the neural network classifier and the accuracies of the naïve Bayes and decision tree classifiers were statistically significant.

You've now learned how to compare any number of classifiers with each other, so it's time to learn how to combine them. The next sections will cover the fusion of classifiers; this is the case where all classifiers contribute to a given classification. Classifier selection, where each classifier is responsible for a particular domain of data points and is supposed to perform well only within its region of influence, won't be covered. But look at the to-do item that refers to the mixture of experts—a technique that falls into the category of classifier selection.

```
bsh % cqTest.evaluate();
       Evaluating classifiers NBCreditClassifier,DTCreditClassifier,NNCreditC

       NBCreditClassifier accuracy: 0.826
       DTCreditClassifier accuracy: 0.8262
       NNCreditClassifier accuracy: 0.7165

       Confidence Interval            : 0.05
       Degrees of Freedom             : 2
       Statistic threshold (chi-square): 5.991

       Q = 2783.821552723059 > 5.991
       The classifiers are different: TRUE

bsh % fTest.evaluate();
       Evaluating classifiers NBCreditClassifier,DTCreditClassifier,NNCreditC

       NBCreditClassifier accuracy: 0.826
       DTCreditClassifier accuracy: 0.8262
       NNCreditClassifier accuracy: 0.7165

       Confidence Interval    : 0.05
       Degrees of Freedom (1st): 2
       Degrees of Freedom (2nd): 39998
       Statistic threshold    : 3.08

       F = 264.49439710228575 > 3.08
       The classifiers are different: TRUE
```

Figure 6.7   The results for Cochran's Q test and the F test applied to all three classifiers simultaneously

6.4   *Bagging: bootstrap aggregating*

The term *bagging*, as we said earlier, is short for *bootstrap aggregating* and was introduced by Breiman. In statistics, the term *bootstrap* refers to a nonparametric method for estimating the sampling distribution of a statistic. What does that mean? Let's say that we have a dataset that contains numbers and we want to evaluate the average value of the distribution from which it was sampled. Note that if you add up all the numbers and divide by the size of the set you get an estimate of the "true" average value of the distribution. The intention of bootstrapping is to improve the estimate of the average value by creating several datasets that are partial replicas of the original dataset by *sampling with replacement*.

In the context of classification, the sample dataset is the labeled data that we have for training and testing. So, the main idea of bootstrap aggregating is straightforward. First, take random samples from your labeled dataset and train one classifier for each sample that you take. Let each one of the classifiers classify a given instance and retain the dominant classification result (majority vote). Once again, random samples aren't created by obtaining new training and testing sets from our system, but through sampling with replacement from our existing dataset.

Notwithstanding the theoretical motivation, be alert: there's a catch. The premise of bagging is that the different classifiers that you get from resampling the same data are going to produce different results. If they don't there's no point in resampling! Classifiers that produce different output when the input is perturbed a bit are called *unstable*. So, we should expect bagging to work well with unstable classifiers, such as neural networks and decision trees. This is related to our earlier observation about the importance of understanding and exploring the nature of our data. It's also related to the danger of overfitting that we discussed in chapter 5.

Bagging attempts to explore the diversity in the data. By sampling a different dataset for training the classifiers, we create classifiers that emphasize different aspects of the data. So, if our data is rich in information then bagging ensures that many aspects of the data will be captured by the classifiers. Bagging will be most appropriate in cases where we have a small training set but we want to classify a much larger dataset. To illustrate this property, we'll use a dataset that has 100 training instances and 10,000 testing instances. Listing 6.16 shows the script that we used to create the data; it's almost identical to listing 6.3, but note the difference in the training size and the noise levels.

> **Listing 6.16   Creating artificial data with a small training set and a lot of noise**

```
UseCaseData useCaseData = new UseCaseData(100,10000);        ❶

UserType.addNoiseLevel("EX",new Double[] {0.5d, 1.5d, 3.0d, 4.0d});      Define
UserType.addNoiseLevel("VG",new Double[] {0.5d, 1.5d, 3.0d, 4.0d});      noise
UserType.addNoiseLevel("GD",new Double[] {0.5d, 1.5d, 3.0d, 4.0d});      levels
UserType.addNoiseLevel("BD",new Double[] {0.5d, 1.5d, 3.0d, 4.0d});      of each
UserType.addNoiseLevel("DN",new Double[] {0.5d, 1.5d, 3.0d, 4.0d});      class

useCaseData.create(false);        ❷
```

❶ The first argument of UseCaseData is the size of the training set. The second argument is the size of the testing set.

❷ This method kicks off the creation of the data. A true value for the argument will override any existing files. A false value will create data only if there are not existing files.

We include the datasets that were produced by listing 6.16 in the distribution that comes with the book. You can create different sets; even better, you can apply the algorithm to your own data. The results will vary based on the diversity that can be created and exploited. In general, as the size of the training set increases, the improvement in the accuracy of classification becomes statistically insignificant. The most significant improvements in bagging have been recorded by intelligently selecting the training sets that are used during the bootstrap process, because when we do that, we maximize the impact on diversity. On a related note, read the work by Friedman et al. on boosting; their main ideas pertain to bagging as well.

6.4.1   *The bagging classifier at work*

Now, it's time to use the bagging algorithm and examine the results that it produces on our dataset. Listing 6.17 shows the steps required to build and execute the class that implements the bagging algorithm—the BaggingCreditClassifier.

Listing 6.17 Evaluating the `BaggingCreditClassifier`

```
UserDataset ds = UserLoader.loadTrainingDataset();

BaggingCreditClassifier bagClassifier =
➥ new BaggingCreditClassifier(ds);                    ❶
bagClassifier.setVerbose(false);

TrainingSet ts1 = bagClassifier.getBootstrapSet();     ❷
DTCreditClassifier dt1 = new DTCreditClassifier(ts1);
dt1.useDefaultAttributes();
dt1.setPruneAfterTraining(true);
bagClassifier.addMember(dt1);
bagClassifier.train();

UserDataset testDS = UserLoader.loadTestDataset();
CreditErrorEstimator bagee1 =
➥ new CreditErrorEstimator(testDS, bagClassifier);
bagee1.run();

TrainingSet ts2 = bagClassifier.getBootstrapSet();
DTCreditClassifier dt2 = new DTCreditClassifier(ts2);
dt2.useDefaultAttributes();
dt2.setPruneAfterTraining(true);
bagClassifier.addMember(dt2);
bagClassifier.train();

CreditErrorEstimator bagee2 =
➥ new CreditErrorEstimator(testDS, bagClassifier);
bagee2.run();
```

❶ | **Set to true to see results**

| **Create CreditErrorEstimator for evaluation**

| **Repeat steps for all members**

❶ Create instance of bagging classifier and point to original training set.

❷ Create the first decision tree, add it as a member of the ensemble, and train the classifier.

You can use any of the three classifiers that we presented in section 6.2. We used the `DTCreditClassifier`, which is a decision tree-based algorithm, due to the fact that decision trees are unstable. You can also use the `NNCreditClassifier`, which is a neural network–based classifier and is also unstable. You can use the `NBCreditClassifier`, which is based on the naïve Bayes algorithm, or you could create a `BaggingCreditClassifier` that contains a mix of all these individual classifiers. We provide more scripts in the code distribution, so you can peruse them to validate that the main steps remain identical.

The output is lengthy, since it contains the confusion matrices. In table 6.8, we've summarized the results in terms of the accuracy and execution time (in milliseconds). It takes about 5 to 10 milliseconds to train each decision tree classifier. As far as the time measurements are concerned, the important thing to note is that both training and runtime are extremely fast; 100,000 instances with 11 attribute values are classified in a couple of seconds.

The data that we created is fairly noisy, hence the low accuracy. But note the improvement as the number of classifiers in the ensemble grows. Note also that the improvement isn't necessarily monotonous. In other words, the accuracy of the

Classifier members	Accuracy	Execution time (ms)
1	0.60517	752
2	0.62158	968
3	0.63714	1173
4	0.62955	1327
5	0.646	1540
6	0.63719	1741
7	0.64258	1945
8	0.63536	2194
9	0.64129	2435
10	0.63625	2662
11	0.64305	2870

Table 6.8   The accuracy and execution time, as a function of the number of classifiers, for the `BaggingCredit-Classifier` used in listing 6.17

ensemble fluctuates as a function of the number of members in the ensemble grows, even though overall the accuracy improves. This means that when you adopt bagging as your strategy for improving the results of your classifier, you'll want to monitor the results and possibly remove members from the ensemble if they don't improve your overall accuracy. One of our to-do items refers to such an exercise as well as a few more tweaks for bagging.

The results that you'll get aren't going to be exactly the same as those of table 6.8 because the samples will be different each time you run the script from listing 6.17. Nevertheless, the order of magnitude for the times and the trend of improvement should be clear and consistent with these results; we ran the script several times and obtained consistent results.

6.4.2   A look under the hood of the bagging classifier

Our main class is the `BaggingCreditClassifier` and is derived from the class `ClassifierEnsemble`, which is an abstract class that you can extend yourself and create different ensemble classifiers based on the same ideas as bagging. The code from the `BaggingCreditClassifier` class is shown in listing 6.18.

Listing 6.18   Bagging as a `ClassifierEnsemble` extension

```
public class BaggingCreditClassifier extends ClassifierEnsemble {

    private UserInstanceBuilder instanceBuilder;                   ⊲─┐ Generates
    private BootstrapTrainingSetBuilder bootstrapTSetBuilder;      ⊲─┘ instances based
                                                                       on user data
    public BaggingCreditClassifier(UserDataset ds) {

        super(BaggingCreditClassifier.class.getSimpleName());       Generates bootstrapped
                                                                     training datasets
```

```
    instanceBuilder = new UserInstanceBuilder(false);

    TrainingSet originalTSet =
➥   instanceBuilder.createTrainingSet(ds);

    bootstrapTSetBuilder =
➥   new BootstrapTrainingSetBuilder(originalTSet);
  }

  public TrainingSet getBootstrapSet() {

    return bootstrapTSetBuilder.buildBootstrapSet();
  }

  public UserInstanceBuilder getInstanceBuilder() {

    return instanceBuilder;
  }

  public Concept classify(User user) {

    return classify(instanceBuilder.createInstance(user));
  }
}
```

Note that there's nothing special in that class as far as algorithms are concerned. The classifier should be able to deal with the credit worthiness data, so it's endowed with a `UserInstanceBuilder` class that can translate our data into the appropriate form that the generic `Classifier` interface requires. In addition, we provide a `Bootstrap-TrainingSetBuilder` for the purpose of creating bootstrapped training sets as described previously. In essence, this is a convenience wrapper class. The real value comes from the `BootstrapTrainingSetBuilder` class and the abstract `Classifier-Ensemble` class. Listing 6.19 shows the source code from the `BootstrapTrainingSet-Builder`, without the Javadoc and the import statements.

Listing 6.19 Auxiliary class for bootstrapping the original training set

```
public class BootstrapTrainingSetBuilder {

 private TrainingSet originalTrainingSet;

 public BootstrapTrainingSetBuilder(
➥   TrainingSet originalTrainingSet) {

   this.originalTrainingSet = originalTrainingSet;
 }

 public TrainingSet buildBootstrapSet() {

   int N = originalTrainingSet.getSize();        ❶

   Map<Integer, Instance> instances =
➥   originalTrainingSet.getInstances();

   Instance[] selectedInstances = new Instance[N];

   Random rnd = new Random();

   int center = rnd.nextInt(N);                  ❷

   int countN =0;
```

```
    while (countN < N) {

      if (countN % (N/5) == 0) {        ❸
        center = rnd.nextInt(N);
      }

      int selectedInstanceId = pickInstanceId(N,center);        ❹

      Instance selectedInstance = instances.get(selectedInstanceId);
      selectedInstances[countN] = selectedInstance;
      countN++;
    }

    TrainingSet tS = new TrainingSet(selectedInstances);

    return tS;
  }

  private int pickInstanceId(int N) {        ❹

    Random rnd = new Random();
    boolean loop = true;
    int selectedInstanceId=-1;

    double scale = (double) (N/2) / 4.0d;

    while (loop) {

      selectedInstanceId = new Double(center +
 ⇒     rnd.nextGaussian()*scale).intValue();

      if (selectedInstanceId >=0 && selectedInstanceId < N) {
        loop=false;
      }
    }
    return selectedInstanceId;
  }
}
```

❶ Every sample training set will have the same number of instances as the original set.

❷ For better diversity select a few points (centers) around which we will draw instances for each training set.

❸ This condition determines the number of instances that will be drawn around each center.

❹ Step 3 and the method of pickInstanceId are crucial because together they define a strategy for selecting the bootstrapped training set. In particular, the two steps consist of identifying a center from the range of possible instances, then drawing an instance from the neighborhood of that center $N/5$ times using a Gaussian distribution. The likelihood (probability) of drawing an instance that's within a certain distance from the center, as a function of N, is controlled by the scale variable.

You could overwrite these methods or write your own, but you should remember that the selection of the training sets is crucial in making bagging work well. In fact, one of the best ways to improve the results of bagging is to use sophisticated training set selection techniques. What kind of sophistication do you think is required? Feel free to experiment with various mechanisms of selection and study the results. You have all the plumbing code ready; this should be fun!

The essential idea behind bagging is that of an ensemble of classifiers. Of course, bagging is just one method of aggregating classifiers; you may have reason to believe that a different way of aggregating classifiers can give you a significant advantage in terms of accuracy. So, instead of providing a bagging-specific implementation, we created an abstract class to illustrate the general ideas that can be amplified and explored further. In fact, we'll use that same abstraction for both bagging and boosting.

6.4.3 *Classifier ensembles*

The abstract class `ClassifierEnsemble`, whose code is shown in listing 6.20, encapsulates the basic elements and methods that you'd need to combine a number of different classifiers, much like bagging does. It doesn't really matter whether the classifiers in the ensemble are different versions of the same classifier or different versions of various classifier types; all that's required is adherence to the `Classifier` interface.

Listing 6.20   An abstract class for constructing ensemble based classifiers

```
public abstract class ClassifierEnsemble implements Classifier {

   private String name;

   private List<Classifier> baseClassifiers =        Classifiers in
      new ArrayList<Classifier>();                    ensemble

   public ClassifierEnsemble(String name) {
      this.name = name;
   }

   public Concept classify(Instance instance) {

      ConceptMajorityVoter voter =                    Classification determined
new ConceptMajorityVoter(instance);                   by majority vote

      for( Classifier baseClassifier : baseClassifiers ) {

         Concept c = baseClassifier.classify(instance);

         voter.addVote(c);          Each classification
      }                            represents a vote

      return voter.getWinner();         Winner selected
   }                                    from ballot

   public boolean train() {
      for( Classifier c : baseClassifiers ) {
         c.train();
      }                     Ensemble is trained when
                            all members are trained
      return true;
   }

   public void addMember(Classifier baseClassifier) {
      baseClassifiers.add(baseClassifier);
```

```
        }
    public void removeMember(Classifier c) {
        baseClassifiers.remove(c);
    }
}
```

The class ConceptMajorityVoter is fairly straightforward: it encapsulates the collection of the votes that each classifier casts for a given instance. This implementation declares a winner according to the simple majority rule. But you can have more complicated selection strategies for determining the classification by the ensemble classifier. Another strategy could account for the specific classifier type by assigning a specific weight to each vote. Another strategy could be assigning a weight that's a function of the (probabilistic) confidence associated with each classification. For completeness, we list the source code of the ConceptMajorityVoter in listing 6.21.

Listing 6.21   A simple selection strategy for an ensemble classifier

```
public class ConceptMajorityVoter {

    private Map<Concept, Integer> votes =
        new HashMap<Concept, Integer>();            ← Keep track of
                                                       votes in HashMap
    private Instance i;

    public ConceptMajorityVoter(Instance i) {
        this.i = i;
    }
                                        Adding vote increases
    public void addVote(Concept c) {  ← number of votes

        Integer conceptVoteCount = votes.get(c);

        if( conceptVoteCount == null ) {
            conceptVoteCount = new Integer(1);
        } else {
            conceptVoteCount = conceptVoteCount + 1;
        }

        votes.put( c, conceptVoteCount );
    }
                                     Implementation
    public Concept getWinner() {  ← of majority rule

        int winnerVoteCount = 0;
        Concept winnerConcept = null;

        for(Map.Entry<Concept, Integer> e : votes.entrySet()) {
            if( e.getValue() > winnerVoteCount ) {
                winnerConcept = e.getKey();
                winnerVoteCount = e.getValue();
            }
        }

        return winnerConcept;
    }
                                          Margin of
    public int getWinnerVoteCount() {  ← victory
```

```
        Concept winner = getWinner();
        return votes.get(winner);
    }
}
```

Finally, we want to mention that there's a sweet spot of training data size for which the diversity, induced by the input variation, is most effective. That sweet spot will depend on the kind of constituent classifiers and the training methodology. If the dataset is small, the gains achieved via a bagged ensemble can't compensate for the decrease in accuracy of individual models, each of which now sees an even smaller training set. On the other end of the spectrum, if the dataset is extremely large and computation time isn't an issue, even a single flexible classifier can be quite adequate.

In summary, bagging harvests its benefits by leveraging the diversity of the training data. If we draw training sets that are representative of that diversity our classifier will be able to "understand" most, if not all, the aspects of our diverse data. If you also read and worked on the related to-do item you're psychologically prepared for boosting!

6.5 *Boosting: an iterative improvement approach*

The main idea behind *boosting* is the incremental growth of the classifier ensemble in such a way that the new classifiers improve the results of classification on the same data that their successors were failing. In bagging, we were creating classifiers of the ensemble independently of each other, in the hope that new members would improve the accuracy of our classifications. As a result, the success of bagging relied on the careful choice of the training set, but it wasn't possible to know a priori if it would work.

In boosting, we iteratively grow the ensemble of classifiers so that the results of our classification improve. Instead of relying on randomly selecting what *could* be appropriate training datasets, we aim to improve the results of classification by carefully picking training sets biased toward those instances that were previously misclassified by the ensemble.

We can draw a parallel between boosting and real-life consulting experience. Let's say we have a committee that's supposed to consult on some corporate financial problem. The problem may be complicated and its solution could depend on a number of subjects. For some of these subjects, say subject X, the members of the committee don't feel comfortable offering advice. In that case, it would make sense to bring in an expert whose specialty is subject X. As soon as we do that, our committee has all the required knowledge to make educated decisions and valuable recommendations about the financial problem under investigation. That's the essence of boosting, which can be summarized as follows: find out what you don't know and bring in someone who does to cover for it!

We'll describe a boosting algorithm introduced by Leo Breiman and called *arc-x4*. Breiman coined the term *arcing* to the class of classifiers that perform *adaptive resampling and combining*. It's similar to another boosting algorithm called AdaBoost—a concatenation of the terms *adaptive* and *boosting*. AdaBoost is a well-known and widely used boosting algorithm that's described in the original paper by Freund and Schapire. You could easily make appropriate modifications to arc-x4 and obtain an implementation of AdaBoost as well. AdaBoost is based on solid theoretical ground and is the result of a rigorous derivation, whereas arc-x4 is an ad hoc algorithm. There are two key differences from an algorithmic point of view and we'll discuss them later.

6.5.1   *The boosting classifier at work*

Now, let's use the arc-x4 algorithm to boost the performance of the decision tree classifier. The script for this purpose is shown in listing 6.22. The layout is similar to the one that you saw for bagging in listing 6.17.

Listing 6.22   Evaluating the `BoostingCreditClassifier`

```
UserDataset ds = UserLoader.loadTrainingDataset();

BoostingCreditClassifier arcx4 = new BoostingCreditClassifier(ds);      ❶

arcx4.setClassifierType("decision tree");       ❷

arcx4.setClassifierPopulation(1);       ❸

arcx4.setVerbose(false);

arcx4.train();

UserDataset testDS = UserLoader.loadTestDataset();

CreditErrorEstimator arcx4ee =
➥   new CreditErrorEstimator(testDS, arcx4);       ❹

arcx4ee.run();

arcx4.setClassifierPopulation(3);
arcx4.train();
CreditErrorEstimator arcx4ee =                     ❺
➥   new CreditErrorEstimator(testDS, arcx4);
arcx4ee.run();
```

❶ Create an instance of the classifier that will use boosting and pass it the reference to the training dataset.

❷ Select the decision tree algorithm as the base classifier of the ensemble.

❸ Define the population of the ensemble; in this case the ensemble has only one member.

❹ Create an instance of the `CreditErrorEstimator` to evaluate the results of the classifier.

❺ Add new members in the ensemble and re-evaluate the classification results.

You can use any one of the classifiers that we presented in section 6.2. In listing 6.22, we used the `DTCreditClassifier` by calling `setClassifierType` with the argument decision tree. It makes sense to use the same base classifier as in listing 6.17, in order to compare the results of boosting with those that we obtained from bagging. The rationale of the choice is the same as before—decision trees are unstable. In addition, decision trees have the fastest execution time, which is convenient when you work in the interactive shell. But you can equally well use the `NNCreditClassifier`, by specifying the string neural network (case doesn't matter), or you can use the `NBCreditClassifier` by specifying the string naive bayes (again case doesn't matter).

Let's digress and note that you can create a "hybrid" `BoostCreditClassifier`, which contains a mix of all these base classifiers rather than using just a single base classifier. That's not a standard variation of AdaBoost or arc-x4, but it makes sense. It's possible that for a certain set of instances, one type of classifier will outperform another, and if you can leverage that fact there's no reason to miss the opportunity for an incremental improvement. Boosting is adaptive, and in principle, you should be able to adapt not only the selection of the training set but also the selection of the classifier type. We suggest that you implement such a generalization in one of our to-do items for this chapter.

Let's now examine the output from the execution of listing 6.22. We've summarized the results in table 6.9 where we show the accuracy and execution time (in milliseconds) of the script in listing 6.22; this table is similar to table 6.8.

Classifier members	Accuracy	Execution time (ms)
1	0.57314	1108
3	0.63862	1638
5	0.64203	2153
7	0.65317	2792
11	0.64668	3947
31	0.65572	9828
41	0.65676	12870
61	0.66044	19032

Table 6.9 The accuracy and execution time, as a function of the number of classifiers, for the `BoostingCredit-Classifier` used in listing 6.22

As you can see, boosting gives us classification results that are slightly better than bagging (table 6.8). In terms of computational performance, we should mention that if we use the naïve Bayes classifier as the base classifier then the training times are still small, and without a perceptible difference from the training times with a decision tree. The accuracy based on the ensemble of the naïve Bayes classifiers was much better than the ensemble with the decision trees, with just 11 members in the ensemble. But the execution times differ significantly. For just 11 classifier members in the ensemble, the execution time for the decision tree-based boosting is about 63 times faster than the execution time of boosting the ensemble that consists of naïve Bayes classifiers.

At this point, you may wonder whether the differences in the accuracy are statistically significant. You can use McNemar's test (see section 6.3.1) and perform a direct comparison between bagging and boosting. Regardless of your choice for the base classifier or any other parameters, you can always compare two classifiers in that way. From an engineering perspective, you want to know the tradeoffs between code complexity, classification accuracy, training and execution time. You should consider the cost of your specific problem as a function of these parameters. In general, the accuracy alone isn't sufficient to make an engineering decision with regard to the choice of algorithm.

6.5.2   *A look under the hood of the boosting classifier*

Our main class is the BoostingCreditClassifier, which is an extension of the class
BoostingARCX4Classifier. In turn, the latter is an extension of the Classifier
Ensemble class much like the BaggingCreditClassifier was. This shouldn't surprise
you since boosting, like bagging, combines different classifiers in the hope of producing
better results. The code from the BoostingCreditClassifier is shown in listing 6.23.

> **Listing 6.23   An implementation that relies on the arc-x4 algorithm**

```
public class BoostingCreditClassifier extends BoostingARCX4Classifier {

    private UserInstanceBuilder instanceBuilder;                      ◁──────┐  Generates
                                                                            │  instances
    private ClassifierMemberType classifierType;                     ◁──────┤  based on
                                                                            │  user data
    public BoostingCreditClassifier(UserDataset ds) {

        this(BoostingCreditClassifier.class.getSimpleName(), ds,        Generates
⇨          new UserInstanceBuilder(false));                             bootstrapped
                                                                        training
    }                                                                   datasets

    public BoostingCreditClassifier(String name, UserDataset ds,
⇨            UserInstanceBuilder instanceBuilder) {

        this(name, instanceBuilder,
⇨      instanceBuilder.createTrainingSet(ds));
    }

    public BoostingCreditClassifier(String name,
⇨      UserInstanceBuilder instanceBuilder, TrainingSet tSet) {

        super(name, tSet);

        this.instanceBuilder = instanceBuilder;
    }

    public UserInstanceBuilder getInstanceBuilder() {
        return instanceBuilder;
    }

    public Concept classify(User user) {

        return classify(instanceBuilder.createInstance(user));       Creates
    }                                                                 new classifier
                                                                      according to
    @Override                                                         classifierType
    public Classifier getClassifierForTraining(TrainingSet set) {  ◁─┘

        Classifier baseClassifier = null;

        switch(classifierType) {

            case NEURAL_NETWORK:
                NNCreditClassifier nnClassifier =
⇨      new NNCreditClassifier(set);
                nnClassifier.setLearningRate(0.01);
                nnClassifier.useDefaultAttributes();
                baseClassifier = nnClassifier;
                break;
```

```
          case DECISION_TREE:
              DTCreditClassifier dtClassifier =
    new DTCreditClassifier(set);
              dtClassifier.useDefaultAttributes();
              dtClassifier.setPruneAfterTraining(true);
              baseClassifier = dtClassifier;
              break;
          case NAIVE_BAYES:
              NBCreditClassifier nbClassifier =
    new NBCreditClassifier(set);
              nbClassifier.useDefaultAttributes();
              baseClassifier = nbClassifier;
              break;
          default:
              throw new RuntimeException("Invalid type!");
      }

      return baseClassifier;
  }

  public ClassifierMemberType getClassifierType() {
    return classifierType;
  }

  public void setClassifierType(String type) {

    if (type.equalsIgnoreCase("decision tree")) {
      this.classifierType = ClassifierMemberType.DECISION_TREE;

    } else if (type.equalsIgnoreCase("neural network")) {
      this.classifierType = ClassifierMemberType.NEURAL_NETWORK;

    } else if (type.equalsIgnoreCase("naive bayes")) {
      this.classifierType = ClassifierMemberType.NAIVE_BAYES;
    }
  }
}
```

Once again, the role of this class is to encapsulate all the parts of the problem. Note that we provide the means to set the type of the base classifier and let the code create the new instances automatically. The arc-x4 algorithm itself can be found in the abstract class BoostingARCX4Classifier, which is shown in listing 6.24 without some auxiliary methods, the Javadoc, and the import statements.

Listing 6.24 An implementation of Breiman's arc-x4 algorithm

```
public abstract class BoostingARCX4Classifier
  extends ClassifierEnsemble {                     ⟵─┐ Ensemble
                                                      │ classifier
  private TrainingSet originalTSet;

  private int classifierPopulation = 2;

  public BoostingARCX4Classifier(String name, TrainingSet tSet) {
     super(name);
     this.originalTSet = tSet;
  }
```

```
public Concept classify(Instance instance) {

    ConceptMajorityVoter voter =
  new ConceptMajorityVoter(instance);

    for( Classifier baseClassifier : baseClassifiers ) {

        Concept c = baseClassifier.classify(instance);

        voter.addVote(c);
    }

    return voter.getWinner();
}

public abstract Classifier
  getClassifierForTraining(TrainingSet set);

public boolean train() {

    baseClassifiers = new ArrayList<Classifier>();

    int size = originalTSet.getSize();

    double[] w = new double[size];

    int[] m = new int[size];

    double w0 = 1.0 / size;

    Arrays.fill(w, w0);
    Arrays.fill(m, 0);

    for(int i = 0; i < classifierPopulation; i++) {

        TrainingSet tSet = buildTSet(originalTSet, w);

        Classifier baseClassifier =
  getClassifierForTraining(tSet);

        baseClassifier.train();

        updateWeights(originalTSet, w, m, baseClassifier);

        baseClassifiers.add(baseClassifier);
    }

    return true;
}

public TrainingSet buildTSet(TrainingSet tSet, double[] w) {

    WeightBasedRandom wRnd = new WeightBasedRandom(w);

    int n = w.length;

    Instance[] sample = new Instance[n];

    Map<Integer, Instance> instances = tSet.getInstances();

    for(int i = 0; i < n; i++) {

        int instanceIndex = wRnd.nextInt();

        sample[i] = instances.get(instanceIndex);
    }
```

Classification determined by majority vote

Create any classifier type

Weights define selection of samples

Number of times instance has been misclassified

Specifies how to build new training set

```
        return new TrainingSet(sample);
    }

    public void updateWeights(TrainingSet tSet, double[] w,
        int[] m, Classifier baseClassifier) {

        int n = w.length;

        for(int i = 0; i < n; i++) {

            Instance instance = tSet.getInstance(i);

            Concept actualConcept =
    baseClassifier.classify(instance);

            Concept expectedConcept = instance.getConcept();

            if( actualConcept == null ||
                !(actualConcept.getName()
        .equals(expectedConcept.getName()) ) ) {
                m[i]++;
            }
        }

        double sum = 0.0;

        for( int i = 0; i < n; i++) {
            sum += ( 1.0 + Math.pow(m[i], 4) );
        }
        for( int i = 0; i < n; i++) {
            w[i] = ( 1.0 + Math.pow(m[i], 4) ) / sum;
        }
    }
}
```

Specifies how to update weights

Fourth power is arbitrary choice

Our implementation is another instance of a ClassifierEnsemble, where the classification is based on the majority vote of the classifier members. The crux of the arc-x4 algorithm is found in its train() method, where we introduce a weight for each instance in the training set. These weights are used in the selection of new training sets during sampling. Initially, all weights are equal to *1/N*, where *N* is the number of instances in the training set. But as soon as the first classifier has been added in the ensemble and is trained, we proceed with an update of the weights through the updateWeights method.

Note that the selection of the new training set, each time that we want to add a new classifier in the ensemble, isn't uniform across the instances but is determined by the newly introduced weights. The class that makes that possible is called WeightBased-Random and its goal is to favor those instances that have a large weight while avoiding the selection of those instances that have small weight.

Every classifier adds its own misclassification in the array m, and in turn, that affects the weights w in the specific way that the method indicates. The number 4 in the name of the algorithm stems from the fourth power of the misclassifications for normalizing and obtaining the value of the weights in the updateWeights method. You can experiment with a different value for the exponent, say 5, and call that the arc-x5 algorithm.

It may produce better or worse results; the outcome will most likely depend on your data. The arbitrary choice of that exponent is why we consider this algorithm ad hoc.

What do you think will happen in the case of the credit classifier? Is it possible to obtain better results by tweaking that value? What other functions can you think of that would relate the number of misclassifications with the weights, in such a way as to improve our sampling for a new training set?

6.6   *Summary*

This chapter introduced the subject of combining classifiers in the context of evaluating the credit worthiness for a mortgage application. Our use case referred to data instances that contained 11 attributes, a fact that brings up the question of how many attributes we really need. During the presentation of these attributes, we had the opportunity to emphasize the importance of understanding your data and the impact of your choices with regard to how the information from the real world is represented in your data. The combination of classifiers may produce significantly better results in some cases, but in other cases a single classifier may be preferable. With a powerful data generator at your disposal, you can further explore the data conditions that favor the use of one or more classifiers.

Of course, in order to assess whether one or more classifiers are better than others, we need the ability to tell whether two or more classifiers have statistically significant differences in their accuracy. We presented four tests that allow you to compare classifiers. The ability to compare classifiers is important because the number of classifiers in an ensemble should be as small as possible while the exploitation of the available information should be maximized. The ability to keep only the best classifiers in an ensemble is crucial. To this end, we presented McNemar's test and the difference of proportions test that can be used to compare two classifiers. We also presented Cochran's Q test and the F test for comparing three or more classifiers.

We've seen that our comparisons rely on statistical tests whose initial premise (null hypothesis) is either proved or disproved based on a numerical comparison between the value of a *statistic* and a *threshold value* that's readily available. All the tests we presented followed the same pattern that involves two steps. First, we evaluated a value for the relevant statistic. Second, we compared the value of the statistic with the threshold value.

Our first ensemble classifier was based on bagging, a technique that aims to improve the accuracy of classification by creating classifiers that are trained on different subsets of the original training set. By doing so, we hope that each time that we sample (with replacement) from the original data, we emphasize different aspects of the data, and therefore are able to increase the total amount of knowledge in the ensemble. Bagging, or bootstrap aggregating, is the tip of the iceberg for what's possible in that area. For that reason, we introduced an abstract class called `Classifier-Ensemble`, which you can use for experimenting, and hopefully, incorporating in your special projects!

A somewhat different approach to ensemble classification is boosting. Instead of selecting randomly new training sets, or even injecting a priori knowledge about the data in the process of selecting new training sets, boosting attempts to drive iteratively toward better results by selecting misclassified instances at a higher rate than correctly classified instances. We presented the implementation of Breiman's arc-x4 boosting algorithm and examined its accuracy and execution time on our test dataset. We broke down the essential parts of the algorithm into three classes—`BoostingCredit-Classifier`, `BoostingARCX4Classifier`, and `WeightBasedRandom`. You can now identify the areas where you can improve the results for our own artificial data, but more importantly for your own real-world data!

This chapter concludes the list of intelligent application tools that we'll cover in this book. In practice, these tools are simply components of a larger picture. In the next chapter, we'll discuss the injection of these elements of intelligence into a news portal application.

6.7 To Do

1 *Attribute selection.* We've chosen 11 attributes for characterizing the credit worthiness of an individual. Why not 10 or 17? Instinctively, you may think that the more attributes we use, the better results we're going to obtain. That's not necessarily the case. The right choice of attributes becomes especially important as the number of available attributes increases. Some algorithms, such as decision trees, are able to identify the information rich attributes by design. Other algorithms aren't as transparent as decision trees, and direct experimentation with different sets of attributes may be required.

How would you go about selecting your attributes? By modifying the defining attributes of the `UserType` classes, some attributes may become irrelevant and others may become dominant. Which classifiers are affected the most from these changes? Can you explain why? You could define your own attributes and expand the attribute space even further. In practice, it's important to understand the nature of the data and the way that the algorithms behave in different regions of the configuration space, in terms of accuracy but also in terms of memory efficiency and computational time.

2 *Decision trees.* Decision trees are used in classification problems due to their simplicity in interpreting the results of the classification. Think of a tree structure where each node is associated with an attribute and every link out of that node corresponds to a particular value of that attribute; strictly speaking, every link is associated with a predicate on that attribute. Every leaf node in that tree is associated with a specific class of our classification problem. That's a decision tree.

To understand how it works, think of the tree's root node situated at the top and all other nodes beneath it. For every instance we want to classify, we start from the root node and examine the value associated with the root attribute. That value will lead us to the next node; by following the appropriate edge, we look at the value of the attribute associated with the first-level node, and so on, until we reach the leaf nodes. Since every leaf node is associated with a class, our classification has been completed. That's pretty straightforward, isn't it?

Of course, in order to use a decision tree for your classification, first you must build the tree! That's not as trivial as using the tree. We invite you to study our implementation and read more about decision trees in the books by Witten and Frank, and Dunham.

3 *Compare two or more neural networks.*   The design of neural network architectures is a fairly complex exercise that requires a good understanding of neural networks and the problem that you're trying to solve. In section 6.2.3, we introduced the `UserCreditNN` class, a custom neural network specifically designed for our credit worthiness use case.

It's instructive to experiment with other neural network architectures and compare the results of the associated classifiers by using the techniques of this chapter. For example, you could create a network that has 11 nodes in the input layer, 5 nodes in the hidden layer, and just 1 node in the output layer. You could experiment with adding one more hidden layer in any one of your existing networks. Even in the context of a single node-wise neural network architecture, different webs of synapses and different biases will lead to different results. Fear nothing and explore as many possibilities as you can.

Is the increased complexity worth the trouble? Given the large number of parameters at your disposal, where would you start to optimize your design and how would you judge its optimality or lack thereof?

Incidentally, we should tell you that we picked this as the "bad" classifier. Since our job was to compare classifiers, we needed a classifier whose results would be quite different from (worse than) the other two. The easiest way to achieve this is to use a neural network that's not optimized—given the plethora of choices in the network design, picking one at random will turn out to be a suboptimal choice with probability close to one!

4 *The χ^2 (chi-square) test between two distributions.*   In section 6.3.1, we introduced the χ^2 statistic for conducting the McNemar test. We can employ the same probability distribution in a different manner. To do this, we need to pose the comparison problem somewhat differently than the McNemar test does. The context of the comparison remains the same—we have two classifiers, a common training set, and a common testing set. If we train the classifiers and test them, can we tell if the results are different in a way that's statistically significant?

Let's consider casting the problem as follows. Recall the confusion matrix we introduced in chapter 5—for each classifier, this matrix was printed in the shell output when we ran the `CreditErrorEstimator`. Let the confusion matrix be denoted by a two-dimensional array, say `int[][] confusion`. If the two classifiers are statistically equivalent it's reasonable to expect that the values of the confusion matrix will be "similar." So, let's calculate the following statistic:

```
double chi2=0;

   for(int i = 0; i < n; i++) {
      for(int j = 0; j < n; j++) {

         int diff = confusion1[i][j]-confusion2[i][j];
         int  sum = confusion1[i][j]+confusion2[i][j];

         chi2 = chi2 + (diff*diff)/sum;
         }
   }
```

where n is the number of classes (in our case n=5), `confusion1` is the confusion matrix of the first classifier, and `confusion2` is the confusion matrix of the second classifier. Write a new test class that extends `Test`, as the `McNemarTest` class does, but evaluates the preceding χ^2 statistic. How would you calculate the threshold value for this statistic? How many degrees of freedom do we have? If the statistic includes only the diagonal elements of the matrix, will it be more valuable? Why?

[Hints: Consult the references in appendix C for the evaluation of chi-square values through incomplete gamma functions. The answer for the degrees of freedom is n-1.]

5 *Mixture of experts—a classifier selection technique.* As we mentioned in the introduction of this chapter, the topic of combining classifiers falls largely into two general directions. One direction is the classifier selection approach, and the other is classifier fusion, such as bagging (section 6.4) and boosting (section 6.5). As software engineers, we can appreciate the beauty and effectiveness of the divide-and-conquer principle that underlies the classifier selection approach.

A particularly interesting and well studied version of classifier selection is the *mixture of (local) experts* (see Jacobs et al.; and Jordan and Jacobs), which originated as a modular version of a multilayer (supervised) neural network. This technique suggests that we can improve the learning rate and our capacity for generalization (correctly classifying instances that we haven't seen before) by using a number of local experts and a gating network (generally speaking, another classifier). The gating network decides which of the experts should be used for each training case, hence at the end of training, each classifier is the expert of a particular domain of the input (of the instances in the training set). For the details of the approach, consult the papers by Jacobs and his coworkers.

Create three neural network classifiers appropriate for the credit worthiness use case and combine them with a fourth network, in the role of the gating network, to build a mixture of experts. In doing so, a number of questions arise. What training method should you use? Are the results from the mixture of experts better than those that we obtained from the single neural network? Is it worth the trouble? What are the advantages and the disadvantages compared to the fusion approaches of bagging and boosting?

6   *Tweaks and tips for bagging.*   In section 6.4, you learned about bagging as a
    method of improving your classification results. Although simple in principle,
    the optimization of the improvement that you can get from bagging requires
    some work. The most critical aspect in the bagging algorithm is the selection of
    the bootstrapped training sets used by the member classifiers of the ensemble.

    Another critical decision is the number of classifiers in the ensemble. In
    other words, how many classifiers should we use? 10? 20? 50? 100? Start in a
    straightforward manner and write a class whose purpose is to investigate the
    improvement obtained by adding a new classifier in the ensemble. The first test
    you'd have to do is to use one of the techniques that we described in section 6.3
    in order to discern whether a difference in the classification results between two
    or more classifiers is statistically significant. If it is, you can perform a second
    test that would check whether the improvement of accuracy is greater than an
    accuracy improvement threshold, whose value you can configure. If both tests
    pass, keep the new classifier in the ensemble; otherwise discard it and pick a
    new one.

    Try the various classifiers and examine the results. What are the differences
    and the similarities between the choices that you make? What happens if you
    mix the type of classifiers? Does bagging still work? Do you get better results or
    worse? Examine that in the context of the class that you just wrote for optimiz-
    ing the accuracy.

    Write your own implementation for the `pickInstanceId` method in the class
    `BootstrapTrainingSetBuilder`. One of the best ways to improve the results of
    bagging is the use of sophisticated training set selection techniques. What kind
    of sophistication do you think is required? Feel free to experiment with various
    mechanisms of selection and study the results. You have all the plumbing code
    ready; this should be fun!

7   *Generalizing boosting through classifier type adaptation.*   In section 6.5, we intro-
    duced boosting and explained how the arc-x4 algorithm works. Breiman states
    that he introduced the arc-x4 algorithm to "demonstrate that arcing works not
    because of the specific form of the arc-fs algorithm, but because of the adaptive
    resampling." (Breiman uses the term arc-fs when he refers to what's widely
    known as AdaBoost.)

    If Breiman is right we could create a `BoostCreditClassifier` that contains a
    mix of base classifiers rather than using a single base classifier. That's not a stan-
    dard variation of AdaBoost or arc-x4, but it makes sense; besides, as we already
    mentioned, arc-x4 is itself an ad hoc algorithm. It's possible that for a certain set
    of instances, one type of classifier will outperform another, and if you can lever-
    age that fact there's no reason to miss the opportunity for an incremental
    improvement. Boosting is adaptive, and in principle, you should be able to
    adapt not only the selection of the training set but also the selection of the clas-
    sifier type.

We suggest that you implement such a generalization. There are a couple of variations that you can do. You could opt to include a representative of each type every time we want to add a member in the ensemble. Alternatively, you may want to create the ensemble based on some predefined proportions of classifier types—for example, 50% decision trees, 30% naïve Bayes, and 20% neural networks.

Think about the tradeoffs and devise a strategy for obtaining maximum benefits in accuracy without making the training or runtime computation times unrealistic. Are the improvements in accuracy sufficiently large to justify the increased complexity and computational effort? How could we further improve the sophistication of the algorithm? In section 6.3 we learned how to compare two or more classifiers. In this case, we're interested in identifying classifiers that are different, so the comparison methods can come handy within the classification algorithm itself!

6.8 **References**

Bell, R., Y. Koren, and C. Volinsky. "Chasing $1,000,000: How we won the Netflix progress prize." *ASA Statistical and Computing Graphics Newsletter*, Vol 18 (2), pp. 4-12, 2007. http://stat-computing.org/newsletter/v182.pdf.

Breiman, L. "Bagging predictors." *Machine Learning*. Vol 24 (2), pp. 123-140, 1996.

Breiman, L. "Arcing classifiers. "*The Annals of Statistics*. Vol 26 (3), pp. 801-849, 1998.

Dietterich, T.G. "Ensemble methods in machine learning." *Multiple Classifier Systems*, (Editors: J. Kittler and F.Roli) volume 1857 of *Lecture Notes in Computer Science*, pp.1-15. Cagliari, Italy. Springer, 2000. http://portal.acm.org/citation.cfm?coll=GUIDE&dl=GUIDE&id=743935.

Freund, Y., and R. E. Schapire. "A decision-theoretic generalization of on-line learning and an application to boosting." *Journal of Computer and System Sciences*. Vol 55 (1), pp. 119-139, 1997.

Friedman, J., T. Hastie, and R. Tibshirani. "Additive logistic regression: A statistical view of boosting." *Annals of Statistics*, Vol 28 (2), pp. 337-407, 2000.

Jacobs, R.A., M. I. Jordan, S. J. Nowlan, and G. E. Hinton. "Adaptive mixtures of local experts." *Neural Computation*. Vol 3, pp. 79-87, 1991.

Jordan, M.I., and R. A. Jacobs. "Hierarchical mixtures of experts and the EM algorithm." *Neural Computation*, Vol 6, pp. 181-214, 1994.

Kuncheva, L.I. *Combining Pattern Classifiers: Methods and Algorithms*. Wiley-Interscience, 2004.

Looney, S.W. (1988). "A statistical technique for comparing the accuracies of several classifiers." *Pattern Recognition Letters*. Vol 8, pp.5-9, 1988.

Putting it all together: an intelligent news portal

This chapter covers:

- Getting and cleansing content from the internet
- Searching for news stories
- Assigning news categories
- Building news groups

Each of the earlier chapters described a particular group of algorithms. We studied search algorithms, recommendation algorithms, clustering algorithms, and classification algorithms. We examined each of these in their own context and their own particular use case. The same algorithms can be used in many other cases, and it's possible to employ all of them to enhance an existing application.

The purpose of this chapter is to show how each algorithm can be leveraged in the setting of a single application. Where can we use a clustering algorithm? How are the results of classification affected by clustering? Can PageRank and DocRank be used for features other than search? How can I write a recommendation engine for my own application by using what I learned in this book? We'll provide answers in this chapter.

We won't write an entire web application; we'll simply place ourselves in the context of such an application and discuss the adoption of intelligent algorithms in it. In other words, we'll discuss the adoption of our algorithms in the context of a hypothetical web application. In particular, our example refers to a news portal, which is inspired by the Google News website.

As we introduce intelligent algorithms in our application, we'll encounter a number of practical issues that you should be aware of. For many intelligent algorithms, the order of operation on the data may be important. Thus, the need for a *meta-algorithm*—an algorithm whose job is to control or combine other[1] algorithms—may be crucial to the success of putting everything together.

This chapter will also give us an opportunity to review all the material we covered in earlier chapters. We'll start by describing the use case of crawling and aggregating the news stories from the Web. We encountered this in chapter 2 but now we can suggest a number of ways that these processes can be improved by leveraging classification. In order to make our results repeatable and establish a data reference frame for our discussion, we'll present and use an extended set of the news stories that we used in chapter 2.

We'll naturally follow up with a section on searching our news stories for various queries. This brings up a lot of interesting questions. In this case (a news portal web application), we aren't searching for results across the entire Web. We're looking for results from a body of documents that has special properties (news stories). We can take advantage of that knowledge and improve the quality of the retrieved results. This is a lesson of general applicability. Nobody knows your data better than you!

In the context of finding what news stories should be grouped together and what news category they should be assigned to (section 7.4), we'll describe a number of topics that arise from the fact that we're using more than one intelligent algorithm to accomplish our goal. If we apply a clustering algorithm to our news stories and subsequently classify the clusters, we'll obtain results that are different from those obtained by first classifying the news stories and later clustering the news stories within each news category. These differences raise a lot of questions that we discuss at length in sections 7.4 and 7.5.

In the last section of this chapter, we bring recommendations into the picture. In particular, we explore the case where our users have the ability to rate the news stories. The entire machinery of recommendation algorithms, developed in chapter 3, is applicable in this case. We'll apply and present the item-based approach and suggest many more extensions.

We've written a large number of to-do action items that should help you explore many more aspects of intelligent algorithms within the context of a news portal; these directions should also be valuable for many other applications. Enjoy!

---

[1] The combination of classifiers that we covered in chapter 6 was a special case of how meta-algorithms emerge and are used in practice.

7.1 *An overview of the functionality*

If you haven't seen the Google News website, point your browser to http://news.google.com/ for a live reference of what we're going to discuss. Once you land on the site, it appears that you've visited yet another portal, but appearances can be deceiving. As we'll see, there are some important differences between the Google News portal and other news portals. We should note from the outset that we're not affiliated in any way with Google and we don't know how and where intelligent techniques are used on the Google News site. We only know the functionality that's publicly available to the end user. Our goal is to present our material from the perspective of a bigger theme, and not to help you replicate a specific website.

What are the differences? Why is the Google News site special? To begin with, it is computer-generated based on content that's collected from thousands of news sources worldwide. The stories are grouped and assigned to categories such as World, U.S., Business, Sci/Tech, and so on. The key is that the grouping and the assignment are performed automatically, without human intervention. After reading chapters 4 and 5, it should be clear that the grouping of news articles can be achieved by clustering and the assignment by classification, hence the relevance of that website for our subject. There are more features of interest to us.

There's a section called Top stories, apparently based on relevance (ranking) metrics similar to what we described in chapter 2. Based on what we've already seen in this book, such a group of stories could be identified by using the PageRank rankings or a content-based ranking method similar to what we described as DocRank. The user rankings on individual articles could be used to determine, or at least affect, these rankings and offer a better personal experience.

Personalization can also be direct and explicit. The Personalize this page link allows you to rearrange the order in which each topic appears on the landing page. It also allows you to introduce custom sections that may reflect your interest in a special category of news. This kind of personalization offers a great mining opportunity for websites with many users. By clustering the customized news content, we can identify groups of users with similar interests. We can also use recommendations by employing the notion of similarity between the articles that users read and how much they like each article. In other words, we can build a recommendation system based on both user ratings and news article content, similar to what we've seen in chapter 3.

Another interesting feature of the Google News site is the section labeled In the News. That's a list of individuals, nonprofit organizations, corporations, governments, and so on that are of "importance" in the news today. Sure, we can build this functionality based merely on basic statistical information, but when you think about it, the importance of a particular name is influenced by several factors, not merely frequency of appearance in the news articles. This is especially true when the content is retrieved from numerous heterogeneous sources, as is the case for a site such as Google News. In these cases, we can greatly benefit from the methods that we encountered in chapter 2—relevance metrics such as PageRank and DocRank.

The News Alerts feature allows you to receive content, via email, based on your own search terms and type of media (for example, news articles, video, blogs, group lists). Alerts should be issued only when the content can be considered "high-value" information by the user, a criterion that's clearly variable from user to user. Intelligent algorithms can come to the rescue once again.

The site designers would've been remiss to ignore localization capabilities, so, naturally, the site is full of customization based on the language used in the news and the geographic location of the user. In our context, these capabilities are important only from the perspective of NLP. For an excellent review of NLP, see the book by Jurafsky and Martin.

Let's get started by describing the process of crawling the news websites and aggregating the news stories on our system for further processing.

7.2 *Getting and cleansing content*

The starting point of a news portal such as Google News is, of course, gathering the news. The articles are collected from various sources on the internet using a crawler. There are several freely available crawlers, but in the interest of convenience and completeness, we'll use a crawler that we wrote for this book; this crawler is a variant of the crawler that we used in chapter 2.

We'll also provide a review of the search prerequisites because now—having gone through six chapters of describing intelligent algorithms—we can look at each stage from a new perspective. Even though you can obtain your own news stories (or any other content) by crawling the Web, our examples must use a fixed set of data in order to be repeatable. At the end of this section, we'll describe the default set of news stories that we'll use for the rest of the book.

7.2.1 *Get set. Get ready. Crawl the Web!*

As you might expect, our news crawler is called `NewsCrawler` and its constructor takes three arguments:

- The base directory for storing the retrieved data
- The depth of the link structure that should be traversed
- The maximum number of total documents that should be retrieved

Let's use it from the BeanShell and crawl the Manning website.[2] Listing 7.1 shows the few steps that we need to take in order to configure the crawler.

Listing 7.1 Crawling the Manning website

```
String rootDir = Ch7Constants.CRAWL_DATA_ROOT_DIR;        ◁─┐ Determine root
                                                             │ directory
NewsCrawler crawler = new NewsCrawler(rootDir, 2, 100);
```

---

[2] Please, be a conscious internet citizen when you crawl. All our internet crawling examples are configured with a small depth and a (relatively) small number of documents to be retrieved.

```
crawler.addSeedUrl("http://www.manning.com");

crawler.run();
```

The first thing we do is to determine the location where the retrieved documents will be stored. By default, we use the location C:/iWeb2/data/ch07/news-crawls, but you can store the content anywhere you like by modifying the value of CRAWL_DATA_ ROOT_DIR. When the crawler starts retrieving the content from the visited URLs, it'll store them in a subdirectory of the root directory. The new subdirectory's name will start with the string *crawl-* and be followed by the numeric value of the crawl's time-stamp in milliseconds, for example crawl-1200697910111. The NewsCrawler delegates its work to the BasicWebCrawler, much like the FetchAndProcessCrawler did in chapter 2.

Let's recall the outcome of the crawler's work. The job of the BasicWebCrawler class is to retrieve the data and parse it. The result of that processing is stored in the subdirectory called processed. For every group of documents that are processed, there are four subdirectories—fetched, knownurls, pagelinks, and processed. The fetched directory contains the raw HTML pages. The knownurls directory contains a single file with all the URL addresses identified during crawling. The pagelinks directory contains a single file with all the links between the visited URL addresses. The structure of the processed directory looks similar to the structure of the fetched directory, but now the content of the web pages has been dissected. Certain web page properties, such as the title of the web page and its URL, are stored separately from the core content. The outlinks from each page have also been extracted and stored separately. If you compare the files from the fetched subdirectories and the files in the processed/content subdirectories, you'll see that the difference lies in removing most of the HTML structure, such as headers, tables, divs, and so on. On an average laptop or desktop with a moderately fast internet connection, the crawler will complete its job in a couple of minutes.

We won't go into an in-depth discussion about the crawler because, as it stands, it does nothing intelligent! But the purpose of giving you a basic crawler with the source code of this book is to entice you into applying intelligent algorithms during crawling. See our first to-do item on that challenge.

7.2.2   *Review of the search prerequisites*

In chapter 2, we examined the basic stages of searching:

- Crawling
- Parsing
- Analyzing
- Indexing
- Searching

For completeness, let's review what's involved during each stage. Parsing and analyzing the retrieved documents is what we call collectively as *cleansing*. The document parsers that we described in chapter 2 are necessary for the transformation of the various documents (such as XML, HTML, Word, PDF) into a common, purely textual, form. For HTML parsing, we're using the code from the NekoHTML project (http://nekohtml.sourceforge.net/). NekoHTML contains a simple HTML parser that can scan HTML files and fix many common mistakes that occur in HTML documents. Its features include adding missing parent elements, automatically closing elements with optional end tags, and handling mismatched inline element tags. NekoHTML is fairly robust and sufficiently fast, but if you're crawling special sites, you may want to write your own parser.

If you plan to crawl PDF documents, you can use the code from the PDFBox project (http://www.pdfbox.org/). It's released under the BSD license and it has plenty of documentation. PDFBox includes the class `LucenePDFDocument` that can be used to obtain a Lucene `Document` object immediately with a single line of code such as the following:

```
Document doc = LucenePDFDocument.convertDocument(File file)
```

Look at the Javadocs for additional information. Similar to the case of PDF documents, there are parsers for Word documents. The Apache POI project (http://poi.apache.org/) provides APIs for manipulating file formats based on Microsoft's OLE 2 Compound Document format by using pure Java. In addition, the TextMining code, available at http://www.textmining.org/, provides a Java library for extracting text from Microsoft Word 97, 2000, XP, and 2003 documents.

The stage of analyzing the documents is also important. Throughout the book, we use the Lucene class `StandardAnalyzer`, which helps us extract the "meaning" of the text from the respective documents. Clearly, NLP is crucial in the successful analysis of the documents. You can find a brief introduction to NLP, and numerous references, in appendix D. The purpose of NLP is to help us retain those words that are most relevant and important in describing the content of the document, while ignoring everything else. If you ignore something that's of interest to you during the analysis stage you'll never be able to leverage that piece of information downstream in your data processing. Conversely, if you include a lot of irrelevant or unimportant words, your processing quality may be jeopardized by the high level of noise in your data. In the case of clustering or classifying news stories, you may not be able to create meaningful story groups or you may end up placing business articles into the sports categories!

Basically, the algorithms for clustering or classification will fail to operate properly if your data is dirty. To put it in terms of an analogy, think of a car that won't run due to an impurity in the fuel mix. No matter how good the car is, it won't run unless its fuel mix is clean and contains the right ratio of gasoline and air necessary for combustion. Cleansing removes the impurities and achieves the proper fuel mix for your algorithms!

The amount of cleansing required for a particular website depends on the complexity of its design. Today's modern websites have a lot of graphics, or media-rich elements, whose content is more difficult to retrieve and process compared to the retrieval of a pure HTML page or a PDF document. For the most part, our code and the tools that we referenced should do a decent job on a general corpus of data collected from the internet.

A professional-grade crawler should be able to detect the language, if not the exact locale, of a website and apply the most appropriate cleansing tools for the job. Once you start crawling, you can land anywhere. You can start from a list of URLs that point to locations in the United States and end up half around the globe in Bangalore (India) or Beijing (China). The crawler should be able to identify how to "read" the content properly.

Although there are standard techniques for identifying the geographic location of a server, it's quite possible to get mixed content or get English postings in India and Chinese content on websites that are located in the United States. Here's where our classifiers can shine once again. For example, the naïve Bayes algorithm is agnostic with respect to languages, so it could be used to identify the language associated with a particular document or part of a document. This would be a different naïve Bayes classifier than the one that you'd use to classify a news story; the same algorithm but a different classifier (for example, NBLanguageDetector). The training dataset for that classifier would involve simple parsing of text without analysis, while the classification concepts would be locales or languages. We won't pursue this example here, but you should keep it in mind if you deal with multilingual text. Think about the possible issues with the various encodings that exist worldwide and what effect that would have on detecting the right language.

7.2.3 *A default set of retrieved and processed news stories*

For the rest of this chapter, we'll use a set of web pages that includes the pages that we've seen in chapter 2. This is necessary in order to make the examples concrete and the exercises repeatable. You can find these pages under the data/ch07/ directory. All the pages can be found under the subdirectory all, and include the following (the choice of content was random):

- Twenty documents related to business news
- Twenty-four documents related to sports
- Twenty-three documents related to health issues and medicine
- Twenty-six documents related to technology news
- Sixteen documents related to U.S. politics
- Twenty documents related to world news

This indicates that our news portal will focus on these six categories by default; we'll discuss how to add custom categories later. For now, let's load our default dataset and look at the news stories. Listing 7.2 shows how to load a set of documents similar to the ones that we used in chapter 2. We're providing two implementations of the NewsDataset interface. The first is CrawlResultsNewsDataset, which can be used for arbitrary (well, almost) documents retrieved from the Web by means of the NewsCrawler class that we saw in listing 7.1. The second implementation is the `FileListNewsDataset` class shown in listing 7.2. The main difference between the two is that, for the `FileListNewsDataset`, the news category is implied by the name of the document; for `CrawlResultsNewsDataset`, the news category that each document belongs in is unknown.

Listing 7.2 Loading the default news stories and invoking a custom news browser

```
NewsDataset dataset = new FileListNewsDataset("DefaultDS");     ┐ Set document
                                                                │ directory
dataset.setDocumentDir("C:/iWeb2/data/ch07/all");          ◄───┘

dataset.setTopTerms(15);    ◄──┐ Number of terms that
                               │ must be retained
dataset.loadTopics();

dataset.loadStories();

NewsUI ui = new NewsUI(dataset);

NewsUI.createAndShowUI(ui);
```

The basic UI, shown in figure 7.1, provides quick access to the content of the news stories and can help us examine the results of our work as we incrementally add intelligent capabilities. In the left panel, you can see the six news categories and their associated news stories; the number of the stories for each topic is shown inside the parentheses. If you click on a particular news story, the content is shown in the right panel.

In summary, the process of collecting and cleansing news stories may seem superficially mundane, but it's truly challenging work. It's difficult to achieve effectiveness and

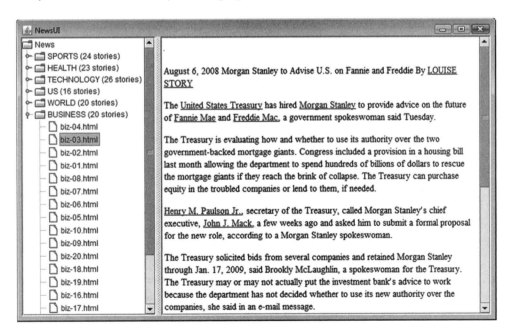

Figure 7.1 A custom user interface for browsing the default news stories

efficiency for large-scale crawling and cleansing of documents from a variety of websites. In these cases, crawling and cleansing can be a fertile ground for applying intelligent algorithms. Let's move on now to the indexing and searching of our news stories.

7.3 *Searching for news stories*

As usual, we'll use Lucene to index and search these documents. But we'll consolidate all the processing functionality for our news portal into a class called `NewsProcessor`. Listing 7.3 creates an instance of the `NewsProcessor`, creates the index for our default dataset, and performs a couple of queries; it's implied that you already executed listing 7.2.

Listing 7.3 Indexing and searching the default news stories

```
NewsProcessor newsProcessor = new NewsProcessor(dataset);

newsProcessor.buildIndexDir();

newsProcessor.runIndexing();

newsProcessor.search("cell",5);

newsProcessor.search("football",5);
```

We discussed indexing and search in chapter 2, so let's now focus on the preceding results and analyze the various elements that can make our news portal a better place for its users! The search for "cell" returns the results shown in figure 7.2.

The document title is the label for a news story as shown on the left panel of the news browser. The document terms are the top 15 terms of each document based on our analysis. The relevance score is the Lucene score for each document. The window of your news browser should be open right now. So, let's click on each of the document titles in the left panel to examine the full content of the articles. The first two results are news about the effect of cellular telephones on our health. The third search result is related to technology news—the use of cellular telephones for locating misplaced objects. The fourth and fifth search result aren't about cellular telephones at all. They're articles about the potential of depressing cancer growth through a high dose of vitamin C.

These results are typical; you can search on Google News itself and a number of articles will appear that refer to different topics. These results bring up a number of important questions. First, when a user searches the news portal for the word "cell," what exactly does she have in mind? Is it stem cell research? Is it some technology gadget? Is it the effect of electromagnetic radiation from cellular telephones on people? It's clear that answering these questions out of context is futile.

Can't we use the PageRank or DocRank algorithms that we studied in chapter 2? Yes, certainly. Our ranking algorithms can help us improve the search results, but only marginally. The greatest benefit of ranking algorithms is to identify the importance of a site with respect to all the other sites that are part of our crawled (hyperlinked) graph. But most of the outlinks in news outlets are self-references or they don't point

```
bsh % newsProcessor.search("cell",5);

Search results using Lucene index scores:
Query: cell

Document Title: health-21.html
Document Terms: warn, limit, phone, cell, children, us, risk,
herberman, ronald, becaus, especi, institut, brain, cancer, dr
Document URL: file:/C:/iWeb2/data/ch07/all/health-21.html -->
Relevance Score: 0.610166192054749

Document Title: health-23.html
Document Terms: phone,concern,cell,us,tumor,research,risk
herberman,pittsburgh,dont,publish,studi,brain,institut,cancer
Document URL: file:/C:/iWeb2/data/ch07/all/health-23.html -->
Relevance Score: 0.537154197692871

Document Title: tech-15.html
Document Terms: control, home, phone, can, your, cell, starner,
you, us, technolog, what, could, kientz, gestur, we
Document URL: file:/C:/iWeb2/data/ch07/all/tech-15.html    -->
Relevance Score: 0.341093242168427

Document Title: health-02.html
Document Terms: work, c, tumour, treatment, cell, inject, suggest
research, dose, bbc, human, mice, becaus, vitamin, cancer,
Document URL: file:/C:/iWeb2/data/ch07/all/health-02.html   -->
Relevance Score: 0.337665110826492

Document Title: health-09.html
Document Terms: telomeras, have, chemic, structur, cell, block
most, activ, bbc, help, new, could, immort, cancer, drug,
Document URL: file:/C:/iWeb2/data/ch07/all/health-09.html      -->
Relevance Score: 0.334201782941818
```

Figure 7.2 Search results for the word "cell" based on indexing alone

to anything else (for example, news reports in PDF format, short news announce-
ments, and so forth), which is what we referred to as dangling nodes in chapter 2.

Don't feel disheartened! We can do a lot more to improve the user's experience.
Another technique that we studied in chapter 2 referred to user clicks, and it seems
that user clicks may be more pertinent to our quest for improving the search results,
in the case of a news portal. Evidently, this isn't something that pays dividends for new
users, but it can have a large payoff in the long run. As we mentioned earlier, relevance is subjective, and that's one of the main reasons why its evaluation is a difficult
task. If you and I are looking results for the query "cell," you may be interested in stem
cell research while I may be interested in the Android platform or Nokia's latest gadget. Thus, the most relevant results for one person can be, and quite often are, different from the most relevant results for another person, even though the query terms
may be identical!

Note that for our news portal, we can leverage user clicks at two levels. First is the level of the individual news stories that the user clicks on, which is similar to the use case of chapter 2. The second level of information is based on the topic that each news article belongs to. Moreover, we can possibly improve our search results by retaining both the query terms and the document terms in the list of attributes for training. That's the subject of the second to-do item for this chapter.

These examples also remind us of the importance of NLP in search. In particular, we'd like to mention three high-level natural language elements that aren't directly accessible from the low-level grammatical or syntactical structure. These are *semantics*, *pragmatics* and *discourse*. Semantics—the knowledge of meaning—is used to leverage our knowledge about the world. Pragmatics refers to our knowledge of the relationship between the meaning of words and the goals or intentions of the user. Discourse refers to knowledge that captures lexical structures larger than single utterances or sentences. The latter notion is particularly important for search results, and its generality goes beyond language processing. It's what we'd call the "big picture" or a "general context" (see also appendix D and its references).

The value of intelligent searching can't be easily overstated. But retrieving relevant news stories through search isn't the only way to present the news of the day to our users. In fact, the standard layout of a news portal reflects the underlying classification scheme—the organization of the page into its various news categories. So, let's move on to examine the assignment of news stories into news categories.

7.4   *Assigning news categories*

The assignment of a news category can be done for an individual news story or for a group (cluster) of news stories. This section will cover both cases. We discussed classifying items in chapter 5 and we'll naturally rely on the algorithms that were presented there for classifying news stories into news categories. But when we examine classification in the broader context of an application that involves additional capabilities such as search, clustering, and recommendations, there are a lot of questions that aren't apparent or relevant if you consider classification as an isolated operation.

The first topic of this section discusses the effect of ordering in the application of our algorithms. As soon as the crawler finishes its job, the news stories have been retrieved but there's no order or structure in them. One possible course of action is to take the entire list of the newly collected stories and form groups out of it. Another possibility would be to first classify each news story into one of the six topics and then group similar stories within each topic. Do you think these two options are equivalent? For a general corpus of news stories they are, most likely, not equivalent. In technical terms we'd say that the two operations don't commute.

The next two sections (7.4.2 and 7.4.3) present the custom news story classifier in detail. You'll see that, once again, the naïve Bayes algorithm proves its versatility and value as a general purpose classifier. Perhaps the most interesting part of this custom classifier is the introduction of a *classification strategy*. Thus, in the last part of this section, we explain what a classification strategy is, why we need it, and how we can use it effectively.

So, let's start assigning news categories to news stories. The two combinations that we'll examine are the classification of the results from clustering and the application of clustering within the classified news stories.

7.4.1 *Order matters!*

We already hinted that by changing the order of operations, we'll obtain different results. But, how different will the results be, and which order is better? The answer to these two questions will depend on both the nature of the data and the algorithms involved. Nevertheless, the general argument in favor of the second approach (first general classification and then clustering) is that the noise of the data after classification is reduced significantly so the job of the clustering algorithm becomes easier.

Let's look at figure 7.3, which shows the results of the combined operations (classification and clustering) for our default news dataset when clustering occurs *before* classification takes place.

The selected article (tech-05) in figure 7.3 is a news story about a research project that Microsoft initiated to replace its legacy family of Windows operating systems. Clearly, this is a technology news story, but it was placed into the general category of

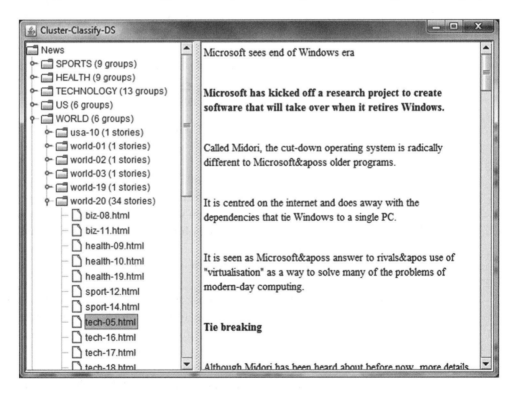

Figure 7.3 Clustering the news stories before classifying them into topics

world news. In particular, it was grouped with a world news story about the resurgence of Russia as a political and economic power, so the two subjects are as remote conceptually as they could possibly be—unless, you have a vivid imagination!

In the same group, under the heading of the article about Russia's resurgence, we find a large number of articles that don't refer to Russia at all and, like article tech-05, don't even belong in the world news category. A total of 34 news stories are in that group, while the total number of news stories in our default dataset is 129. The breakdown of the stories by category is as follows: 20 stories belong in the business category, 23 stories belong in the health category, 24 stories belong in the sports category, 26 stories belong in the technology category, 16 stories belong in the U.S. category, and 20 stories belong to the world category. So, a group of 34 news stories is clearly unbalanced, and unless our clustering algorithm is highly tuned, this is likely to happen.

Listing 7.4 demonstrates how you can create these news groups and display them in our custom viewer. You can execute the script now and peruse the grouping structure and the placement of the news stories into their respective topics.

Listing 7.4   Creating news groups by clustering before classifying the stories

```
NewsDataset trainingDS = new FileListNewsDataset("TrainingDS");
trainingDS.setDocumentDir("C:/iWeb2/data/ch07/training");     Create training/
trainingDS.init();                                           testing datasets

NewsDataset ds1 = new FileListNewsDataset("Cluster-Classify-DS");
ds1.setDocumentDir("C:/iWeb2/data/ch07/all");
ds1.init();

NewsProcessor newsProcessor = new NewsProcessor(trainingDS);

newsProcessor.trainClassifier();            Cluster news
                                            stories
newsProcessor.createClusters(ds1);

newsProcessor.classifyClusters(ds1);        Classify grouped
                                            news stories
NewsUI ui1 = new NewsUI(ds1);
NewsUI.createAndShowUI(ui1);
```

We'll return to figure 7.3 and discuss more details of the structure that has been created based on listing 7.4. But let's now look at the structure that would be created by inverting the order of operations—the order in which clustering takes place *after* classification. Figure 7.4 displays the news groups for the same dataset as figure 7.3 but with clustering following classification.

A few things are immediately clear from comparing figures 7.3 and 7.4. In figure 7.4, the technology news stories are now grouped together and have been (correctly) assigned to the technology category. All the news stories that are grouped with the story world-20 are related and refer to Russia's resurgence. Moreover, the business- and health-related articles are now absent from that group. This is certainly a better arrangement of our news stories than what we had before, but a few quirks still exist. The technology articles tech-16, tech-17, and tech-18 all refer to email spam and are rightfully in the same group. But the Microsoft-related news story in tech-05 isn't directly related to them and shouldn't be in the same group.

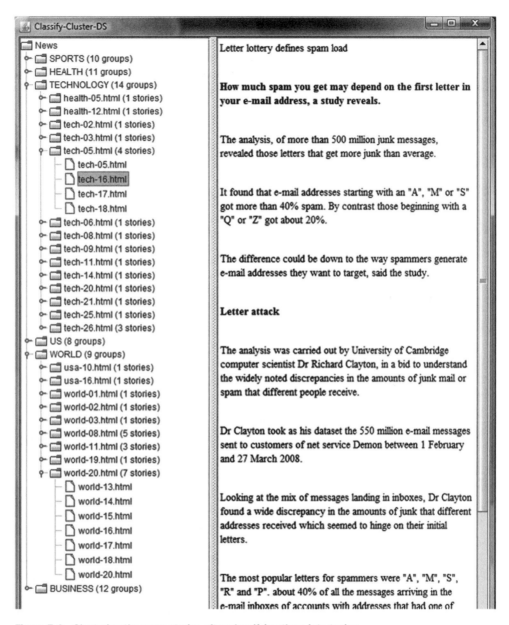

Figure 7.4 Clustering the news stories after classifying them into topics

Listing 7.5 demonstrates how you can create these news groups and display them in our custom viewer. It's identical to listing 7.4 for the most part. There is one important difference. As promised, we've added code that swaps the order of operation for clustering and classification. Naturally, the name of the methods that we invoke has also changed, since classification now applies to all the stories individually (rather than to the clusters as a whole) and clustering happens only within each topic. We use a new instance of the FileListNewsDataset class, called ds2, so that we can operate on an identical copy of the data but display them separately. If you use the same instance (ds1), you won't be able to compare the two approaches! If you didn't exit from the shell that you executed listing 7.4, you can start typing in the shell from the line that creates the NewsDataset ds2.

Listing 7.5   Creating news groups by clustering after classifying the stories

```
NewsDataset trainingDS = new FileListNewsDataset("TrainingDS");
trainingDS.setDocumentDir("C:/iWeb2/data/ch07/training");
trainingDS.init();

NewsDataset ds1 = new FileListNewsDataset("Cluster-Classify-DS");
ds1.setDocumentDir("C:/iWeb2/data/ch07/all");
ds1.init();

NewsProcessor newsProcessor = new NewsProcessor(trainingDS);

newsProcessor.trainClassifier();

newsProcessor.createClusters(ds1);

newsProcessor.classifyClusters(ds1);

NewsUI ui1 = new NewsUI(ds1);
NewsUI.createAndShowUI(ui1);

NewsDataset ds2 = new FileListNewsDataset("Classify-Cluster-DS");
ds2.setDocumentDir("C:/iWeb2/data/ch07/all");
ds2.init();

newsProcessor.classifyStories(ds2);                          ◁─── Classify all
                                                                  news stories
newsProcessor.createClustersWithinTopics(ds2);    ◁─── Cluster news stories
                                                         within each topic
NewsUI ui2 = new NewsUI(ds2);
NewsUI.createAndShowUI(ui2);
```

Now, both Swing clients—ui1 and ui2—should still be visible. Resize the window of figure 7.3 (Cluster-Classify-DS) and the window of figure 7.4 (Classify-Cluster-DS) and put them side-by-side to examine the structure of the groups and the way that each method allocated the news stories. In figure 7.5, we show only the first level of the node hierarchy, with the browser area minimized; on your screen, you can expand that view so that half of the screen shows the left window and the other half shows the right window.

In both cases, the data that was clustered and classified was the same, but the two different orderings of the clustering and classification operations created the two different structures shown in figure 7.5. It becomes clear, through the juxtaposition of the structures, that the cluster-classify ordering results in fewer and larger clusters, while the classify-cluster ordering results in a larger number of clusters that are fairly narrow and clean in their content.

Let's look inside the world category where we find the largest discrepancy in the number of groups; six groups were formed during the cluster-classify approach and

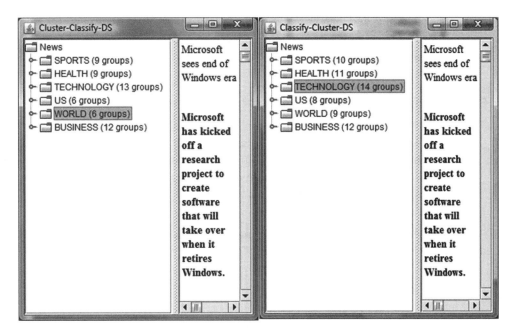

Figure 7.5 Juxtaposition of the two different tree structures shown in figures 7.3 and 7.4

nine groups were formed during the classify-cluster approach. The news story usa-10 has been misclassified by both methods, and is contained in a "clean" group without other news stories.

Now, note that we applied both methods on a superset of the training dataset. This indicates that the textual content of that news story isn't close to any other news story in our collection. It tells us also that its content is much closer to the training documents that refer to the world news category than any other document from the rest of the news categories. This implies that we should include this instance (news story usa-10) into our training set! It's exactly this kind of analysis, or quality assurance if you prefer, that augments the body of knowledge in our system.

The usa-16 group of news stories was also misclassified during the classify-cluster approach, but that group wasn't even formed during the cluster-classify approach. If you look inside the group labeled world-20, you'll find the news story usa-16 grouped there with another 33 stories. What happened? During the cluster-classify approach, we start clustering with a list of news stories whose content is very diverse. As a result, large groups such as world-20 appear to be robust and the clustering algorithm can't break them into smaller pieces; of course, by fine-tuning the parameters, you can influence the level of granularity, but the main problem isn't resolved. During the classify-cluster approach, the initial classification results in a compartmentalization of the documents that made the job of clustering much easier. Thus, with a lot of the noise reduced between documents that landed in the world news category, the clustering algorithm was able to detect that the news story usa-16 doesn't belong in any of the other clusters and, like story usa-10, should go in its own group. Incidentally, we should mention that often people will refer to clusters that consist of a single member as *singletons*, a term that must be familiar to you, a software professional, from the famous singleton pattern.

7.4.2   *Classifying with the NewsProcessor class*

Now, let's take a closer look into the inner workings of classification with the News-Processor class. We'll break down the description of each important step into its own set of listings. Let's start with the training phase for the NewsProcessor, shown in listing 7.6. This consists of training the classifier, since there's no training involved for the clustering operation, but note that there's more than defining the classifier and calling the train method.

> **Listing 7.6   Training a naïve Bayes classifier and selecting a classification strategy**

```
public void trainClassifier() {

   if( topicSelector == null ) {

      NBStoryClassifier storyClassifier =
 new NBStoryClassifier("NewsStoryClassifier",trainingDataset);

      storyClassifier.train();

      ClassificationStrategyImpl defaultTopicSelector =      ◁──┐ Select classification
 new ClassificationStrategyImpl();                                │   strategy

      defaultTopicSelector.setStoryClassifier(storyClassifier);  ◁──┐

      topicSelector = defaultTopicSelector;                          │
   }                                                     Assign classifier
}                                                           to strategy  ┘
```

The name of the class NBStoryClassifier indicates something that you probably expected. We're going to leverage the powerful naïve Bayes classifier that we encountered in chapter 2 and revisited in chapter 5. The NBStoryClassifier class implements the core Classifier interface, like all classifiers ought to do, and contains the mechanics that'll translate the specific news story data into the "language" that the NaiveBayes classifier uses—the Concept and Instance classes.

We'll look at the NBStoryClassifier class shortly, but first, let's discuss the selection of classification strategy that takes place in listing 7.6. What's this Classification-StrategyImpl class doing? It's a class that we didn't encounter before. Why do we need it? Because all the classification examples that we worked on earlier in the book were concerned with classifying a list of instances into their respective concepts, that's why. Here, in our news portal example, we must deal with the classification of *groups of instances* (news groups) into their respective concepts (news categories). There's more than one way to do this, so we need a strategy of deciding what to do.

One strategy would be to select the most "representative" story of the group and classify it, then wherever the representative is assigned, the group is assigned; that's similar to how the Electoral College (in the U.S.) works. Another strategy would be classifying all stories combined with a *majority vote* rule. Before you look at the code, try to think of other possible strategies and ponder the differences that each can impart in the final news structure.

In summary, the process of classification for our `NewsProcessor` class is more involved than what we've seen so far. It relies on two classes—the `NBStoryClassifier` and the `ClassificationStrategyImpl`. The first enables the use of our naïve Bayes classifier, while the second is responsible for encapsulating the decision strategy that we want to follow when we classify a news group.

7.4.3 Meet the classifier

To go one level deeper in the code, let's look closer at each one of these two classes. The code from the `NBStoryClassifier` is shown in listing 7.7. As usual we've removed some methods, Javadoc comments, and so on. Apart from the essential `train` and `classify` methods that every `Classifier` must implement, there are a number of auxiliary methods that are responsible for creating an `Instance` for a news story and a `Concept` for a news `Category`.

Listing 7.7 A news story classifier that uses the Naïve Bayes algorithm

```java
public class NBStoryClassifier implements Classifier {

    private List<ClassificationResult> conceptScores;
    private NaiveBayes nbClassifier;
    private boolean verbose = true;

    public NBStoryClassifier(String name, NewsDataset ds) {

        TrainingSet tSet = createTrainingSet(ds);

        nbClassifier = new NaiveBayes(name, tSet);                    ❶
    }

    public TrainingSet createTrainingSet(NewsDataset ds) {

        int nStories = ds.getSize();
        List<Instance> allTrainingInstances =
          new ArrayList<Instance>(nStories);

        Iterator<NewsStory> iter = ds.getIteratorOverStories();

        while( iter.hasNext() ) {
          NewsStory newsStory = iter.next();

          Instance instance = toInstance(newsStory);                 ❷
          allTrainingInstances.add(instance);
        }

        Instance[] instances =
          allTrainingInstances.toArray(new Instance[nStories]);

        return new TrainingSet(instances);
    }

    public boolean train() {
        TrainingSet tSet = nbClassifier.getTset();
```

```
      for(String attributeName : tSet.getAttributeNameSet() ) {
         nbClassifier.trainOnAttribute(attributeName);
      }
      return nbClassifier.train();
   }

   public Instance toInstance(NewsStory newsStory) {              ❷

      Concept concept              = toConcept(newsStory.getTopic());      ◄─────┐
      String[]             terms = newsStory.getTopNTerms();                     │
      StringAttribute[] attributes = new StringAttribute[terms.length];          │
                                                                                 │
      for(int i = 0; i < terms.length; i++) {                                    │
         String name = terms[i];                                                 │
         String value = "Y";                                                     │
         attributes[i] = new StringAttribute(name, value);                       │
      }                                                                   ❸      │
      return new BaseInstance(concept, attributes);                              │
   }                                                                             │
                                                                                 │
   private Map<String, NewsCategory> allTopics =                                 │
   new HashMap<String, NewsCategory>();                                          │
                                                                                 │
   private Map<String, Concept> allConcepts =                                    │
   new HashMap<String, Concept>();                                               │
                                                                                 │
   public Concept toConcept(NewsCategory t) {                            ◄───────┘

      if( t == null ) return null;

      String topicName = t.getName();
      Concept c = allConcepts.get(topicName);
      if( c == null ) {
         c = new BaseConcept(t.getName());
         allConcepts.put(topicName, c);
      }
      return c;
   }

   public Concept classify(Instance instance) {              ❹

      conceptScores       = new ArrayList<ClassificationResult>();
      Concept bestConcept = null;
      double       bestP = 0.0;
      TrainingSet    tSet = nbClassifier.getTset();

      for (Concept c : tSet.getConceptSet()) {
         double p = nbClassifier.getProbability(c, instance);

         ClassificationResult cR = new ClassificationResult(c, p);
         conceptScores.add(cR);

         if( p >= bestP ) {
            bestConcept = c;
            bestP = p;
         }
      }
      return bestConcept;
   }
}
```

❶ The `createTrainingSet` method is the primary responsibility of the `NBStory-Classifier`. We intend to delegate the task of classification to our standard Naive-Bayes implementation, but to do that we need a `TrainingSet` object.

❷ The `toInstance` method takes a `NewsStory` object as its input and creates a `BaseInstance` object. In order to create a `BaseInstance` object, we need two things. We need a `Concept` object to which the `Instance` belongs and we need a list of attributes and their values. The number of attributes depends on the number of "top" terms that a news story has. The default value (set equal to 25) is determined in the class `FileListNewsDataset`. We used that value implicitly in listing 7.5, when we created the training dataset and the two testing datasets (`ds1` and `ds2`). Altering the number of top terms will change the results of classification. To change that value, use the method `setTopTerms`, immediately before you call the `init` method on the dataset, and observe the differences in the results compared with what you obtained earlier.

Alternatively, you could change the implementation of the `toInstance` method, so that it doesn't train the classifier on all top terms. This exercise is also described in the third to-do item of this chapter.

❸ The `toConcept` method is the second important auxiliary method for building our training set, and the `toInstance` method relies on it. Its implementation is straightforward and there's little room for variation here. We take the name of the `NewsCategory` and create an object of the `BaseConcept` class, while keeping track of all the concepts that we've encountered so far.

❹ If you compare this `classify` method implementation with the implementation of the `classify` method in the `NaiveBayes` class, you'll realize that they're almost identical. The difference is that here, we collect the classification scores for all concepts and store it in the `conceptScores` variable, which will be available until the next time the `classify` method is invoked. This will give us more options later, when we use the `ClassificationStrategyImpl` to assign a news category to each news story or news group.

The purpose of the `ClassificationStrategyImpl` class is to capture the definition of the two possible approaches in classifying news stories. The first is the classification of a news group to a news category. The second is the classification of a news story to a news category. Let's examine how the class works.

7.4.4 *Classification strategy: going beyond low-level assignments*

The `ClassificationStrategyImpl` class implements the interface `ClassificationStrategy`, which reflects the two possible approaches to classifying news stories. In particular, the `assignTopicToCluster` and `assignTopicToStory` methods, respectively, are responsible for encapsulating these approaches—the term *topic* as used here is equivalent to a news category. Without further ado, let's see exactly what this class does by looking at its code in listing 7.8; the listing doesn't contain the complete source code of the class.

Listing 7.8 `ClassificationStrategyImpl`: **defining a classification strategy**

```
public class ClassificationStrategyImpl implements ClassificationStrategy {

    private NBStoryClassifier storyClassifier;

    public void assignTopicToCluster(NewsStoryGroup cluster) {          ❶

        List<NewsStory> newsStories = cluster.getStories();
        NewsStory     rpStory = selectRepresentativeStory(newsStories);     ❷

        NewsCategory bestTopic = selectBestMatchingTopic(rpStory);      ❸

        cluster.setTopic(bestTopic);              ❹
        cluster.setRepresentativeStory(rpStory);
    }

    public void assignTopicToStory(NewsStory newsStory) {          ❺

        Instance instance = storyClassifier.toInstance(newsStory);
        Concept concept = storyClassifier.classify(instance);

        NewsCategory bestTopic = storyClassifier.toTopic(concept);
        newsStory.setTopic(bestTopic);
    }

    private NewsStory selectRepresentativeStory(List<NewsStory> newsStories) {

        return selectLongestStory(newsStories);
    }                                                                          ❻

    private NewsStory selectLongestStory(List<NewsStory> newsStories) {

        NewsStory representativeStory = null;
        int maxContentLength = 0;

        for(NewsStory newsStory : newsStories) {

            int storyContentLength = newsStory.getContent().getText().length();

            if( storyContentLength > maxContentLength ) {

                maxContentLength = storyContentLength;

                representativeStory = newsStory;
            }
        }

        return representativeStory;
    }

    private NewsCategory selectBestMatchingTopic(NewsStory newsStory) {        ❸

        Instance instance = storyClassifier.toInstance(newsStory);
        Concept   concept = storyClassifier.classify(instance);

        return storyClassifier.toTopic(concept);
    }
}
```

❶ The `assignTopicToCluster` method encapsulates the steps that we need to take to decide what news category should be assigned to a given news group. This particular implementation is simple. It identifies one news story from the group as the representative of the group, classifies the representative story, and keeps track of both the news category (topic) and the representative for the cluster. The fourth to-do item of this chapter invites you to explore more advanced strategies for assigning a news category to a group.

❷ The selection of the representative story relies exclusively on the method `select-LongestStory`, but this can also be more sophisticated; once again, see the fourth to-do item.

❸ You may wonder whether we should've used the `assignTopicToStory` method here rather than the `selectBestMatchingTopic` method. After all, the latter simply invokes the classifier and is no different from the former. But the two methods don't have to be the same, and that's why we explicitly call a different method.

❹ This step records the assignments of the representative story and the corresponding news category.

❺ As noted earlier, this implementation is equivalent to the implementation of the `selectBestMatchingTopic` method. It's the job of the `NBStoryClassifier` class to classify a news story into a news category. This method isn't particularly useful when it simply delegates the classification to the `NBStoryClassifier`; we could've used the classifier to begin with. The value of this method becomes clear when the result of classification is postprocessed or when the news story itself is preprocessed before we pass it on to the classifier.

❻ The `selectLongestStory` method provides a simple heuristic of identifying a representative story for a list of news stories. The idea behind this choice is that the larger the size of the news story, the more overlap it'll have with every other news story. This isn't very sophisticated and we could improve significantly on it based on our discussion in the previous chapters, especially chapter 4. Some ideas that you can explore are provided in the fourth to-do item.

We conclude that the `ClassificationStrategyImpl` class plays the role of a meta-algorithm. In other words, it's a construction where we can inject business logic or sophisticated combination techniques to help us make the best choice possible based on what we know (data) and what we can do (low-level or base algorithms). In chapter 6, we examined a number of techniques that can help us combine classifiers. These techniques, which are also meta-algorithms, could be applied here along with other heuristics or business rules to optimize the allocation of the news stories into news categories.

Let's return to the `NewsProcessor` itself. Listing 7.9 shows us how the `ClassificationStrategyImpl` class is used in its two classification methods—`classifyClusters` and `classifyStories`. There's no direct involvement of the `NBStoryClassifier` class; the `ClassificationStrategyImpl` class is the façade for all the classification-related work. Within the `NewsProcessor` itself, classification for both news clusters and news stories is reduced to a single line of code.

Listing 7.9 Assigning news categories to news groups and news stories

```
public void classifyClusters(NewsDataset ds) {          Classify all groups
                                                        in given dataset
  List<NewsStoryGroup> clusters = ds.getStoryGroups();
```

```
    for(NewsStoryGroup cluster : clusters) {
        topicSelector.assignTopicToCluster(cluster);
    }
}
public void classifyStories(NewsDataset ds) {

    Iterator<NewsStory> iter = ds.getIteratorOverStories();

    while(iter.hasNext()) {

        NewsStory newsStory = iter.next();

        topicSelector.assignTopicToStory(newsStory)

    }
}
```

Delegate to
ClassificationStrategyImpl

**Classify all stories
in given dataset**

Delegate to
ClassificationStrategyImpl

This section concludes our review of the details about classifying news clusters and news stories. We showed that order matters in the results of classification. We also described how the broader context of classification—the possibility of classifying individual news stories or groups of news stories—enlarges the set of options that are available to us for designing an effective solution. In particular, the notion of classification strategy emerged naturally to deal with the fact that higher-level classification decisions might need to be made when we classify news groups. Now, we need to describe in more detail how we formed these news groups to begin with.

7.5   *Building news groups with the NewsProcessor class*

We described clustering in chapter 4, so you won't be surprised to find out that we relied on those algorithms for grouping news stories. In listing 7.5, we encountered two main methods for grouping news stories. The first was the createClusters method and the second was the createClustersWithinTopics method. When you first look at the code in listing 7.10, these two methods seem to rely on different classes for performing the clustering operations. But both methods rely on the ROCK algorithm that we saw in section 4.5.1.

Listing 7.10   The two clustering methods of the NewsProcessor

```
public void createClusters(NewsDataset ds) {

    NewsClusterBuilder clusterBuilder = new NewsClusterBuilder();

    clusterBuilder.setNewsDataset(ds);

    clusterBuilder.cluster();

}
public void createClustersWithinTopics(NewsDataset ds) {

    TopicalNewsClusterBuilder clusterBuilder =
        new TopicalNewsClusterBuilder();

    clusterBuilder.setNewsDataset(ds);

    clusterBuilder.cluster();

}
```

**Use
NewsClusterBuilder**

**Use
TopicalNewsCluster**

If both methods eventually rely on the ROCK algorithm, why did we create two separate classes? The main difference between the current implementation of these two classes is that the first one clusters all the stories in a `NewsDataset`, the other clusters all the stories inside each `NewsCategory` of the `NewsDataset`. Similar to the discussion that we had in the previous section about classification, it's possible to improve the results of clustering if the implementation of these two cases is handled differently. The distinction between the two will become clearer as our exposition progresses. Let's start by looking into the creation of clusters without taking into account the news categories.

7.5.1 Clustering general news stories

The `createClusters` method, applied on our default news story dataset, produces the clusters that are shown in figure 7.6. There are 55 clusters in total—you can't see them all in the figure but you'll be able to see them all in the Swing client. In particular, there are 42 clusters that are singletons, 2 clusters with two stories, 5 clusters with three stories, 1 cluster with four stories, 2 clusters with five stories, 1 cluster with six stories, 1 cluster with 14 stories, and a single cluster with 34 stories!

These numbers are of relative importance. On a general set of news stories, you'd expect that the clusters would be of roughly equal size and that most stories would be clustered rather than not (the number of singletons would be a small percentage of the overall number of clusters). If the cluster distribution is known then we can evalu-

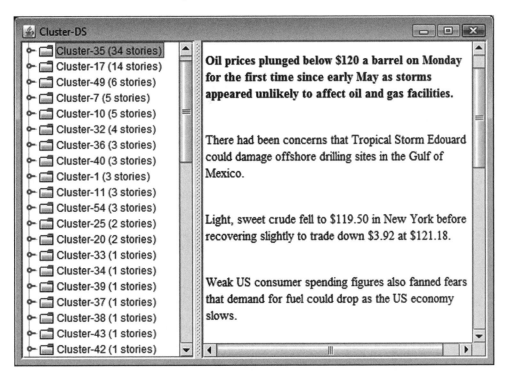

Figure 7.6   The results of clustering the default news dataset before classifying the news stories

ate the performance of our clustering algorithm. Identifying an "ideal" cluster is somewhat subjective and depends on what we want a cluster to be. For example, take a look at our default news dataset: how would you cluster the news stories? In order to be more specific and narrow down the number of stories, take a look at all the news stories whose filename begins with *biz-*. What stories would you group together? Why? See the fifth to-do item about this important point.

Now, let's examine the results that are shown in figure 7.6. You can create the Swing client that contains the results from figure 7.6 by executing the script in listing 7.11. The first problem with clustering the news stories is the big cluster that contains 34 stories. This is problematic because we know that there are 129 news stories divided more or less equally among six big subjects. So, this cluster's size is 26% of the entire news dataset and is larger than the largest possible group given the division of the news stories by subject. These are two good reasons for considering this cluster as being too large. This quantitative, back-of-the-envelope assessment can be corroborated by the qualitative assessment that we can perform by perusing the 34 news stories in the Swing client. Similarly, we can argue that Cluster-17, with 14 stories, is also large. Look at these news stories and review section 4.5.1 to refresh your memory with regard to the inner workings of the ROCK algorithm.

Listing 7.11   Clustering news stories without reference to the news categories

```
NewsDataset ds = new FileListNewsDataset("Cluster-DS");      Load default
ds.setDocumentDir("C:/iWeb2/data/ch07/all");                 news dataset
ds.init();

NewsProcessor newsProcessor = new NewsProcessor();           Cluster news
newsProcessor.createClusters(ds);                            stories

NewsUI ui = new NewsUI(ds);           Show only
ui.showClustersOnly(true);            clusters
NewsUI.createAndShowUI(ui);
```

It seems that the default values for the number of clusters and the threshold value for creating a link between two data points (news stories) allow the creation of a *supercluster*. Naturally, the first thing we need to look into is setting these two parameters, which takes place in the `cluster` method of the `NewsClusterBuilder`, as shown in listing 7.12.

Listing 7.12   The clustering method of the `NewsClusterBuilder`

```
public void cluster() {

    DataPoint[] dataPoints = createDataPoints(ds);       Desired number
    int k = dataPoints.length / 3;                       of clusters

    double linkThreshold = 0.15;      Threshold for forming link

    ROCKAlgorithm rock = new ROCKAlgorithm(dataPoints, k, linkThreshold);

    Dendrogram dnd = rock.cluster();

    List<NewsStoryGroup> storyGroups = createStoryGroups(dnd);
```

```
    for(NewsStoryGroup cluster : storyGroups) {
        ds.addStoryGroup(cluster);
    }
}
```

As you can see, in this method the number of desired clusters is set equal to one third of the dataset's size. We ask from the algorithm to construct approximately 43 clusters. There's nothing special about that choice. Experiment with the value of k and observe the effect this has on the largest cluster that's formed. To do this, you can replace the method `cluster()` with the overriding method `cluster(int k, double linkThreshold)`, which can also be found in the `NewsClusterBuilder`. Changing the variable `linkThreshold` will also affect your results, so you shouldn't change them simultaneously. Vary one parameter while keeping everything else the same.

The second problem with the clustering distribution of figure 7.6 is the large number of singletons (clusters that contain a single element). We know that this number can't be that large because we constructed the news stories by hand! What part of the ROCK algorithm do you think will have the largest impact on the number of singletons? Don't focus only on the number of desired clusters of the link threshold parameter. If you didn't review section 4.5.1 yet, please do so now. What if we write a different implementation of the `ROCKAlgorithm`? What would you change? See the sixth to-do item for more hints and analysis in that direction.

To go deeper into the results, let's focus on the news stories whose filename starts with the prefix *biz-*. Figure 7.7 shows three clusters that contain business news. The

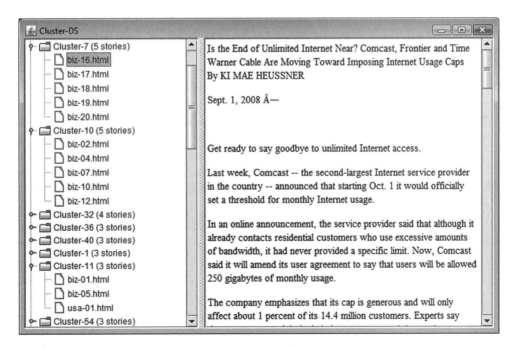

Figure 7.7   Inspecting the three business news story clusters that are shown expanded (left panel)

figure shows that a story from the category U.S. (news stories whose filename starts with the prefix *usa-*) has been included in the third cluster, where we have two business news stories. It turns out that including this story is correct; click on each article to convince yourself that the stories are related. This type of cluster would be harder to create if the news stories had first been assigned to news categories. In that case, the news story usa-01 might have been separated from the biz-01 and biz-05 news stories during the classification phase.

This brings up an interesting point about intelligent algorithms and the possible effects that emerge from combining them. It is not necessary to think of the two clustering approaches as mutually exclusive. It's possible to apply both and reap the benefits of each.

If it turns out that clustering news stories *after* classification generates clusters of higher quality, this doesn't imply that the reverse order is valueless. The value of clustering before classification might be found in *cross-referencing*. By cross-referencing, we mean that we can have a separate panel on our website that indicates related stories from other news categories. This feature isn't the same as recommendations, even though it may be presented in a similar way to the end user: for example, "If you liked this story, you may be interested in the following stories." Cross-referencing is about building an underlying semantic web across your dataset. I hope that this gives you a glimpse of the possibilities that emerge by using a combination of intelligent algorithms. By merely examining their order, we arrived naturally at an interesting new functionality!

Our inspection of Cluster-7 and Cluster-10 brings up another interesting point. The structure of our clusters has only one level—there are no clusters within clusters. This was partly by construction, because the Google News portal presents the stories in such a layout. Nevertheless, it's possible to add value by creating hierarchical relationships and creating groups of news groups.

Let's identify that value, first from a practical perspective. In Cluster-7, we have five stories that are indeed related. But the strength of that relevance isn't the same for all news stories. The biz-17 and biz-20 news stories are two different accounts of the same event—the constraint on network throughput on some users by Comcast. The biz-18 and biz-19 news stories, similarly, are two different reports on a Time Warner Cable experiment regarding internet usage. The last news story of Cluster-7, biz-16, is of a more general nature but still directly related to both of the events reported by the rest of the news stories.

A human might have distributed these news stories differently. It makes sense to have these stories under the same "roof" but group together biz-17 and biz-20, as well as biz-18 and biz-19, while leaving as a single entry the news story biz-16 due to its more general description. Such a structure would be more compelling and user friendly. One possible way to achieve this is to apply the clustering algorithm more than once, successively.

In fact, it doesn't even have to be the same algorithm, and typically it isn't. It is common practice to apply first the k-means algorithm and then the ROCK algorithm within the individual k-clusters. This approach is commonly used in order to improve the quality of the clusters as well as the performance characteristics of clustering itself.

We invite you to experiment with this approach, as applied to our present example, in the seventh to-do item of this chapter.

7.5.2 Clustering news stories within a news category

The `createClustersWithinTopics` method, applied on our default news story dataset, produces the clusters that are shown in figure 7.8. Note that there are now 64 clusters. In particular, there are 45 clusters that are singletons, 4 clusters with 2 stories, 6 clusters with 3 stories, 2 clusters with 4 stories, 3 clusters with 5 stories, 1 cluster with 6 stories, 1 cluster with 7 stories, 1 cluster with 8 stories, and 1 cluster with 14 stories, as in the previous section.

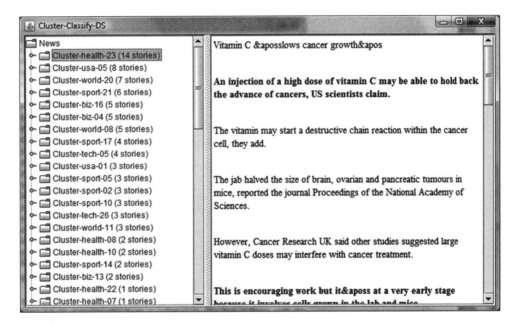

Figure 7.8   The results of clustering the default news dataset after classifying the news stories

The names of the clusters now indicate the news category (topic) within which each cluster was formed. This distribution of clusters seems to be better than before; compare it with the results shown in figure 7.6. We got rid of the supercluster while the number of clusters with two, three, and four news stories increased. Unfortunately, the number of singletons has also increased. Listing 7.13 shows the BeanShell script that creates the results of figure 7.8. Execute that script now, so that you have a handy reference to the structure as we discuss these results. The steps in that listing are straightforward and are similar to those in listing 7.5.

Listing 7.13   Clustering news stories that have been assigned to news categories

```
NewsDataset trainingDS = new FileListNewsDataset("TrainingDS");
trainingDS.setDocumentDir("C:/iWeb2/data/ch07/training");
```

```
trainingDS.init();

NewsDataset ds = new FileListNewsDataset("Classify-Cluster-DS");
ds.setDocumentDir("C:/iWeb2/data/ch07/all");
ds.init();

NewsProcessor newsProcessor = new NewsProcessor(trainingDS);

newsProcessor.trainClassifier();

newsProcessor.classifyStories(ds);

newsProcessor.createClustersWithinTopics(ds);

NewsUI ui = new NewsUI(ds);
ui.showClustersOnly(true);
NewsUI.createAndShowUI(ui);
```

If you expand the largest cluster—Cluster-health-23—you'll realize that its content is identical to the content of Cluster-17, which we identified in figure 7.6. Not only is the number of news stories identical, the actual new stories that belong to the two clusters are identical, as shown in figure 7.9. As far as this cluster is concerned, the order of operations didn't make a difference.

The invariance of this cluster is important and can be explained as follows. Neither the story tech-04 nor the story tech-15 belongs in the training set of the classifier, so it's not easy for the classifier to assign them to the proper news category. The news

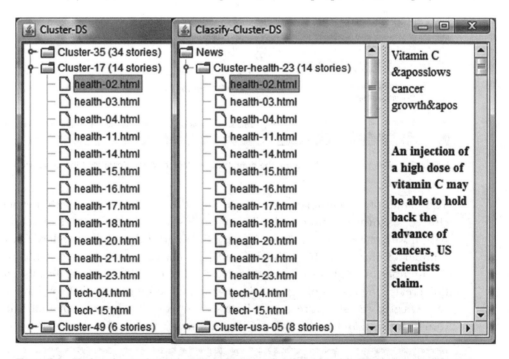

Figure 7.9   The invariance of a large cluster after swapping the order of clustering and classification. The leftmost panel shows the results of clustering when clustering comes first. The middle panel shows the results of clustering when classification comes first.

story health-16 is included in the training set, and its content is related to the usage of mobile phones, which overlaps with the content of the two technical stories. It seems that this overlap is more significant than the overlap of the news stories that belong in the training set and are assigned in the technology category. Once these two technical news stories are misplaced, our best chance would be that they remain as singletons or that they cluster together—within the wrong news category, of course.

At any rate, the content of the 14 news stories appears similar to both the clustering and the classification algorithms. From a practical perspective, in the case of clustering after classification, this situation can be remedied by enriching our training set. When we do have misclassified elements, we want the clustering to be finer within the topics.

A deeper look into the results reveals that many of the clusters, formed within each news category, are identical to the clusters that we found in the case of clustering before classification. This means that the greatest gain was breaking up the supercluster. We should certainly be cautious not to generalize this finding for an arbitrary news dataset, but we expect it to be true when the training set provides sufficient coverage of the news categories.

Let's look into setting the default values for the number of clusters and the threshold value for creating a link between two data points (news stories), which takes place in the `cluster` method of the `TopicalNewsClusterBuilder`, as shown in listing 7.14. These parameters can change the number of singletons that we obtain in the final results. This is true regardless of the order of clustering and classification. But changing these parameters should have a greater impact when clustering after classification because the sets of data points that are passed as input to the clustering algorithm have reduced noise level.

Listing 7.14 The clustering method of the `TopicalNewsClusterBuilder`

```
public void cluster() {

  for(NewsCategory topic : ds.getTopics() ) {

    List<NewsStory> stories = ds.getStories(topic);
    DataPoint[] dataPoints = createDataPoints(stories);

    int k = dataPoints.length / 3;      ◁── Desired number of clusters

    double linkThreshold = 0.15;      ◁── Threshold for forming a link

    ROCKAlgorithm rock = new ROCKAlgorithm(dataPoints, k, linkThreshold);

    Dendrogram dnd = rock.cluster();

    List<NewsStoryGroup> storyGroups = createStoryGroups(topic, dnd);

    for(NewsStoryGroup cluster : storyGroups) {
      ds.addStoryGroup(cluster);
    }
  }
}
```

Listing 7.14 is similar to listing 7.12. The main difference is the outer loop that defines a new scope for each news category. Does this difference in implementation merit the existence of two separate classes for handling the clustering of news stories? As we've seen, the current implementation does avoid the formation of superclusters, but more importantly, it paves the way for an implementation where the number of clusters and the threshold value for creating a link between two data points can become a function of the news category. You can begin exploring the possibilities that open with such an approach by reading the eighth to-do item.

We've now covered the two most important ways of clustering our news stories— clustering individual news stories and clustering news stories within a news category. We've completed the introduction of every intelligent algorithm that we described in this book, except the recommendation algorithms. The subject of the next section introduces an item-based recommendation algorithm in our news portal. In particu- lar, we'll explore the case where our users have the ability to rate the news stories and we want to use these ratings to dynamically arrange the content of the portal for each user.

7.6   *Dynamic content based on the user's ratings*

If we have ratings of the news stories then we can recommend news stories that a user hasn't viewed yet. In chapter 3, we discussed the two broad categories of techniques that allow us to create recommendations—collaborative filtering and the content-based approach. We pointed out that, in the process of building our online music store exam- ple, we've created the infrastructure that you need for writing a general recommenda- tion system for your own application. It's time to test that claim. Let's create a recommendation engine for our news stories based on the code from chapter 3. If you need to review chapter 3, or haven't read it yet, now is a good time to do so.

We'll start by creating a file that contains the ratings of the users. As you might recall, the basic concepts of a recommendation engine are the Items, Users, and Rat- ings. In this chapter, our news stories correspond to items. The file ratings.txt, which you can find inside the C:\iWeb2\data\ch07\ratings directory, contains the data that are shown in table 7.1.

User	News story	Rating
	Usa-04	4
	Usa-05	3
A	Biz-05	5
	Biz-01	4
	World-16	5
	Usa-01	5
	Sport-04	3
B	Sport-03	4
	Biz-05	5
	Tech-06	2

Table 7.1   Fifteen ratings from three users of the news portal

User	News story	Rating
	World-15	3
	World-16	5
C	Usa-04	4
	Biz-01	4
	Usa-01	5

Table 7.1   Fifteen ratings from three users of the news portal *(continued)*

In table 7.1, there are 15 ratings provided by three users (A, B, and C). In section 7.5, we repeatedly encountered a cluster that contained the articles biz-01, biz-05, and usa-01. We devised the ratings so that the news stories biz-01 and biz-05 are shared between user A and C, and between user A and B, respectively. By mere inspection, we expect that the news story usa-01 should be among the recommended stories for user A. Let's execute the script shown in listing 7.15 and see what happens!

Listing 7.15   Recommending news stories based on ratings

```
NewsDataset ds = new FileListNewsDataset("NewsDataset");
ds.setDocumentDir("C:/iWeb2/data/ch07/all");
ds.setTopTerms(25);
ds.setUserAndRatingsFilename("c:/iWeb2/data/ch07/ratings/ratings.txt");
ds.init();

StoryRecommender delphi = new StoryRecommender(ds);        ◁──┐ Create recommendation
delphi.calculateRecommendations();                            │ engine

delphi.recommendStories("1");
```

The results are shown in figure 7.10, and the news story usa-01 is indeed one of the recommended stories. This may not be impressive for the small number of news stories, users, and ratings that we use in this example, but the same code can be used for much larger datasets with satisfactory results. Note that our recommender skips the news stories that user A has already rated.

```
bsh % delphi.recommendStories("1");
Skipping item:biz-01.html
Skipping item:biz-05.html
Skipping item:usa-05.html
Skipping item:usa-04.html
Skipping item:world-16.html

Recommendations for user UserA:
Item: usa-01.html          , predicted rating: 5.000000
Item: sport-03.html        , predicted rating: 4.000000
Item: world-15.html        , predicted rating: 3.000000
Item: sport-04.html        , predicted rating: 3.000000
Item: health-16.html       , predicted rating: 2.500000
bsh %
```

Figure 7.10   Recommendations for user A based on the ratings of table 7.1

Let's take a look into the StoryRecommender class, which made these recommendations possible. Listing 7.16 shows its complete source code. By leveraging the recommendation engine Delphi, we've created a custom news story recommendation engine with only a few lines of code. This is the same Delphi class that we encountered in chapter 3.

Listing 7.16   StoryRecommender: producing user recommendations for news stories

```
public class StoryRecommender {

  private DatasetAdapter rDs;
  private Recommender delphi;

  public StoryRecommender(NewsDataset ds) {
      this.rDs = new DatasetAdapter(ds);
  }

  public void calculateRecommendations() {

    Delphi d = new Delphi(rDs,                              ⎤ Create recommendation
      RecommendationType.ITEM_PENALTY_BASED, false);    ◁──⎦ engine
    d.setVerbose(true);

    this.delphi = d;
  }

  public List<PredictedNewsStoryRating>
    recommendStories(String newsUserId) {

    if( delphi == null ) {
      String msg = "Recommender not initialized.";
      throw new RuntimeException(msg);
    }

    User user = rDs.getUserForNewsUserId(newsUserId);

    List<PredictedItemRating> predictedRatings = delphi.recommend(user);

    List<PredictedNewsStoryRating> ratings =
      new ArrayList<PredictedNewsStoryRating>();

    for(PredictedItemRating iR : predictedRatings) {

        PredictedNewsStoryRating r = new PredictedNewsStoryRating();
        r.setUserId(newsUserId);
        r.setRating(iR.getRating());

        NewsStory newsStory =
      rDs.getNewsStoryForItemId(iR.getItemId());
        r.setStoryId(newsStory.getId());

        ratings.add(r);
    }

    return ratings;
  }
}
```

Apart from the necessary translations between the specific news story terminology and the general purpose dataset interface of chapter 3, which are taken care of by the

`DatasetAdapter` class, we've used nothing else. The `Delphi` recommendation engine is based on item-based similarities with penalties (its type is `Recommendation-Type.ITEM_PENALTY_BASED`). You can experiment with the other types that are available for our recommendation engine.

The `StoryRecommender` class, and its auxiliary classes such as `DatasetAdapter` and `PredictedNewsStoryRating`, can act as a template for your own application. The general idea is simple: transform your data so that it can map onto `Items`, `Users`, and `Ratings`. Then delegate recommendations to the `Delphi` recommendation engine; you can tinker with the available recommendation types to find the one that best suits your goal. Your data may be persisted and structured in a somewhat different way, but it shouldn't be hard to transform it into our general-purpose classes.

7.7   *Summary*

The chapter demonstrated the use of the intelligent algorithms that we examined so far, in the setting of a web application; more specifically, in the context of a news portal such as Google News. We've seen that the value of using intelligent algorithms starts from the beginning, with the possibility of intelligent crawling. Naturally, the material from our second chapter was also applicable in the news portal example for enabling searching based on indices and beyond!

Initially, the place of intelligent algorithms and their value in any given application might be hard to recognize. Nevertheless, as we start asking questions, it becomes evident that these algorithms can improve the level of service that the users of the application get in quite unexpected ways. We've seen that a clustering algorithm might be used not just for grouping similar news stories but also for enhancing the visibility of relevant news stories by *cross-referencing*.

We've seen also that we can use a single algorithm multiple times or different algorithms in sequence. But it turns out that the order of the sequence matters. We demonstrated that property by explicitly inverting the order of clustering and classification on our news stories. The results of clustering news stories after the classification stage were better than the results of clustering the news stories before classification. This observation is quite general and likely to happen with your data too, whether or not news stories.

Another interesting fact was revealed from using the clustering and classification algorithms in sequence. We showed how to deal with the classification of groups themselves. Up to now, we'd seen only classification of simple objects such as emails or credit card transactions. Here, we described how to classify a single news story as well as a group of news stories. There are many ways that this can be done, so the construction of a meta-algorithm can be expedient in these cases.

It's practically impossible to answer all questions related to applying intelligent algorithms in a way that would be applicable to all applications. Nevertheless, we hope that we've sketched out how you should approach the introduction of intelligent algorithms. We also think that, after reading this chapter, it should be clear that you can construct components that combine several intelligent algorithms for a given purpose. Review the questions raised in the text and explore the many suggestions that we provide in the to-do action items. We're certain that you'll find them useful in your own work.

7.8   To do

1   *Add intelligent features to the* NewsCrawler.   Our NewsCrawler is good for getting started with a small code base. But if you simply want to retrieve the content from a list of base URLs, many other crawlers are available that are probably much better than ours. The reason for writing this small crawler is we want to point out a number of areas where intelligent algorithms can make crawling much more efficient and effective. In this to-do item, we'd like to discuss these potential improvements and hopefully motivate you enough to implement them!

Let's consider the case of websites with spam or inappropriate material—you can define as inappropriate whatever you like, or rather you don't like! These are websites that you probably don't have an interest in crawling. Even though you might not target these sites intentionally, your crawler may end up in one of them by accident. So, it would be nice if the crawler could identify these sites and avoid them. How would you do that?

In the email spam use case that we worked on in chapter 5, we used the naïve Bayes classifier and rules-based classifier to filter out the spam email. We could do the same here. Our crawler could sample the pages and classify them as legitimate for retrieval or not. For the naïve Bayes classifier, you'd need to have some sample web pages from both categories; that would be your training set. For the rule-based classifier, you'll need some rules. For example, if the page contains the word *xyz* then skip it.

The same algorithms can be used for a slightly different use case. If you want to target (rather than filter out) certain web pages, you can create a crawler whose focus is on Java-related articles, or even more specifically on Java open source projects. In that case, you'd start from a list of known URLs, or the link results of a Google search, but you'd download a website only if the classifiers tell you that its content is relevant to your subject.

You could build intelligence on top of these results. If a link from site A takes me to site B and site B is deemed inappropriate, it might be expedient to count the number of links that emanate from site A and lead to such sites. We could use that percentage directly as a threshold to build a link graph that we'd analyze with a method similar to the one used by PageRank. These are only a few ideas for you to work on. If you implement them and you like the results and the capability, try to come up with similar ideas for embedding intelligent algorithms in crawling. It should be rewarding as a learning experience and it might turn out to be useful in your work.

2   *Improve the search results of the news portal by leveraging user clicks.*   In chapter 2, we saw that the interaction of a user with a search engine defines his or her own areas of interest and own subjectivity. We introduced a naïve Bayes classifier to

leverage the user's clicks and improve the search results. As you may recall, we assumed that you've collected the clicks of the users as indicated in the file user-clicks.csv, located in the data/ch02 directory. That comma-separated file contained three fields: the user ID, the terms of the search query, and a string that contained the URL.

Similarly, you can create a file that captures user clicks in order to improve the search results of the news portal. What should the training attributes be now? Try the following recipe. Select as training attributes:

- The user ID
- The terms of the search query
- The terms of the document that was selected
- The topic of the document that was selected

Can you justify these choices? Why did we replace the URL with the topic? Why did we introduce the terms of the document? How would you proceed in correcting the ranking score? Write down your ideas and implement them.

For the same user and the same query terms, you should have more than one entry in the user clicks file. In the example from chapter 2, the number of times that a click appeared in that file made its URL a better candidate for our search results. The same will be true for the various topics in the case of a news portal. Typically, the same user will read a number of different topic stories for the same query because his interest may vary over time or because he may be looking for additional information on a particular topic.

In the case of the portal, an interesting problem to solve is the following. If I have a number of stories under the same category and my classifier is trained to identify the topic, how will that help me boost the most interesting stories for a given user? Is it possible? If not, what can we do to address that problem?

3 *Evaluate the effect of the attribute selection on the results of our news portal.* Our choice of attributes for a news story was based on the top terms that can be extracted from it. It's clear from the code in listing 7.7 that each top term becomes a training attribute for the classifier. There are clearly many more choices than that!

The obvious modification of the toInstance method in listing 7.7 is to create a single string attribute that contains the entire set of top terms, perhaps separated by space when we concatenate them, to make it legible for us. Do you think that this will result in better or worse classifications? Whatever your opinion might be, try to justify it conceptually and then implement the change to see what happens!

Note the way that we construct the StringAttribute instances inside the toInstance method. In effect, the string attributes are becoming Boolean variables! Another modification to the code would be geared toward a fixed set of top terms and assign as attribute values the actual string values of the top terms. You can do this by executing the following steps:

– Create a parameter that will determine the number of training attributes
– Create a name for each of these attributes by adopting a simple convention; for example, use a fixed term and enumerate them—attr-1, attr-2, and so on.
– Assign the value that corresponds to each attribute based on the order of the top terms. That means, the attribute attr-1 takes its value based on the first top term, the attribute attr-2 takes its value based on the second top term, and so on.

With such a construction, rerun our examples and observe the results. What do you think is going to happen? Do you think that this approach will provide us with better results? If so, why do you think that?

What issues, if any, do you anticipate? Let's say that you want to use 32 attributes and, for whatever reason, certain stories don't have 32 top terms, which means that the last attributes (in the enumeration from 1 to 32) won't have a corresponding top term. What should the value of these attributes be? Does it matter?

4 *Create a sophisticated implementation of the* `ClassificationStrategyImpl` *class.* In listing 7.8, we described a basic implementation for the `ClassificationStrategy` of our news processor. In that implementation, the `assignTopicToStory` method is rudimentary. So, let's examine whether other implementations are possible and whether they'd would be beneficial.

Let's consider the case where we apply two classifiers to obtain our classification results. Unlike the methods of combining classifiers that we discussed in chapter 6, here we simply want to use one classifier after the other. You may think that this is odd, but consider the following scenario. We train our naïve Bayes classifier based on the content of each web page, but this doesn't involve any contextual knowledge or metainformation about the content.

If your web page was pulled from ESPN the likelihood that it refers to sports is fairly high. We can build rules based on such metatags that web pages have and enforce the rules once the naïve Bayes classifier finishes its job. In other words, we let the probabilistic classifier take a first sweep at classifying the news stories and subsequently enforce a number of rules that we presume to be true regardless of the content itself. Go ahead and implement such a classification strategy in the `assignTopicToStory` method and compare it with the results of the original implementation.

This approach should give you a significant improvement in the accuracy of automated classification! Of course, you could devise other strategies that might be even better. We encourage you to do so and compare the results. Note that the serial application of classifiers isn't as straightforward when we want to classify a cluster because the news stories of a given news group almost certainly originate from different sources. For a news group, this approach might be more difficult. So, let's turn our attention to the second important method of the `ClassificationStrategyImpl` class.

The particular implementation of `assignTopicToCluster` is fairly simple. It identifies one news story from the group as the representative of the group, classifies the representative story, and keeps track of both the news category (topic) and the representative for the cluster. The selection of the representative story relies exclusively on the method `selectLongestStory`, which provides a simple heuristic of identifying a representative story for a list of news stories. The idea behind this choice is that the larger the size of the news story, the more overlap it'll have with every other news story.

This isn't very sophisticated and we can improve on it significantly. In chapter 4, when we were describing the k-means algorithm, we introduced the notion of a centroid. Implement a `selectRepresentativeStory` method that identifies as a representative story the news story that's closest to the centroid. How would you approach this? Think about the fact that you're comparing documents and experiment with different distance metrics.

Finally, implement an `assignTopicToCluster` method that doesn't rely on a single representative story but rather implements a majority vote among the members of the news group. Should all members be considered? If not, how can we decide who should vote?

5 *Is there a best clustering distribution?* Identifying an ideal cluster is somewhat subjective and certainly depends on what we want a cluster to be. Look at our default news dataset: how would you cluster the news stories? In order to be more specific and narrow the number of stories, look at all the news stories whose filename begins with *biz-*. What stories would you group together? Why?

To answer such questions systematically, you must define a measure that defines the "goodness" of a cluster formation. This will lead you naturally to the following question: what should the cluster be measured with? In comparison to what is a cluster better or worse? In the case of classification, there's a structure (typically hierarchical) and a training set that establish a frame of reference with respect to which we measure the quality of our classification. In clustering, we must devise other means of measuring the quality of a cluster because there's no reference frame. So, the measure must dependent on internal information. What attributes of the cluster's structure would you choose for your metric?

6 *Tweaking the ROCK.* The second problem with the clustering distribution of figure 7.6 is the large number of singletons (clusters that contain a single element). We know that this number can't be that large because we constructed the news stories by hand.

What part of the ROCK algorithm do you think will have the largest impact on the number of singletons? What would the effect of the number of desired clusters be? How about the link threshold parameter?

What if we write a different implementation of the `ROCKAlgorithm`? There are several parameters of the algorithm that are implied. Perhaps, the most fundamental is the choice of similarity measure for constructing the link matrix. What other similarity measure would be appropriate? Is it possible to create a completely custom approach for our news portal? Consider the possibility of using our naïve Bayes classifier for assigning a *probability of linkage* rather than a similarity measure.

7 *Hierarchical clustering of news stories.* Presenting information in a hierarchical structure is a much more effective way of organizing information that will be consumed by humans. The use of hierarchical structures abounds. The folders and files on your computer are presented in hierarchical (tree) format. The catalogs of online stores are also organized as hierarchies. These structures are more compelling and user friendly compared to a flat list or a simple one-level grouping.

We can create hierarchical cluster structures by applying a clustering algorithm more than once. In fact, it doesn't even have to be the same algorithm. Consider for example the clustering of our news stories by first applying the *k*-means algorithm and subsequently the ROCK algorithm on each cluster identified by the *k*-means. Swapping the execution order between the two algorithms and using a single algorithm are two viable alternatives.

What advantages do you see in each case? How would you proceed with such an implementation? Look at the problem not only from the perspective of cluster quality but also from the performance (computational cost) point of view.

8 *Fine tuning clustering for each news category.* In listing 7.14, we described the `cluster` method of the `TopicalNewsClusterBuilder`. Upon closer examination, you'll be convinced that there's nothing topical about the code, other than the fact that, for each news category, we cluster only the news stories within it. Of course, the name of the class would be a misnomer if we leave it like that. So, let's investigate some options.

What about the use of an array of integers and an array of doubles, say `int k[]` and `double linkThreshold[]`, for representing the number of desired clusters and the link threshold values, respectively. Now, you can use different values for these two parameters for each news category, but what should these values be? How would you choose the best value for each parameter?

Given that each news category will have its own representative topics, what other modifications can you make to improve the clustering within each news category? Brainstorm and experiment with your ideas; there's not only one answer!

7.9   References

Jurafsky, D., and J. H. Martin (2008). *Speech and Language Processing: An Introduction to Natural Language Processing, Computational Linguistics and Speech Recognition,* Second Edition. Prentice Hall (Series in Artificial Intelligence), 2008, pp 1024. http://www.cs.colorado.edu/~martin/slp.html.

appendix A:
Introduction to BeanShell

We use BeanShell throughout this book to remove the fine-grained details and focus on the high-level steps of an algorithm. The BeanShell scripts that we provide throughout the book present an overview of the algorithms. In addition, they facilitate quick experimentation and interactive learning. We found a lot of value, and had a lot of fun, while using the BeanShell scripts. We tested many ideas involving the topics that we developed in the course of writing the book, so we believe that you'll also appreciate the value of BeanShell once you become accustomed to it. So what's this BeanShell thing anyway?

A.1   What is BeanShell?

BeanShell is a lightweight scripting language that's compatible with the Java language. In fact, BeanShell dynamically executes standard Java syntax and extends it with common scripting conveniences such as loose types, commands, and method closures like those in Perl and JavaScript. It was written by Pat Niemeyer, and you can find its implementation in the open source project aptly called BeanShell (http://www.beanshell.org).

There's been an effort to standardize the scripting language and incorporate it in a future JDK. As the Java Specification Request 274 states:

> BeanShell is a VM hosted language, supporting dynamic execution of the full Java grammar and semantics as well as transparent access to Java objects and APIs. Additional scripting and convenience features are brought into the language as a strict superset of the Java language syntax. In this way BeanShell attempts to minimize both the syntactic and runtime barriers between Java application code and scripts, easing development and facilitating migration between scripts and static Java.

You may wonder at this point: if it's more or less Java, what's the point of using BeanShell? Let's try to answer that question.

A.2   Why use BeanShell?

For the purposes of this book, BeanShell is an environment that helps you learn about and experiment with intelligent algorithms. From a learning perspective, you can start with the APIs that we've defined and the scripts that we've written, but as you gain more and more experience, you can choose to expose more of the details of an algorithm as part of the BeanShell scripts.

From a research and development perspective, you may want to use BeanShell to quickly check the results of some tweaks in your algorithm. Alternatively, you might want to interact with algorithms through the command line of the interpreter for examining individual responses. For example, you may have just trained a classifier and want to use it as an oracle to find out about the classes of specific instances. If you don't know what instances these should be then it's convenient and valuable to interactively interrogate the classifier. We hope that these justifications provide you with the necessary and sufficient motivation. So, let's see how we can quickly get BeanShell up and running.

A.3   Running BeanShell

You can run BeanShell and execute the scripts of this book as long as you have a Java runtime available and the BeanShell JAR file (bsh.jar) in your classpath. Our source code distribution contains version 2.0b4 of BeanShell. We also include Windows and *nix script files that can load the BeanShell interpreter in a console window; these can be found in the `deploy\bin` directory of our distribution.

In what follows, we'll assume that your working environment is Microsoft Windows; you should be able to adjust the scripts in a similar manner in any other environment where the Java runtime is available. We should also mention our assumption that the book source code is located in the directory `C:\iWeb2`. That location is referenced by the `%IWEB2_HOME%` environment variable and all relative references are with respect to that root directory. If you want to place the source code elsewhere in your system, you should change the scripts accordingly. Open a command prompt: go to Start, click on Run ..., and type `cmd` in the text box. Change the directory to `c:\iweb2\deploy\bin`. You should be able to see the Windows script file called bsc.bat.

Aside from the location of the source code, the script also assumes that the environment variable `%JAVA_HOME%` has been set and is visible in the environment of the command prompt. If that's not the case you should at least have the Java executable of your choice in your PATH environment variable. Note that we haven't tested any code with versions of Java prior to 1.5. We recommend that you install the latest JDK (version 6) from Sun.

Finally, since you're executing (or better yet interpreting) a Java program, you can adjust the options of the JVM from the command line according to your needs and the specifications of your system. Our recommended settings for the heap of the JVM are `-Xms256M -Xmx1280M`, but these values may be too large for your system. Be aware of that fact and adjust your values accordingly, if you encounter any issues.

A.4   References

The BeanShell open source project. http://www.beanshell.org/home.html.

JSR 274: The BeanShell Scripting Language. Java Specification Requests. http://jcp.org/en/jsr/detail?id=274.

appendix B:
Web crawling

This appendix provides an overview of web crawling components, a brief description of the implementation details for the crawler provided with the book, and a few open-source crawlers written in Java.

B.1   An overview of crawler components

Web crawlers are used to discover, download, and store content from the Web. As we've seen in chapter 2, a web crawler is just a part of a larger application such as a search engine.

A typical web crawler has the following components:

- A repository module to keep track of all URLs known to the crawler.
- A document download module that retrieves documents from the Web using provided set of URLs.
- A document parsing module that's responsible for extracting the raw content out of a variety of document formats, such as HTML, PDF, Microsoft Word. The parsers are also responsible for extracting URLs contained in the document and other data that can be useful during indexing phase—in particular, metadata information.
- A repository module that stores retrieved document metadata and content extracted from the raw documents during the crawling process.
- A URL normalization module that transforms URLs into standard form, so that they can be compared, evaluated, and so on.
- A URL filtering module, so that the crawler can skip undesirable URLs.

Design and implementation of individual components depend on what you're planning to crawl and the scale that the crawler is required to handle. In the simplest cases when you want to collect a couple of pages from a known website, complete crawler implementation can fit on one page of code. For intranet websites, you can get away with a fairly simple implementation as well. But in an implementation capable of handling large-scale document collection from the Web, the crawler will be implemented as a set of applications distributed across a network of hardware nodes. These nodes can even be geographically distributed to be closer to the source of data. We've included a set of references at the end of this section that describe implementation concerns for large-scale crawling.

B.1.1 The stages of crawling

The operation of a typical crawler involves the following two stages:

1 The URL repository of the crawler is initialized with a list of URLs (commonly known as seed URLs) and starts web crawling.
2 The crawler loads the seed of the URLs that haven't been visited, in order to identify the scope of its work.

For every eligible URL, the web crawler has to:

1 Fetch the URL content.
2 Parse the fetched documents in order to extract the outgoing URLs and the document content.
3 Persist the information that we want to retain.
4 Normalize the newly discovered URLs.
5 Filter out the URLs that the crawler should ignore.
6 Update the URL repository with the list of new URLs to crawl.
7 Repeat step 2 until the desired depth of discovery has been reached.

There are two broad categories of crawlers: general-purpose and focused. General-purpose crawlers collect all documents they can get their hands on. They can rely on URL-filtering techniques to restrict URLs that will be crawled. Focused crawlers are used to discover content related to a specific topic of interest. All crawlers can employ the techniques that were covered in this book to their advantage.

B.1.2 Our simple crawler

Our simple web crawler can download pages from the Web or a local filesystem. In addition to HTML documents, it can handle Microsoft Word documents. As we mentioned earlier, this is a demo crawler whose purpose is to facilitate your experimentation with the intelligent techniques that were presented in this book. The code has been kept clean and simple so that you can easily review what's happening at every step of the processing. Each document is stored in a separate file and the crawler uses plain text file format, so that you can review the content easily. You can find all the source code related to the crawler under the `iweb2.ch2.webcrawler` package.

We demonstrate how the web crawler works in our listings. Every time the crawler runs, it'll create a new `crawl-<timestamp>` directory to store all the relevant data. Within the crawl directory, the following set of subdirectories and files will be created:

- `<crawl-dir>/knownurls/knownurlsdb.dat`—This file contains the list of URLs that are known to the crawler.
- `<crawl-dir>/fetched/`—This directory contains the raw documents that are downloaded by the crawler. Documents are downloaded and processed in batches; the default batch size is 10.
- `<crawl-dir>/fetched/<batch-number>/<doc-id>.fetched`—Each file stores the raw content of a particular document.
- `<crawl-dir>/fetched/<batch-number>/<doc-id>.meta`—Each file contains the metadata of a document's content; the metadata information is specific to the transport protocol.
- `<crawl-dir>/processed/`—This directory contains the documents in processed form. It contains a separate directory for each processed batch of URLs.
- `<crawl-dir>/processed/<batch-number>/content/<doc-id>.content`—Each document contains the content after parsing. If you change the parser the content of these documents may change.
- `<crawl-dir>/processed/<batch-number>/outlinks/<doc-id>.outlinks`—Each file contains all the links that were detected by the document parser, in the respective parent document.
- `<crawl-dir>/processed/<batch-number>/properties/<doc-id>.properties`—Each file contains document properties such as the document type, the title, the URL, and so on.
- `<crawl-dir>/processed/<batch-number>/txt/<doc-id>.txt`—Each file contains only the textual content of the retrieved document, as extracted by the parser.
- `<crawl-dir>/pagelinks/pagelinkdb.dat`—This file contains the data about the outlinks for all the processed URLs. It contains only data about the outlink URLs that passed through the URL filter.

B.1.3 Open source web crawlers

There are two major Java-based projects—Nutch and Heritrix—that offer a web crawler implementation. Nutch is an Apache Lucene subproject that you can visit at: http://lucene.apache.org/nutch/. The project web site contains a step-by-step tutorial on how to install and run the application, which of course includes the web crawler. Unlike our own crawler, Nutch stores multiple pages per data file. This makes it difficult to review results of small crawls, but for large crawls, this has better I/O performance.

Heritrix is the Internet Archive's open source web crawler. It's used to archive large portions of the Web. The project's web site is http://crawler.archive.org/. The Heritrix project is focused on large-scale crawling and is released under the liberal LGPL license.

Another open source library that might be of interest to you is provided by the Apache Tika project, which you can visit at http://lucene.apache.org/tika/. Tika is a toolkit for detecting and extracting metadata and structured text content from various documents using existing parser libraries.

You can find more details on various aspects of crawler design in Heydon and Najork, and in Gomes and Silva. An overview of issues that must be considered when designing high-performance scalable web crawlers is provided in Boswell, as well as Shkapenyuk and Suel. For more details on focused crawling, consult the paper by Chakrabarti et al.

B.2   References

Boswell, D. "Distributed High-performance Web Crawlers: A Survey of the State of the Art." 2003. http://www.cs.ucsd.edu/~dboswell/PastWork/WebCrawlingSurvey.pdf.

Gomes, D. and M. Silva. "The Viuva Negra crawler: An experience report." *Software—Practice & Experience*, Volume 38 (2), pp. 161-188, 2006.

Heydon, A. and M. Najork. "Mercator: A Scalable, Extensible Web Crawler." Compaq Systems Research Center, 1999.

Chakrabarti, S., M. Berg, and B. Dom. "Focused crawling: a new approach to topic-specific Web resource discovery." WWW8 International World Wide Web Conference, vol. 31, pp. 1623-1640. Toronto, 1999. http://www8.org/w8-papers/5a-search-query/crawling/index.html.

Shkapenyuk, V. and T. Suel. "Design and Implementation of a High-Performance Distributed Web Crawler." Polytechnic University: Brooklyn, NY, 2001. http://cis.poly.edu/suel/papers/crawl.pdf.

appendix C:
Mathematical refresher

Throughout this book, we assumed little about the mathematical background of our audience. This appendix presents some of the mathematical formulas that we used in our algorithms, but never wrote explicitly in their standard form. The classic book that combines a solid mathematical description together with numerical algorithms is *Numerical Recipes: The Art of Scientific Computing* by William H. Pres et al. That book is a must-have reference for a large number of topics related to the development of intelligent algorithms.

C.1 Vectors and matrices

In the context of elementary mathematics and physics, a vector is the mathematical representation of an arrow. The most common and intuitive example is an arrow that connects two points, say A and B on a plane. In the formulas that we used, a vector is represented by a one-dimensional array. In other words, it's an ordered set of numbers. We typically denote vectors with a bold Latin letter, such as x. A 10-dimensional vector would be an ordered set of numbers x_i, where the index i takes values between 1 and 10 (inclusive)—or 0 and 9 (inclusive), if you start counting from 0.

Think of a two-dimensional matrix as a table with rows and columns. Each matrix element corresponds to a cell in the table. In the formulas that we used, a matrix is represented by a two-dimensional array. We typically denote matrices with capital Latin letters that are formatted as bold and italic, such as A. Like vectors, matrices can be denoted by their individual ordered elements. In other words, the matrix A can also be written as A_{ij}, where the two indices can have different ranges. The matrix that's formed by swapping the order of the indices is called the *transpose* of the original matrix. So, A_{ji} is the transpose matrix of A_{ij}; clearly, the reverse is also true!

Matrices don't have to be two-dimensional; they can be n-dimensional, where n is an arbitrary integer. A n-dimensional matrix will have n indices, of course. Vectors can be thought of as a special case of one-dimensional matrices. Matrices have many interesting properties and can be used symbolically to perform manipulations, just like we use x and y variables to denote some unknown in elementary algebra. As far as symbolic manipulations are concerned, you can think of matrices as numbers! But unlike ordinary numbers, two matrices don't necessarily commute when they multiply each other. So, in general, when we deal with two matrices A and B, it's possible that $A\,B \neq B\,A$.

In summary, for most practical purposes, think of a vector as a one-dimensional Java array and a matrix as a two- or (more generally) n-dimensional Java array. The literature on vectors and matrices is vast. You can find numerous textbooks that cover the subject in-depth and at various levels of sophistication; we cite some of the classic textbooks in the references.

C.2 *Measuring distances*

We've seen in chapter 3 that there are many ways to measure the distance between two points, say A and B. Let's see how all these different ways of measuring translate into formulas in terms of vectors. If each point is represented by a vector (a and b for A and B, respectively) then the difference between these two vectors is another vector, say x, whose magnitude provides a measure of the distance between the two points.

The most common distance is the Euclidean distance, also known as the L^2 *distance* or L^2 *norm*. As you can imagine, the Euclidean distance is a special case of a general distance formula called the L^p *norm*, where p can be any real number greater or equal to 1. The formula for the L^p norm is the following:

$$\|x\|_p = \left(\sum\nolimits_{i=1}^{n} |\,x_i\,|^p \right)^{\frac{1}{p}}$$

The Euclidean distance is obtained by setting p=2. The "city block" or "taxi cab" distance—discussed in the first to-do item of chapter 3—is obtained by setting p=1. Of course, in the preceding formula, the vector x is the difference between the two vectors whose distance we want to measure—x = b - a.

Another distance formula that we used extensively is related to the *cosine similarity* metric. In order to define the formula that we used for the cosine similarity, we need to define the inner product of two vectors (often called the *dot product*). The inner product of two vectors measures the *projection* of one vector onto another. In figure C.1, we show two (two-dimensional) vectors on a plane. When the two vectors are perpendicular to each other, the projection of one vector onto the other is minimum (equal to zero). When the two vectors are aligned, the projection is maximum.

We used a freely available applet to capture these images. You can experiment with this and other applets online at http://www.cs.brown.edu/exploratories/freeSoftware/

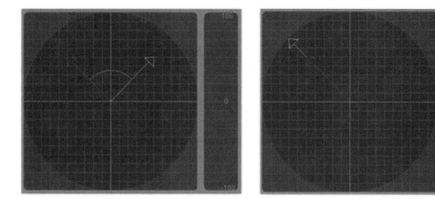

Figure C.1 **The inner product of two vectors that are perpendicular (orthogonal) to each other (left) and aligned (right)**

catalogs/linear_algebra.html. The formula for the inner product of two (n-dimensional) vectors a and b is the following:

$$\mathbf{a} \cdot \mathbf{b} = \sum_{i=1}^{n} a_i b_i = a_1 b_1 + a_2 b_2 + \ldots + a_n b_n$$

Based on the inner product, we defined our cosine similarity through the formula:

$$\cos(\theta) = \frac{\mathbf{a} \cdot \mathbf{b}}{(\mathbf{a} \cdot \mathbf{a})(\mathbf{b} \cdot \mathbf{b})},$$

where Θ is the angle between the two vectors, a and b. The code for this formula is given in the class `iweb2.ch3.collaborative.similarity.CosineSimilarityMea-sure`. Some people use the value of the angle itself by applying the arc cosine function on the right of the equation (`Math.acos`). But that's a matter of convention if you stick with similarities. It becomes important if the quantity involved must satisfy the requirements of a mathematical norm, as does the L^p norm, for example.

If you want to build your own norms and measure distances in a way that fits your problem's needs, you should read a book on functional analysis. We recommend *Elements of the Theory of Functions and Functional Analysis* by A.N. Kolmogorov and S.V. Fomin. The measurement of distances, from a mathematical perspective, is related to the study of metric spaces. Some knowledge of set theory is required in order to properly understand the convergence of sequences, hence the concepts of limit points, open and closed sets, and so on. There are myriad books on functional analysis; we recommend Kolmogorov's book because it's concise, complete, and inexpensive to purchase.

C.3   *Advanced matrix methods*

If your problem has already been "translated" into the matrix language, you have a tremendous arsenal of methods and techniques at your disposal. You have the opportunity to study the properties of your system in detail, and with the rigor that only mathematics can offer. Of course, this might not be as straightforward as it sounds. It's possible that only some of these methods are applicable in your case, plus, the mental correspondence of matrix concepts to the characteristics of your problem is as much an art as it is a science. Nevertheless, if you're mathematically inclined and intellectually adventurous, we highly recommend books that apply advanced matrix methods in data mining.

One such recent book by Lars Eldén covers intelligent algorithms, just like our book, and is titled *Matrix Methods in Data Mining and Pattern Recognition*. This book covers the fundamentals of vectors and matrices, linear systems of equations and least squares methods, orthogonality of vectors and matrices, various decompositions of matrices (QR and SVD), and nonnegative matrix factorization. Of particular interest to the readers of our book might be section 9.1, which presents the k-means algorithm. The rest of the book uses the tools of matrix calculus to address problems such as the classification of handwritten digits, text mining, the PageRank algorithm (that we saw in chapter 2), automatic keyword and key sentence extraction, and face recognition using tensor SVD. References to the scientific computing literature abound, so we highly recommend that book for delving deeper into some of the algorithms that we presented in this book.

C.4   *References*

Eldén, L. *Matrix Methods in Data Mining and Pattern Recognition.* (Series: Fundamentals of Algorithms). SIAM: Society for Industrial and Applied Mathematics, 2007.

Kolmogorov, A.N., and S.V. Fomin. *Elements of the Theory of Functions and Functional Analysis.* Dover Publications, Inc. New York, 1961.

Lay, D.C. *Linear Algebra and Its Applications (Third Edition).* Addison Wesley, 2005.

Press, W.H., S. A. Teukolsky, W.T. Vetterling, and B.P. Flannery (2007). *Numerical Recipes: The Art of Scientific Computing (Third Edition).* Cambridge University Press, 2007.

Trefethen, L.N., and D. Bau. *Numerical Linear Algebra.* SIAM: Society for Industrial and Applied Mathematics, 1997.

appendix D: Natural language processing

We've used NLP throughout the book. NLP refers to a set of techniques and methods for processing written and spoken (usually human) languages. In practical terms, it helps us deal with text and audio records for the purpose of analyzing their content. As you can imagine, the field is as vast as it is interesting.

Work on NLP dates back to the early years of AI. In fact, the famous Turing test was cast in terms of a computer's ability to communicate with a human over a cable line, without the human being able to distinguish whether or not the entity on the other side of the cable is human; for a nice review of the Turing test, see Saygin et al. In a field that old, you can find several branches that tackle the same problem from different angles. Thus, terms such as *computational linguistics* and *speech synthesis* refer to research areas that address the same (or closely related) kind of problems as NLP.

An excellent reference on NLP is *Speech and Language Processing* by Daniel Jurafsky and James Martin. The authors break down the engineering of natural language into the following components:

- *Phonetics and phonology*—The study of word pronunciation and word recognition based on the human voice.
- *Language morphology*—The study of the patterns of word forms that carry meaning in a human language; for example, recognizing that *phone* is to *phonology* what *hydro* is to *hydrology*.
- *Language syntax*—The study of constructing sentences in natural languages. There's a well known prophecy—given by the oracle of Delphi to a soldier before he headed for war—that reveals nicely the paramount importance of syntax. The (ancient Greek) words are as follows: "ηξειζ αφφηξειζ θυηξειζ."

The same words can be interpreted in two ways. In the first (optimistic) interpretation, the oracle says, "You'll go, you'll come back, you won't die in war." In the second interpretation, the oracle says, "You'll go, you won't come back, you'll die in war." Knowing the correct syntax for interpreting Apollo's message was vital!

- *Semantics*—The study of what words mean within a specific context. For example, *cool* in U.S. English can be interpreted as "neither warm nor very cold" but also as "confident and worry free" or as "marked by indifference or disdain," depending on the context.
- *Pragmatics*—The study of the relationship between the meaning of the words and the intentions or goals of the communication.
- *Discourse*—The study of linguistic units that are larger than a single utterance.

Jurafsky and Martin provide a delightful exposition of all these. In addition, they offer a comprehensive review of the subject that includes speech synthesis and speech recognition, statistical parsing, temporal expression analysis, and even conversational agents and machine translation.

On a more practical note, there are many open source projects whose work is related to NLP and are well worth your time if you're interested in working with textual or other linguistic representations. A project called UIMA was initiated at IBM more than a decade ago and is now standardized by OASIS (http://www.oasis-open.org/). UIMA stands for Unstructured Information Management Applications and refers to software systems that analyze large volumes of unstructured information (such as the freeform text of business reports, analyses, and contracts). The project is now maintained in the Apache incubator at http://incubator.apache.org/uima/. Due to its longevity, the project is stable and quite active.

Another stable project is GATE (General Architecture for Text Engineering), which has been in development at the University of Sheffield since 1995 and has excellent supporting documentation. It's the best place to start if you're looking for hands-on examples of language processing that touch on a wide spectrum of topics from Jurafsky and Martin's list. According to the project's documentation, it consists of three elements:

- An architecture that describes how to build language processing systems that are made up of individual components.
- A framework that's written in Java and provides the underlying APIs.
- A graphical development environment. The project can be found at http://gate.ac.uk/.

You might also be interested in the MinorThird project written (primarily) by William Cohen, a professor at Carnegie Mellon University in the machine learning department. The project is described by its founders as follows: "MinorThird is a collection of Java classes for storing text, annotating text, and learning to extract entities and categorize text." It's hosted on http://sourceforge.net and is distributed under the BSD license, but you should read the notes on third-party libraries before you embed it in production code. Notwithstanding the legal notes, the library contains a rich set of NLP methods to help you analyze text. Other notable open source NLP libraries include a precursor of MinorThird called SecondString, and an umbrella project called openNLP; both of these projects can be found on http://sourceforge.netas well.

D.1 *References*

Cohen, W.W. "Minorthird: Methods for Identifying Names and Ontological Relations in Text using Heuristics for Inducing Regularities from Data." http://minorthird.source-forge.net, 2004.

Jurafsky, D. and J. Martin. *Speech and Language Processing,* Second Edition. Prentice Hall (Series in Artificial Intelligence), 2008.

Saygin, A.P., I. Cicekli, and V. Akman. "Turing Test: 50 Years Later." *Minds and Machines* 10 (4) pp. 463-518, 2000.

Turing, A. "Computing Machinery and Intelligence." *Mind,* 59 (236), pp. 433-460, 1950.

appendix E:
Neural networks

In chapter 5, we introduced the central ideas of neural networks. We also demonstrated how to build a simple neural network, train it, and use it in a practical scenario. The general subject of neural networks is vast; we only touched on the tip of the iceberg. It's difficult to discuss the fundamentals of neural networks without using mathematical terminology. We hope that we did a good job explaining the basic concepts, but a deeper understanding of the inner workings requires a dive into the specialized literature.

To ease the transition from *Algorithms of the Intelligent Web* to the highly specialized ones on neural networks, we'd like to recommend two books that provide easily accessible introductions to the mathematical description of neural networks. *Machine Learning* by Tom Mitchell is an excellent introductory book in machine learning and we highly recommend it as a general reference. In particular, the chapter on artificial neural networks includes the back-propagation algorithm, and its mathematical derivation; a detailed example on face recognition; alternative error functions; alternative error minimization procedures; and dynamic modification of the network structure.

As a first step in the general literature we recommend *Information Theory, Inference, and Learning Algorithms* by David MacKay. It has more sophisticated (and more recent) introductory coverage of artificial neural networks. It begins with an overview of neural networks and a detailed exposition of the single neuron as a classifier. It thoroughly examines the capacity of a single neuron and offers a probabilistic interpretation of the neural network learning process. MacKay provides an introduction to the so-called *Boltzmann machines* (a fascinating topic for those with a physics background) as a stochastic Hopfield network. Bayesian neural networks are also used as a springboard for introducing Gaussian processes, which are well-established statistical models. We should mention that the algorithms in MacKay's book are implemented in a free, open source, mathematical programming language called

Octave. The execution platform for this language is available for all major operating systems, so it's easy to experiment with the code.

In the category of books that focus on the study of neural networks, a must read on the subject is *Self-Organizing Maps* by Tuevo Kohonen, one of the grand masters of neural networks. Aside from masterfully covering the subject of unsupervised learning with neural networks, the book offers a clear and concise chapter on mathematical preliminaries as well as one of the best presentations of the learning vector quantization technique. This dense, graduate-level book is as much a delight to read as it is original.

Neural Networks in Finance: Gaining Predictive Edge in the Market by Paul D. McNelis focuses, as the title implies, on the application of neural networks in finance. After a few introductory chapters, it covers the modeling of several financial problems such as the Black-Sholes option pricing model, the modeling of corporate bonds, time series forecasting, credit card default and bank failures, as well as the modeling of inflation and deflation.

We also want to mention the book *Complex-valued Neural Networks* by Akira Hirose. This book provides a systematic exposition of the new and expanding field of complex-valued neural networks. These networks can be valuable in areas such as adaptive radar systems, the processing of digital elevation maps, and speech synthesis. In general, any area whose problem domain is naturally represented by complex-valued quantities may benefit from the inherent representation of these networks in terms of complex numbers. Clearly, this isn't an introductory book, but it can offer you new ideas and expose you to the possibilities in generalizing neural network design. It will also reveal the challenges involved in generalizing the design of neural networks. For a larger list of books that are related to the study of neural networks, check out the references.

E.1 References

Arbib, M.A., S. Amari, NetLibrary, Inc., and P. H. Arbib. *The Handbook of Brain Theory and Neural Networks.* MIT Press, 2003.

Bishop, C.M., *Neural Networks for Pattern Recognition.* Oxford University Press, 1996.

Dreyfus, G. *Neural Networks.* Springer, 2005.

Haykin, S. *Neural Networks: A Comprehensive Foundation, Second Edition.* Prentice Hall, 1998.

Kohonen, T. *Self-Organizing Maps,* Third Edition. Springer, 2000.

MacKay, D.J.C. *Information Theory, Inference, & Learning Algorithms.* Cambridge University Press, 2003.

Maier, K.D., C. Beckstein, R. Blickhan, W. Erhard, and D. Fey. "A multi-layer-perceptron neural network hardware based on 3D massively parallel optoelectronic circuits." Proceedings of the *6th International Conference on Parallel Interconnects*, pp. 73-80, 1999.

Mandic, D.P., and J. A. Chambers. *Recurrent Neural Networks for Prediction: Learnning algorithms, architecture, and stability.* John Wiley & Sons, Inc., 2001.

Mitchell, T. *Machine Learning.* McGraw Hill Higher Education, 1997.

Neapolitan, R.E.. *Learning Bayesian Networks.* Prentice Hall, 2003.

Ripley, B.D. *Pattern Recognition and Neural Networks.* Cambridge University Press, 2008.

index

MORE TITLES FROM MANNING

Collective Intelligence in Action

by Satnam Alag

ISBN: 1-933988-31-2
424 pages
$44.99
October 2008

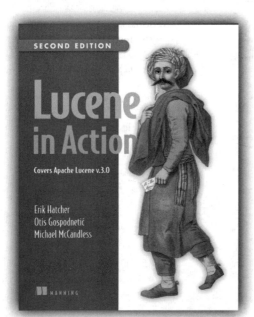

Lucene in Action, Second Edition

Covers Apache Lucene v.3.0

by Erik Hatcher, Otis Gospodnetić, and
  Michael McCandless

ISBN: 1-933988-17-7
475 pages
$44.99
September 2009

For ordering information go to www.manning.com